REMEMBERING
THE
COVENANT
A COMMENTARY ON
THE BOOK OF MORMON

VOLUME 4

Denver C. Snuffer, Jr.

Published in the United States by Mill Creek Press.
Mill Creek Press is a registered trademark of Mill Creek Press, LLC.
www.millcreekpress.com

ISBN-10: 0-9891503-3-X
ISBN-13: 978-0-9891503-3-0

Printed in the United States of America on acid-free paper.

First Edition

Cover design by Mill Creek Press.

CONTENTS

VOLUME 4

RESTORATION AND APOSTASY

Your Life in Context

I've been reading modern church history, recently from primary sources including diaries as part of my work on a new book. I've been struck by how difficult it is for people to put their own lives into context as they live them. The history inside of which they live dominates their thoughts, beliefs, perceptions and interpretations. It is almost impossible for people to disconnect from their surroundings and view history as they live it.

We rarely have it occur to us that we are part of a current, a flow of people, events and even thought in all the moments of our lives. But we can act independent of that flow by making a choice.

I am astonished by the arrogance of office, position, and wealth. When any person is put into a position in which their circumstances grant them advantages over their fellow man, it is hard to retain empathy for how well intended but terribly misinformed actions always affect others. Such things certainly do not make any person a bad man, but always reduces them from what they might have become.

It was essential to Christ's life that He be born in obscurity, associated with the least of His society, be deprived of wealth and official power. He could not have accomplished His mission were He in a position to preside. He needed to be persecuted to fully awaken to the injustices men impose on others. Even so little a matter as tempting Him by interrogations designed to trip Him up made Him greater than He would have been had people deferred to His standing. He was challenged, not coddled. He grew from grace to grace until He was called the Son of God, because of the things which He suffered.

Almost without exception when a soul awakens to the historic context in which they live they immediately find themselves at odds with the surrounding culture. In this also the Lord was The Great Example.

On Thanksgiving I find myself appreciating our Lord and His difficult life all the more.

Dolores Umbridge

In the Harry Potter series, I like how Dolores Umbridge turns questioning her actions into questioning the Ministry of Magic. And by extension questioning the Minister of Magic. What a power-hungry wench she was. She parlayed herself and her every move or decision by extension into the acts of the very pinnacle of their social authority. It is a sort of pathology you only see in very unhealthy social groups who are ruled by fear and intimidation. I thought it was brilliant of J.K. Rowling to envision such a character.

Perfect Love

Perfect love casts out all fear. (Moroni 8:16)

Peter gave instruction about how the church ought to operate. It was never through fear or intimidation; but through gentle example:

"I exhort, who am also an elder, and a witness of the sufferings of Christ, and also a partaker of the glory that shall be revealed: Feed the flock of God which is among you, taking the oversight thereof, not by constraint, but willingly; not for filthy lucre, but of a ready mind; Neither as being lords over God's heritage, but being ensamples to the flock. And when the chief Shepherd shall appear, ye shall receive a crown of glory that fadeth not away." (1 Peter 5:1–4)

What a marvel the Gospel of Jesus Christ is in all its details. When it appears on the earth, it appears in weakness, does not force itself upon the world, and persuades others to the truth. When it is lost, then religion turns into the means to control and exercise compulsion. It becomes all that Catholicism was. Though, in truth, once the Protestant Reformation gathered power it greatly improved Catholicism by reducing its capacity to rule and reign with compulsion and intimidation. By disposition men tend to abuse power whenever they think they hold it. (D&C 121:39–40) Just like men, institutions are best when humbled, and worst when they reign with pride and power.

How delightful it is when fiction, like the Potter series, captures a character which puts a timeless conflict into a modern yarn.

Provo Tabernacle

The destruction of the Provo Tabernacle by the fire last night makes me mourn. I heard President Kimball speak there. We had some of our student Stake Conferences there. Later I attended the funeral of Rex Lee, the Dean of the J. Reuben Clark Law School while I attended. I also attended Hugh Nibley's funeral there. It was hallowed ground because of those memories.

I assume it was arson, because of so many recent fires in LDS owned buildings. Seems a foolish gesture, even if you hate the Church. Nothing important is ever accomplished by destroying the creative labors of others. If someone hates the Church, perhaps they ought to go build up their own. There is no equivalency made by tearing down. A person may be able to burn a building, but it does not make them any more important or great. A man may have shot John Lennon, but that did not alter the killer's importance. It merely made his insignificance more public.

There are two great forces at work. One is entropy. Everything is getting colder, darker, and dissolving. This force is unrelenting, and can be found everywhere in the physical world. Opposing it, however, is something which is creative, renewing, and equally unrelenting. I believe this force which renews life, introduces new energy and forms new systems to be God's work. It is, in a word, love. Or, in the vernacular of the scriptures, it is charity.

When the labors of hundreds have been assembled to create a place of worship, a thing of beauty and a refuge for Saints, that act of charity will endure beyond any subsequent act of vandalism. It cannot be lessened; though it may be broken or burned. The testimony of sacrifice establishes an enduring legacy.

I hope the Tabernacle will be rebuilt. I hope also the memory of the original will not fade from those who went there for such events as Brother Nibley's funeral, Dean Lee's funeral, and President Kimball's address.

Solstice

Tuesday marks the darkest day of the year, with the longest night. During that night the moon will be eclipsed, most prominently in the North American continent.

Traditionally that night marks the moment when darkness has its greatest reign, to be then conquered by the returning light. The following day beginning the return of light and the defeat of darkness.

Christ's answer completely frustrates man's capacity to control the kingdom of heaven. It is not a franchise, giving Pharisees any authority or right. It is not even capable of being "observed" by those who are blind to its appearance. But it is nevertheless real. It is "within" some few who qualify.

Sacrifice of Isaac

There were ancient Jewish traditions which held that Abraham actually killed Isaac on the mount and the Lord brought Isaac back to life. The reference in Hebrews 11:17–19 seems to be based upon this earlier tradition[1372] in contrast to the Genesis account.[1373]

(If Abraham actually slew Isaac, and Isaac was raised from the dead, the trial of Abraham and the test of Isaac is more analogous to Christ's sacrifice than we imagine.

Hugh Nibley writes about these earlier traditions in *Abraham in Egypt*, 329–344, 372–375.

We imagine the difficulties of the ancients to be less than they were. Their faith was established through trial, sacrifice, obedience, and consecration. Not to the will of man or men, but to the will of God. When men attempt to displace obedience to God into submis-

---

[1372] Hebrews 11:17–19 "By faith Abraham, when he was tried, offered up Isaac: and he that had received the promises offered up his only begotten *son*, Of whom it was said, That in Isaac shall thy seed be called: Accounting that God *was* able to raise *him* up, even from the dead; from whence also he received him in a figure."

[1373] Genesis 22:9–13 "And they came to the place which God had told him of; and Abraham built an altar there, and laid the wood in order, and bound Isaac his son, and laid him on the altar upon the wood. And Abraham stretched forth his hand, and took the knife to slay his son. And the angel of the Lord called unto him out of heaven, and said, Abraham, Abraham: and he said, Here *am* I. And he said, Lay not thine hand upon the lad, neither do thou any thing unto him: for now I know that thou fearest God, seeing thou hast not withheld thy son, thine only *son* from me. And Abraham lifted up his eyes, and looked, and behold behind *him* a ram caught in a thicket by his horns: and Abraham went and took the ram, and offered him up for a burnt offering in the stead of his son."

sion to the will of men, then it is not merely an error, it is idolatry. It is an abomination.

More often than not, obedience to God causes conflict with your fellow man. It did not get these ancient Saints applause, position, praise or notice.

Religion in Rome

The following is taken from *Cicero: The Life and Times of Rome's Greatest Politician*, by Anthony Everitt, p. 55:

"Religion was not so much a set of personal beliefs as precisely laid-down ways of living in harmony with the expectations of the gods. In fact, by the end of the Republic educated men believed less in the literal truth of the apparatus of religious doctrine than in a vaguer notion of the validity of tradition."

How controlling are traditions.

They blind us to any view other than the one we've inherited and keep us from examining what, exactly, the source of the tradition was or what it was originally intended to accomplish.

The Battle

The battle we are all called upon to fight is not external. Some people spend their time stirring people up to alarm them about carnal security. They are trying to sell something. There are fortunes being made by proponents of fear. But the audience for such things are only being distracted from a much greater, more immediate battle. Until the internal condition of the individual has been conquered and brought into alignment with heaven, there is no amount of political, social, economic or military security which will matter in the long run.

I think it more advisable to seek for and listen to the Lord, and secondarily those teachers who will convert you to the Lord; rather than any other advice or movement advocated by those promoting causes. Teachers ought to point to Him. Not to themselves. No one but the Lord is coming to rescue you; and no group will be able to overcome error apart from Him. Ultimately the battle we each face is the Lord's. We must cooperate with Him for Him to be able to win it. When He does, however, the victory is ours for we are the ones who He redeems.

The path back to the Lord's presence is an individual one. It is not likely to be accomplished while in an audience. There is no "support group" needed. It is you. What goes on inside you. What you love most. He will one day associate with a group in a city; but that group will be comprised of individuals who have previously met Him.

It surprises me how little discernment there is among those claiming to seek truth. Many of them will take in ideas from foolish, vain and proud sources with as much enthusiasm as from a true one. How is it that people cannot tell the difference between them? Does not a true message sound much different from a false one? Is merely associating some lesser virtue with a cause enough to have it distract? What is more plain than the admonishment to seek first the kingdom of God and His righteousness?

Restoration and Apostasy

There really is no static position in nature. The full moon of two nights ago is now replaced by the waning gibbous immediately as the light begins to be lost. Nor does the half-moon last longer than a single night, followed by the waning crescent. When the moon's light is altogether stricken, the new moon phase begins with the waxing crescent which is, at first, only a sliver. But it follows nightly through the waxing crescent, to the half moon, to the waxing gibbous, to the full moon. Always in motion. Always either growing or receding in light.

So also with the sun. From solstice to equinox, to solstice to equinox, it grows, then dims. Never static. It is impossible to freeze the light. It will grow or it will fade.

All things in nature testify of the truth. This includes things in the "heavens" or sky above, as well as things on, in and under the earth.[1374]

It is not possible for an individual, nor a collection of individuals, to remain static. They are either involved with restoring truth or in apostasy from it; never merely "preserving" it. Those who claim to merely preserve the truth given them are concealing the fact of their apostasy. They are soothing their conscience. Caretakers simply cannot exist.

All great truths are simple, and they are testified of in nature as well as in scripture.

Zion Is Not Yet

In response to a question I received earlier today about whether Zion presently exists in some form I responded:

"Zion has not begun in an organized city-form and could not do so at the moment. Some of what would be required to establish Zion may have been returned, but only in the most incipient form at present, and not such that it can stand on its own. If the hounds of hell have been released to balance things because of Zion's "appearance" then it is wholly disproportionate at present. The evil is far more numerous, far more widely planted, far stronger, and securely fastened here

---

[1374] Moses 6:63 "And behold, all things have their likeness, and all things are created and made to bear record of me, both things which are temporal, and things which are spiritual; things which are in the heavens above, and things which are on the earth, and things which are in the earth, and things which are under the earth, both above and beneath: all things bear record of me."

than the tiniest shoots of a diminutive Zion. Even the idea of starting a small gathering is not possible at present."

It was an interesting enough question I thought the answer worth posting.

I've been learning more over the last months about many things of interest to me. It is wonderful to have more time to study and meditate. The Gospel as restored through Joseph Smith contains a great deal more than we've chosen to respect and explore. This is a mixed blessing, of course. We neglect it at our peril. But we are still in recent enough time to the events that the record is with us. Wars, unrest, upheavals and destructions have not eliminated the libraries of material still available for our study. So, if we are interested, we can learn a great deal in our day.

It is foolish to trust your salvation to another. It is more foolish to trust anything to a committee or organization where compromises and agendas conflict with truth almost at every turn. History has no ego, but the purveyors of legacies who hope to mold history to support their agendas are always driven by ambition to trim, add, censor, reinterpret, and contradict. If religion matters, and if Joseph Smith was indeed a prophet, then we ought to try and get as unfiltered an account as possible. Then, with what account you settle as true, you ought then to inquire of the Lord to see if He by revelation has something further to open to your view.

I'm amazed at how much the Lord would want us to know, if we only showed interest enough to make an inquiry, with real intent, having faith in Him.

If the mammalian prophet from Puxatony (or Al Gore for that matter) can be trusted, things are going to be warmer soon. I'd like that. Trading light and warmth for dark and cold is an annual pilgrimage nature takes us through to remind us of eternal things.

Book of Abraham

The last lesson I taught the Priests in my ward I went over the history of the Book of Abraham. There are a host of arguments made against Joseph Smith, his translation and the authenticity of the Book of Abraham which rely upon ignorance to persuade.

The Book of Abraham is one of the strongest proofs of Joseph Smith's credibility as a prophet who restored ancient knowledge and did so using the power of God. But only if you have read enough to know the lay of the terrain.

I brought the following books with me to the class:

- *Abraham in Egypt* (Nibley)
- *The Joseph Smith Papyri: An Egyptian Endowment* (Nibley)
- *Astronomy, Papyrus and Covenant* (Hauglid)
- *An Approach to the Book of Abraham* (Nibley)
- *One Eternal Round* (Nibley)
- *The Blessings of Abraham* (Clark)
- *Traditions about the Early Life of Abraham* (Tvedtnes, Gee)
- *The Hor Book of Breathings* (Rhodes)
- *A Guide to the Joseph Smith Papyri* (Gee)
- Vol. 2 of *The History of the Church* (Joseph Smith)

Critics of Joseph have provoked a tremendous effort to account for the Book of Abraham. If you are interested in the topic, the results of that effort are worth reading. I find that all topics related to the restoration are interesting to me.

I have spent a few days with scholars with backgrounds in Egyptology. There is a great deal to learn about the earliest days of Egypt and the Egyptian influence on ancient Israel. Many of our Psalms are taken directly from Egypt. Abraham sojourned there, Joseph served there, the twelve tribes resided there, Moses was raised there in the royal courts, Jeremiah fled there, and Christ lived several years there. Egypt was a repository of arcane knowledge which remains interesting to Latter-day Saints.

Ten Parables

My purpose in writing *Ten Parables* was to take an ancient literary form and use it to illustrate the path back to God. It was intended to replicate the underlying meaning of the temple endowment, but without employing theatrical presentations, signs, tokens or key words. Instead the process is portrayed through parables involving characters in the stories moving from a state of disassociation with God, through understanding His attributes and manner, adopting His virtues and conduct, then back to a reconciliation with Him, at last reaching His presence by satisfying angelic sentinels and obtaining His tutelage.

The book is actually only one story: the process of redemption. It was written to be readable in the same time as it would take to attend a temple endowment session. However, its meaning can take many days of reflection to fully unlock. It is intended to provoke action or changes within the reader who sees the messages.

Some people have seen the value of that little book and, as a consequence, have gained some considerable benefits in their own search into the mysteries of godliness. Others have regarded it as nothing more than a little story book, and I suppose gained varying degrees of entertainment from it.

We are all entitled to see as much or as little as we choose to see. That is the beauty of communications that employ symbols. It does not force the listener to understand a thing. It only invites.

Beloved

The Lord inquired of John, who is called "Beloved:"

"John, my beloved, what desirest thou? For if you shall ask what you will, it shall be granted unto you." (D&C 7:1)

This is what the Lord offers, at some point, to those who meet with Him as He confirms their exaltation. I've explained this in *Beloved Enos*. It is part of the privilege He extends to those who come to know Him.

A person could ask anything of Him. In the case of John, however, the request was completely selfless (one of the reasons he is "Beloved" by Christ). It reflects the same heart as the Lord's.

"And I said unto him, Lord, give unto me power over death, that I may live and bring souls unto thee." (D&C 7:2)

That is, John desired this not for his own sake, but for the sake of those to whom he could minister. He wanted to bring souls to Christ.

"And the Lord said unto me, Verily, verily, I say unto thee, because thou desirest this thou shalt tarry until I come in my glory, and shalt prophesy before nations, kindreds, tongues and people." (D&C 7:3)

The ministry of John would continue. There would be "nations" who would receive his prophesy. What do you suppose it means for John to be able to prophesy before "nations?" Do "nations" mean modern states, or do they mean family divisions or subsets, like the ancient tribes of Israel, which were called "nations?" Do the terms "nations, kindreds, tongues and people" have a family meaning? What family? Has the gospel been intended primarily for one family of redeemed souls all along? If so, then, how does one connect to that family? What is John doing?

The Lord explained to Peter that, concerning John, "he has undertaken a greater work; therefore I will make him as flaming fire and a ministering angel; he shall minister for those who shall be heirs of salvation who dwell on the earth" (D&C 7:6).

It is an interesting question to ask what John has been doing.

What do you suppose it means to be "as flaming fire and a ministering angel?" What jurisdiction does John have if he "shall minister for those who shall be heirs of salvation who dwell on the earth?" Does this require John to be involved with all who are to become "heirs of salvation who dwell on the earth?" In what way would he be involved?

These are interesting things to contemplate. All the more so because these ideas are somewhat at odds with the idea that God has finished His work and given his power to men, as we claim. Nephi disagrees with the idea[1375], but that hasn't affected our views much. We're really quite certain we have everything we need without John.

My Kingdom

I was asked an interesting question. I thought the question and answer might be worth posting.

> "In 3 Nephi 28, the 9 disciples are promised that when they die they will go to "my Kingdom" meaning Christ's. However, the other 3 who tarry are promised to go to the "Kingdom of my Father." Are they different? They must be, but how? In what way? Different levels of exaltation? This same thing is discussed in D&C 7. Peter is promised "My Kingdom" while John is promised the greater blessing. I'm assuming it's "my Father's Kingdom" like the 3 Nephite disciples."

[1375] 2 Nephi 28:5 "And they deny the power of God, the Holy One of Israel; and they say unto the people: Hearken unto us, and hear ye our precept; for behold there is no God today, for the Lord and the Redeemer hath done his work, and he hath given his power unto men;"

I've written about this in *Beloved Enos*. The offer is extended to all those whose calling and election is confirmed. The 9 chose to move into the post-mortal inheritance at their death. That is, they would not be required to return here for anything else, but would be judged, crowned, and exalted upon death. Because this is a blessing conferred by the Son, it is "His Kingdom" into which they will move. When the work is at last completed and delivered to the Father—at the end of the earth's temporal existence—it becomes the Father's at that point. The 3 will be awaiting that moment to receive that inheritance. The 9 will enter into the "Son's" until then, and will likewise be among those who are received by the Father, in the due order of things.

[My answer provoked a follow up question:]

"But doesn't Peter, James and John have the earthly role of teaching Adam and Eve (us) further light and knowledge as shown in the temple? Do they send ministering angels or maybe even John since Peter and James don't come to earth anymore?"

I answered:

Peter, James, and John were added to the endowment by Brigham Young, but weren't part of what Joseph originally portrayed. They were added to remove required narration. When added, they are a "type," and not intended to be the personalities or individuals. Much like Elias is a "title" and not a name. Peter, James, and John are in the endowment types, or "titles"—not intended to be the actual persons who were known by those names while in mortality.

The endowment used to include the words, "You should consider yourselves respectively as if Adam and Eve . . . This is simply figurative so far as the man and woman are concerned." The same could be said about other roles—which all represent truths, but the truths are not tied to personal identities. You are Adam. The endowment is about your life. Those true ministers who are sent are explained in D&C 130:5[1376], which include those who do (i.e. currently living individuals who have gained a message from the Father and Son to be delivered) or have (i.e., those who have left mortality and are returning as angelic, or resurrected, or translated individuals, who have gained a message from the Father and Son to be delivered) belonged to this earth.

I should add: Without ministering of angels there is no longer any faith, as Moroni explained.[1377] Only a fool would take their own message and portray it as coming from God. As Joseph Smith put it, "only fools trifle with the souls of men." [I've noted, however, an endless abundance of fools here. The Historic Christian religions are filled with them . . . Unfortunately, they've crept into the restored faith, as well.]

P.S. A reminder—I do answer questions from time to time. However, before you ask me a question, *read* or *review* the books I have written (there are 6 of them). Much of what is written in the books following *The Second Comforter* is written because of the questions I am asked most often. Therefore, I suspect you'll find things in what I've already written which make it unnecessary to ask.

Home Evening

We have Family Home Evening on Sunday night, because of all the activities our family has. Between softball, soccer, lacrosse, girl scouts, Young Women, school play, and gymnastics we don't have an available evening other than Sunday. Today the sister Missionaries

---

[1376] D&C 130:5 "I answer, Yes. But there are no angels who minister to this earth but those who do belong or have belonged to it."

[1377] Moroni 7:37 "Behold I say unto you, Nay; for it is by faith that miracles are wrought; and it is by faith that angels appear and minister unto men; wherefore, if these things have ceased wo be unto the children of men, for it is because of unbelief, and all is vain."

were visiting, and were included in the lesson and treat. One of the sisters has been out five days. She's from Hawaii. The other is from Ohio and is the trainer senior companion. Our next door neighbor has a daughter currently serving a mission in Kirtland, Ohio. She returns home in four days.

We are going to have the returning sister missionary speak to the Priests Quorum next month. The Bishop had to approve it, but he agreed a returning missionary is appropriate to instruct the Priests, even though she is a sister.

I was thinking about my home ward. We have a doctor who has serious physical ailments due to another physician's malpractice. He is going to undergo experimental surgery at the U of U Medical Center to attempt to undo the serious disability currently afflicting him. (My ward includes so many physicians that as I write this I can't be sure I've counted them all.) We have a member of the Draper Temple Presidency, Inner City Missionaries, English as a Second Language Missionaries, a Federal Judge, several families who have experienced the deaths of children, former Mission Presidents, skeptics, musicians, accountants, the strong and the weak. We have the faithful and the faithless in my ward. We have a family in which the father served a mission in Madagascar, where he met his wife. We have several families from Hong Kong and two from Korea. Our ward is a remarkable mix of ages, backgrounds, personalities and abilities.

I was thinking about how wonderful it is to have this arbitrary ward boundary where we are associated together by geographic division and not by preference for one another. We are expected to serve one another and with one another. Of all the benefits which come from the church, the association as a ward family with different, diverse people you have not sought to find is perhaps one of the greatest. It lets us stretch to serve. In many ways it mirrors our own families, where relationships are given us by God and choices others make in marriages. We do not control the make-up of our extended families, but are expected to love them anyway.

Elimination

I was asked about elimination of penalties in the temple ceremonies. It made me think of the following:

There was a general unease about the use of penalties. The solution was to eliminate them. Perhaps if temple goers were instructed in the value and the significance of the penalties, they would not have been uncomfortable with them. They may have even been kept in the endowment ceremony.

In an abstract way, God sending His Son to be killed is an idea that could cause unease. However, we've made a great effort to study the Lord's sacrifice, to understand it and appreciate it. His sacrifice is not viewed as offensive, but rather as the source of gratitude, even awe, about what the Father and the Son were willing to do to rescue us from eternal disappointment.

Similarly, there are reasons to value, even cherish the penalties which were once a part of the temple rites. But not everyone considered their importance. A significant number of active saints just associated them with Masonic rituals, thought they were borrowed anyway, and never attributed anything more to them.

Old Testament covenant making was always associated with cutting. A marking, or cut, upon sacred clothing anciently also testified to the willingness to undergo a penalty if a vow or covenant with God was not fulfilled. God's covenant with Abraham involved God swearing by His own life (for He could swear by nothing higher); the covenant being sealed by the divided carcasses of sacrificed animals.[1378] That great horror of darkness[1379] was a revelation of outer darkness into which God would descend if He failed to keep the covenant. The burning lamp[1380] which passed between the slaughtered, divided carcasses was the Lord's act sealing the covenant and swearing by His own life to fulfill all He promised to Abraham.

We may have lost respect and understanding, but that does not alter truth. Our loss of light does not make God's brilliance any less. It just reduces our own association with, and understanding of Him. Today we seem pretty content to have others speak to God for us rather than to undertake the fearful responsibilities associated with coming into the presence of a living God.[1381]

And so we settle for inspirational ditties in lieu of doctrine.

Pleasantries in place of repentance.

[1378] Genesis 1 "And he said, Lord God, whereby shall I know that I shall inherit it? And he said unto him, Take me an heifer of three years old, and a she goat of three years old, and a ram of three years old, and a turtledove, and a young pigeon. And he took unto him all these, and divided them in the midst, and laid each piece one against another: but the birds divided he not. And when the fowls came down upon the carcasses, Abram drove them away. And when the sun was going down, a deep sleep fell upon Abram; and, lo, an horror of great darkness fell upon him. And he said unto Abram, Know of a surety that thy seed shall be a stranger in a land *that is* not theirs, and shall serve them; and they shall afflict them four hundred years; And also that nation, whom they shall serve, will I judge: and afterward shall they come out with great substance. And thou shalt go to thy fathers in peace; thou shalt be buried in a good old age. But in the fourth generation they shall come hither again: for the iniquity of the Amorites *is* not yet full. And it came to pass, that, when the sun went down, and it was dark, behold a smoking furnace, and a burning lamp that passed between those pieces. In the same day the Lord made a covenant with Abram, saying, Unto thy seed have I given this land, from the river of Egypt unto the great river, the river Euphrates: The Kenites, and the Kenizzites, and the Kadmonites, And the Hittites, and the Perizzites, and the Rephaims, And the Amorites, and the Canaanites, and the Girgashites, and the Jebusites."
Hebrews 6:13–15 "For when God made promise to Abraham, because he could swear by no greater, he sware by himself, Saying, Surely blessing I will bless thee, and multiplying I will multiply thee. And so, after he had patiently endured, he obtained the promise."

[1379] Genesis 15:12 "And when the sun was going down, a deep sleep fell upon Abram; and, lo, an horror of great darkness fell upon him."

[1380] Genesis 15:17 "And it came to pass, that, when the sun went down, and it was dark, behold a smoking furnace, and a burning lamp that passed between those pieces."

[1381] Hebrews 10:31 "*It is* a fearful thing to fall into the hands of the living God."

Humor in place of sobriety.

We prefer our guides to be blind, because we think they hold onto the handrail better. Of course, when we proclaim them to be the handrail, it doesn't matter what path they take any longer, does it?

We've become (or perhaps stayed) "too low, too mean, too vulgar" to claim we are the people of God—as Joseph Smith put it from Liberty Jail.

We'll all arrive in Hell stained with deplorable sins of every magnitude but all with a good self image. The lessons there will be titled:

- "Why Fire is Good for Us"
- "Burning Shows God's Love to Us"
- "When We Feel Pain, We Get Gain"
- "God Loves a Fiery People"
- "Odds Are We're All Glorious"
- "Burning Will Keep Us Bright"
- "The Fire Belongs to the Refiner"
- "Fissile not Fizzle"
- "We are the Refining and Becoming Refined"

I never took offense at the penalties. I regret their elimination. However, I attended the temple so often that they are indelibly etched into my mind. Even today, I cannot attend without walking through in my mind the remainder of the covenant. They assure me of the exactness expected of us when we enter into a covenant with God. I like that reminder. It helps me to hold myself up to scrutiny which I might not otherwise expect. Though I fail, it is not because I approach the altar of God with anything less than complete respect for Him and His ways. My own impurity cannot detract from His complete purity. My weakness does not limit His forgiveness and mercy. But I have never detected in Him the least particle of imperfection, darkness or unholiness.

Patience

I was recently in a discussion with a fellow regarding the topic of patience.

Moses spent 40 years in the Pharaoh's courts. He apparently knew most of that time that he was to deliver Israel out of bondage. He killed the Egyptian, in part, because of his knowledge he would one day deliver them. Stephen explained, just prior to his martyrdom, the story of Moses. Stephen declared that Moses knew his calling from God made him the deliverer of Israel.[1382] Moses presumed the Israelites would recognize him as the one promised to deliver them. He killed the Egyptian to identify himself to the Israelites. They were unimpressed, did not recognize him, and rejected his claim.

Seeing he had been rejected and betrayed by the Israelites, Moses fled for his life.[1383]

Then, after another 40 years passed while he made a new life for himself in the wilderness, the "voice of the Lord" came to him and called him at last to perform as Israel's deliverer.[1384]

[1382] Acts 7:24–25 "And seeing one *of them* suffer wrong, he defended *him,* and avenged him that was oppressed, and smote the Egyptian: For he supposed his brethren would have understood how that God by his hand would deliver them: but they understood not."

[1383] Acts 7:26–29 "And the next day he shewed himself unto them as they strove, and would have set them at one again, saying, Sirs, ye are brethren; why do ye wrong one to another? But he that did his neighbour wrong thrust him away, saying, Who made thee a ruler and a judge over us? Wilt thou kill me, as thou diddest the Egyptian yesterday? Then fled Moses at this saying, and was a stranger in the land of Madian, where he begat two sons."

[1384] Acts 7:30–34 "And when forty years were expired, there appeared to him in the wilderness of mount Sina an angel of the Lord in a flame of fire in a bush. When Moses saw *it,* he wondered at the sight: and as he drew near to behold *it,* the voice of the Lord came unto him, *Saying,* I *am* the God of thy fathers, the God of Abraham, and the God of Isaac, and the God of Jacob. Then Moses trembled, and durst not behold. Then said the Lord to him, Put off thy shoes from thy feet: for the place where thou standest is holy ground. I have seen, I have seen the affliction of my people which is in Egypt, and I have heard their groaning, and am come down to deliver them. And now come, I will send thee into Egypt."

Moses knew his mission from his youth. But when he attempted on his own to begin that mission, his attempt failed. He was nearly killed for it and had to flee for his life.

After 40 years spent in the wilderness of Sinai, the time came and Moses was commissioned directly by the Lord to go forward.

WE control nothing. *WE* have no right to move the Lord's hand. We may ask, but He alone commands. *Timing is entirely the Lord's.* Although we may know what we have been assigned to do, it is the Lord alone who will decide when the assignment can be performed.

Christ wanted to begin His Father's work at 12.[1385] It would be another 18 years before the Lord would be permitted to begin. In the interim, He "waited upon the Lord for the time of his ministry to come. And he served under his father, and he spake not as other men, neither could he be taught; for he needed not that any man should teach him. And after many years, the hour of his ministry drew nigh" (JST-Matthew 3:24–26). Although fully prepared for "many years" before, the Lord "waited" on His Father for 18 years.

If Moses waited 40 years, and produced only disaster when he attempted to begin his mission early, and Christ waited "many years" for "the hour of his ministry to draw nigh," then what possible reason can any of us give for refusing to submit in patience to the Lord's timing for our lives, mission, ministry, assignments and calling?

[1385] Luke 2:41–49 "Now his parents went to Jerusalem every year at the feast of the passover. And when he was twelve years old, they went up to Jerusalem after the custom of the feast. And when they had fulfilled the days, as they returned, the child Jesus tarried behind in Jerusalem; and Joseph and his mother knew not *of it.* But they, supposing him to have been in the company, went a day's journey; and they sought him among *their* kinsfolk and acquaintance. And when they found him not, they turned back again to Jerusalem, seeking him. And it came to pass, that after three days they found him in the temple, sitting in the midst of the doctors, both hearing them, and asking them questions. And all that heard him were astonished at his understanding and answers. And when they saw him, they were amazed: and his mother said unto him, Son, why hast thou thus dealt with us? behold, thy father and I have sought thee sorrowing. And he said unto them, How is it that ye sought me? wist ye not that I must be about my Father's business?"

Among the many lessons of mortality, Christ learned patience.[1386] **How arrogant must we be to presume we can tell better than the Lord when a blessing should come?** How little understanding would we get if the Lord responded to our impatience and excused us from the necessity to first learn this noble trait of patience?

Learning and Living

There is a considerable gulf between being aware of a teaching or doctrine and living it. I've noticed how it is often the case that we confuse our knowledge about an idea with the notion we are in possession of the attribute.

Learning doctrine and living it are two entirely different things.

The query by Alma the Younger in the Book of Mormon, "Are ye stripped of pride?" is more than meaningful.[1387] It is clarifying. The lens we see ourselves through is distorted as long as pride is part of our makeup.

I don't know of any way to strip ourselves of pride other than to suffer setback, loss, difficulty, disappointment, or anguish. I've never been able to do so on my own. Without suffering, I cannot see myself in the correct light.

There are only a few people I know who have received God's greatest approval; who have had the heavens opened to them and heard the voice of God. Almost without exception, they suffer from physical ailments, struggle with aging and reduced physical abilities, have losses, or bear anguish. These burdens have benefited them. Without a strong, corrosive encounter with difficulty they could not strip themselves of pride.

[1386] Hebrews 5:8 "Though he were a Son, yet learned he obedience by the things which he suffered;"

[1387] Alma 5:8 "And now I ask of you, my brethren, were they destroyed? Behold, I say unto you, Nay, they were not."

For the most part, organized religion does not do what is necessary to break down the hard, prideful hearts of followers. The prophecy of Isaiah is as current as this moment:

> "That this is a rebellious people, lying children, children that will not hear the law of the Lord: Which say to the seers, See not; and to the prophets, Prophesy not unto us right things, speak unto us smooth things, prophesy deceits: Get you out of the way, turn aside out of the path, cause the Holy One of Israel to cease from before us." (Isaiah 30:9–11)

We want to be taught a positive religion. We want praise. If something challenges our good self-image we think it unhelpful, negative and even devilish. But the truth is that until we have broken down before God, seen ourselves in our horrible weakness, foolishness and pride, and acquired a broken heart and contrite spirit, we will remain lying children that will not hear the law of the Lord. When our prophets will only speak smooth things to us we are only being deceived. We are compelling the Holy One of Israel to cease from among us.

But we do feel good about ourselves. We do think we prosper, and all is right.

More blessed, therefore, are those who will do the will of the Lord and not merely acknowledge it. Those who will break down their pride and realize they know nothing until they know God. When they meet Him, He will "reveal all things" to you[1388], because you will at last see yourself as you really are.[1389]

Everything else is vanity.

[1388] D&C 101:32 "Yea, verily I say unto you, in that day when the Lord shall come, he shall reveal all things—"

[1389] 1 John 3:2 "Beloved, now are we the sons of God, and it doth not yet appear what we shall be: but we know that, when he shall appear, we shall be like him; for we shall see him as he is."

Easter

I was the speaker in my ward on Easter Sunday. Although the talk was not written I'm going to try to summarize what was said. (I never "write" a talk. Just take a list of scriptures with me, which on this occasion I never used.)

In the months before I entered law school, I worked in Provo alongside a fellow named Jay Wirig. Jay had been a missionary in the 70's in Hong Kong. While there, he suffered a collapsed lung. He was diagnosed and then sent by the doctor to see a specialist to be treated. His companion took him to the specialist's office, which was up a flight of stairs. That isn't much of a problem unless you have a collapsed lung.

When he arrived in the office, an unpretentious, elderly, Chinese fellow—in a spartan office—used a stethoscope to listen all about his chest and back. Then the fellow got out a tool that looked like a phillips-head screw driver, but had four razor tips on the end. Without warning or anesthetic the doctor stabbed him in the upper chest. It hurt. Then he fished a tube in the hole he'd just made, attached the tube to a suction bottle, and within a short while the lung re-inflated and pain went away—except for the wound on the upper chest. The doctor has no bedside manner, did not bother explaining what he was going to do or why. He just proceeded without regard to the patient's feelings to administer what would cure the ailment.

When Jay returned to home after the mission ended, he suffered recurring collapsed lungs. Eventually, they recommended surgery. The surgery required them to enter his chest cavity through his underarm. When you open on the side, rather than through the solar plexus, the rib spreader crushes cartilage, pulls muscles and ligaments, and inflicts a great deal of trauma. He was kept in the same post surgical ward as the heart patients. The much older heart patients had their chests opened through the far less traumatic means of opening and spreading at the solar plexus. Therefore, the elderly patients were feeling quite well post-surgery, while Jay was in agony. He took some grief from the older patients, because here was a 20–something year-old young man complaining while they were not.

Poor bedside manner by physicians can make the patients they treat feel anxious and alienated, even if the medical treatment they provide is curative. Even if they ultimately do what is right, good and healing, doctors can leave the patient feeling victimized rather than cared for.

Similarly, lawyers can be insensitive to client's feelings, becoming far more attentive to legal principles, theories and arguments than the underlying people affected by the dispute. When I was in law school, I co-authored a book on family law. Because of that, I wanted to practice family law when I graduated. In Utah that means primarily divorces, although it includes the occasional adoption and guardianship. I took divorce cases for about three years before I just could not stand that area of law any longer. It was too bitter, too divisive and too inadequate. It would take another three years before I finished all the cases I had pending, but when finished, I stopped practicing family law. Although I got good results for my clients, I was unable to identify with their emotional needs.

Some years later, after my own divorce, I saw this in a whole different light. As a result of going through the legal process for my own divorce, I concluded the law should not be used to deal with family dissolution. It should be handled by mental health counselors, who have adequate sensitivity for the horror and pain experienced any time a family is broken apart by divorce.

We have a ward infested with lawyers and doctors. I would venture, perhaps every one of us can look back and see those we have helped professionally, but who we have failed inter-personally. We may have solved the legal or medical problem, but at the price of injuring the spirit of those we helped.

When Christ suffered, He gained knowledge. His knowledge is not limited to the physical cure, but includes the spiritual and mental anguish of our disappointments, losses, failures, illnesses, injuries and limitations. He said very little about what He went through. The longest single explanation given by Him is in D&C 19:15. There He states:

> Therefore I command you to repent—repent, lest I smite you by the rod of my mouth, and by my wrath, and by my anger, and your sufferings be sore—how sore you know not, how exquisite you know not, yea, how hard to bear you know not.

Now this sounds like the Old Testament God. However, this is a warning based on the established laws by which all things operate. Sooner or later, all of us will come back into the presence of God. When we do we will either have repented and be prepared to be in His presence, or we will not have repented and we will withdraw in shame and agony. This is explained in Mormon 9:

> . . . Do ye suppose that ye could be happy to dwell with that holy Being, when your souls are racked with a consciousness of guilt that ye have ever abused his laws?

> Behold, I say unto you that ye would be more miserable to dwell with a holy and just God, under a consciousness of your filthiness before him, than ye would to dwell with the damned souls in hell.

> For behold, when ye shall be brought to see your nakedness before God, and also the glory of God, and the holiness of Jesus Christ, it will kindle a flame of unquenchable fire upon you. (Mormon 9:3–5)

Joseph Smith said a man is his own tormentor and accuser. That is, when we see ourselves as we truly are, and can reckon our own unworthiness from the presence of a "just and holy being," we will recoil in horror at our filthiness. We will see how vain we have been.

It is this problem Christ is warning us to guard ourselves against. It is a plea from Him to repent, so we may remove from ourselves this burden of guilt. This is the greatest gift of the Atonement. All other benefits of His suffering pale in comparison with this compassionate result of His suffering for our sins. The explanation continues:

> For behold, I, God, have suffered these things for all, that they might not suffer if they would repent; But if they would not repent they must suffer even as I; Which suffering caused myself, even God, the greatest of all, to tremble because of pain, and to bleed at every pore, and to suffer both body and spirit—and would that I might not drink the bitter cup, and shrink— (D&C 19:16–18)

This is describing a specific event and time. The only Gospel which records the event is Luke. Luke 22 tell us:

> And he was withdrawn from them about a stone's cast, and kneeled down, and prayed, Saying, Father, if thou be willing, remove this cup from me: nevertheless not my will, but thine, be done. And there appeared an angel unto him from heaven, strengthening him. And being in an agony he prayed more earnestly: and his sweat was as it were great drops of blood falling down to the ground. (Luke 22:41–44)

For Him to suffer as we will if we choose not to repent, He was required to assume our sins, feel our anguish and unworthiness in the presence of a "just and holy God," and then come back into harmony with Him. Hence the need for the "angel" to appear to Him from heaven. Unless He confronted exactly what we are called on to confront, He could not minister to us. He could not heal us. He could not take upon Him our sins.

And so He became as unworthy as any of us. No matter what malignant thing you have suffered, who you have abused or neglected, or what harm you have caused or endured, Christ has felt the anguish of that while in the presence of a "just and holy being." He knew His sheep would flee while He suffered. But He also knew the Father would never leave Him:

> Behold, the hour cometh, yea, is now come, that ye shall be scattered, every man to his own, and shall leave me alone: and yet I am not alone, because the Father is with me. (John 16:32)

Suffering the guilt of filthiness in the presence of His Father, He overcame and subdued all enemies to righteousness. He felt shame, but returned it to compassion. He felt agony and rejection, but overcame it with charity. By this means He gained the knowledge necessary to heal all our sins, remove all our guilt, and subdue all our anxieties in the presence of holiness.

Isaiah says this:

> . . . by his knowledge shall my righteous servant justify many; for he shall bear their iniquities. (Isaiah 53:11)

By bearing or taking upon Himself the guilt which divides us from the Father, Christ knows perfectly how to conduct you safely back to the Father's presence. As Christ explains in D&C 19, it requires us to "repent"—because if we fail to repent we must suffer, just as He did. Except our own suffering for our own sins is not curative. It is not redeeming. It is only justice. For us, we seek to claim mercy. Mercy comes from Christ's Atonement which can and does render those who take part in it altogether clean.

His explanation continues:

Nevertheless, glory be to the Father, and I partook and finished my preparations unto the children of men. (D&C 19:19)

He has prepared it for us. But it is our choice to take hold upon it. For that, our personal decision to repent remains at the core.

Christ's capacity to heal us was gained through the Atonement. He possesses compassion in another measure beyond us. For Him the power of His compassion exceeds mere sympathy. It is a power to heal. His compassion removes from us the burdens we feel.

Joseph Smith wrote from Liberty Jail about the injustice of the Saints' suffering from the Missouri mob attacks. As he listed his complaints, and clamored for justice against his enemies, his mind became a blur of emotion and events. With "the avidity of lightening" his mind turned over and over again the injustice of it all. Then, when his mind could take it no more, Joseph fell into a detached state of profound openness to God's voice. Then the voice of inspiration came to him and said:

My son, peace be unto thy soul; thine adversity and thine afflictions shall be but a small moment; And then, if thou endure it well, God shall exalt thee on high; thou shalt triumph over all thy foes. (D&C 121:7–8)

On the other side of this statement from God, Joseph was still in jail, under the same horrid conditions, with the same captors. But having heard the voice of God declaring, "peace be unto thy soul," the compassion of Christ removed the pain of suffering. Now the conditions of his lamentable imprisonment became tolerable. For Christ's compassion removes, empowers, enables, and enlivens. It frees us from the torments we suffer. Through Him we can bear all things.

Of all the Lord provided, an escape from our torments crowns His Atoning sacrifice. It empowers Him to liberate us from all our burdens. His compassion is a power, not a sentiment.

1252 REMEMBERING THE COVENANT

Mother's Day

Today is Mother's Day. Many of you will be getting a phone call from your missionary. My daughter will speak in Sacrament today. It's a different daughter than the one who spoke for the last two years on Mother's Day. Seems we can't have it come without one of our daughters speaking.

My mother died years ago. I always remember her always on this date. She was a remarkable, stern, intelligent, spry, curious and faithful woman. Every morning at breakfast she would read a verse from the Bible to us, even though I did my best to feign disinterest. She persisted. Somehow, despite my own neglect of reading the Bible, when the missionaries taught me, I already knew most of the material they used from the Bible. Although she was not Mormon, her teaching was absolutely necessary for me to become what I am now.

She drug me to the Baptist Church every week, always hoping I'd become a Baptist. But the only church I ever joined was The Church of Jesus Christ of Latter-day Saints. That was troubling to a devout Baptist. I've often said that throughout my childhood she was afraid I would go to hell. Then I became a Mormon and removed all doubt.

If your mother is still here, take time for her today. And if she's gone, like mine, then take some time for your wife as mother of your children. I'm planning to go prepare dinner and then clean up afterwards. (Even if I go to KFC and use paper plates.)

Early Morning Seminary

I've been substituting an early morning seminary class this week. It's a Doctrine & Covenants course, and we've been covering Sections 132, 133 and 135. These include the eternal marriage covenant, plural wives, prophecy of Christ's Second Coming, and martyrdom of both Joseph and Hyrum.

I drew a layout of the Carthage Jail yesterday morning, described the movements of each of the four in the upper room (Joseph, Hyrum, John Taylor and Willard Richards) during and after the attack, then discussed what happened between the killing and the time the bodies made it back to Nauvoo.

Joseph's last words, "Oh Lord my God . . . " is a shorthand reference to the distress call for the Third Degree, or Master Mason. The entire call is, "Oh Lord my God, is there no help for the widow's son?" Invoking the call, requires all other Masons to rally to help the one in distress. Joseph was aware members of the mob who came to kill him were Masons. By addressing the call to the mob, Joseph was putting the Masons on their sworn duty to provide relief. He was putting them to the test of their oath, which they failed.

It is good to stay in touch with younger Latter-day Saints through teaching opportunities. I teach Priests in my own ward. There are two interesting observations I've made. First, younger minds are more open and willing to be taught. They are interested in thinking or considering ideas. The more you can inform them, the better able they are to gain perspective about the Gospel. They possess a resource which diminishes with time—teachability (to use the vocabulary of scripture, humility). Second, the youth who have grown up using the current form of institutional teaching materials are woefully less informed than those who grew up forty years ago. They are every bit as interested and curious as past generations, but the material used to inform them has been so diminished in content that they are left with the most superficial of understanding of the Gospel. All you parents need to assume responsibility for fixing that with your own children. The institutional approach narrows the scope each year, leaving less and less substance taught.

I've studied the restored Gospel and church history for over 40 years. I continue to search more carefully into the subject year by year. There are so many things to appreciate. I think the most interesting, gripping and important subject you can study is the restored Gospel. Not through the kind of superficial inspirational drivel now sold by Deseret Book. You can go round and round with that kind of crap—won't make one bit of progress there. You'll be briefly entertained, and then lulled to sleep by such quasi-religious infotainment. You will never awaken to your awful situation by being coddled, inspired and reassured that "All is well in Zion." If you intend to actually come to grips with the Gospel, you need to read the Book of Mormon, other scriptures, everything you can find about Joseph Smith, and original material or works based on original materials taken from then contemporary sources. The bibliography from the new book I'm working on has a number of great sources worth considering.

But the Gospel is not study alone. The purpose of study is to inform our conduct, our thoughts and our words. What truths we learn need to be put into action and lived. It is in the living that the power of the Gospel is released. As we "do" what we are instructed, we find ourselves in company with angels and Heavenly messengers.

That process which Joseph Smith describes in the *Joseph Smith-History* found in the *Pearl of Great Price*, still works. For any soul who decides to try it.

Utah Women in the Law

This evening I attended a gathering at the Little America Grand Hotel paying tribute to the first 100 women admitted to practice law in Utah. It wasn't until the 1970's that the total women admitted to practice law in Utah reached the 100 mark.

Utah Supreme Court Chief Justice Christine Durham was one of two keynote speakers, Elder Dallin Oaks was the other. Chief Justice Durham was the 72nd woman admitted to practice in Utah's history.

Now she is the state's Chief Justice. She and Elder Oaks served together temporarily on the Utah Supreme Court. She was added to the court in 1982, Elder Oaks departed in 1984 for church service. It was an interesting evening. I am glad I was able to attend, and take my wife, and daughter, Lindsay.

There were excerpts from court opinions in the late 1800's from both Utah and Wisconsin when the first women were applying to practice law in both states. Surprisingly, the attitude from Wisconsin was condescending, critical, and discouraging toward women who wanted to be lawyers. But from Utah, there was praise and encouragement—even the expectation that women would add some degree of dignity and compassion to the profession.

Events like these serve to remind us how greatly things have changed in relatively recent times. Some of the things we take for granted have only recently occurred.

Societies which fail to educate, and allow women to influence every aspect of their lives are diminished by the failing. Advancement to the entire culture is tied to the education and contribution of women. They should be allowed every opportunity possible.

Utah Sound Money Act

On June 2nd, I attended the ceremony at the Capitol Building acknowledging the signing of the Utah Sound Money Act. The act makes gold and silver coin legal tender in Utah. It is designed to allow a form of currency to be used that will have intrinsic value. Its value will not be tied to monetary policy.

The prediction now is that billions of dollars in capital will migrate into Utah because of the ability to purchase and store (in Utah) gold and silver as currency. By treating it as currency, any inflationary value increases to the gold and silver will not be taxed as a gain. You can't tax money. It is now treated as money under Utah law.

Given all the recent, direful economic news, the idea of stabilizing monetary value by a precious metal form of currency seems prudent. Utah may be the first state to adopt the idea, but there are fourteen other states with similar legislation being considered.

The US Constitution allows a state to adopt gold and silver coin as currency for the state. Utah's move is in keeping with that Constitutional power. It also seems wise, given the announced determination by the central bank to "monetize the debt"—meaning the debt will be paid by printing more dollars. The inevitable result of expanding the money supply, and not simultaneously increasing goods and services will be inflationary. When a nation resorts to financing national expenditures by printing paper money, sooner or later the paper money becomes valueless. Oftentimes dramatically.

The prudence of migrating some money into a form having more value than that bestowed on it by a printing press, managed by a profligate government, seems wise.

D–Day

Early this morning in 1944, my father and Hugh Nibley were storming onto the beach at Normandy. Oddly, both of them were older GI's, and were the same age at the time. My father landed on Omaha Beach, against terrible German emplacements firing down from a cliff above, without any tank support. Hugh Nibley landed on Utah Beach, where he arrived in a Jeep that drove through craters caused by the incoming German artillery fire.

It is hard to comprehend the chaos of that day. As my father was dying fifty years later, it was about that day he chose to speak. He wondered if the many more years he had been given than those he saw die that day had been well lived.

Therefore, when Saving Private Ryan came out years later, I concluded the universal result of living, when so many others died, was the same. The added years given the survivors were always viewed as a stewardship, a gift. One they would need to report on to their friends when they at last joined them in death.

That is not a bad way to live a life. Viewing it as a gift. A probation. An opportunity to do something worthwhile with the precious and limited time given to each of us.

Catholic Business Network, Utah State Treasurer

I attended a meeting of the Catholic Business Network this week where Utah State Treasurer, Richard Ellis gave a talk. His remarks about the economy of Utah were very insightful, and reaffirmed how well the state government has been managed.

Right now the federal stimulus money is ending, and states are panicked about the loss of those "bail out dollars." Utah, however, has already budgeted to proceed without the need of any further federal contribution. If the money ends, Utah will be unaffected.

There are over $8 billion in new construction projects currently underway in Utah. These are just the top 20 projects. Hundreds of other projects are not included in that number.

Utah's housing bubble lagged behind the national average, did not reach the same levels, and therefore did not result in the same kinds of crippling losses. Although Utah has been affected, and many people are in a great deal of financial stress, it is comparatively less significant than the national economic turmoil.

The growth of Utah's population has averaged over 9% since the last census, one of the highest in the nation. Sooner or later that growth will require new housing to be built. Housing must recover for the overall economy to return to steady growth. New housing is what drives all durable good sales.

It was an interesting meeting. I asked a question about the likelihood of a double-dip recession. Mr. Ellis was reluctant to predict it is coming. However, if it comes, Utah will be better equipped to cope than most the rest of the country. Though national economic downturns do affect Utah, they are ameliorated by state government's careful management, balanced budget, careful pension management, and rainy-day funding. I think State Treasurer Richard Ellis is a credit to Utah.

Guidance from the Spirit

I've been reflecting on a commonly held belief concerning the Holy Ghost. Among Latter-day Saints the assertion is widely believed that the Holy Ghost will always leave a "good feeling" as the evidence of a message coming from God. This is in contrast with Joseph Smith's correct description of the Holy Ghost as delivering "intelligence" or "sudden insight" or, to use scriptural language, "light and truth." The feelings which follow an authentic encounter with the Holy Ghost can be anything from fear and dread to joy and rejoicing. Our emotional reaction to the message can vary depending upon the information we've been given. But "feeling good" about something is separate from the Holy Ghost.

When the message from God calls to repentance, the reaction can be best described as anger, or distress, or fear; but is not likely to be described as leaving a "good feeling." The message of repentance always requires change. It will always confront the error and require you to alter what you are doing.

I have noticed some reactions to what I've written measure what has been written against the standard of a "good feeling" and, as a result, some have concluded I'm not worth reading. I suppose against that standard Abinadi would have been rejected. Samuel the Lamanite, too. John the Baptist, Elijah, Christ, Peter, Paul, Joseph Smith, Noah, Enoch, John the Beloved, as well. Certainly Nephi, Jacob, Alma, Mormon, and Moroni. In fact, I can't think of a single authentic message which did not include as its most important content information which violates the "feeling good" standard. I think care should be taken when a standard gets employed. Use a false standard and you risk reaching a false result.

This is one of the criticisms made by Grant Palmer in his *Insider's* book. He took aim at a false notion ("feeling good" means the Holy Ghost) and then leveled criticism against the false notion. Though a lifelong employee of the Church Education System, he was ignorant of the correct standard and lost his faith in the Holy Ghost's ability to enlighten because of it. His criticism was justified, but not the standard. He, like many Latter-day Saints, confuses something which inspires with a witness from the Spirit. You can be inspired by music, movies, plays and thrilling speeches coming from unenlightened sources which bring no light and truth. You may be entertained, but you are not given greater light and truth or intelligence from such thrilling encounters.

The one thing I do know, and the truth I can proclaim is this: Truth will come through and confirm itself when measured against the standard of: 1) imparting truth and light, which is intelligence; and 2) whether the message leads to greater belief in, understanding of and testimony of Christ. These standards do not involve "feeling good." They do, however, involve enlightenment and edification. Even if the result of gaining more light is to see yourself in a new way, requiring repentance, confession of sin, re-baptism, breaking your heart and becoming contrite in spirit. Anyone who can teach a message which will pass this standard, whether they are high or low, rich or poor, great or obscure, has given something of value.

Joseph the Prophet

Although Joseph Smith revealed many, previously unknown things, his ministry was devoted primarily to bringing others into fellowship with God. The ordinances, scriptures, revelations, and teachings restored through him were not intended to titillate, but to instruct on how to reconnect with God.

From his emphasis on the promise in James 1:5 ("if any of you lack wisdom, let him ask of God . . . and it shall be given him") leading to the First Vision, to the promise of Moroni 10:4 ("I would exhort you that ye would ask God, the Eternal Father, in the name of Christ, if these things are not true; and . . . he will manifest the truth of it unto you"), to D&C 93:1 ("It shall come to pass that every soul who forsaketh his sins and cometh unto me, and calleth on my name, and obeyeth my voice, and keepeth my commandments, shall see my face and know that I am"), and in numerous other places throughout his ministry, Joseph reiterated both the possibility and importance of each soul coming directly to God.

This is the role of a true messenger. It is to bring others into harmony with God. Not to titillate them with new information, leaving them without knowledge of God. When someone delivers a new message that does not include knowledge about how the audience may come to God themselves, then the primary intent is always to make others dependent on the messenger. It is vanity. It is prideful. It is to call attention to themselves in an effort to place themselves above their fellow man, and interject themselves between the person and God. It is priestcraft.

The "welfare of Zion" consists of teaching others how to come to God themselves, and receive the heavenly promises directly from God.[1390] Zion will be composed exclusively of those who can endure the presence of God. Therefore, it is necessary for everyone to come

---

[1390] 2 Nephi 26:29 "He commandeth that there shall be no priestcrafts; for, behold, priestcrafts are that men preach and set themselves up for a light unto the world, that they may get gain and praise of the world; but they seek not the welfare of Zion."

up to the heavenly mount by their own repentance and remembrance of the Lord.

It is foolishness to separate information about the Lord's doings from instruction on how to become redeemed. It is vanity to spread new, and personal revelation about the afterlife, God, man, prophecy, visionary encounters, and spiritual experiences if the primary reason does not focus on instructing how the audience can come to God themselves. It is also dangerous to trust teachings which fail to give you guidance on how you can find God for yourself. If all that is delivered is a message about some great experience, the experience was not intended for you. It isn't important. It is the way to find God that will save you. Not someone else's new, and exciting spiritual manifestation.

I've shared almost nothing of the things I have learned. But I've tried to share everything about how you can "come and see"[1391]. Still, however, there are very few who can detect the difference. Still there remain those who are tossed to and fro by the sleight of men.[1392]

Here's how things really work:

New revelation for the church comes from the top. It is not binding upon anyone unless it comes through the correct channel, and then is sustained as binding upon the church. Whether you like that system or not, that is the system. *However*, every church member is obligated to teach one another the doctrines of the kingdom. Expounding, exhorting, teaching, and instructing is a common obligation imposed upon us all. Therefore, everything I have written, all I have taught, and the things I have testified about are confined to elaborating upon the established doctrines of the church, the revela-

---

[1391] John 1:46 "And Nathanael said unto him, Can there any good thing come out of Nazareth? Philip saith unto him, Come and see."

[1392] Ephesians 4:14 "That we *henceforth* be no more children, tossed to and fro, and carried about with every wind of doctrine, by the sleight of men, *and* cunning craftiness, whereby they lie in wait to deceive;"

tions in the Book of Mormon, the other standard works, and Joseph Smith's teachings. I've said almost nothing about my personal revelations because they were intended for me. They will not help you. They equip me to be able to preach, teach, exhort and expound, but just publishing what I know to the world will not aid any other person in their individual journey.

Salvation for you is a journey exactly like the journey undertaken by Joseph Smith. Which is also identical to the journey undertaken by Abraham, Isaac and Jacob. Which was modeled upon the pattern coming down through Noah. Who was a contemporary with Enoch, both of whom undertook the same journey. Which originated with Adam, who came back into God's presence three years previous to his death, and received "comfort" from the Lord.[1393] The Lord is the promised Comforter who will come to all of us on the same conditions[1394]. I was asked, and wrote a manual on that process in the first book, *The Second Comforter: Conversing With the Lord Through the Veil*. The purpose of the book has nothing to do with my own recognition or importance. Throughout the book my many failings are discussed. The book is about the reader, and how the reader can come to know God.

Still people will go to great trouble, and spare no effort to find someone who will only give a titillating peek behind the veil, but who

---

[1393] D&C 107:53–55 "Three years previous to the death of Adam, he called Seth, Enos, Cainan, Mahalaleel, Jared, Enoch, and Methuselah, who were all high priests, with the residue of his posterity who were righteous, into the valley of Adam-ondi-Ahman, and there bestowed upon them his last blessing. And the Lord appeared unto them, and they rose up and blessed Adam, and called him Michael, the prince, the archangel. And the Lord administered comfort unto Adam, and said unto him: I have set thee to be at the head; a multitude of nations shall come of thee, and thou art a prince over them forever."

[1394] John 14:23 "Jesus answered and said unto him, If a man love me, he will keep my words: and my Father will love him, and we will come unto him, and make our abode with him."
D&C 130:3 "John 14:23—The appearing of the Father and the Son, in that verse, is a personal appearance; and the idea that the Father and the Son dwell in a man's heart is an old sectarian notion, and is false."

will do nothing to instruct you on how you can meet God here, be redeemed from the fall of man, and come back into God's presence. This is the purpose of the Gospel, and the definition of redemption.[1395] Telling about personal experience cannot help another. Testifying to the process, however, is the burden of all true teaching.

I am a fool, and anyone who thinks otherwise is misled. My only relevance is the common obligation imposed upon us all to preach, teach, exhort and expound. I confine all I do to that obligation. The only thing I can offer anyone is to point them to the One who is filled with truth and light, which is intelligence.[1396] And still there are those who cannot discern between what and how I teach, and how others who are practicing only priestcraft do so. I am saddened, not particularly surprised, but saddened. These are the times we live in.[1397]

What more could have been done than the Lord has already done? Is it not us, not He, upon whom the blame must be lain?

The Latter-day famine continues unabated still. Not because there isn't something worth consuming, but because we crave only the weakest of gruel, which cannot sustain life. Therefore, let us all feast away and still become famished until at last we perish without hope, having wasted the days of our probation. We didn't care much for Joseph's message in his day, and we fail to even notice it in ours.

[1395] Ether 3:13 "And when he had said these words, behold, the Lord showed himself unto him, and said: Because thou knowest these things ye are redeemed from the fall; therefore ye are brought back into my presence; therefore I show myself unto you."

[1396] D&C 93:36 "The glory of God is intelligence, or, in other words, light and truth."

[1397] Isaiah 29:9–10 "Stay yourselves, and wonder; cry ye out, and cry: they are drunken, but not with wine; they stagger, but not with strong drink. For the Lord hath poured out upon you the spirit of deep sleep, and hath closed your eyes: the prophets and your rulers, the seers hath he covered."

Adultery

That's a title that ought to get readers.

I've been thinking about adultery since the 4th, when my wife, the bishop's wife and I were talking about the abysmal job we do of teaching anything on the subject. The bishop's wife is a nurse, and she does rape-kit exams at local hospitals. Her view of the condition of young Latter-day Saints' understanding alarms her. Both perpetrators and victims are often Latter-day Saints. The casual way in which young women put themselves at risk reflects poor teaching, warning and counsel. She tries to educate, but there's a lot of soft-selling going on instead of candid teaching and warning.

I wrote a paper for the stake presidency when I was on the high council. As a result, there was a series of 5th Sunday adult meetings conducted by a member of the stake presidency in our stake. The paper later became the basis of one chapter in *Eighteen Verses*.

Out of wedlock children who are raised by single mothers has become one of the great tragedies of our day. Children raised by a single mother, without fathers present comprise about 70 percent of juvenile murderers, drug abusers, suicides and runaways. While I was on the high council, adultery was the top reason for temple marriages breaking up in our stake.

Parents have the primary responsibility for teaching youth about this subject. It is important enough that you should be candid with your children. They deserve to be taught, to be warned, to understand the cultural atmosphere of casual sex is ultimately destructive of life itself. It imprisons.

If you love your children, teach them. And set a good example before them. The church is not responsible for teaching your children, you are. They aren't going to be doing the job only you can perform.

Well, on another topic, I finally enjoyed being able to do legally what used to require sneaking up to Evanston, Wyoming, and smuggling back contraband to Utah to accomplish . . . Aerial fireworks are now legal in Utah. I suspect that has kept several million dollars in Utah for the 4th, and will keep even more here for the 24th. (That's Pioneer Day, a State holiday in Utah.) We may not get drunk in Utah, but we do blow the hell out of things as a workable substitute.— Well, perhaps I ought to qualify that: Some few of us, who celebrate around our neighbors, and invite our street, where our bishop lives to our 4th of July party, don't get drunk in Utah. As for those out of sight, I can't account for them.

Forsake, come, call, obey, keep, see, and *know*.

I had a discussion about the difficulty of rising above the sins of this world. It was provoked by the recent post on adultery. It has in turn led to these additional thoughts.

It is impossible to become altogether clean in this fallen world. We can do our best, but in the end we're going to find we are lacking. The scriptures admit this. The proposition is so fundamentally understood among most saints that it goes without saying. We're all in need of redemption from an outside power, someone with greater virtue and power than we have, who can lift us from our condition into something higher, cleaner, and more godly. This is the role of Christ. His atoning sacrifice equipped Him to accomplish this.

The atonement, however, is not magic. Through it, Christ accomplished some very specific things, and has the power to lead us all back to the presence of God, the Father. The process was difficult for Him and is necessarily difficult for us.

Christ participated in the ordinance of the atonement to acquire two things. First, knowledge.[1398] It is through His knowledge He is able to "justify many." The knowledge was acquired through His suffering the pains of all mankind. That allowed Him to know ex-

---

[1398] Isaiah 53:11 "He shall see of the travail of his soul, *and* shall be satisfied: by his knowledge shall my righteous servant justify many; for he shall bear their iniquities."

actly what weaknesses afflict mankind, and how to overcome them. This allows Him to succor, or relieve, or teach mankind how to overcome every form of guilt, affliction, and weakness.[1399] This knowledge was gained by suffering guilt and remorse for sins He did not commit exactly as if He were the one who committed them. He performed this great burden before His Father, who would never leave Him; even in His hour of temptation, despite the fact that all His followers would abandon Him.[1400] When He suffered the guilt of all mankind, it was necessary for His Father to draw near to Him.[1401] This was required because it is impossible for Christ to know how to redeem mankind from the guilt and shame of sin unless He experiences the pains of uncleanliness before God the Father, as mankind will do if they are unclean in the day of judgment.[1402] Unlike all of us, however, Christ knows how to overcome this shame because He has done so.

Second, Christ acquired the keys of death and hell by suffering, reconciling, dying, rising, and reuniting with the Father.[1403] Because

---

[1399] Alma 7:11–12 "And he shall go forth, suffering pains and afflictions and temptations of every kind; and this that the word might be fulfilled which saith he will take upon him the pains and the sicknesses of his people. And he will take upon him death, that he may loose the bands of death which bind his people; and he will take upon him their infirmities, that his bowels may be filled with mercy, according to the flesh, that he may know according to the flesh how to succor his people according to their infirmities."

[1400] John 16:32 "Behold, the hour cometh, yea, is now come, that ye shall be scattered, every man to his own, and shall leave me alone: and yet I am not alone, because the Father is with me."

[1401] Luke 22:42–43 "Saying, Father, if thou be willing, remove this cup from me: nevertheless not my will, but thine, be done. And there appeared an angel unto him from heaven, strengthening him."

[1402] Mormon 9:4–5 "Behold, I say unto you that ye would be more miserable to dwell with a holy and just God, under a consciousness of your filthiness before him, than ye would to dwell with the damned souls in hell. For behold, when ye shall be brought to see your nakedness before God, and also the glory of God, and the holiness of Jesus Christ, it will kindle a flame of unquenchable fire upon you."

[1403] Revelation 1:18 "*I am* he that liveth, and was dead; and, behold, I am alive for evermore, Amen; and have the keys of hell and of death."

the keys of death and hell belong to Him, He has the power of forgiveness. He can forgive all men all offenses. But He requires us to forgive others.[1404] If we fail to forgive others, we cannot be forgiven.[1405]

We do not move from our state of evil to redemption by Christ's sacrifice alone. It is required for us to follow Him.[1406] We follow Him when we allow Him to succor us, to impart knowledge to us, and to forgive others through His knowledge gained from the atonement.

Through the keys of death and hell, Christ's atonement cleanses us from our errors, our failings, and our deliberate wrong choices. He provides cleansing from those failings. But His atonement does not change our character unless we follow Him. The atonement, if properly acted upon, frees us to develop character like His, unencumbered by the guilt of what we've failed to do. He removes our guilt. But developing character like His is our responsibility.

We cannot be passive and obtain what He offers. We are required to actively pursue the redemption we seek through Him. When the sin is removed from us, we are free to pursue virtue without the crippling effects of remorse which He removes from us.[1407] When freed from the guilt of sin, the past mistakes no longer haunt us. Our sins are no longer remembered by the Lord, and we are free to con-

---

[1404] D&C 64:9–10 "Wherefore, I say unto you, that ye ought to forgive one another; for he that forgiveth not his brother his trespasses standeth condemned before the Lord; for there remaineth in him the greater sin. I, the Lord, will forgive whom I will forgive, but of you it is required to forgive all men."

[1405] Matthew 6:15 "But if ye forgive not men their trespasses, neither will your Father forgive your trespasses."

[1406] John 10:27 "My sheep hear my voice, and I know them, and they follow me:"

[1407] Alma 24:10 "And I also thank my God, yea, my great God, that he hath granted unto us that we might repent of these things, and also that he hath forgiven us of those our many sins and murders which we have committed, and taken away the guilt from our hearts, through the merits of his Son."

fess and forsake them.[1408] The reason we can publicly confess them is because they are no longer us. They do not define us. It is no longer our sin, nor our character. We have chosen to follow Him into a new life.

The development of a godly character happens in stages, gradually. We are forgiven in an instant, suddenly.[1409] When forgiven we necessarily turn to a new life, in which sharing the joy of forgiveness and the joy of redemption through Christ is our abiding desire.[1410] The mind changes in proportion to the joy found in the new life.[1411] Such new people are no longer the sons of men, but they become the sons of God.[1412] They know the joy of having the voice of the Father declare to them that they have been begotten by the Father and are the sons of God.[1413]

[1408] D&C 58:42–43 "Behold, he who has repented of his sins, the same is forgiven, and I, the Lord, remember them no more. By this ye may know if a man repenteth of his sins—behold, he will confess them and forsake them."

[1409] Alma 36:18–20 "Now, as my mind caught hold upon this thought, I cried within my heart: O Jesus, thou Son of God, have mercy on me, who am in the gall of bitterness, and am encircled about by the everlasting chains of death. And now, behold, when I thought this, I could remember my pains no more; yea, I was harrowed up by the memory of my sins no more. And oh, what joy, and what marvelous light I did behold; yea, my soul was filled with joy as exceeding as was my pain!"

[1410] Alma 36:24 "Yea, and from that time even until now, I have labored without ceasing, that I might bring souls unto repentance; that I might bring them to taste of the exceeding joy of which I did taste; that they might also be born of God, and be filled with the Holy Ghost."

[1411] Romans 8:5–6 "For they that are after the flesh do mind the things of the flesh; but they that are after the Spirit the things of the Spirit. For to be carnally minded *is* death; but to be spiritually minded *is* life and peace."

[1412] Romans 8:14–17 "For as many as are led by the Spirit of God, they are the sons of God. For ye have not received the spirit of bondage again to fear; but ye have received the Spirit of adoption, whereby we cry, Abba, Father. The Spirit itself beareth witness with our spirit, that we are the children of God: And if children, then heirs; heirs of God, and joint-heirs with Christ; if so be that we suffer with *him,* that we may be also glorified together."

[1413] Psalms 2:7 "I will declare the decree: the Lord hath said unto me, Thou *art* my Son; this day have I begotten thee."

Remaining mired in the flesh is evidence a man has not been redeemed, not been succored by Christ, not accepted the saving knowledge which He can impart, and has not risen up to receive salvation. The atonement is not active in such lives. The fullness of the atonement is the fullness of knowledge, which comes by following Him and abiding the conditions. No one can receive what He offers unless they conform to the conditions He has established for redemption.[1414]

This is the Gospel of Christ. This is the news which comes from the Lord—the Messenger of Salvation. Those who know Him will declare these things in unmistakable words to allow others to come and partake of the same fruit of the tree of life. All the other virtues, causes, programs and, "inspirational stories" are distractions which, if indulged in to the neglect of these other things, will damn you.

> "Verily, thus saith the Lord: It shall come to pass that every soul who forsaketh his sins and cometh unto me, and calleth on my name, and obeyeth my voice, and keepeth my commandments, shall see my face and know that I am; And that I am the true light that lighteth every man that cometh into the world; And that I am in the Father, and the Father in me, and the Father and I are one—The Father because he gave me of his fulness, and the Son because I was in the world and made flesh my tabernacle, and dwelt among the sons of men." (D&C 93:1–4)

I am not that Light. But I have seen that Light and can testify He lives, and His atoning work continues today among all of those who will receive Him. If you will receive Him, He will not leave you comfortless, but He will come and take up His abode with you.[1415] Not

---

[1414] D&C 93:27–28 "And no man receiveth a fulness unless he keepeth his commandments. He that keepeth his commandments receiveth truth and light, until he is glorified in truth and knoweth all things."

[1415] John 14:18 "I will not leave you comfortless: I will come to you."

only Him, but the Father also.[1416] This is literal, and the idea this is only an abode "in your heart" is false; for they will come and make themselves known to you.[1417] Eternal life is to know Him.[1418] This means to come into His presence again.[1419]

These things are the Gospel of Jesus Christ. Anyone who teaches otherwise is in error and a deceiver.

Distracted

There are too many distractions. We're like small children whose eyes are captured by every shiny object passing before us. We lose focus.

The Gospel has a core we don't even understand. We think we're getting somewhere when we debate environmental issues in light of Mormonism, or immigration policy, or conservative versus liberal political solutions, or dress, grooming, word of wisdom, and ten thousand other irrelevancies.

Until the core is corrected and our souls are saved, no amount of energy or focus devoted to the periphery will get us anywhere.

How are you saved? How are you born again? What ordinances are required? Are they symbols? If symbols, what do they symbolize? What critical things must a man know to be saved? What does it mean "a man cannot be saved in ignorance?" What does it mean to

---

[1416] John 14:23 "Jesus answered and said unto him, If a man love me, he will keep my words: and my Father will love him, and we will come unto him, and make our abode with him."

[1417] D&C 130:3 "John 14:23—The appearing of the Father and the Son, in that verse, is a personal appearance; and the idea that the Father and the Son dwell in a man's heart is an old sectarian notion, and is false."

[1418] John 17:3 "And this is life eternal, that they might know thee the only true God, and Jesus Christ, whom thou hast sent."

[1419] Ether 3:19 "And because of the knowledge of this man he could not be kept from beholding within the veil; and he saw the finger of Jesus, which, when he saw, he fell with fear; for he knew that it was the finger of the Lord; and he had faith no longer, for he knew, nothing doubting."

have "life eternal" through Christ Jesus? Since Alvin was saved in the Celestial Kingdom before the Gospel was restored, what does Section 137 really mean? What about the rest of the revelation from which Section 137 was drawn? Since it involves salvation of a man who died before the fullness of the Gospel returned, how applicable is that section to the condition we find ourselves in today?

Until we understand the core, there is no topic on the periphery worth giving any attention.

Prodigal Son

Luke preserved this now familiar parable of the Lord's:

And he said, A certain man had two sons: And the younger of them said to his father, Father, give me the portion of goods that falleth to me. And he divided unto them his living. And not many days after the younger son gathered all together, and took his journey into a far country, and there wasted his substance with riotous living. And when he had spent all, there arose a mighty famine in that land; and he began to be in want.

And he went and joined himself to a citizen of that country; and he sent him into his fields to feed swine. And he would fain have filled his belly with the husks that the swine did eat: and no man gave unto him. And when he came to himself, he said, How many hired servants of my father's have bread enough and to spare, and I perish with hunger! I will arise and go to my father, and will say unto him, Father, I have sinned against heaven, and before thee, And am no more worthy to be called thy son: make me as one of thy hired servants.

And he arose, and came to his father. But when he was yet a great way off, his father saw him, and had compassion, and ran, and fell on his neck, and kissed him. And the son said unto him, Father, I have sinned against heaven, and in thy sight, and am no more worthy to be called thy son. But the father said to his servants, Bring forth the best robe, and put it on him; and put a ring on his hand, and shoes on his feet: And bring hither the fatted calf, and kill it; and let us eat, and be merry: For this my son was dead, and is alive again; he was lost, and is found. And they began to be merry.

Now his elder son was in the field: and as he came and drew nigh to the house, he heard musick and dancing. And he called one of the servants, and asked what these things meant. And he said unto him, Thy brother is come; and thy father hath killed the fatted calf, because he hath received him safe and sound. And he was angry, and would not go in: therefore came his father out, and intreated him. And he answering said to his father, Lo, these many years do I serve thee, neither transgressed I at any time thy commandment: and yet thou never gavest me a kid, that I might make merry with my friends: But as soon as this thy son was come, which hath devoured thy living with harlots, thou hast killed for him the fatted calf.

And he said unto him, Son, thou art ever with me, and all that I have is thine. It was meet that we should make merry, and be glad: for this thy brother was dead, and is alive again; and was lost, and is found. (Luke 15:11–32)

When all is said and done in the story, the wayward son is given a "ring on his hand," the "best robe," "shoes on his feet," and invited into "the feast."

What does the "ring" on his hand signify?

What does "the best robe" signify?

What do "shoes" symbolize?

What is "the feast" offered by his father?

The faithful son refuses to enter into the feast, stands in judgment of the wayward, but repentant son, and does not join the feast.

What does the refusal to come into the "feast" signify?

What does his "anger" symbolize?

What does his protest of "neither transgressed I at any time thy commandment" signify?

At the end of the parable, who is "alive?" Is it the repentant son who feasts with his father, or the resentful but ostensibly faithful son, who refuses to join the feast? Which of the two is now "dead?"

What does this parable really tell us about those who think themselves better than repentant sinners?

Charity in Teaching

It is both unkind and ineffective to teach truths to those who are unprepared to understand them. A person who has learned and accepted a truth has an obligation to be as kind and patient with those she explains it to as the Lord was in bringing her to the understanding she was given.

You never want someone to reject truth. But if you're going to teach something that hasn't been understood before, you have an obligation to make the matter clear. You should prepare the the audience by laying a foundation using existing scripture, teachings and knowledge to show how the new concept fits into the existing framework. Just declaring something without a foundation to support it often offends instead of enlightens. It alienates rather than invites.

I'm somewhat concerned about those who try to get an understanding of what I've taught, but who haven't read what I've written. In the material, I walk through existing concepts, accepted doctrines, recognized scripture, and language of Joseph Smith to first lay the foundation. Much of that may be familiar; some of it may be surprising, but I take the time to lay it out. Then, after clearing the path to the next ideas, using the existing body of recognized material, I go forward with something that may be new, or difficult, or challenging.

The book I am working on right now will introduce some important information that most people are unfamiliar with. But it will walk through, in the same patient way, building the foundation from which the conclusions are inevitable, and fit it into the framework of all that is known already. I know there are those who are unkind, impatient, or who don't care about the audience. They will want to blurt out the conclusions, and only move quickly to the startling points. That is inevitable, I suppose. But anyone who does that is neither a good teacher, nor are they kind to their audience. They don't care if someone rejects truth. They just want to be involved in the sensational, the surprising and the titillating.

Anyone who is going to teach has an obligation to bring along, in a kindly way, those they seek to reclaim from error. That's how Joseph put it. If you think you have some truth and want to remove an error, you have an obligation to proceed in a proper and affectionate manner to reclaim them.[1420] When a new truth is introduced in a harsh, challenging, unkind way it will be disturbing, upsetting and alienating. Such a person is not a teacher, but instead an enemy to the truth. They make it hard for people to find their way back to God. It is wrong.

True teachers will always adapt to their audience and show kindness and patience to those they teach. When they are called upon by

---

[1420] JS–H 1:28 "During the space of time which intervened between the time I had the vision and the year eighteen hundred and twenty-three—having been forbidden to join any of the religious sects of the day, and being of very tender years, and persecuted by those who ought to have been my friends and to have treated me kindly, and if they supposed me to be deluded to have endeavored in a proper and affectionate manner to have reclaimed me—I was left to all kinds of temptations; and, mingling with all kinds of society, I frequently fell into many foolish errors, and displayed the weakness of youth, and the foibles of human nature; which, I am sorry to say, led me into divers temptations, offensive in the sight of God. In making this confession, no one need suppose me guilty of any great or malignant sins. A disposition to commit such was never in my nature. But I was guilty of levity, and sometimes associated with jovial company, etc., not consistent with that character which ought to be maintained by one who was called of God as I had been. But this will not seem very strange to any one who recollects my youth, and is acquainted with my native cheery temperament."

the spirit to rebuke with sharpness, they will afterwards show an increase of love, to make it possible to accept the inspired rebuke.[1421] They want to bring people to a position where truth spreads, is accepted, and all can rejoice in the new light and knowledge shared between them.

This is not to say that all truth a person has should be always be shared. Unless the right circumstances arise, with a properly prepared student to instruct, some kinds of knowledge cannot be shared. But to the extent something is appropriate for instruction, the lesson should be adapted to the capacity and preparation of the audience. Some material may be appropriate with one person that would be inappropriate for another. Until an audience has first been taught basic information, they are unprepared to hear something further. We don't discuss some things with investigators, but leave it until later for them to be taught. It takes about four years for a convert to receive the basics of the church. It takes years before some information can be put into context. Rushing to expose people to information is not only hasty, but oftentimes destructive. If you intend to be a teacher, and not an enemy to someone's salvation, you should only proceed in the appropriate way, using kindness, meekness, gentleness, pure knowledge and love unfeigned.[1422] Not haste, shock, surprise and ambush.

[1421] D&C 121:43–44 "Reproving betimes with sharpness, when moved upon by the Holy Ghost; and then showing forth afterwards an increase of love toward him whom thou hast reproved, lest he esteem thee to be his enemy; That he may know that thy faithfulness is stronger than the cords of death."

[1422] D&C 121:41–42 "No power or influence can or ought to be maintained by virtue of the priesthood, only by persuasion, by long-suffering, by gentleness and meekness, and by love unfeigned; By kindness, and pure knowledge, which shall greatly enlarge the soul without hypocrisy, and without guile—"

We Are the Gentiles

I had an interesting question asked about the "remnant" I thought worth addressing here.

There should be no confusion about the identity of the "remnant" spoken of in the Book of Mormon. It refers to the descendants of Lehi (at times further divided into those descended from Nephi, Jacob and Joseph—all Lehi's sons). The European stock who migrated to North America and dispossessed the indigenous people are invariably referred to as "gentiles" in the Book of Mormon. Throughout it is the case that the European descendants are "gentiles" and never anything else.

You can start in 1 Nephi and go through the end. The "gentiles" are us—the Latter-day Saints (to the extent we are primarily European-descended and not Native American).

Joseph Smith received the dedicatory prayer for the Kirtland Temple by revelation. In the prayer he refers to the church as being "identified with the gentiles." (D&C 109:60)

It does not matter if we descend from Israel. Nor if we have actual genetic markers which would make us Ephraimites, or Levites, or of the tribe of Judah, or any of the other tribes of Israel. Unless we are Native American, we are not the "remnant" discussed in the Book of Mormon.

There are many references to early church leaders being descended from Israelite bloodlines. Even if that is the case, however, the Book of Mormon usage refers to us as "gentiles" unless descended from Lehi.

No Man Will Save You

There isn't going to be any man or group of men who save you. There is literally a single way, and a single source. That is Christ.[1423] Whether you are able to receive salvation or not is entirely dependent on how you respond to Him, not to other people.[1424]

There are no magic ordinances that will reconcile you to Him.[1425] Ordinances may be mandatory, but they do not save. They are evidence we are willing to submit to Him[1426], but they are not the full scope of submission required for salvation.[1427]

It has never been enough to attend meetings, perform outward ordinances and be part of a group that meets to discuss the scriptures from time to time. Every one must individually accept responsibility for coming to Christ and doing what He asks.[1428]

[1423] Mosiah 3:17 "And moreover, I say unto you, that there shall be no other name given nor any other way nor means whereby salvation can come unto the children of men, only in and through the name of Christ, the Lord Omnipotent."

[1424] 2 Nephi 9:41 "O then, my beloved brethren, come unto the Lord, the Holy One. Remember that his paths are righteous. Behold, the way for man is narrow, but it lieth in a straight course before him, and the keeper of the gate is the Holy One of Israel; and he employeth no servant there; and there is none other way save it be by the gate; for he cannot be deceived, for the Lord God is his name."

[1425] 2 Nephi 25:23 "For we labor diligently to write, to persuade our children, and also our brethren, to believe in Christ, and to be reconciled to God; for we know that it is by grace that we are saved, after all we can do."

[1426] 2 Nephi 31:5 "And now, if the Lamb of God, he being holy, should have need to be baptized by water, to fulfil all righteousness, O then, how much more need have we, being unholy, to be baptized, yea, even by water!"

[1427] Luke 6:46 "And why call ye me, Lord, Lord, and do not the things which I say?"

[1428] Luke 6:45–49 "A good man out of the good treasure of his heart bringeth forth that which is good; and an evil man out of the evil treasure of his heart bringeth forth that which is evil: for of the abundance of the heart his mouth speaketh. And why call ye me, Lord, Lord, and do not the things which I say? Whosoever cometh to me, and heareth my sayings, and doeth them, I will shew you to whom he is like: He is like a man which built an house, and digged deep, and laid the foundation on a rock: and when the flood arose, the stream beat vehemently upon that house, and could not shake it: for it was founded upon a rock. But he that heareth, and doeth not, is like a man that without a foundation built an house upon the earth; against which the stream did beat vehemently, and immediately it fell; and the ruin of that house was great."

The relentless message of the Book of Mormon is that we must all repent. We are not secure in our standing before God until we repent, come down in the depths of humility and become accepted by Him. When He ministers to us, we can know our standing before Him. Until then, we cannot know.[1429]

There is no "boss" who will bring you along to salvation.

There are no comforting words you need to hear that will make you secure in your sins.[1430]

There is no hopeful message that needs to be shared about how everyone will probably be saved at the last day.[1431]

You don't need me, nor any other man. You need to reconcile yourself to Christ. Anyone who wants to place themselves between you and the Lord will, if you let them, bring you and them to hell.

[1429] JS–H 1:29 "In consequence of these things, I often felt condemned for my weakness and imperfections; when, on the evening of the above-mentioned twenty-first of September, after I had retired to my bed for the night, I betook myself to prayer and supplication to Almighty God for forgiveness of all my sins and follies, and also for a manifestation to me, that I might know of my state and standing before him; for I had full confidence in obtaining a divine manifestation, as I previously had one."

[1430] 2 Nephi 28:21 "And others will he pacify, and lull them away into carnal security, that they will say: All is well in Zion; yea, Zion prospereth, all is well—and thus the devil cheateth their souls, and leadeth them away carefully down to hell."

[1431] 2 Nephi 28:22 "And behold, others he flattereth away, and telleth them there is no hell; and he saith unto them: I am no devil, for there is none—and thus he whispereth in their ears, until he grasps them with his awful chains, from whence there is no deliverance."

Passing the Heavenly Gift

New Book

I will have a new book out soon and want to clarify a few things in advance of its release.

First, this is not a book for everyone. Some people have become aware of problems in church history. They have struggled with what they've learned. As a result there have been crises of faith among some of the brightest and most inquisitive among us. This is a tragic loss. The new book is written to help those who are already aware of problems to come to grips with the issues and see how it all still makes sense. There are those who are perfectly content with the oftentimes fanciful accounts of our history which gloss over problems and ignore contradictions. For such people reading the new book will be startling and perhaps a faith challenging experience. The book will perhaps upset them more than reassure them. I do not want to do that for any Latter-day Saint. I would hope they would decide to pass on reading the book and continue to be content with whatever assumptions please them about our past.

Second, I am very concerned that many of the most important points of the book will be taken completely out of context and shared by overeager readers who want to show off their new understanding. That can be destructive. The book is prepared carefully, with precepts constructed, historic proof gathered, explanations crafted with care and an overall harmony between parts. Taking some of the information out of context and blurting it out as an isolated event, quote, or idea will not help anyone. The unkind person doing so may get to show off, but they tear down rather than build up. None but fools will trifle with the souls of men (see *TPJS*, 137).

The book will not read like the traditional accounts of what has happened. The point of departure for the book is the scriptures. No historian's theme is used to substitute a retelling of events. Instead the book relies on the scriptures, primarily the Book of Mormon, as the basis from which to construct the events of our dispensation. So far as I know, this is the only time our history has been told with an eye on what the scriptures say about us instead of our own vanity and pride. Therefore, it is quite different than what you've been reading about us in other accounts.

Passing the Heavenly Gift

The new book, titled *Passing the Heavenly Gift*, is now available on Amazon.com.

I have explained previously that the book may not be for everyone. If you elect to read it, you should read it all. Reading the entire book is necessary so that you will understand the full meaning of the material. Foundational things are discussed that will be revisited later to show how they fit into a larger picture—then revisited again to complete the construction of the matter from beginning to end. If you do not complete the whole book, you will not be able to evaluate the matter.

I do not expect many will enjoy the book. Although I believe anyone who reads it will be benefited by its contents. The object is to be faith promoting. Not in the sense that it will create false or naive hope, but instead it will inform you of the responsibilities resting upon anyone who seeks to know Christ. The result of the Gospel has always been intended to bring us joy. I think this book offers a greater opportunity for you to come to find joy in this life than the errors which merely use flattery or praise to distract you from the truth.

For any who elect to read it, I would hope if you choose to recommend it to others you will permit them to discover the contents of the book for themselves. Editorial summaries or statements taken out of context in this book will be more misleading than they would be with any other book I've written.

A Fair and Full Hearing

The new book has hardly become available to anyone. However, I did receive some feedback from a friend who has not attended church for many years. He was one of the more conscientious saints. He learned and studied and reflected for several decades as an active member. He served in several bishoprics, high priest group leaderships and as a gospel doctrine teacher. His study led him to a number of unfavorable conclusions about the church and its history. He read the new book, *Passing the Heavenly Gift*, and called to tell me he had returned to sacrament meeting a week ago, and for the first time in nearly a decade took the Sacrament.

I've already been called "apostate," as well as "on the road to apostasy" from some who have not read the book and have no intention to do so. I suppose there will be a great deal of that. But it is a small thing. The truth is that this book, as all I've written, testifies to the truth as I understand it. It has already done some good in one reader's life. If the only price to be paid for reclaiming another's faith is to endure some evil speaking about myself, it is truly only a small thing.

Another person's ignorance can never define your own faith. Some people do not study our faith, but claim to practice it. If Mormonism truly is of God (as I believe), then it is important enough to warrant the closest of study. When any matter is studied with great care, issues will surface. Quandaries will arise. There will be gaps, problems and failings. Human weaknesses will be exposed. Some things will get quite messy.

The underlying truth, however, deserves a fair and full hearing. Study of Mormonism which goes only far enough to discover the quandaries has not proceeded far enough. It should search into it deeply enough, prayerfully enough, and searchingly enough to find the answers.

When one person has sought deeply and another has not, there is a gap between the understanding of the two which makes a common understanding problematic. The one in possession of less is really not in a position to correctly judge the one in possession of more. Oddly, however, the one who has less is altogether more likely to judge the one with more, while the one with more is equipped to look more kindly upon the other. After all, the one with more has struggled from the lesser position.

I understand the criticism I've received. I expected it. No one needs to defend me. No one needs to argue the point, get angry or deal unkindly with people who have not yet studied enough to form an appropriate conclusion. Only a fool judges a matter before they hear it. Such souls warrant our kindly efforts to persuade, not our censure or condemnation. We all carry foolishness, learning year by year, struggling to overcome the many things we've neglected in our study, prayers and contemplation. God does not grade on a curve. Therefore, when you begin to think you've outshone your fellow man, you should reflect again on Moses' reaction to seeing the Man of Holiness: "Now for this cause I know man is nothing, which thing I never had supposed".[1432] None of us have anything to boast of, even if you know more than your fellow man. We all know less than He who is "more intelligent than them all".[1433]

Whenever I contemplate the gulf between He who is Holiness and myself, and the great charity required from Him to condescend for me, I can hardly bear the thought of feeling triumph because of the ignorance of my fellow saints. How unkind. How foolish. How uncharitable. More than that, how very unlike the Lord whom we all claim to serve.

I teach the Priests in my Ward. I love the calling and love their openness, their eagerness and desire to learn. The last lesson I taught was about sex, based in the scriptures, and candidly covered the topic in a way which I hoped would both inform and edify. I was genuinely thanked by these 16 to 18 year old young men afterwards. I hope their lives will be better for the lesson.

So, also, I hope any who read *Passing the Heavenly Gift* will find their lives better for having read it. If you find yourself upset by it, I'd hope you would realize at least one person has returned to church after many years of absence because it restored in him a desire to fellowship with the saints, and again partake of the Sacrament. That one soul's renewal was to me, worth any petty or foolish reactions that may now come from others.

[1432] Moses 1:10 "And it came to pass that it was for the space of many hours before Moses did again receive his natural strength like unto man; and he said unto himself: Now, for this cause I know that man is nothing, which thing I never had supposed."

[1433] Abraham 3:19 "And the Lord said unto me: These two facts do exist, that there are two spirits, one being more intelligent than the other; there shall be another more intelligent than they; I am the Lord thy God, I am more intelligent than they all."

A Lesson to the Priests

I was asked by someone who also teaches priests about the lesson to the priests on sex I mentioned on this blog. Here is a brief summary of what was covered:

When Adam was alone it was "not good" in God's view.[1434]

The story of Eve's creation is allegorical, not actual. The allegory says she was made "from a rib" taken "from Adam's side."[1435] This is not intended as an actual explanation of her creation, but instead as a description of the way she is to be regarded. Part of him. Taken from his side, making her his intimately connected associate in whom he should recognize companionship runs within himself. Her presence is intended to satisfy what was before "not good" about Adam's condition. She is literally not only a part of him, but also completes him. This completion is the "image of God" because God is both a Father and a Mother.[1436] Among mankind, when you see the "image of God" you will always see a couple who are as one.[1437] [As an aside, I would add this is why there were two angels upon the Mercy Seat.[1438] He would not permit them to behold His image without seeing what is also symbolized in Adam and Eve.]

[1434] Genesis 2:18 "And the Lord God said, *It is* not good that the man should be alone; I will make him an help meet for him."

[1435] Genesis 2:21–23 "And the Lord God caused a deep sleep to fall upon Adam, and he slept: and he took one of his ribs, and closed up the flesh instead thereof; And the rib, which the Lord God had taken from man, made he a woman, and brought her unto the man. And Adam said, This *is* now bone of my bones, and flesh of my flesh: she shall be called Woman, because she was taken out of Man."

[1436] Genesis 1:27 "So God created man in his *own* image, in the image of God created he him; male and female created he them."

[1437] 1 Corinthians 11:11 "Nevertheless neither is the man without the woman, neither the woman without the man, in the Lord."

[1438] Exodus 25:22 "And there I will meet with thee, and I will commune with thee from above the mercy seat, from between the two cherubims which *are* upon the ark of the testimony, of all *things* which I will give thee in commandment unto the children of Israel."

The purpose of the creation of the two was that they may "become one" or unified.[1439]

The first commandment given after the two are joined by God was to "be fruitful and multiply".[1440]

When they were expelled from the Garden, Adam "knew his wife" which is a euphemism. The word "know" or "knew" is a reference made throughout the Old and New Testaments to sexual intercourse. As a consequence of this Eve became pregnant.[1441]

This is fulfilling the commandment to "be fruitful," and is the way intended for new human life to be brought into the world. When joined by God (temple marriage) and then used to produce a family, the union of the man and woman is pleasing to God. It is order. It is harmony. It produces life, peace and "fulfills the measure of creation" which "brings joy." Unfortunately, when it is employed in other ways, it produces pain, misery and sometimes catastrophic results.

Keeping the power of procreation inside the bounds which produce joy was included in the 10 commandments.[1442]

David was a man after God's own heart. As a youth, he had such faith to follow God that although still a lad he was able, with God's

---

[1439] Genesis 2:24 "Therefore shall a man leave his father and his mother, and shall cleave unto his wife: and they shall be one flesh."

[1440] Genesis 1:27–28 "So God created man in his *own* image, in the image of God created he him; male and female created he them. And God blessed them, and God said unto them, Be fruitful, and multiply, and replenish the earth, and subdue it: and have dominion over the fish of the sea, and over the fowl of the air, and over every living thing that moveth upon the earth."

[1441] Genesis 4:1 "And Adam knew Eve his wife; and she conceived, and bare Cain, and said, I have gotten a man from the Lord."

[1442] Exodus 20:14, 17 "Thou shalt not commit adultery. Thou shalt not covet thy neighbour's house, thou shalt not covet thy neighbour's wife, nor his manservant, nor his maidservant, nor his ox, nor his ass, nor any thing that *is* thy neighbour's."

help, to slay Goliath.[1443] He was so favored by God, that God made him His son, established his throne, and promised him He would watch over him.[1444]

But David committed adultery.[1445] To conceal the sin, he committed murder.[1446] As a result of these sins, he fell from his exaltation.[1447] The result was that a man "after the Lord's own heart" lost everything

---

[1443] 1 Samuel 17:34–37, 45–46 "And David said unto Saul, Thy servant kept his father's sheep, and there came a lion, and a bear, and took a lamb out of the flock: And I went out after him, and smote him, and delivered *it* out of his mouth: and when he arose against me, I caught *him* by his beard, and smote him, and slew him. Thy servant slew both the lion and the bear: and this uncircumcised Philistine shall be as one of them, seeing he hath defied the armies of the living God. David said moreover, The Lord that delivered me out of the paw of the lion, and out of the paw of the bear, he will deliver me out of the hand of this Philistine. And Saul said unto David, Go, and the Lord be with thee. Then said David to the Philistine, Thou comest to me with a sword, and with a spear, and with a shield: but I come to thee in the name of the Lord of hosts, the God of the armies of Israel, whom thou hast defied. This day will the Lord deliver thee into mine hand; and I will smite thee, and take thine head from thee; and I will give the carcases of the host of the Philistines this day unto the fowls of the air, and to the wild beasts of the earth; that all the earth may know that there is a God in Israel."

[1444] 2 Samuel 7:14–16 "I will be his father, and he shall be my son. If he commit iniquity, I will chasten him with the rod of men, and with the stripes of the children of men: But my mercy shall not depart away from him, as I took *it* from Saul, whom I put away before thee. And thine house and thy kingdom shall be established for ever before thee: thy throne shall be established for ever."

[1445] 2 Samuel 11:2–5 "And it came to pass in an eveningtide, that David arose from off his bed, and walked upon the roof of the king's house: and from the roof he saw a woman washing herself; and the woman *was* very beautiful to look upon. And David sent and enquired after the woman. And *one* said, Is not this Bath-sheba, the daughter of Eliam, the wife of Uriah the Hittite? And David sent messengers, and took her; and she came in unto him, and he lay with her; for she was purified from her uncleanness: and she returned unto her house. And the woman conceived, and sent and told David, and said, I *am* with child."

[1446] 2 Samuel 11:14–15 "And it came to pass in the morning, that David wrote a letter to Joab, and sent *it* by the hand of Uriah. And he wrote in the letter, saying, Set ye Uriah in the forefront of the hottest battle, and retire ye from him, that he may be smitten, and die."

[1447] D&C 132:39 "David's wives and concubines were given unto him of me, by the hand of Nathan, my servant, and others of the prophets who had the keys of this power; and in none of these things did he sin against me save in the case of Uriah and his wife; and, therefore he hath fallen from his exaltation, and received his portion; and he shall not inherit them out of the world, for I gave them unto another, saith the Lord."

because the power of procreation was not used in the way to produce joy, but instead used to gratify lust.

When the solution to an unwanted pregnancy is abortion, then the person has elected, like David, to do something akin to murder. This is forbidden.[1448]

Adultery and lust leading to adultery deprive us of the Spirit.[1449]

The purpose of sexual relations is to have joy. To bring you children. To put those children into a setting where they are loved by both a father and a mother. When it is used in any other way, it produces misery. Almost all crime in the United States is related directly or indirectly to violating this commandment. Even what seems to be unrelated crime often occurs because the person involved was not raised in a home environment where they had a father and mother.

It is a right of every child to come into a family where they have the benefit of the family as established by God. The father and mother are literally symbols of God. They are in His image and likeness. When the image is imprinted upon the child in their early years and innocence, they develop a stability and foundation that is their right as an inheritance from God. Conforming to God's pattern is intended as a gift from Him to every child.

I then took a few moments to speak about individual fathers of the respective young men, including one whose father has passed away. The deceased father was a great man, whose influence is still felt by his son. I expressed my genuine affection for his father, who, although now no longer among us, left a great influence on others in addition to his son. I challenged all of the young priests to become

---

[1448] D&C 59:6 "Thou shalt love thy neighbor as thyself. Thou shalt not steal; neither commit adultery, nor kill, nor do anything like unto it."

[1449] D&C 42:22–24 "Thou shalt love thy wife with all thy heart, and shalt cleave unto her and none else. And he that looketh upon a woman to lust after her shall deny the faith, and shall not have the Spirit; and if he repents not he shall be cast out. Thou shalt not commit adultery; and he that committeth adultery, and repenteth not, shall be cast out."

fathers who will bring their children into an environment where they will look with gratitude and affection upon them as fathers.

" . . . speak unto us smooth things . . ."

There is a false notion that is so invidious it precludes us from emerging from our current widespread spiritual slump. The false notion is that anything from God will invariably be "lovely" or "of good report" as implied by the 13th Article of Faith. This false mantra however, is so wrong it alone empowers the darkness to grow all around us.

If you only need to listen to the voices of praise, and adulation which speak to you that "all is well in Zion" then you can never recognize an authentic call from the Lord to repent. Instead, like Laman and Lemuel, you will erroneously think any message that condemns your misbehavior is "sharp" or "angry".[1450] Yet Nephi's only intention was to seek "the eternal welfare" of Laman and Lemuel.[1451]

When we will only listen to vanity and praise, we are not much different than those who only wanted "smooth things" anciently.[1452]

The cure for some illness requires a knife to be used first before healing can begin. The purpose is not to injure, but only to heal.

[1450] 2 Nephi 1:26 "And ye have murmured because he hath been plain unto you. Ye say that he hath used sharpness; ye say that he hath been angry with you; but behold, his sharpness was the sharpness of the power of the word of God, which was in him; and that which ye call anger was the truth, according to that which is in God, which he could not restrain, manifesting boldly concerning your iniquities."

[1451] 2 Nephi 1:25 "And I exceedingly fear and tremble because of you, lest he shall suffer again; for behold, ye have accused him that he sought power and authority over you; but I know that he hath not sought for power nor authority over you, but he hath sought the glory of God, and your own eternal welfare."

[1452] Isaiah 30:10 "Which say to the seers, See not; and to the prophets, Prophesy not unto us right things, speak unto us smooth things, prophesy deceits:"

Joseph Smith's Limited Plural Marriage Sealings

Yesterday, while at a college baseball game, I got an inquiry from David C. asking the following:

A few people have contacted me and told me of "apparent errors" in your book... primarily that Joseph Smith performed a lot more plural marriages. This in part of an email I received from a friend:

"Under the plural marriage section of Denver's book, I remember that he mentions that only 1 other plural marriage was performed for another man besides Joseph before his death . . . making his case that not many others lived it. When I came across that a couple nights ago, I was pretty sure there were more . . . Brigham, Heber, Will Clayton, etc. I came across 2 different books tonight, one *The Refiner's Fire* by JL Brooke, said that there were over 20 different men who also participated before Joseph's death. The other *The Persistence of Polygamy* by Bringhurst and Craig Foster (Pres. of FAIR) states on page 126, quoting from Brian C Hales' extensive research and soon to come book, that 34 plural marriages were done for Joseph, and 29 for other men before Joseph's death. These they called sealing ceremonies. Many of these brethren that later lived PM in Joseph's time were also performing PM sealings before they lived the law themselves, page 128.

The reference this inquiry makes to the "apparent error" in my book *Passing the Heavenly Gift* can be found on the bottom of page 163 and top of page 164 and includes footnote 210. What I wrote on those pages is as follows:

"Of the 23 marriages sealed by Joseph prior to his death, other than his own, only one involved a plural wife. If eternal wives was necessary for exaltation, as was taught in the second phase, proof of that cannot be established through Joseph's actions." This is accompanied by a footnote which gives all the names and cites to Lisle G. Brown's work *The Holy Order in Nauvoo*, appendix 1. You can find *The Holy Order in Nauvoo* online, if you look for it. There you can read the names, or you can look at footnote 210 in my book where they are also set out.

The question raised in the email is confusing two issues. The specific topic being discussed in my book involves the narrow issue of the connection between exaltation and plural wives. I explain that eternal marriage is necessary, but plural wives is not. I distinguish between Section 132 (and other statements) during Joseph's lifetime and what became an absolute requirement for exaltation during the phase of Mormonism immediately following his death.

Another recent book contains the same list as the Lisle G. Brown article cited above. It is Devery S. Anderson and Gary James Bergera's book *Joseph Smith's Quorum of the Anointed, 1842–1845*. The list can be found in that book on pp. xxxiv-xxxv.

To put the two different issues into contrast, you need to focus on the topic I am discussing, namely the relationship between requirements for exaltation and plural wives. Joseph's ultimate indication of what was required for exaltation is not found in civil unions, or even church marriages he performed. It is found in the final ordinances, including the second anointing, in which exaltation was assured and a person was sealed up to eternal life. That final step is found in Joseph's organized Quorum of the Anointed, as it was then called.

Joseph Smith performed civil marriages. Joseph performed religious marriages. But the link between exaltation, eternal life, sealing up to a kingdom as an eternal inheritance, is to be found unconditionally in the final order he organized known as the Quorum of the Anointed. My book is focused only on that step.

Joseph was able and did perform civil marriages. Joseph also performed other forms of religious marriages. However, on the subject of sealing an eternal union, with the promise of eternal life, that kind of union represents something different. In that form of union we find what Joseph understood would be a marital union that would include exaltation.

In the context of that form of union which is associated by Joseph with exaltation itself, there was, apart from his own, only one other plural marriage. Therefore, if plural wives was *required* for exaltation, as taught subsequently by Brigham Young, the proof for that cannot be based upon Joseph Smith's actions.

In the second book cited above (*Joseph Smith's Quorum of the Anointed, 1842–1845*), they observe this about the final Quorum of Anointed which represent heirs of exaltation in Joseph's practices: "Still, many polygamists were not admitted into the quorum during Joseph's lifetime. Of the twenty-eight men who are presumed to have entered plural marriage during Joseph's lifetime, sixteen (57 percent) joined the quorum prior to Joseph's death; twelve (43 percent) did not. Acceptance of plural marriage did not automatically assure admission into the quorum. (See Table 2.)" (*Ibid.* p. xxiii; the referenced Table is the same list as I was referring to in footnote 210 on page 163 of *Passing the Heavenly Gift.*

Joseph Smith's Quorum of the Anointed, 1842–1845 also, referring to those who were polygamists and included in the Quorum before Joseph's death, observes: "No plural wife received the ordinance prior to Joseph's death. '[D]uring the lifetime of Joseph Smith,' Quinn concluded, 'polygamy was only an appendage 'to the highest order of the priesthood' [the second anointing] established on 28 September 1843'" (Ibid. pp. xxxv-xxxvi, citing to Quinn, *Latter-day Saint Prayer Circles*, 88.)

When I write, I try to be very specific. When speaking about a limited topic (i.e., the requirements for exaltation established by the actions taken by Joseph Smith), I am not referring to other topics. Nor did I take the added step of suggesting that the unsealed plural wives might be evidence of concubinage, or marital relationships which were not intended to continue after this life. That subject isn't even raised in my book. So the better approach would be that the topic I am discussing be read narrowly, and the context I am addressing be carefully considered, before assuming there are "apparent errors."

People assume deep topics and carefully composed language can be read with the same superficiality as reading a text message. I do not write that way. In fact, someone who has hastened through the book probably won't even understand it. The careful reader will find a good deal more in everything I've written than will the casual reader. It took careful, solemn, ponderous thoughts to learn what I've learned. Reading it in casual haste will never yield to such a reader what can be found.

As I also mention in the latest book, everything I've written is focused only on one topic. There has only been one theme to it all. Therefore if someone is interested in being redeemed from the fall, they will find there is a description of the path back in these commonly-themed books. Whether it involves discussion of The Book of Mormon, my testimony of Christ, or church history, it is all centered in redemption of the reader from the fall.

Surfing for Gossip

I don't read other blogs or follow what's happening in the blogosphere. But my wife, who maintains this site for me, does. She has the ability to track stuff all around the 'net, and also has traffic information given her through the site itself. And from time to time she updates me on what she thinks I would be interested in learning about the various gossip mongers who feel free to discuss me.

I do not think I'm worth a minute of anyone's time as a topic to discuss. I really do not matter one bit. Some of the things I've written are quite important. Those ideas are worth time, even a good deal of time, spent in careful contemplation. Some things I've been privileged to write are important enough that a careful soul will make it a matter of prayer, as well. But me? That's just a waste of time. There's nothing about a man worth anyone's time as a topic of gossip, speculation or discussion.

Apparently some number of folks have come to this blog for a week or so to find what I've said about President Boyd K. Packer. He's someone I've quoted more frequently than perhaps any other living church leader. I have a great deal of regard, respect, even admiration for him. Some of the talks he has given have been quite profound and worth reading by everyone. I've also lamented the conflict that developed between him and Paul Toscano. I wish that whole episode had not happened. But, as I've said before, I put the blame on Paul, not on President Packer, for provoking the conflict. I wish Paul were still a member of the church. We are the poorer for his absence.

I'm not sure why anyone would be interested in comments I've made on President Packer, but mentioning him again here will at least give this in answer to a search.

I've been hoping to drive the Alpine Loop when the colors change. They're changing now. Hope I can find time to do that.

General Conference is coming soon. I always go to the Marriott Center at BYU for Priesthood. It's a tradition. I'm looking forward to doing so again in a week or so. I think General Conference Priesthood should be done in a large group. Apart from the Conference Center itself, I think the BYU Marriott Center may be the largest assembly in the world. At least I think they've mentioned that before. Perhaps now the MTC has more.

For Sunday's sessions I like to take a drive with my family and listen in the car. Seems more like an "event" when we do that.And I think the kids like doing that. Oftentimes we'll drive by the Conference Center to see the anti-Mormon stuff. It's always entertaining to see folks spending their time blasting our religion under the pretext of establishing theirs. Not sure how that's supposed to work. But nevertheless someone thinks that is worth their effort. Maybe go the Alpine Loop on Sunday.

My wife tells me some people are offended by others using the word "crap"—when she said so I inquired if "bovine feces" would be a better substitute. She didn't know.

Saw Stewie and Brian step in and try to rescue Christmas last night. It turned into a home invasion. I laughed so hard I nearly hurt myself. I laugh at the idiocy on the TV. My wife laughs at me. So we both get entertained.

I'm reading a book by a Catholic Theologian who teaches at a Protestant Theological Seminary in New York. Interesting book. When I finish I think I'll put some of his stuff on the blog. His focus is the post-Apostolic era from about 70 A.D. to 125 A.D. It's an interesting moment of rapid change. I disagree with some of his retelling, and I reject his Catholic lens, but nevertheless he has some important things to say.

Well, to return to what started this ramble, watch your gossip. My wife may be watching you.

Response to Question

When you write something, a reader can put into what you've written something that is not there. Some of the questions I get asked result from misreading the information, rather than confining the things I've written to the writing itself. I got one this morning which I thought was worthwhile enough to put on the blog.

The question related to the role of the Holy Ghost. In effect, the person I spoke with thought I "denigrated the role of the Holy

Ghost" by focusing upon Christ. I responded I did not believe that was the case.

First, I explained in everything I've written, beginning with *The Second Comforter*, that it is the role of the Holy Ghost to prepare and bring us to Christ. Without the Holy Ghost we cannot come to Christ. Further, in that same book I acknowledged the Holy Ghost's foundational role by telling the reader that they must receive a witness from the Holy Ghost as they read the book or they do not have the required two witnesses. Without the Holy Ghost's ratifying confirmation, I tell the reader to discard what I've written. Far from denigrating the Holy Ghost's role, I have made it a central part of the process, without it no person can come unto Christ.

It is not overemphasis on Christ at the expense of the Holy Ghost, but rather it is showing how the members of the Godhead work together. Just as Christ taught, the Comforter (Holy Ghost) will abide with us and bring us to Him. The Holy Ghost's vital role is unchanged. But to ignore the continuation of the ministry of the members of the Godhead, particularly the role of Christ as a continuing minister of salvation, is to cast aside His promise as the Second Comforter.

He also asked about his conclusion that our "priesthood line of authority" was meaningless. I explained that was not anything I'd written or thought. Rather quite to the contrary, the church extends an authoritative invitation in ordination to the priesthood which is a vital prerequisite to acting on the invitation and receiving the "power of heaven." Without an authoritative invitation, I do not see how a person can obtain the "power of heaven." In fact, there are recent talks in General Conference which lament the absence of "power in the priesthood" within the church. I've cited to those before. The church itself has recognized and taught the need for going beyond mere ordination into receiving power in the priesthood. Therefore, what I've written is consistent with, and respects, the church's rights, as well as the necessity of ordination through the church system.

When we finished talking, he said I'd removed his concerns. Said he would go back and read it again with less emotion.

I spent the day defending the latest book yesterday. I received much welcomed criticism, which allowed me to answer questions. I enjoyed the opportunity very much. Criticism does not bother me. It allows me to understand what the reader has misapprehended, or leaped to conclude, which in turn better informs me about how others can err in attributing motives or positions. I also got some needed corrections (editing never ends), and spelling corrections which are needed. To me it is all worthwhile and quite interesting.

Today I'm going to teach the Priests about testimony. I hope to discuss my own conversion story with them. Some of them are going to be missionaries soon and I want them to know how the potential convert thinks as they approach a monumental change to their life by joining the church.

I do not think I'll mention this to them: Within the first year of joining I'd received visits from angels, and been attacked by the adversary and a hoard of his minions. My life was threatened by those who are darkness itself, and was delivered by beings of light. As a new convert, who had recently joined after studying Joseph Smith's experience, I thought this was normal for Mormons. I thought this kind of stuff happened to everyone. I learned, however, that it was not and I should not talk about such things because some became easily offended. So the things I say are heavily redacted that no one may know anything other than I am a believer in Mormonism, with a witness of our Lord. I do in fact have a witness and testimony of Christ. I also have a testimony of Joseph Smith. I have empathy for those who have once believed and find they can no longer. To them I write what I hope will persuade them to believe in Christ that they will return and join in fellowship with the saints.

As to others who misunderstand what I've written, it is a small thing to be evil spoken of when the criticism is not warranted. If even one person is brought to see the truth in Christ, any price required to be paid is modest.

Controlled Revelation

Joseph Smith did not attempt to control or limit people's revelations except in only one regard. When it came to revelation involving governing the church, that was limited to him alone, as President.[1453] Reading *The Joseph Smith Papers*, however, it is clear that for Joseph, it came as a matter of some considerable satisfaction to him that others received revelation as well.

The declarations of Joseph's revelations raise two interesting questions: First, if Joseph's status as the prophet, seer and revelator are foundational, then can any subsequent person change anything restored through Joseph? Even if there is another person elected through common consent to be the president of the church, is such an office holder free from the obligation to receive Joseph's words as God's words? Are we all, including subsequent office holders, required

---

[1453] D&C 43:2–5 "For behold, verily, verily, I say unto you, that ye have received a commandment for a law unto my church, through him whom I have appointed unto you to receive commandments and revelations from my hand. And this ye shall know assuredly—that there is none other appointed unto you to receive commandments and revelations until he be taken, if he abide in me. But verily, verily, I say unto you, that none else shall be appointed unto this gift except it be through him; for if it be taken from him he shall not have power except to appoint another in his stead. And this shall be a law unto you, that ye receive not the teachings of any that shall come before you as revelations or commandments;"
D&C 21:4–5 "Wherefore, meaning the church, thou shalt give heed unto all his words and commandments which he shall give unto you as he receiveth them, walking in all holiness before me; For his word ye shall receive, as if from mine own mouth, in all patience and faith."
D&C 28:2 "But, behold, verily, verily, I say unto thee, no one shall be appointed to receive commandments and revelations in this church excepting my servant Joseph Smith, Jun., for he receiveth them even as Moses."

to "give heed unto all his [Joseph's] words and commandments, which he [Joseph] shall give unto you as he receiveth them"? Or instead, does Joseph get relegated to obsolescence once he has been replaced by President Brigham Young, and so on?

Secondly, the question arises whether possession of the office Joseph held (church president) automatically entitles such an office holder to be in every whit exactly like Joseph. That is, do subsequent office holders also get the automatic right to claim everyone in the church must give heed to their words, too?

In Joseph's case, the only way to replace him in his position was for Joseph himself to designate his successor/replacement. This is set out in the revelation to Joseph as follows:

> "[N]one else shall be appointed unto this gift except it be through him [Joseph]; for if it is taken from him [Joseph] he shall not have power except to appoint another in his stead." (D&C 43:4)

Implicit in the revelation, if you read it carefully, is that Joseph's choice of the one who would succeed him would necessarily come by revelation to Joseph.

> "And this shall be a law unto you, that ye receive not the teachings of any that shall come before you as revelations or commandments; And this I give unto you that you may not be deceived, that you may know they are not of me. For verily I say unto you, that he that is ordained of me shall come in at the gate and be ordained as I have told you before, to teach those revelations, which you have received and shall receive through him [Joseph] whom I have appointed." (D&C 43:5–7).

In Joseph's case, he did receive a revelation which identified who would replace him, just as the revelation provided.

"[T]hat my servant Hyrum may take the office of Priesthood and Patriarch, which was appointed unto him by his father, by blessing and also by right; That from henceforth he shall hold the keys of the Patriarchal blessings upon the heads of all my people, That whoever he blesses shall be blessed, and whoever he curses shall be cursed; that whatsoever he shall bind on earth shall be bound in heaven; and whatsoever he shall loose on earth shall be loosed in heaven. And from this time forth I appoint unto him that he may be a prophet, and a seer, and a revelator unto my church, as well as my servant Joseph . . . " (D&C 124:91–94)

Hyrum, however, died in Carthage Jail before Joseph. The issue of "succession" was decided by common consent in the votes taken in Nauvoo following Joseph's death. Then there is all that stuff about Joseph giving "the keys of the kingdom" to "the council." But "the kingdom" was the Council of Fifty, not the church. The "council" to whom Joseph made the remark was the Fifty, not the Twelve. But we sorted that out in Nauvoo by common consent, choosing to follow the Twelve.

Revelation is foundational to the church. No one comes into the church without revelation. Missionaries ask investigators to ask God, based on Moroni 10:4, and get their own answer to prayer. A convert is expected to have received a personal revelation before becoming a Mormon.

This gives rise to some other interesting issues: Moroni 10:4 has as its scope the truthfulness of the Book of Mormon. But Moroni 10:5 expands the scope so that a sincere inquirer "may know the truth of all things." Therefore, there is no limit on what a person might inquire about and receive a revelation concerning.

Now a convert who has discovered that they have already obtained an answer to prayer is likely (as I was) to continue to inquire. Converts who have had such an experience become rather like Joseph Smith following his first vision. That is, they "had full confidence in obtaining a divine manifestation, as [they] previously had one" (JS–H 1:29). So people who have succeeded in obtaining an answer to prayer go on to make further inquiries and get further answers. The scope of such inquiries can be, as Moroni 10:5 informs us, into literally *anything*. They can get to know "the truth of all things" by making such inquiries.

The interesting issue arises when the church then informs the convert that they can't have revelations involving things which the church wants to control. They can't ask and get an answer about anything that contradicts or opposes what the church says. If they do so, they are told they have a false revelation, or they are being inspired by the devil.

A great problem arises when someone who has received authentic revelation, and has been inspired as a consequence of that revelation to join the church, is then told by the church that their subsequent revelation is false, or of the devil. The convert must then choose. Revelation led them into the church in the first instance. If the church then tells them their continuing revelation is false or of the devil, they must grapple with whether the original revelation which led them to convert was also false and of the devil? Of course, if they reach that conclusion they leave the church. The other choice is that the revelation, both the original and the following revelations, are from God. If that is the conclusion they reach, then they know the church is overreaching. This gives rise to a continual anxiety about the church's motives, and reliability about things which matter most.

Joseph's delight in the revelations others received is akin to Moses' delight in the same thing:

"Enviest thou for my sake? would God that all the Lord's people were prophets, and that the Lord would put his spirit upon them!" (Numbers 11:29)

The church's jealousy on the same topic makes an interesting contrast, where those who have revelation oftentimes know God has spoken to them, but also know the church will not tolerate revelation which goes any further than knowing the Book of Mormon is true, Therefore, you have an obligation to join the institution which publishes and proclaims that book.

These are big topics. They are worth a lot of careful thought. One conclusion which leaps to mind, however, is that the loose grip Joseph and Moses took on the reigns of control extended to management decisions at the highest level. At lower levels people were free to develop their gifts, including revelation, without any molesting by the top. Our own scriptures say as much. To the church is given a variety of gifts, disbursed throughout the body:

"To some is given one, and to some is given another, that all may be profited thereby. To some it is given by the Holy Ghost to know that Jesus Christ is the Son of God, and that he was crucified for the sins of the world. To others it is given to believe on their words, that they also might have eternal life if they continue faithful. And again, to some it is given by the Holy Ghost to know the differences of administration, as it will be pleasing unto the same Lord, according as the Lord will, suiting his mercies according to the conditions of the children of men. And again, it is given by the Holy Ghost to some to know the diversities of operations, whether they be of God, that the manifestations of the Spirit may be given to every man to profit withal. And again, verily I say unto you, to some is given, by the Spirit of God, the word of wisdom. To another is given the word of knowledge, that all may be taught to be wise and to have knowledge. And again, to some it is given to have faith to be healed; And to others it is given to have faith to heal. And again, to some is given the working of miracles; And to others it is given to prophesy; And to others the discerning of spirits. And again, it is given to some to speak with tongues; And to another is given the interpretation of tongues. And all these gifts come from God, for the benefit of the children of God." (D&C 46:12–26)

Well, if they all come from God, and are spread to people throughout the church, it would seem incredibly wrong-headed to condemn such things or to attempt to limit them. It is an interesting thing to try and limit the Spirit. As Christ put it,

> "The wind bloweth where it listeth, and thou hearest the sound thereof, but canst not tell whence it cometh, and whither it goeth: so is every one that is born of the Spirit." (John 3:8)

> Such things are free indeed. To hedge them in, correlate them, and attempt to subjugate them, oftentimes does not convince or persuade those being controlled.

Fortunately, history generally sorts it out correctly. And today's heroes become tomorrows villains—just as today's fools become tomorrow's venerated examples. How we sort it out in our brief moment here is not necessarily how either the Lord or those in the future will do so.

Well, enough of that. I do so look forward to General Conference this coming weekend. I'm hoping to get some input on the things which really do matter most. There are so many important questions facing us today. It will be nice to hear what counsel we are given on these many perplexities.

Some Random Updates

My wife brought a matter to my attention which I thought I'd comment about again. I put up some cautions about how the new book was going to have those who wanted to take sensational state-ments out of context and put them on the Internet in isolation, separated from the many sources carefully assembled to lay a foundation to understand the statements. That has begun. I'd only remind those who are interested that anything can be made to look sensational if it is divorced from context. I could make the most benign of Joseph Smith's statements look fanatical and rob them of all meaning if I wanted to do so. But to understand the Prophet, it takes careful, even prayerful, study.

I have no agenda apart from explaining the truth as I understand it. But when I explain it, I give (particularly in the case of the latest book) enough historic and scriptural support that any conclusions are only an extension of what the Prophet, or the Book of Mormon, or the history itself compels us to conclude. The conclusions are rather anticlimactic. They are only the result of the accumulated and disclosed body of information preceding them. When, therefore, someone takes merely the conclusion and represents it as an accurate statement of what I've written, it is so gross a distortion that it is essentially untrue. Time, care, patience and great effort was taken to show the history for the benefit of the reader. Divorcing all that from a single sentence and parading it as what I think is, at best, a disservice.

But people crave the 'sound-bite' solution to everything. Therefore the cunning and fearful want to rush to expose and distort, in hopes to mislead and inoculate people from learning some things which help them find their way to the Lord. As I say in the book, I've been ministered to by the Lord. I'd caution those who want to distort what I've written to be careful, therefore, and prayerful (as I have been) in how they elect to proceed.

The souls of men are something no one should trifle with. I've never done so. I'd encourage others to avoid doing so unless they are certain they are on the Lord's errand.

Repentance

The first step for repentance is always to recognize something is wrong and needs changing. Oddly, that is a more difficult challenge than it ought to be. We all like to think of ourselves as being in the right way. It makes people mad to suggest otherwise.

Membership in The Church of Jesus Christ of Latter-day Saints was never intended to be temporary, with people cycling in and then out of the church. Once they come aboard they should stay aboard. The Gospel, as restored through Joseph Smith, has a delightful and expanding source of almost endless truth available to all of us. We were not meant to be bored, flattered and comfortable. Instead we were meant to be challenged, provoked, delighted and engaged in the relentless search deeper and deeper into the mysteries of God. When we take it and instead make it flat, curtailed and predictable, we often attract only temporary members. People who come for the doctrine at first, and then leave because the new faith offering answers at last to their questions, ends in a repetition of brief and superficial answers to probing questions after a brief cycle of a few years. I wish all men were motivated to study deeply for themselves, but they are not. For such people, they rely upon others to bring them along further and further in the right Path. When they falter because we aren't teaching them invigorating, challenging material each week, they presume we have nothing to offer. The truth is we have a lifetime of rewarding information available for their endless edification and growth. But, when they will not search into it for themselves, they do not find it.

We make a mistake when we discourage the search or claim they *must* confine what they investigate to our limited approved church curriculum. They get the mistaken impression that is because our official manuals are all the Gospel offers. They presume we are no better informed than are the other mainstream churches, whose memberships are static or dropping.

In our Region of the church (we're about to have a Regional Conference in two weeks), one of the greatest problems we face is adult apostasy stemming from reading critical things about the church's history on the Internet. A great number of adults are dismayed when they learn of things from hostile, even bitterly opposed sources working to remove faith in the restored Gospel. There are some people assigned by the church to investigate this problem, and who are discussing how to address it. I suggested to my stake president that my book, *Passing the Heavenly Gift*, might be of use. I know of twelve men now who have returned to activity in the church after reading the book. These are bright men, well read and engaged in searching into things which matter to them. They had all reached the conclusion the church was not being honest about its history and therefore ended their activity with the church. After reading the book, however, they decided it was not as they presumed, and the Lord does indeed have a destiny for the Latter-day Saints, foretold by the Prophets in the Book of Mormon and revealed to Joseph Smith.

I have found nothing quite as engaging, challenging and hopeful as the Gospel of Jesus Christ. To me, it is exactly as Nephi put it: "delicious." It takes a great deal of effort to make the excitement of eternal truth into something stale and boring. That effort ought to be spent letting the Gospel understanding expand, under the tutelage of a benign church, tolerant of inquiry and discussion that is open ended and tolerant. The discussions are going to happen. Any efforts to stop them will only drive them into places where the truth may not receive an invitation to even contribute.

There is nothing so wonderful as the truths we were handed by Joseph Smith. All those who awaken to his great ministry still "seek counsel, and authority, and blessings constantly from under [his] hand" (D&C 122:2). The truth never had a better friend than Joseph Smith. Even when it put him into conflict with all the world, he nevertheless declared the truth. That is because truth compels the recipient to declare: "I had actually seen a light, and in the midst of that light I saw two Personages, and they did in reality speak to me; and though I was hated and persecuted for saying that I had seen a vision, yet it was true; and while they were persecuting me, reviling me, and speaking all manner of evil against me falsely for so saying, I was led to say in my heart: Why persecute me for telling the truth. I have actually seen a vision; and who am I that I can withstand God, or why does the world think to make me deny what I have actually seen? For I had seen a vision; I knew it, and I knew that God knew it, and I could not deny it, neither dared I do it; at least I knew that by so doing I would offend God, and come under condemnation." (JS–H 1:25.) Praise to the man, indeed!

I could not have repented (at least not in an effective way) if I had not listened to what Joseph taught. In that sense, he brought me to Christ. Therefore, although Christ is the Redeemer and Savior, it was Joseph Smith who taught me how to return to the Lord. No man can save another. Yet there are those we owe some gratitude for the light they brought. Not because they are more than men (for all men are weak and prone to err), but because the Lord worked with them despite their weakness.

Reply to Questions

I was asked in an email to clarify some topics. I am posting this in response:

The appearance in 1836 in the Kirtland Temple does not appear to have fulfilled the return of Elijah. This is a topic the church is grappling with at the moment. Not at the bottom, where I live and write, but at the top. Though there are continuing statements made in public, behind the scenes there is a debate going on over the meaning of Elijah's appearance, when Joseph Smith received the sealing power, how he received it, and whether the history should be revisited and clarified. I am setting out what I believe. It is for others to decide for themselves what they believe. But this is not as settled a subject as some public statements made for generations by the church make it appear.

Why does Joseph Smith omit mention of Elijah in his letter to the saints in September, 1842 (Section 128) if Elijah's return was completed in Kirtland in 1836?

Why does Oliver Cowdery never mention Elijah in his testimony about the restoration, though he does mention Moroni, the voice of God, John the Baptist and Peter, James, and John?

Why does Joseph Smith speak of the return of Elijah as a future event in both January and March of 1844 if the Kirtland appearance satisfied the promise made in Malachi?

These are serious questions. There are people trying to answer them right now. I've provided my answer. Anyone is free to disagree with it. Anyone is free to decide it for themselves.

I don't think I am Elijah, and that's so stupid a proposition that I have a hard time even dignifying it with an answer. I want to say: "Are you serious???!!" But I'll leave it with, "No."

The sealing keys came to Joseph, like they came and were conferred upon Melchizedek and Nephi the same way. I explained it in *Passing the Heavenly Gift.* I'm not going to repeat it again here. It comes in only one way, that is by the Voice of God.

I've never said any church leader was "evil" or "of the devil." On the contrary, I've continually said they are the only ones entitled to lead the church, and no one has a right to interfere with their leading. No one has the right to call someone to any office in the church, collect tithing, or lead people away from the church. But EVERY-

ONE has a duty to testify of the truth and to teach one another the doctrines of the kingdom. Therefore we are all under some obligation to declare what we believe, explain why, and defend it using the scriptures and declarations of the prophets. As to the analogy of church presidents to "Popes" that is J. Reuben Clark's terminology, as you can see in the book, and is not mine. I defer to him for that characterization. It is relevant to see how a member of the First Presidency viewed the role of the President and for that reason was included. I do not say whether I agree or disagree with his characterization, I only provide it. In fact, I do very little evaluating or concluding in *Passing the Heavenly Gift*. I merely set out what was said, done or written with the exception of one chapter which presumes, for purposes of that chapter, that the things promised in Section 124 were not delivered. Then, in light of that presumption, I explain what would then be the case. The book is an alternative view of history, which people are free to consider and reject. It is proposed as a way to grapple with inconsistencies and glaring problems which are not adequately reconcilable with the current stories we tell one another. I believe it is faith promoting. Particularly for those who are aware of the problems with our history. But, it is only faith promoting if you read the entire book. Reading only the first part will not be faith promoting, because it acknowledges the many problems and acquaints readers with the reasons why there is a crisis of faith among some of the most serious students of our history. I do not try to hide anything. It is or should be clear I'm not trying to shirk from difficulties. After setting it out, I then explain why I believe God's hand still lingers over the church and the saints. What is amusing to me is that one apostate reader thought it was too much an apologetic work (i.e. a defense of the church) for him to finish reading it. In other words, he thought it TOO faith promoting.

I do think the words of a dispensation head, in any dispensation, are binding upon all who follow. I do not think any prophet subsequent to Moses had the right to change Moses' teachings, for they were binding upon them. Until the Lord makes a change and opens a New Dispensation (which I expect Him to do personally), what Joseph Smith brought us is binding upon everyone, including all following prophets. We are told to be obedient to what we have received from him.[1454] I believe that is still true. Meaning that no one, regardless of position or rank, can ignore what came through Joseph Smith except to their peril. Until a New Dispensation arrives, what Joseph Smith launched is supposed to remain intact.

"Elias" for our day is, I believe, Joseph Smith.

I expect Elijah to return the same way he departed. That's one of the great assignments to him. He must return because he will reopen the way through which others will follow. It will be, I believe, the same person as departed and not someone who self-proclaims or self-identifies as being "Elijah." It will be him. Not another. Anyone making that claim would (to me at least) be someone who does not understand the scriptures and is not to be take seriously.

I think that covers it. But I have to say the mischief comes from speculating, interpreting, or emotionally reacting to the words I've written or spoken. Not in the words themselves. I try to be clear. The words are not attempting to "suggest" anything. Only to explain what I believe and why I believe as I do. They are the result of a great deal of work, which is set out in the text or footnotes, or bibliography.

[1454] D&C 28:2–3 "But, behold, verily, verily, I say unto thee, no one shall be appointed to receive commandments and revelations in this church excepting my servant Joseph Smith, Jun., for he receiveth them even as Moses. And thou shalt be obedient unto the things which I shall give unto him, even as Aaron, to declare faithfully the commandments and the revelations, with power and authority unto the church."

An Email Response

I got another email inquiry which I responded to yesterday I thought I ought to put up here. This inquiry related to *Passing the Heavenly Gift*:

[The email linked to several conversations of some length.] Well, that's a lot to read. I did scan some of it, but not all. I do not mind being criticized, nor people disagreeing with me. They're free to do so. And I mean both criticize me and disagree. The problem is that criticizing me is sort of a misadventure, because doing that detracts from the underlying real questions. Who cares a fig about me? I hope no-one. But the stuff I write about—meaning an attempt to discuss the Gospel—that is important and certainly worth spending some time thinking about and discussing.

Without the benefit of reading all those posts (I stopped reading when it got noxious), I'll respond as follows:

First, I've explained in what I've written (some approximate one million words now) what I think and why. There's no reason to re-write it again to answer questions. If they'd read what I wrote they'd know the answers. They'd even know the reasons for the answers. It's lazy to try to shortcut things and just interpose questions based on false assumptions and interpretations that are, in many cases, so off kilter that even answering is distorting. I think every one of these questions are answered in what I've written far better than in the responses below.

Despite this, and really even anticipating that these answers don't contribute anything to the discussion, here's a brief reply:

Does he actually claim in the first quote that all the keys of the priesthood are not held by Thomas S. Monson?

No. I don't take a position on that. In one chapter I entertain the possibility of that and discuss how important the church remains anyway. As to whether he has them all, that is a matter between him and the Lord. When he became President, I prayed and was told to sustain him and I do. That's enough for me. The Book of Mormon clearly identifies us (the Latter-day Saints) as gentiles. Joseph Smith said we were "identified with the gentiles" in the dedicatory prayer for the Kirtland Temple (D&C 109:60). Book of Mormon prophecies clearly indicate there will be an apostasy or sorts by the gentile church (us). We either have (in the past) or will (in the future) reject the fullness. I show how a reasonable interpretation of our history could reach the conclusion it was in the past. If it isn't then it is in our future. But if the Book of Mormon can be trusted on the point, and I think it can, then we'll reject the fullness of the Gospel at some point. But that's a quick and altogether distorted treatment of a topic worthy of so much attention and so much care that I've written a 170,000 word book on the subject which will do a better job than a snapshot.

Q: Does Bro. Snuffer actually believe that the sealing power is not with the Church and was lost?

No. Don't take a position on that, either. The sealing power is conferred in one way and that way is described in the scriptures. I take some lengths to explain, using scripture, the matter. Beyond laying out the process I never say anything about what the church has. I do explain the church's claims. And I also use the church's explanations to show where the church's authority comes from.

Q: That the GAs over the Church's curriculum are not teaching what God has instructed them to include in our Church manuals?

I'm not sure I understand this question. Where has God instructed someone to do something about curriculum? There are committees that do this stuff. In the fourth phase everything is attributed to the president, and that process is laid out in the book. This question is a product of that process. But I really don't understand the question. So far as I've seen, there is nowhere a claim made that God was involved in writing or developing the church's curriculum.

Q: We have a 'devalued gospel' in the LDS Church?

There are a list of 72 approved subjects allowed to be taught, as a result of the Correlation process. The Gospel allows everyone to learn all the mysteries of God. It is, you know, given unto many to know the mysteries of God. And those who will give more heed to the matter learn more, those who give less heed learn less.[1455] By the Spirit we can know the truth of all things.[1456] Limiting the scope of discussion to the list of approved topics is removing some of the great, even important topics from our permitted discussions. Therefore the most important subjects have now gravitated away from Sacrament, Sunday School and Priesthood/Relief Society and into the Internet. I have seen unapproved subjects on your blog's index.

I have also shown that David O. McKay was not the champion of Correlation, but was instead concerned it would lead to the church's apostasy. Now Correlation claims he was the one who was inspired to bring it forward, even that it was revealed to him by God and is

---

[1455] Alma 12:9–11 "And now Alma began to expound these things unto him, saying: It is given unto many to know the mysteries of God; nevertheless they are laid under a strict command that they shall not impart only according to the portion of his word which he doth grant unto the children of men, according to the heed and diligence which they give unto him. And therefore, he that will harden his heart, the same receiveth the lesser portion of the word; and he that will not harden his heart, to him is given the greater portion of the word, until it is given unto him to know the mysteries of God until he know them in full. And they that will harden their hearts, to them is given the lesser portion of the word until they know nothing concerning his mysteries; and then they are taken captive by the devil, and led by his will down to destruction. Now this is what is meant by the chains of hell."

[1456] Moroni 10:5 "And by the power of the Holy Ghost ye may know the truth of all things."

proof of revelation to the church's President on the matter. These claims are opposite to President McKay's concern that it was both wrong and would endanger the church of apostasy by consolidating power in the hands of the top, when people were always intended to be free to learn, discuss, believe and act consistent with what they understood. That's all laid out in the book as well. And giving a cryptic response is really more misleading than helpful. Read the book and you'll have the answer. And answers to many other things about which we should be open and free to discuss among friendly, believing Saints.

That is the end of the email response. I should note also that in the first 7 books I wrote I presumed the church's traditional narrative is true and accurate. I wrote them in contemplation of the church's traditional claims about history, and therefore anyone who reads those will not have their understanding challenged on the matter.

History of Elijah Doctrine

The talk on Elijah given in Spanish Fork and posted on this blog last week is a continuation of the development of information found in *Passing the Heavenly Gift*. The foundation for why the Elijah issue required further discussion is found in the book. Some people have listened to the talk without first reading the book. Therefore they are unacquainted with the background information which shows the importance of re-examining the Elijah tradition inside the church. I will give a brief explanation here, although you won't really understand the reason for the talk unless you read the book.

Briefly, and without repeating all the historic records, journals and sources from which the history is explained in the book, this is what happened: Elijah came to visit the Kirtland Temple in 1836 according to the third person account written by Warren Cowdery in the back of the 3rd volume of revelations in Kirtland. It is the last entry made, and the source of all the later claims made about Elijah, his purpose and appearance. The account is third-person, (i.e., The Lord appeared to them . . . said to them . . . , etc.) but when it was later discovered it was reworded to the first person (i.e., the Lord appeared to us . . . said to us . . . , etc.). You can read the original document, actually see a photostatic reproduction of the original, in the *Joseph Smith Papers*. I give the cite in *Passing the Heavenly Gift*.

The record Joseph Smith left makes no mention of Elijah's appearance. The record Oliver Cowdery left makes no mention of Elijah's appearance. Joseph died without every explaining anything about the event, or making any mention of it. Oliver also. Both of them testified about visitations they received, and wrote about who had come to empower them, but neither of them ever mention Elijah.

In talks in Nauvoo, Joseph refers on every occasion he mentions Elijah as a future event. Not as a past event. He explains Elijah "will return," not that he has returned.

Joseph Smith received the sealing power in a revelation given sometime in the early 1830's, which was recorded in 1843. I take some effort to lay out the chronology in the book, and the information can be reviewed there.

When Joseph Smith died, there is no contemporaneous source to verify the appearance of Elijah in 1836, and the appearance was not known at that time.

There is no mention of the Elijah appearance in 1836, nor 1837, nor 1838 nor '39, '40, '41, '42, '43 nor in 1844, though Joseph does say there will be a future return. After Joseph Smith's death, there was nothing said or known in 1844, '45, '46, '47, '48, '49, '50 nor for years thereafter. When the Kirtland Revelation Book was reviewed in the 1850's the first notice resulted in the revelation being published for the first time in November of the year it was found. Along with the publication was an explanation given by Orson Pratt explaining it was quite significant. He garbles the chronology in that article, and the chronology ever since was taken from his first editorial. Since then the chronology has remained the same as Orson declared, even though he erred in attributing the revelation recorded on July 12, 1843 to having been given on that date. The revelation was received much earlier, the first part in 1829. I also walk through that in *Passing the Heavenly Gift*.

Since the 1850's when the revelation was found (which is now Section 110) about the Kirtland Temple appearance of Elijah, and then published for the first time in the Deseret News, there have been hundreds of statements which rely upon Orson Pratt's original analysis accompanying the announcement of finding the record.

By the time the words were discovered, Warren Cowdery who wrote it down was dead. He could not explain where it came from because we couldn't ask him. Oliver died shortly before Warren, and he also could not be asked. And, of course, Joseph died before either of them, and so he could not be asked either. Therefore the two witnesses left nothing about it, could not be asked, and the scribe who recorded it could not be asked either.

I walk through all these events using the historical records, scriptures and lengthy explanations. It is a topic which takes a lot of material to set out in full, but has been done in the book.

The talk on Elijah's mission posted on this blog was taking the topic and discussing what the still future mission of Elijah would necessarily involve. Since Joseph expected it to happen in the future when he spoke about it in January and March, 1844, there must be a future mission for him. Because if Joseph, who was present in the Kirtland Temple in 1836 when the Warren Cowdery recorded event took place thought there was still a future mission for Elijah, then it would be important to notice that and give some thought to what it could involve. I've done that. Hence the contents of the talk.

Now, if you disagree with history and you are perfectly content with what Orson Pratt bequeathed us as the accompanying commentary when the account was discovered, then you needn't give this one further thought. There have been generations come and go with that explanation regarded as the absolute truth and the basis for our Temple work. So you'll be in good company. But there are those serious minded individuals who are trying to sort this out right now at high levels of the Church who know these are important issues which are NOT as settled as the past pronouncements make it appear. In fact, I doubt the current explanations will last much longer because the record simply does not support the conclusions we have urged. The place to start is not after the 1850's discovery, when there were conclusions leaped to by Orson Pratt which then became the operative explanation thereafter. The place to start is instead from 1836 to 1844 in the records of that time. What was Joseph saying? What was Oliver saying? Why did both of them leave out mention of Elijah in their testimonies of who had come to visit with them? Where did Section 110 come from? That is, who did Warren Cowdery consult with to learn the material he wrote into the book? I work on that in both the book and the talk.

I think Elijah has a ministry still future. I think it is connected to the very things Joseph Smith was speaking about in January and March, 1844. And I explain what that is in the talk linked on this blog.

The Power of God's Word

I've been reflecting on the power of God's word. It is so remarkable a source of power that Christ was called the Word of God, because He embodies the Father's will so completely.[1457]

God's word alone is what ordains to Melchizedek Priesthood.[1458] "It was delivered unto men by the calling of his own voice . . . "

God's word alone conferred sealing authority upon Nephi.[1459]

God's word along conferred the sealing authority upon Joseph Smith.[1460]

[1457] John 1:1 "In the beginning was the Word, and the Word was with God, and the Word was God."

[1458] JST Genesis 14:27–29 "And thus, having been approved of God, he was ordained an high priest after the order of the covenant which God made with Enoch, It being after the order of the Son of God; which order came, not by man, nor the will of man; neither by father nor mother; neither by beginning of days nor end of years; but of God; And it was delivered unto men by the calling of his own voice, according to his own will, unto as many as believed on his name."

[1459] Helaman 10:3, 5–10 "And it came to pass as he was thus pondering—being much cast down because of the wickedness of the people of the Nephites, their secret works of darkness, and their murderings, and their plunderings, and all manner of iniquities—and it came to pass as he was thus pondering in his heart, behold, a voice came unto him saying: And now, because thou hast done this with such unwearyingness, behold, I will bless thee forever; and I will make thee mighty in word and in deed, in faith and in works; yea, even that all things shall be done unto thee according to thy word, for thou shalt not ask that which is contrary to my will. Behold, thou art Nephi, and I am God. Behold, I declare it unto thee in the presence of mine angels, that ye shall have power over this people, and shall smite the earth with famine, and with pestilence, and destruction, according to the wickedness of this people. Behold, I give unto you power, that whatsoever ye shall seal on earth shall be sealed in heaven; and whatsoever ye shall loose on earth shall be loosed in heaven; and thus shall ye have power among this people. And thus, if ye shall say unto this temple it shall be rent in twain, it shall be done. And if ye shall say unto this mountain, Be thou cast down and become smooth, it shall be done. And behold, if ye shall say that God shall smite this people, it shall come to pass."

[1460] D&C 132:46 "And verily, verily, I say unto you, that whatsoever you seal on earth shall be sealed in heaven; and whatsoever you bind on earth, in my name and by my word, saith the Lord, it shall be eternally bound in the heavens; and whosoever sins you remit on earth shall be remitted eternally in the heavens; and whosoever sins you retain on earth shall be retained in heaven."

God's word is the only constant, which will never fail, whether He speaks it or He authorizes someone else to speak it, it is the same.[1461]

In a very real sense, the power of the priesthood consists in obtaining God's word. For when He will answer you it is possible to have His word on all things. D&C 132:45 (for Joseph);[1462] D&C 124:95 (for Hyrum);[1463] Helaman 10:5 (for Nephi).[1464]

Those who have God's word know how to proceed in all things. Those who do not are always uncertain what they should do and what their standing is before Him.

Borrowed Doctrine

I've just finished a conversation with a daughter who is in college in another state. Some doctrinal issues were on the agenda stemming from interpretations of the Book of Revelation. She had an encounter with a Relief Society teacher who introduced her to some ideas which are largely borrowed from Evangelical sources, adopted by Mormon writers, and now being repeated as if they were true. That conversation provokes this post.

We should be careful about importing doctrine and interpretations from other traditional Christian sources. The reason "the professors

---

[1461] D&C 1:38 "What I the Lord have spoken, I have spoken, and I excuse not myself; and though the heavens and the earth pass away, my word shall not pass away, but shall all be fulfilled, whether by mine own voice or by the voice of my servants, it is the same."

[1462] D&C 132:45 "For I have conferred upon you the keys and power of the priesthood, wherein I restore all things, and make known unto you all things in due time."

[1463] D&C 124:95 "That he may act in concert also with my servant Joseph; and that he shall receive counsel from my servant Joseph, who shall show unto him the keys whereby he may ask and receive, and be crowned with the same blessing, and glory, and honor, and priesthood, and gifts of the priesthood, that once were put upon him that was my servant Oliver Cowdery;"

[1464] Helaman 10:5 "And now, because thou hast done this with such unwearyingness, behold, I will bless thee forever; and I will make thee mighty in word and in deed, in faith and in works; yea, even that all things shall be done unto thee according to thy word, for thou shalt not ask that which is contrary to my will."

[of traditional Christianity] are all corrupt" is not because they are bad people (JS–H 1:19).[1465] It is because their doctrine is wrong. They do not have the truth. They entertain ideas which are not informed by heaven, and rely upon men to speculate about meaning, without knowing a thing about heaven.

Joseph remarked that "A man is saved no faster than he gets knowledge, for if he does not get knowledge he will be brought into captivity by some evil power in the other world" (TPJS, 217). The meaning of "knowledge" is, of course, the key to that statement. For the only "knowledge" which can save it to "know God" for yourself.[1466] The means of knowing this God is, of course, revelation and His personal ministry. His personal ministry will bring the faithful to the Father, as well. Both the Son and the Father will take their abode with you.[1467] This is the knowledge that saves.

The Christian world cannot save, their doctrines are corrupt, because they do not have the required knowledge to be able to teach. Therefore, they are "all corrupt" because their minds are corrupt. They cannot save themselves, much less inform us of anything which will aid us in knowing God.

Even reading Joseph's teachings will not save us. His knowledge and his covenant is not ours. We must find the required knowledge for ourselves. "Reading the experience of others, or the revelations

---

[1465] JS–H 1:19 "I was answered that I must join none of them, for they were all wrong; and the Personage who addressed me said that all their creeds were an abomination in his sight; that those professors were all corrupt; that: "they draw near to me with their lips, but their hearts are far from me, they teach for doctrines the commandments of men, having a form of godliness, but they deny the power thereof."

[1466] John 17:3 "And this is life eternal, that they might know thee the only true God, and Jesus Christ, whom thou hast sent."
D&C 132:24 "This is eternal lives—to know the only wise and true God, and Jesus Christ, whom he hath sent. I am he. Receive ye, therefore, my law."

[1467] John 14:18, 23 "I will not leave you comfortless: I will come to you. Jesus answered and said unto him, If a man love me, he will keep my words: and my Father will love him, and we will come unto him, and make our abode with him."

given to them, can never give us a comprehensive view of our condition and true relation to God." (*TPJS*, 324). Even Joseph's revelations, and Joseph's scriptures are inadequate. They must be obtained by each individual or they will be left without saving knowledge.

How do we get good doctrine, good information and a valid covenant with God for ourselves? It is through knowledge from Him. ". . . could you gaze into heaven five minutes you would know more than you would by reading all that ever was written on the subject" (*TPJS*, 324). This is true because we then gain knowledge that saves us. We know God.

I don't give a fig for lengthy quotes of man's speculation about the "truth" as they understand it. I care only for the revelations from heaven. Men who have never gazed into heaven simply do not know the truth. Good men, honest men, and men of the highest intent who know nothing about the heavens cannot help anyone to find their way to God.

There are, of course, disappointments along the way when you gain knowledge. You find that you learn things you do not want to know. You become disconnected with this world as you attach to the higher world. I read the *Doctrines of Salvation* from Joseph Fielding Smith as a convert to the church, believing it to be filled with truth. I accepted the notion he advances, that

> "Christ has himself declared that the manifestations we might have of the Spirit of Christ, or from a visitation from an angel, a tangible resurrected being, would not leave the impression and would not convince us and place within us that something which we cannot get away from which we receive through a manifestation of the Holy Ghost. Personal visitations might become dim as time goes on, but this guidance of the Holy Ghost is renewed and continued, day after day, year after year, if we live to be worthy of it." (*Doctrines of Salvation* 1:44)

I believed that at one point. I thought it good doctrine. I was troubled and disappointed to learn this was wrong. I did not want to know Joseph Fielding Smith was in error. But I learned it. Visitations are more, not less, powerful than the Holy Ghost. The scriptures prove it. For an angel will not come to visit you without being fully armed by the power of the Holy Ghost. Indeed, they speak by the power of the Holy Ghost when they visit.[1468] I wish I did not know Joseph Fielding Smith was wrong. I wish I did not realize he had never been visited by an angel, for only by lacking such an experience could he make this error. But we seek "knowledge" to be saved, and therefore we should find ourselves informed by heaven alone, and not men, even very good men, trying to tell us about things they can only guess to be true.

There is a great deal of difference between saving knowledge, which comes from heaven, and error, speculation and man's own doctrine, which cannot help us. We should never find ourselves among those who "teach for doctrine the commandments of men."[1469] Get connected to heaven and you needn't be dependent upon any *man* for your salvation. Not even Joseph Smith wanted you to do that by depending on him. Such things make you darkened in your mind, because you neglect the duty which God has imposed upon you (*TPJS*, 238).

[1468] 2 Nephi 32:2–3 "Do ye not remember that I said unto you that after ye had received the Holy Ghost ye could speak with the tongue of angels? And now, how could ye speak with the tongue of angels save it were by the Holy Ghost? Angels speak by the power of the Holy Ghost; wherefore, they speak the words of Christ. Wherefore, I said unto you, feast upon the words of Christ; for behold, the words of Christ will tell you all things what ye should do."

[1469] JS–H 1:19 "I was answered that I must join none of them, for they were all wrong; and the Personage who addressed me said that all their creeds were an abomination in his sight; that those professors were all corrupt; that: "they draw near to me with their lips, but their hearts are far from me, they teach for doctrines the commandments of men, having a form of godliness, but they deny the power thereof.""

I do not point to me, or to another man, or to any group of men, no matter how well intentioned. I point to Christ, who alone can save you. You will not be rescued by another. No office can do it. No ordinance can do it. Only Christ has the power to save.[1470]

The most dogmatic and well studied Mormons are often the furthest away from heaven. Proud, confident, insistent they possess great knowledge, all the while little more than a child of hell, bound in darkness, and unable to recognize the truth. They will, as Joseph put it, "be brought into captivity by some evil power in the other world" (*TPJS*, 217) because they are already captive by a spirit of contention, which Christ told us all is of the devil.[1471]

We should declare the truth, point to Christ, and say what we know to be true from our knowledge. It is up to others to accept or reject what is true. We cannot be saved; NONE of us can be saved unless we have saving knowledge which comes from Christ. You would know this if the heavens were opened to you and angels ministered to you. This is why the Book of Mormon authors so often confirmed their message did not originate from them, but came as a result of the Lord or His angels requiring the message to be delivered.

I do not care if anyone believes a thing I have ever said or written. But I do care if someone decides they will close the gate of heaven by the false things they preach, all the while declaring they are Christ's. How can they know the Master when they oppose knowledge of Him? It is more than an enigma. It is a tragedy.

[1470] Mosiah 3:17 "And moreover, I say unto you, that there shall be no other name given nor any other way nor means whereby salvation can come unto the children of men, only in and through the name of Christ, the Lord Omnipotent."
Mosiah 5:8 "And under this head ye are made free, and there is no other head whereby ye can be made free. There is no other name given whereby salvation cometh; therefore, I would that ye should take upon you the name of Christ, all you that have entered into the covenant with God that ye should be obedient unto the end of your lives."

[1471] 3 Nephi 11:29 "For verily, verily I say unto you, he that hath the spirit of contention is not of me, but is of the devil, who is the father of contention, and he stirreth up the hearts of men to contend with anger, one with another."

Our Many Cares

Our many cares often focus on things which do not matter. Christ told us what matters. It is not what we can get from God, but what we do for Him, what we give up for His sake, that has value. If we lose our fathers and mothers—are rejected by those we are closest to in this life— for His sake, we are in the right way.[1472] When we are entrusted with something by Him, it is not for our benefit, but for the benefit of others while in His service.[1473] In the parable about the talents, the talents were given for the Lord's sake, not the servants. The servant was accountable for what he did for the Lord

---

[1472] Matthew 10:35–39 "For I am come to set a man at variance against his father, and the daughter against her mother, and the daughter in law against her mother in law. And a man's foes *shall be* they of his own household. He that loveth father or mother more than me is not worthy of me: and he that loveth son or daughter more than me is not worthy of me. And he that taketh not his cross, and followeth after me, is not worthy of me. He that findeth his life shall lose it: and he that loseth his life for my sake shall find it."

[1473] Matthew 25:14–30 "For *the kingdom of heaven is* as a man travelling into a far country, *who* called his own servants, and delivered unto them his goods. And unto one he gave five talents, to another two, and to another one; to every man according to his several ability; and straightway took his journey. Then he that had received the five talents went and traded with the same, and made *them* other five talents. And likewise he that *had received* two, he also gained other two. But he that had received one went and digged in the earth, and hid his lord's money. After a long time the lord of those servants cometh, and reckoneth with them. And so he that had received five talents came and brought other five talents, saying, Lord, thou deliveredst unto me five talents: behold, I have gained beside them five talents more. His lord said unto him, Well done, *thou* good and faithful servant: thou hast been faithful over a few things, I will make thee ruler over many things: enter thou into the joy of thy lord. He also that had received two talents came and said, Lord, thou deliveredst unto me two talents: behold, I have gained two other talents beside them. His lord said unto him, Well done, good and faithful servant; thou hast been faithful over a few things, I will make thee ruler over many things: enter thou into the joy of thy lord. Then he which had received the one talent came and said, Lord, I knew thee that thou art an hard man, reaping where thou hast not sown, and gathering where thou hast not strawed: And I was afraid, and went and hid thy talent in the earth: lo, *there* thou hast *that is* thine. His lord answered and said unto him, *Thou* wicked and slothful servant, thou knewest that I reap where I sowed not, and gather where I have not strawed: Thou oughtest therefore to have put my money to the exchangers, and *then* at my coming I should have received mine own with usury. Take therefore the talent from him, and give *it* unto him which hath ten talents. For unto every one that hath shall be given, and he shall have abundance: but from him that hath not shall be taken away even that which he hath. And cast ye the unprofitable servant into outer darkness: there shall be weeping and gnashing of teeth."

with what was given. It was not about the servant, nor the pride of being entrusted, nor the praise of men. It was only about doing the will of the Lord and glorifying Him.

When we claim we've done great things in the Lord's name, we miss the point.[1474] The kingdom, and the power and the glory is the Fathers, not ours.[1475]

What little we have must all be given to Him if we hope to please our Lord.[1476] Until we give all we have to Him, we have nothing.

This is more than enough to occupy all our days. How is it then we have time to fret about so much else? How do we have time for endless debate and group discussions which circle about but fail to reach the truth; without ever noticing how little we have given to Him? Why do we ever contemplate with pride what we've received, what we own, what office or station we occupy, or how great we have become down in this dark well? What use is it to succeed here? What great thing is it you have here that will endure for even a thousand years? "And when he had called the people unto him with his disciples also, he said unto them, Whosoever will come after me, let him deny himself, and take up his cross, and follow me. For whosoever will save his life shall lose it; but whosoever shall lose his life for my sake and the gospel's, the same shall save it. For what shall it profit a

---

[1474] Matthew 7:21–23 "Not every one that saith unto me, Lord, Lord, shall enter into the kingdom of heaven; but he that doeth the will of my Father which is in heaven. Many will say to me in that day, Lord, Lord, have we not prophesied in thy name? and in thy name have cast out devils? and in thy name done many wonderful works? And then will I profess unto them, I never knew you: depart from me, ye that work iniquity."

[1475] Matthew 6:13 "And lead us not into temptation, but deliver us from evil: For thine is the kingdom, and the power, and the glory, for ever. Amen."

[1476] Luke 21:1–4 "And he looked up, and saw the rich men casting their gifts into the treasury. And he saw also a certain poor widow casting in thither two mites. And he said, Of a truth I say unto you, that this poor widow hath cast in more than they all: For all these have of their abundance cast in unto the offerings of God: but she of her penury hath cast in all the living that she had."

man, if he shall gain the whole world, and lose his own soul? Or what shall a man give in exchange for his soul?"[1477]

Jesus' Doctrine

Jesus complained to the Nephites about their religious arguments. He called such disagreements over religion "contention" and said it was His doctrine that "such things should be done away."[1478] Seems we want to believe in Christ, but reject His doctrine. He was quite unrelenting on the point:

> "Verily I say unto you, he that hath the spirit of contention is not of me, but is of the devil, who is the father of contention, and he stirreth up the hearts of men to contend with anger, one with another." (3 Nephi 11:29.)

It is interesting how He did it. Because He disagreed with the presiding authorities of His day on almost every particular of their then-current religious observances. But He managed to declare what He believed, to teach what He thought comprised the higher, underlying purpose of the law, without contending. He answered their oftentimes hostile questions forthrightly, and unequivocally but not through contention.

He goes on to declare His doctrine, which is the doctrine given to Him by the Father:

> "I bear record of the Father, and the Father beareth record of me, and the Holy Ghost beareth record of the Father and me;

[1477] Mark 8:34–37 "And when he had called the people *unto him* with his disciples also, he said unto them, Whosoever will come after me, let him deny himself, and take up his cross, and follow me. For whosoever will save his life shall lose it; but whosoever shall lose his life for my sake and the gospel's, the same shall save it. For what shall it profit a man, if he shall gain the whole world, and lose his own soul? Or what shall a man give in exchange for his soul?"

[1478] 3 Nephi 11:30 "Behold, this is not my doctrine, to stir up the hearts of men with anger, one against another; but this is my doctrine, that such things should be done away."

and I bear record that the Father commandeth all men, everywhere, to repent and believe in me. And whosoever believeth in me, and is baptized, the same shall be saved; and they are they who shall inherit the kingdom of God. And whoso believeth not in me, and is not baptized, shall be damned. Verily, verily, I say unto you, that this is my doctrine, and I bear record of it from the Father; and whoso believeth in me believeth in the Father also; and unto him will the Father bear record of me, for he will visit him with fire and with the Holy Ghost. And thus will the Father bear record of me, and the Holy Ghost will bear record unto him of the Father and me; for the Father, and I, and the Holy Ghost are one." (3 Nephi 11:32–36.)

His doctrine is to "bear record of the Father." And His doctrine is the "Father will bear record of Him." And the "Holy Ghost will bear record of both Him and the Father." For they are all one.

It is nice, I suppose, when someone bears their testimony. I do it. I hear others do it. I see some folks swooning when they hear someone they think holds an important office in the church bearing a testimony. But we are supposed to get our testimony from Christ and from the Father and from the Holy Ghost.

We are all told by Christ that "all men everywhere" are commanded to repent. That is all inclusive. There isn't some special, elect few who are so nigh to heaven they are not required to repent. Everyone. Relentlessly. We are all in desperate need of repentance. We don't need a healthy self-image. We don't need reassurance that we are loved, even doted upon by God. We don't need to be indulged in our sins, told we are just born with problems we should accept, or given any excuse to turn away from facing our weaknesses. They are, after all, gifts from Him to humble us.[1479] They were given to humble us, to drive us onto our knees, and to commend us to Christ. We are commanded to repent from them, and they are a gift to remind us of our dependence upon Him.

When someone cries out that we are in desperate need of repentance today, however, they are called "negative" and "unkind" and "not at all like Christ." They imagine Christ as a limp-wristed, happy-go-lucky chap who is indulgent and promiscuously forgiving. I do not imagine such a being; but instead a Counselor of Righteousness, whose every word is designed to make me become more like Him. Whose every sacrifice was designed to bring greater light into my mind and heart. Who stretches and pulls me relentlessly forward and upward, bringing me to my knees as I view in horror my many failings. I see a Man of Holiness who cannot tolerate any degree of unrighteousness; but who is ever ready to heal and instruct. A God indeed. Who works to bring others to become like Him.

"Wait!" shouts someone, "I have a testimony of 'the church'!" Well, that's nice, I suppose. I find the church important, too. I fellowship there every Sunday. I enjoy immensely my ward. But that isn't Christ's doctrine. My testimony should come from Christ bearing record to me of the Father, and the Father then bearing testimony or record to me of the Son, and the Holy Ghost bearing testimony to me of the Father and the Son. That is His doctrine. And Christ is quite emphatic on that point, as well:

> "And whoso shall declare more or less than this, and establish it for my doctrine, the same cometh of evil, and is not built upon my rock but he buildeth upon a sandy foundation, and

---

[1479] Ether 12:27 "And if men come unto me I will show unto them their weakness. I give unto men weakness that they may be humble; and my grace is sufficient for all men that humble themselves before me; for if they humble themselves before me, and have faith in me, then will I make weak things become strong unto them."

the gates of hell stand open to receive such when the floods come and the winds beat upon them." (3 Nephi 11:40)

I've been bearing testimony of Christ in books I have written for some time now. But the testimony I bear is that He lives and is altogether willing to bear testimony to you. And the Father, also, is willing to do so. And also the Holy Ghost.

I do not believe God was meant to be experienced second- and third-hand. I do not believe we are supposed to "know about God" but were instead, according to Christ's doctrine, to "know God." He will make Himself known to you. Not vicariously through a Pope, or a Bishop, or an Archbishop, or a Cardinal, or a Stake President, or some other preacher. He, Christ, and He, the Father and the Holy Ghost are the ones who are to declare themselves to you. Then you aren't building on the sandy, unstable foundation comprised of the many varieties of the hireling intermediary who gets acclaim here, praise and adoration here, as an inappropriate surrogate for He alone who can save. When men get put between the individual and God almost every individual immediately begins to exercise control, and dominion and compulsion over others. It is a wise God who restricts His delegation of "power" to such a degree that it cannot be exercised unrighteously.[1480]

God is knowable. He comforts.

Draper Temple Visit

Last week we took our Priests to the Draper Temple to do baptisms. It was a busy evening. I talked the Bishop into doing baptisms, and I was able to do confirmations. This left me dry.

[1480] D&C 121:41 "No power or influence can or ought to be maintained by virtue of the priesthood, only by persuasion, by long-suffering, by gentleness and meekness, and by love unfeigned;"

Then I rushed home to pick up my wife and we returned to attend the last endowment session of the evening with her brother. He was taking out his own endowment for the first time in a "live session."

A neighbor of mine was in the Celestial Room as a worker and he told me the temples were all overbooked for weddings last Friday. The 11–11–11 date was in high demand for weddings. He had a sheet with numbers on it. I forget the totals, but it was to be the largest single day of weddings in the Draper Temple history. Apparently there was a lottery for the 11:00 time frame.

The Draper Temple is quite lovely. I liked the Jordan River Temple (which was our district before the Draper Temple was built). It was very efficient. With six session rooms you can get a session every 20 minutes. I liked the convenience of that. When we lost that district assignment, the Draper Temple was so busy that I started going to the Oquirrh Temple. That is an amazingly beautiful facility. It was the temple I attended temporarily. It had a wonderful spirit about it. Then the police shot and killed that fellow on the temple grounds and I haven't been back. It's a personal thing, I suppose.

We helped with the Draper Temple Open House as a stake and as a family when it was first open. We enjoyed that experience.

The Temple I like most is the Manti Temple. Like Salt Lake, it is live with real people instead of a film. It is not crowded. The pioneer workmanship is interesting and beautiful. I also think the outside architecture is among the most beautiful of any of the Temples.

The Priests were taught today about how to find ancestors for whom work can be done through the "Ancestry.com" website. The hope is that between the visit this week and the information provided in today's lesson, these young men will find themselves interested in finding their ancestors. That would be good. Our lives are not ours alone. Our ancestors have an interest in how we live and what we do with the time we have allotted to us in mortality. As Joseph put it:

> "The spirits of the just are enveloped in flaming fire, . . . are not far from us, and know and understand our thoughts, feelings, and emotions . . . and are often pained therewith." (*TPJS*, 326)

Temples can remind us we are not living for our own interests, but also owe an obligation to those who went before in our family lines.

Reactions to Passing the Heavenly Gift

I had a conversation this morning with a friend whose years-long alienation from the church has been healed through reading *Passing the Heavenly Gift*. I have also had a discussion yesterday about how another man was deeply offended by the content and thought it was nearly apostate to have written it. One man who withdrew from membership in the church told me he could not finish reading it because it was too "faith promoting" and "apologetic" and could not be regarded as true history because of its pro-church bias. Another man told me that it finally told the truth and liberated him to continue in church activity while feeling at home again among the Saints. I also heard a woman bear her testimony for the first time in years, in part because of the book's effect upon her heart.

The book has been praised as inspired by a reader who told me they felt close to the Holy Ghost as they read every page; and it has been denounced as the product of an evil and aspiring man.

Well, I'm not going to react to the reactions. But I want it clear that first, the only motive I have is to deal honestly with what I know is a current problem friends I know are struggling to solve. People who want to believe in the Restoration, but who cannot find any peace in the details of the history. I have looked at the problems and the book is an honest explanation of how I cope with the issues.

No one needs to read the book. Anyone who does read it is put to the inconvenience of buying or borrowing a copy. I do not advocate it, but only offer it. If you are untroubled by church history issues, then go your way and give it no thought. If you struggle with problems from the church's past, then I offer it to help.

I do not advocate any position. I offer my understanding for whatever value someone may take from it. I never speak up in church and argue my views. I sit silent for the most part and leave people to enjoy their own understanding. On occasion I'm asked to teach or talk in Sacrament. When asked, I teach the assigned topic in the way I think brings the greatest understanding to the topic. As far as I know, there are only a very few people in my home Ward who are even aware I have written a single book. And of those who may know, I believe most have not read anything I've written.

I have no following, as far as I am aware. If there is anyone who claims to be following me, the only advice I would give them is to quit. I do not want a follower. Like any other Latter-day Saint, I offer my testimony and I give what I hope will help others understand difficult issues. If there is anyone worth following it is the Lord alone. I know of no man who can help anyone be saved. It does no good to claim you are "of Paul" or are "of Cephas" or you are "of Moses" or "Apollos" or some other man. That merits a Telestial condemnation comparable to what is merited by the liars, and whoremongers and adulterers.[1481] Therefore I do not commend any man as someone to claim you follow.

Harold Bloom Article

Harold Bloom has written an interesting article in the New York Times titled "Will This Election Be the Mormon Breakthrough"—it includes Professor Bloom's observations about how dramatically Mormonism has changed from its origins.

Harold Bloom is a serious student of religion. He one time admired Mormonism. The article I linked to earlier today is a reflection of his disillusionment because of the changes which the faith has undergone since the 1990's. What he once thought would be a revolutionary religion, with vitality that would revolutionize the world, is now gone.

Mormonism was designed to change the world, not to be changed by it.

Mormonism was intended to alter how people understood and relate to God; not to become an Americanized version of Roman Catholicism with a magisterial hierarchy viewed as God's "Vicars" holding keys to heaven through which sycophants could obtain Divine favor.

[1481] D&C 76:98–105 "And the glory of the telestial is one, even as the glory of the stars is one; for as one star differs from another star in glory, even so differs one from another in glory in the telestial world; For these are they who are of Paul, and of Apollos, and of Cephas. These are they who say they are some of one and some of another—some of Christ and some of John, and some of Moses, and some of Elias, and some of Esaias, and some of Isaiah, and some of Enoch; But received not the gospel, neither the testimony of Jesus, neither the prophets, neither the everlasting covenant. Last of all, these all are they who will not be gathered with the saints, to be caught up unto the church of the Firstborn, and received into the cloud. These are they who are liars, and sorcerers, and adulterers, and whoremongers, and whosoever loves and makes a lie. These are they who suffer the wrath of God on earth. These are they who suffer the vengeance of eternal fire."

Bloom laments the transition and, because of it, has let the tarnishing recent changes to Mormonism alter his earlier, much more positive assessment of Joseph and the faith founded through him.

Bloom's conclusion that Mormonism is now just another Protestant religion is a conclusion he was disappointed to reach. But, having reached it, he does not hold back on his disappointment.

When it began, Mormonism denounced the idea of following men. It captured in rapid prose the idea that following men, even inspired men who were authentic prophets who spoke with God, merited damnation to hell alongside the wicked:

> "For these are they who are of Paul, and of Apollos, and of Cephas. These are they who say they are some of one and some of another—some of Christ and some of John, and some of Moses, and some of Elias, and some of Esaias, and some of Isaiah, and some of Enoch; But received not the gospel . . . will not be gathered with the saints, to be caught up unto the church of the Firstborn, and received into the cloud. These are they who are liars, and sorcerers, and adulterers, and whoremongers, and whosoever loves and makes a lie. These are they who suffer the wrath of God on earth. These are they who suffer the vengeance of eternal fire." (D&C 76:99–105)

Joseph Smith elaborated on this idea in a sermon to the Relief Society in Nauvoo, telling them:

> "the people should each one stand for himself, and depend on no man or men in that state of corruption of the Jewish church—that righteous persons could only deliver their own souls—applied it to the present state [1842] of the Church of Jesus Christ of Latter-day Saints—said if the people departed from the Lord, they must fall—that they were depending on the Prophet, hence were darkened in their minds, in consequence of neglecting the duties devolving upon themselves. . . " (TPJS, 238)

Today we have inverted that idea. Now if you do not "depend on the Prophet" you are considered to have a darkened mind.

It is a fundamental principle of fourth phase Mormonism that all anyone needs to do is "Follow the Prophet" (meaning the President of the church) and everything else will take care of itself. There is little else required. Tithing and some dietary restrictions, and a few meetings are needed.

Today if there is the slightest hint by someone that "Following the Prophet" as your primary faith will merit only "the wrath of God on earth" and "the vengeance of eternal fire" because we must not say we follow any man-—well that is taken as weakness of faith, or worse. It can be regarded as a substantial error in doctrine or under-standing. Or, worse still, as evidence that you don't believe God at all. You are, therefore, damned.

Well, Bloom's criticism is biting, to be sure. But it is borne from his disappointment in what we've become in only a few short years of transition. The pace of the changes are accelerating, too. In an-other two decades it will be even more difficult to recognize Mormon-ism as the faith restored through Joseph. The caretakers now point to change as evidence of inspiration; instead of worrying change may be provoking ire.[1482] Fortunately, for us, there is no need to really consider the ideas which arise from anywhere other than the recog-nized authorities. We can always trust that God will protect us with a mighty hand. Our freedom to err has literally been circumscribed by His power and commitment to save us. We are not free to apostatize from His ways, but are instead guaranteed we cannot fall away as was the case with every earlier dispensation of God's Gospel. Any idea

---

[1482] Isaiah 24:5 "The earth also is defiled under the inhabitants thereof; because they have transgressed the laws, changed the ordinance, broken the everlasting covenant."
Malachi 3:7 "Even from the days of your fathers ye are gone away from mine ordi-nances, and have not kept *them*. Return unto me, and I will return unto you, saith the Lord of hosts. But ye said, Wherein shall we return?"

we can do the same thing as every earlier era of man's interaction with God belittles God's power. It challenges His overriding hand which has restored the truth for the last time to the earth, and nothing can ever change His determination to keep it here. Even our neglect, rebellion, sins and stupidity is nothing compared to God's commitment to letting us keep the fullness of the Gospel of Jesus Christ. We got it. We've got keys that cannot tarnish. And, all of this is to the envy of every other Christian denomination; because there's just nothing anyone can do to change that. Not even us. Right?

Gospel Study

There are issues some Saints believe are fully resolved which, upon closer study, turn out to be much less clear. I'm quite comfortable with investigating claims, history and doctrine even when it creates long periods of uncertainty while I research the topic. I've spent years following the trail on some issues before reaching a conclusion.

I'm converted to the restored Gospel. I have absolute confidence in Joseph Smith's calling as a latter-day Prophet. His life is worth careful study. Even minute details are sometimes quite important. The available material for studying his life has greatly expanded in recent years, and is in the process of expanding further as *The Joseph Smith Papers* project continues.

Some Saints are anxiety ridden when something new is raised about the Prophet, the church's history or doctrine which they thought was "settled." But that is largely because they are insecure about the search into truth. I understand that and even sympathize with it. But I came into the faith as a convert, and therefore it required a search by me in the first place.

When I write about the conclusions I have reached the "audience" is not necessarily intended to include life-long members of the church who have a sedentary approach to their religion and who hope the church's formal programs represent everything God wants them to know. I am pleased to leave them alone. They aren't interested in the search, don't care to learn anything new, and have little in common with the religion I believe. I do not write for them. To the extent my writing causes alarm for them, I understand. But I'm really not trying to tell them anything.

Those who believe the faith, want to explore its depths, and enjoy reading the thoughts of similarly motivated Saints are the only people who should have any interest in what I write.

Mormonism was (originally) intended to include "all truth." But the available information in 1844 has now transformed. It is transforming now almost daily. But not by sampling opinions—that is completely worthless to the search for truth. It is instead through uncovering history, studying the past and opening the heavens.

The church was intended to be a repository of truth. That does not require wealth, political influence, property or numbers. Truth is alien here and will not be rewarded in this world. When the world welcomes "Mormonism" then you can know compromises have been made to enable it to become popular. The Book of Mormon sounds an alarm on that topic. It is one of the great sources of truth. And it exposes the modern world, and ourselves, to relentless criticism and warning. However comfortable others may become with their faith, I find it serves best as an alarm, warning me of the perils of life in this fallen sphere.

Christ the Opener

Christ is the one who opens the heavens.[1483] It is at His command the heavens open and close.

[1483] Ether 4:9 "And at my command the heavens are opened and are shut; and at my word the earth shall shake; and at my command the inhabitants thereof shall pass away, even so as by fire."

Those to whom the heavens remain closed and to whom angels no longer minister are practicing a faith which is vain.[1484]

Nephi warned us against a faith which claims Christ had finished His work and given His power to men.[1485]

Neither God nor His Gospel change.[1486]

I care nothing for men or their precepts. Man's precepts will only condemn us at the last day.[1487] I care only about Him at whose command the heavens are opened; and for those whom He sends through the opening He causes to occur. All else is vanity—because it cannot save.

Thanksgiving

I'd been thinking of putting something up about Thanksgiving and using some New Testament things I've been reflecting on, but it changed today when I got my mail. Now I thought I'd just put up a short comment on another matter.

The practice of law is largely just work and the means for providing for my family. I like to be able to assist in solving problems between people, but oftentimes the work involves disputes which are intractable among people who want to vent against an opposing party. It is a real privilege to work for someone whose cause is just

---

[1484] Moroni 7:37 "Behold I say unto you, Nay; for it is by faith that miracles are wrought; and it is by faith that angels appear and minister unto men; wherefore, if these things have ceased wo be unto the children of men, for it is because of unbelief, and all is vain."

[1485] 2 Nephi 28:5 "And they deny the power of God, the Holy One of Israel; and they say unto the people: Hearken unto us, and hear ye our precept; for behold there is no God today, for the Lord and the Redeemer hath done his work, and he hath given his power unto men;"

[1486] Moroni 8:18 "For I know that God is not a partial God, neither a changeable being; but he is unchangeable from all eternity to all eternity."

[1487] 2 Nephi 28:26–27 "Yea, wo be unto him that hearkeneth unto the precepts of men, and denieth the power of God, and the gift of the Holy Ghost! Yea, wo be unto him that saith: We have received, and we need no more!"

and who has been put upon in an improper way. That, however, is not always the client.

I have a client who has spent several years in prison on a conviction of a felony which he did not commit. The system failed. I did not represent him in his trial, nor in the appeal which followed. But I was asked to assist him once the Appellate court had denied his appeal. After four years in prison there are limited options to try and get him freed from prison. He has a great deal to be angry over, and little reason to be giving thanks for how his life has been afflicted from a system which has, in his case, failed.

Nevertheless, today I got a hand-made card in the mail from him, thanking me for the work we are doing on his behalf to seek his freedom again. Tomorrow I am going to have my children read his card, sent from prison, and use it to celebrate our own many, many blessings.

We all have much to be grateful for. A man I met after he read some of my books died of brain cancer last week. I was able to talk with him before his death. I tried to cheer him, but found it was instead him who was cheering me.

Life is difficult for everyone. But every life is also filled with blessings. Whether we notice the blessings seems to be entirely optional. But what seems almost mandatory is that we notice the problems, the slights, the disappointments and the failings we each endure here. Tomorrow, however, I intend to be not only superficially grateful, but genuinely so; and to reflect on recent events and the home-made card I received from prison to remind me once again how God blesses me almost beyond measure.

Recent Conversations

I have a few requests for the talk mentioned on this blog. I will send those out later today to the ones who have requested them.

This morning I finished reading the Book of Mormon again. I've lost count of how many times I've read it through now. Dozens, if not hundreds. It still contains new information and powerful doctrine that I haven't noticed before. It is apparent they had the Temple rites. They were in possession of greater knowledge than we have among ourselves.

A few days ago I had a conversation with a former Mormon who became Catholic when he left the church. He finished reading *Passing the Heavenly Gift* and wanted to talk to me about it. It was a wonderful conversation. He talked openly about his experience as a Latter-day Saint and how much the church changed during the four decades he was a member. He talked about how much he liked being a member at first, and how he thought it was the church that changed and not him. He thought it had become increasingly dictatorial and harsh over the years he belonged, and he was at last completely alienated from it.

I mentioned the historic excesses of the Catholic Church, the terrors exercised by their priestly authorities during the Dark Ages and the atrocities of the Inquisition. He admitted their historic shortcomings, but thought these errors were now all behind the Catholics. They had learned from their mistakes, and were now keenly aware that they cannot dictate to people in a modern, pluralistic and secular society. They were now more broad-minded, tolerant and accepting of freedom to think and behave than perhaps almost any other Christian faith. There are things such as abortion and homosexuality, which the Catholic Church condemns, but despite this, whenever personal failure occurs the church's role is to forgive and to support. There is almost no thought given to church discipline, even in the case of transgressing priests who engage in pedophilia, and homosexual abuses. They accept and rehabilitate, condemn sin, but do not cast away the sinners.

As we talked, he said he expected that Mormonism, which is still in its infancy, will make the historic errors of the Catholic Church rather than to learn from history. He believed Catholicism's great mistakes were in the past, but he thought Mormonism's great mistakes are still in its future. He thought it was unlikely my LDS faith would learn from what I'd written in my book and turn away from its current direction. He thought my book offered an opportunity for Mormonism to reassess itself and turn into a more open, hopeful, helpful and tolerant faith because it would be necessarily more humble if it faced down its history.

Well, there were things we could agree on and things we will respectfully disagree. But I respect his faith because it is sincerely held. And he respects mine because he knows of my devotion to it. I enjoyed the open discussion. Neither of us felt threatened by the conversation and neither of us was trying to convert the other. We respected the choices each made in their faith.

As my wife and I walked and talked later that night, we discussed the problem of fear that is often an undercurrent when discussing religion with other people. Whether consciously or unconsciously fear is a great problem when the topic is religion. We puzzled over why that is the case.

With Latter-day Saints, the idea of a "testimony" can be an impediment to increased learning. That should not be the case. A person should be able to have a testimony and learn something new, even if it has the effect of changing their testimony. In fact, it is impossible for a testimony to grow if the new things must always conform to what is presently known. If a person's understanding is limited, incomplete, or even mistaken, then when a new idea that conflicts with these incomplete, limited or mistaken ideas is encountered, the temptation is always to resort to measuring the new ideas by the old, mistaken ones.

The Nephites followed the Law of Moses. But when Christ taught them He informed them the Law was fulfilled in Him.[1488] Can you imagine what the result would have been if the Nephites chose to measure Christ's message against their "testimony of the Law of Moses." They would have rejected our Savior, knowing that He was false and trying to deceive them because He was teaching something that conflicted with their prior testimony.

Fear is a tool used to limit inquiry. Fear is a tool used to keep people from repenting and facing God. The path to God can only be found when you refuse to share in the confederacy of fear held by your fellow man.[1489] For those controlled by their fears, they will view Christ's way as a stumbling block and an offense.[1490]

What if your testimony is incomplete? What if your understanding is wrong? How can God ever work to your satisfaction if you refuse to acknowledge His gifts among His people?[1491]

As our conversation continued, my wife was of the view that fear is one of the most effective ways to prevent learning. It shuts more

---

[1488] 3 Nephi 15:2–4 "And it came to pass that when Jesus had said these words he perceived that there were some among them who marveled, and wondered what he would concerning the law of Moses; for they understood not the saying that old things had passed away, and that all things had become new. And he said unto them: Marvel not that I said unto you that old things had passed away, and that all things had become new. Behold, I say unto you that the law is fulfilled that was given unto Moses."

[1489] Isaiah 8:11–13 (see also 2 Nephi 18:11–13) "For the Lord spake thus to me with a strong hand, and instructed me that I should not walk in the way of this people, saying, Say ye not, A confederacy, to all *them to* whom this people shall say, A confederacy; neither fear ye their fear, nor be afraid. Sanctify the Lord of hosts himself; and *let* him *be* your fear, and *let* him *be* your dread."

[1490] Isaiah 8:14–15 (see also 2 Nephi 18:14–15) "And he shall be for a sanctuary; but for a stone of stumbling and for a rock of offence to both the houses of Israel, for a gin and for a snare to the inhabitants of Jerusalem. And many among them shall stumble, and fall, and be broken, and be snared, and be taken."

[1491] Moroni 10:24–25 "And now I speak unto all the ends of the earth—that if the day cometh that the power and gifts of God shall be done away among you, it shall be because of unbelief. And wo be unto the children of men if this be the case; for there shall be none that doeth good among you, no not one. For if there be one among you that doeth good, he shall work by the power and gifts of God."

minds and curtails God's gifts more than any other tool in Satan's arsenal. It takes faith to allow your beliefs to be corrected by the Lord's continuing revelations. He always imparts things that are un-expected, and which require you to adjust what you are thinking to a new, and greater light.

Two Suggestions

There are two suggestions I'd offer to you. First, when you read the scriptural accounts of answers to prayer, ask yourself if there is additional information given by God beyond the topic raised by the prayer or petition to God, in the answer received. The prayer or peti-tion is what the prophet wanted to know. The answer, when it goes beyond that, is what God wanted to be known.

In the First Vision, Joseph wanted to know what church to join. He learned not to join any of them. But it was the rest of the infor-mation which was the Lord's agenda, not Joseph's.

When the Brother of Jared asked about lighting, that was his concern. The answer solved the problem, but went well beyond that. The answer included a revelation about the entire earth's history and destiny.

Section 76 resulted from an inquiry about "heaven" but included a great deal more.

Section 107 satisfied the inquiry about how to organize the church, but it went well beyond that.

It is the additional information which tells you what the Lord wants us to know. Where He would like our attention directed. Follow that suggestion and you'll find a great deal of what we often overlook.

Second, I'd suggest you read *Passing the Heavenly Gift* as a doctrinal exposition, rather than a history. The history can be disorienting and upsetting, even though it was intended for an audience which was already aware of issues and needed to be reoriented and comforted.

If you are content with the traditional story, the book wasn't written for you. But if you elect to read it anyway, then read it as an exposition of what the original doctrine was at the beginning with Joseph Smith.

Editing and Expanding

I've been working with the transcript of the Elijah Talk for the last week. It is expanding from what was done in the oral presentation. I had a two-hour timeframe to speak in that evening. Therefore the material was adapted to be presented in that time. For the transcript, however, I don't feel the same constraint. Therefore I have been expanding the information to reflect other related ideas which would not fit into the time allowed.

I've also been adding footnotes and showing the sources from which the ideas were taken. There are over 190 footnotes in the first 28 pages. Right now the paper appears to be some 37 pages long, but it has a tendency to continue to expand as I edit further into the document. When finished I expect it may grow to 43 or so pages. But then it will be edited to reduce redundancy, etc. and shrink again.

At the moment, I'm hoping to have it done by next weekend, but make no promises. It will be made available for anyone interested. Given the length, however, it cannot be put up here as a post. Instead it will either be sent as a pdf copy by email, or posted as a pdf you can either download or read on-line.

I've been struck by the quantity of scriptures which were relied on in the talk. It isn't clear that the ideas come from scripture until you go back through and cite to the sources. Then the entire talk becomes a foray into the Standard Works.

This effort reminds me once again just how delightful the faith restored through Joseph Smith was intended to be for those who follow it. It is a feast that includes "all truth." Mormons should be the most open, inquisitive, searching minds in the universe. The faith spreads from antiquity to all eternity. We are the only folks claiming to be Christian whose scriptures include Egyptian hieroglyphs, some of which are left unexplained and for the reader to search out. In other words, our scriptures raise questions which they deliberately do not answer. We are forewarned, therefore, by our own Standard Works, that we have a job to undertake for ourselves if we want to learn the truth. What a delight it is to be Mormon.

I hope those who want to cut off discussion, curtail thought, stop the search for truth, and censor differing views realize they advocate apostasy from the original vital, living, delightful religion of Christ. If they succeed, they reduce our restored faith to just another dead faith, without living root or branch, separated from the living vine, who is Christ. So long, however, as there remains even one soul willing to search for the truth in Christ, the Restoration remains alive.

Answer to Inquiry

I received criticism about using John D. Lee as a source in *Passing the Heavenly Gift*. My response was this:

Though he was excommunicated from the church, convicted of the crime and executed for his role in Mountain Meadows, the church reinstated John D. Lee to full fellowship in 1962. His temple ordinances were restored, and so far as the church is concerned all his blessings returned.

There are things in the church's archives that have never been made public. Therefore, the church knows things about John D. Lee's role in the incident that have not been made available for me to review. In the recent book, *Massacre at Mountain Meadows*, one of the LDS Church Historians (Richard Turley) makes a number of acknowledgements about the event. I presume he was acquainted with material in the archives when he did so.

The primary sources for my views are the work of Juanita Brooks and the recent Richard Turley books, *not* John D. Lee's work. However, I think it is now a mistake to ignore what was said in Lee's book. If the church believed he deserved reinstatement of all blessings, including his temple rites after what he wrote about the event, then I think it is a mistake to just ignore it.

I read Lee's book with his attitude at the time it was written fully in mind. There were competing motivations. On the one hand, he was decidedly disaffected and felt betrayed by Brigham Young and the church. On the other hand, he was about to die and wanted to part this world telling the truth. Each reader will have to decide for himself which motivation prevailed. I found parts of the book were not credible to my mind because the incident was too remote and his retelling seemed to have too much detail for me to believe it wasn't being embellished. But there were other parts which were very believable. His acknowledgements of wrongdoing and acceptance of his faults, particularly in his own family and among his plural wives, seemed to me to be an authentic effort of a man about to die to set matters straight.

In the end, I think his work is something that needs to be read and considered. I wanted corroboration to important details, but since the church has more information than has been given to the public, and decided in the light of that information to fully reinstate John D. Lee, it is no longer appropriate to dismiss him out of hand.

I also considered the criticism that his lawyer could have altered the text to make it more salacious before publication. I reached my own conclusion about that and do not think there was enough of that to warrant the conclusion that the text represents the story of the lawyer, and not John D. Lee's. Anyone reading it should consider the historical criticisms made about the book.

We drove to Las Vegas in a snow storm on Friday. My daughter's last softball games were down there. The drive down was exciting. We lost count of the wrecks we passed, or, in one occasion, drove through. Stayed in Circus Circus. I learned that Las Vegas still considers men who wear their uncontrolled lusts on their countenances, who are willing to pay money to titillate themselves in their desperate hormonal slavery, "Gentlemen." They organize "clubs" for them. Somehow there are enough of them to apparently make a profit from catering to their weaknesses.

TURNS AND RETURNS

Cycles of Truth

The ordinances have been the same since Adam, according to Joseph Smith. He explained that "[Jesus] set the ordinances to be the same forever and ever" (*TPJS,* 168). Also, "Ordinances instituted in the heavens before the foundations of the world, in the priesthood, for the salvation of men, are not to be altered or changed." (*Ibid.,* 308). This is why Joseph "restored" the Gospel, but did not bring anything new. It was a return to the earlier, forgotten truths.

Christ was careful to explain what was "fulfilled" in Him and what remained still intact from His earlier dealings with mankind. He "fulfilled" and brought to an end the Law of Moses. It ended. It was fulfilled. But everything else remained and was still in effect. Part of His explanation was as follows:

> And he said unto them: Marvel not that I said unto you that old things had passed away, and that all things had become new. Behold, I say unto you that the law is fulfilled that was given unto Moses. Behold, I am he that gave the law, and I am he who covenanted with my people Israel; therefore, the law in me is fulfilled, for I have come to fulfil the law; therefore it

hath an end. Behold, I do not destroy the prophets, for as many as have not been fulfilled in me, verily I say unto you, shall all be fulfilled. And because I said unto you that old things have passed away, I do not destroy that which hath been spoken concerning things which are to come. For behold, the covenant which I have made with my people is not all fulfilled; but the law which was given unto Moses hath an end in me. (3 Nephi 15:3–8)

Was Abraham a prophet? Did he live before Moses? Was the covenant with him fulfilled in Christ's fulfillment of the Law of Moses? If Abraham preceded Moses by more than three centuries, how is the later Law of Moses related to the earlier covenant?

Here is part of the covenant between Abraham and God, to endure throughout all generations of those who claim part of Abraham's covenant:

And I will establish my covenant between me and thee and thy seed after thee in their generations for an everlasting covenant, to be a God unto thee, and to thy seed after thee. And I will give unto thee, and to thy seed after thee, the land wherein thou art a stranger, all the land of Canaan, for an everlasting possession; and I will be their God.

And God said unto Abraham, Thou shalt keep my covenant therefore, thou, and thy seed after thee in their generations. This is my covenant, which ye shall keep, between me and you and thy seed after thee; Every man child among you shall be circumcised. And ye shall circumcise the flesh of your foreskin; and it shall be a token of the covenant betwixt me and you. And he that is eight days old shall be circumcised among you, every man child in your generations, he that is born in the house, or bought with money of any stranger, which is not of thy seed. He that is born in thy house, and he that is bought with thy money, must needs be circumcised: and my

covenant shall be in your flesh for an everlasting covenant."
(Genesis 17:7–13)

Since the covenants between God and man were established in
the heavens before the foundations of the world, as Joseph explained,
I suspect the covenant of circumcision did not originate with Abraham. I suspect it was restored through him, but came down from the
beginning. I believe if we had a full record we would find that originally the covenant was established through Adam. That it was originally intended to be performed by the male in contemplation of
marriage. That the covenant of marriage, like all covenants, required
the shedding of blood to be in effect. For the man, circumcision sealed
with the shedding of blood his covenant to marry. For the wife, the
virgin sacrificed blood at the marriage. But those things are now long
forgotten, lost to time, and could only be known today by revelation.

If Joseph's statement is correct, and Adam had the fullness of
the Gospel, then every prophet from the beginning has only "restored" lost truth. It has been a search to return to the original truth.
After all, Christ came to Adam three years previous to his death and
comforted him.[1492] Such an event strongly indicates Adam had the
fullness. The Gospel is, therefore, in all likelihood a search into the
ancient order of things, not a leap forward into something new. In
order to go forward, we will need to go back.

[1492] D&C 107:53–57 "Three years previous to the death of Adam, he called Seth, Enos,
Cainan, Mahalaleel, Jared, Enoch, and Methuselah, who were all high priests, with the
residue of his posterity who were righteous, into the valley of Adam-ondi-Ahman, and
there bestowed upon them his last blessing. And the Lord appeared unto them, and
they rose up and blessed Adam, and called him Michael, the prince, the archangel. And
the Lord administered comfort unto Adam, and said unto him: I have set thee to be at
the head; a multitude of nations shall come of thee, and thou art a prince over them
forever. And Adam stood up in the midst of the congregation; and, notwithstanding he
was bowed down with age, being full of the Holy Ghost, predicted whatsoever should
befall his posterity unto the latest generation. These things were all written in the book
of Enoch, and are to be testified of in due time."

It is an interesting question to contemplate whether the Lord was serious about the token becoming a memorial of His "covenant [which] shall be in your flesh for an everlasting covenant." Also, although the New Testament debates over "those of the circumcision" determined not to require circumcision of adult converts, they did not have 3 Nephi 15 to inform their debate.[1493]

I would doubt there will be any uncircumcised males included in the latter-day Zion. It is, at least for me, an interesting question to contemplate.

Sacrifice

This world is the place of sacrifice. We all came here to make sacrifices. We wanted to come here, we knew it would require sacrifice to produce the faith necessary for salvation, and we gladly came.

Christ is the great Prototype of the "saved man" according to the Lectures on Faith. He came and gave Himself as a sacrifice, and we are to "follow Him" if we are to be saved.

We came here to lay on the altar everything, our desires, appetites, passions, and everything with which the Lord has blessed us. Abraham put his beloved son on the altar, intending to kill him and then burn his remains, because God asked it of him. He did not refuse. However bitter, terrible and painful the request, the Lord asked it of Abraham and he proceeded to offer it.

No one obtains the faith necessary for salvation unless they are prepared to sacrifice all things to God. Faith for salvation cannot otherwise be obtained. Read the *Lectures on Faith* again. You'll see it is all set out there.

[1493] For New Testament references, see Romans 2 & 4, Galatians 5, and many other places.

Flattery and Repentance

It is the mark of a false message that it relies on flattery.[1494]

It is the mark of a true message that it calls for repentance (D&C 6:9; 11:9; Mosiah 18:20; 25:22).

Christ's message is always to "repent" and then to "come to Him" (Moroni 7:34).

There has never been a bona fide, reliable, infallible source of truth which cannot be compromised in this world. But there has always been a bona fide, reliable, infallible message of truth which does not compromise. It is the message of repentance.

Answer to Moroni 8:8

I got asked about Moroni 8:8 and the issue of "circumcision" posted earlier.

Moroni 8 is a letter from Mormon to his son, Moroni. In the 8th verse he (Mormon) quotes the Savior as having said, in relation to infant baptism, the following: "I came into the world not to call the righteous but sinners to repentance; the whole need no physician, but they that are sick; wherefore, little children are whole, for they are

---

[1494] Alma 46:5 "And they had been led by the flatteries of Amalickiah, that if they would support him and establish him to be their king that he would make them rulers over the people."

Alma 61:4 "And it is those who have sought to take away the judgment-seat from me that have been the cause of this great iniquity; for they have used great flattery, and they have led away the hearts of many people, which will be the cause of sore affliction among us; they have withheld our provisions, and have daunted our freemen that they have not come unto you."

Jacob 7:4 "And he was learned, that he had a perfect knowledge of the language of the people; wherefore, he could use much flattery, and much power of speech, according to the power of the devil."

Mosiah 27:8 "Now the sons of Mosiah were numbered among the unbelievers; and also one of the sons of Alma was numbered among them, he being called Alma, after his father; nevertheless, he became a very wicked and an idolatrous man. And he was a man of many words, and did speak much flattery to the people; therefore he led many of the people to do after the manner of his iniquities."

2 Nephi 28:22 "And behold, others he flattereth away, and telleth them there is no hell; and he saith unto them: I am no devil, for there is none—and thus he whispereth in their ears, until he grasps them with his awful chains, from whence there is no deliverance."

not capable of committing sin; wherefore the curse of Adam is taken from them in me, that it hath no power over them; and the law of circumcision is done away in me." My response is this:

First, the comment is about "little children" who do not need ordinances. They do not need baptism, and they do not need circumcision. Little children are exempt and the requirements are fulfilled in every respect by Christ's atonement. Therefore, they needn't be baptized, needn't be confirmed, needn't have circumcision; and they needn't comply with any of the requirements for salvation because Christ atoned for all sin arising from the Fall of Adam. They, "little children" that is, are not sick and therefore do not need a physician.

The teaching leaves open, however, the question about adults. Originally circumcision was an adult ordinance. When restored through Abraham, it was made an infant ceremony. The Law of Moses kept it something for infants. Christ removed all accountability for any law in the atonement for all infants, through the age of 8, who are not accountable before Him.

The issue, however, is whether this is satisfied for adults as well. Moroni 8:8 does not address that question. The earlier post does attempt to address it.

Out of Season Fruit

I've been asked several times about the comment that Adam and Eve partook of the fruit "out of season" in the Elijah Talk. Since it's come up more than once, here's an answer I gave to one of those who inquired:

They would have eventually received the command to partake. If they had waited for that command, the "fall" would have introduced the kind of opposition experienced during the Millennium rather than the kind we now have. Opposites only required: 1) change and 2) death. Both will be present during the Millennium.

The Garden of Eden is an allegory, and we all pass through a "Fall from Eden" to come here. But there are many other worlds.[1495] Among these countless others, ours fell the greatest.[1496] We are singular in our fallen state, and qualify as the "most wicked" of any of God's creations. Here we suffer, but with the opportunity to grow by making sacrifice. We all came here to offer sacrifice. Just being here is a form of sacrifice, and we will all submit to death to leave here.

Destination

I was asked at what point a car ceases to be a car. If it runs out of gas and cannot move is it still a car?

What if the engine is broken, and therefore it would not matter if there was gas, once it is broken is it still a car?

What if both the engine and transmission are beyond repair?

What if you cannot even push it because the tires and wheels are gone and it is sitting on blocks beside the road. Is it still a car?

If it bears some superficial resemblance to a car, is it still a car no matter what condition it is in or whether it works or not?

After thinking for a few minutes I responded: It was never meant to be a car. It was always about the destination. When the car stops for whatever reason, you get out and walk toward the destination and have gratitude for how far the car was able to take you before it

---

[1495] D&C 76:24 "That by him, and through him, and of him, the worlds are and were created, and the inhabitants thereof are begotten sons and daughters unto God."

[1496] Moses 7:36–37 "Wherefore, I can stretch forth mine hands and hold all the creations which I have made; and mine eye can pierce them also, and among all the workmanship of mine hands there has not been so great wickedness as among thy brethren. But behold, their sins shall be upon the heads of their fathers; Satan shall be their father, and misery shall be their doom; and the whole heavens shall weep over them, even all the workmanship of mine hands; wherefore should not the heavens weep, seeing these shall suffer?"

stopped. It was never about the car in the first place. *You* must keep moving. He was grateful.

Wickedness and Destruction

The cycle of wickedness and destruction often includes a complete inability of the wicked to detect their grave errors. They have their religion, and are comfortable with it. They think their pretenses are enough.

Ezekiel saw a vision of the destruction of the "chosen people" beginning at their Temple. The destroyers were told to wait before the slaughter began. First an angel would mark the foreheads of those who "sigh and cry for all the abominations that be done in the midst thereof".[1497] Meaning there were a few among the chosen, who knew their religious practices were used to justify abominable behavior. These few did not just condemn the wicked, they "sighed" and "cried" for their fellow saints. They prayed, made intercession, hoped for more time, and urged repentance.

The larger group, however, were content with their abominations and thought themselves righteous. They were not marked, nor spared. The command was given to slay them all, utterly, and spare none "both maids and little children, and women."[1498]

In the vision Ezekiel saw the destruction begin at the Temple.[1499] It began there because it was the Temple which these corrupt people believed to be proof of their great righteousness and also their favor with God. Therefore the destruction needed to begin there.

[1497] Ezekiel 9:4 "And the Lord said unto him, Go through the midst of the city, through the midst of Jerusalem, and set a mark upon the foreheads of the men that sigh and that cry for all the abominations that be done in the midst thereof."

[1498] Ezekiel 9:6 "Slay utterly old *and* young, both maids, and little children, and women: but come not near any man upon whom *is* the mark; and begin at my sanctuary. Then they began at the ancient men which *were* before the house."

[1499] Ibid.

The angel faithfully marked only those who were aware of the abominations and who would not join in with it.[1500] When the destruction began, the Lord was committed to His judgment, and declared "mine eye shall not spare, neither will I have pity, but I will recompense their way upon their head."[1501]

Ezekiel 9 is a useful chapter to consider. It reinforces the importance of repentance when it is offered. When the offering ends, it is followed by judgment and destruction.

How odd it is that the self-proclaimed "righteous" are almost without exception those who are most wicked, fallen, abominable and proud. You rarely encounter a corrupt group in the Book of Mormon who are not also quite involved in a false religion. The false religions in the Book of Mormon frequently teach that the followers are righteous and highly favored of God.[1502]

Wouldn't it be amazing if this kind of mistake could be made again by people who think themselves holy, better than others who do not enjoy the fullness of God's favor/Gospel, and destined for salvation while all others were doomed to an inferior kingdom? It's

---

[1500] Ezekiel 9:11 "And, behold, the man clothed with linen, which *had* the inkhorn by his side, reported the matter, saying, I have done as thou hast commanded me."

[1501] Ezekiel 9:10 "And as for me also, mine eye shall not spare, neither will I have pity, *but* I will recompense their way upon their head."

[1502] Alma 31:14–18 "Therefore, whosoever desired to worship must go forth and stand upon the top thereof, and stretch forth his hands towards heaven, and cry with a loud voice, saying: Holy, holy God; we believe that thou art God, and we believe that thou art holy, and that thou wast a spirit, and that thou art a spirit, and that thou wilt be a spirit forever. Holy God, we believe that thou hast separated us from our brethren; and we do not believe in the tradition of our brethren, which was handed down to them by the childishness of their fathers; but we believe that thou hast elected us to be thy holy children; and also thou hast made it known unto us that there shall be no Christ. But thou art the same yesterday, today, and forever; and thou hast elected us that we shall be saved, whilst all around us are elected to be cast by thy wrath down to hell; for the which holiness, O God, we thank thee; and we also thank thee that thou hast elected us, that we may not be led away after the foolish traditions of our brethren, which doth bind them down to a belief of Christ, which doth lead their hearts to wander far from thee, our God. And again we thank thee, O God, that we are a chosen and a holy people. Amen."

almost too ridiculous to even consider. Those things are behind us now, aren't they? Because we are promised salvation, and for us to fail would be for God to fail, and we know He's not going to do that.

History Is the Stuff

Almost always when an institution or group claims to have authority from God, the primary enforcement tool used to establish control over others is fear. Authority from God relieves the claimant to the authority of any need to display merit apart from the claim of authority itself. The Catholics were able to engage in excesses, abuses, even outright institutional evil, but these great wrongs were regarded as unimportant because of the claim to have authority from God.

God's holiness was embodied in "keys" given from Peter. They were thought to allow holders of the authority to seal in heaven. This silenced the critics. The fear of being kept from heaven or consigned to hell was enough to rule over the souls of men. They could claim they acted from a higher plane, with God's ways remaining mysterious, even incomprehensible to the common man. The power of God can judge others, but no may can judge God under this system.

If mental coercion did not work, then credulous and cruel believers could be employed to intimidate and get control. If more was needed, the Catholic hierarchy felt no inhibition at using violence to be able to rule and reign over the souls of men.

The Pope did not need to display virtue, only power. He did not need to produce revelation or expound on how men could entertain angels, only to appear in the seat of power, displaying the incidents of authority, wealth, privilege, standing above the common man in a place filled with art, treasure, statuary surrounded by supporters. These trappings were a substitute for revelation and authentic fruits from heaven.

This formula worked to keep all of Christendom subordinate to the rule of oftentimes wicked, even cruel, men. For nearly a thousand years it monopolized power over men. Because these pontiffs claimed to hold God's authority, people feared them and were loathe to challenge them. When the bedrock of an institution's claims rests on authority, these failings are almost always eventually unavoidable. God's power is so resilient, so powerful, so vital for salvation that almost all men will surrender to it or be forced to submit when a group trusts that it exists.

These are powerful forces. When released upon the stage of history, they are meant to be held by only the meek, the humble, and the servants of all. Never by the proud, the vain, and the ambitious. But it is always the proud, the vain and the ambitious who are drawn to seek to hold such authority. Hence the many sycophants who always congregate at Rome.

We see some of this very excess on display within radical Islam today. Brutality is justified by God's power; God's right to kill. No one questions God's right in such matters. But what man is there who can be certain of God's will until he has stood in His presence and learned how great a gulf exists between the foolishness of man and the holiness of God? But those are rare indeed. It is far easier to claim to speak FOR God than to actually speak WITH God. Whole cable networks are filled with clamoring clergy claiming to speak for Him. They'll be the first to burn, because the command to not take the Lord's name in vain is, after all, one of the Ten Commandments.

History is the stuff from which most clearly the warnings of scripture take form in flesh and blood. All the warnings are there, but we frequently believe them only applicable to those we know to have fallen. But the lessons were always meant for us . . .

A Visit to Temple Square

We took all the kids who are home, our foreign exchange student from Slovakia, and a friend of my daughter's to visit Temple Square last evening. The place was crowded. That's an understatement—it was packed! At times the sidewalks were "side stands," because no one seemed to know you could walk on them.

The impatient crowding and the cold made the overall experience less than I'd hoped. After crowding about in the Square itself, we maneuvered to the east, exiting the Square onto former Main Street by the large reflecting pool. There wasn't any relief there from the congestion and stern faces. People seemed quite determined, though it was hard to see of what.

We found some open space between the two sides of City Creek on the frozen grass and took a few group pictures with the eastern face of the Temple in the background. Then visited the Nativity scenes from other countries in the court area between the Administration Building and the Church Office Building. My daughter's friend needed to visit the restroom, so we set out for the North Visitor's Center, using the sidewalk on North Temple to avoid the congestion. As we entered North Temple there was a beggar on the ground. Now that the church owns the property, beggars are not allowed into Temple Square, Main Street, or in the campus area to the east. I gave some money to my daughter who is home from the University of Wyoming, and she gave to the beggar. That helped improve the spirit of the evening. Reminded us of the condition we occupy in relation to God.[1503]

At last, arriving in the Visitor's Center it was even more crowded than outside. There was a small rivulet of movement against the

---

[1503] Mosiah 4:19 "For behold, are we not all beggars? Do we not all depend upon the same Being, even God, for all the substance which we have, for both food and raiment, and for gold, and for silver, and for all the riches which we have of every kind?"

north wall before the desk, and at the moment we arrived the rivulet was occupied by outward bound Sister Missionaries headed back out to the frigid throngs. I noticed a wool cap on the floor, picked it up and held it high above my head for the owner to notice and come to reclaim. No one did. After a few minutes of holding it up, I asked a Sister Missionary with a Swiss Flag beside her name tag if there was a "lost and found." She said it was at the desk beside the north wall. So I entered the rivulet and headed inward. Those who were not visiting the restroom followed me. We settled beside the lost and found north desk to await the return of our missing company.

In the North Visitor's Center there was a youth choir in the southeast corner of the main floor singing some forgettable Christmas tune. I was taken by the expressions on the faces of those in the crowd as they either pressed into one another trying to move, or stood about in exasperation. The event was not what they had hoped for either. I lapsed into a quiet thoughtfulness of the circumstances, and wondered at how little joy seemed to be all about me in this crowded place.

Then it happened. It only took six notes to recognize the coming hymn. A cascade of memories of that song came back to me. The first time I remember recognizing it was in high school, when two of my classmates sang a duet. Debbie Penn was one of them, and I forget who accompanied her. When I first heard it I was stirred to reflection. For years it has been my favorite Christmas Hymn, even though it is terribly difficult to sing it well. On occasion, as I try to sing along, I will mutilate it. I cannot do the hymn justice, and I hope the Lord recognizes in my sincerity a slain sacrifice offered in honest devotion. Then the female voices joined in the melody:

O Holy Night, the stars are brightly shining,

It is the night of the dear Saviour's birth.

They were perfect. Here was the greatest of Christmas Hymns being presented by the loveliest of chorus voices. I was transfixed. The crowds began to disappear and I was in deep reflection.

It *was* a holy night. That night represented more than just His birth. It represented also the beginning of an infinite sacrifice. It is difficult to adequately state how great the condescension of God in coming here. His great condescension began by coming into the flesh.[1504]

He explained to the Nephites His great status before His birth. He was the one who gave the Law to Moses on the Mount.[1505] The glory He displayed on the Mount was inexpressible. Moses attempted to convey some idea using precious stone and referring to the bright glory of heaven itself. (See Exodus 24:10[1506], but the translation is not a fair expression of the idea in Hebrew in which "the clear, bright glory of heaven" should probably replace "the body of heaven in his clearness.")

A great, glorious Law Giver, whose glory was like the brightness of Heaven itself, condescended to become confined to a body of dust. Condescension indeed! Even before offering Himself as a sacrifice, He descended from glory to dwell here in the dust among our fallen race. The enormity of that step can hardly be put into words.

[1504] 1 Nephi 11:16–20 "And he said unto me: Knowest thou the condescension of God? And I said unto him: I know that he loveth his children; nevertheless, I do not know the meaning of all things. And he said unto me: Behold, the virgin whom thou seest is the mother of the Son of God, after the manner of the flesh. And it came to pass that I beheld that she was carried away in the Spirit; and after she had been carried away in the Spirit for the space of a time the angel spake unto me, saying: Look! And I looked and beheld the virgin again, bearing a child in her arms."

[1505] 3 Nephi 15:4–5 "Behold, I say unto you that the law is fulfilled that was given unto Moses. Behold, I am he that gave the law, and I am he who covenanted with my people Israel; therefore, the law in me is fulfilled, for I have come to fulfil the law; therefore it hath an end."

[1506] Exodus 24:10 "And they saw the God of Israel: and *there was* under his feet as it were a paved work of a sapphire stone, and as it were the body of heaven in *his* clearness."

A thrill of hope the weary world rejoices,

For yonder breaks a new and glorious morn . . .

Here, in the newly born body of our Lord, was Hope come down to this fallen world. What humility exists in the God of Glory who would choose to come here. We are all important because God came from His lofty position down to be among us, to rescue us all. What greater proof of man's worth can there be than this great condescension by a Holy Being?

Fall on your knees! Oh hear the angel voices! . . .

The angels came to announce His birth. In their joy they could not contain their feelings, and words alone would not do. They broke out in hymns of praise. Only the combined voices of a glorious chorus could give vent to the feelings within the message of His coming![1507] Enoch saw this coming, and also rejoiced at the Lamb destined to be slain, at last coming into the flesh![1508]

The crowd before me in the Visitor's Center transformed. They were not longer a busy, distracted, stern body pressing against one another. Each of them showed the merit of a God who came to dwell with them. They are all holy. They are all His handiwork.

Truly He taught us to love one another,

His law is love and His gospel is peace.

Chains He shall break, for the slave is our brother . . .

[1507] Luke 2:13–14 "And suddenly there was with the angel a multitude of the heavenly host praising God, and saying, Glory to God in the highest, and on earth peace, good will toward men."

[1508] Moses 7:47 "And behold, Enoch saw the day of the coming of the Son of Man, even in the flesh; and his soul rejoiced, saying: The Righteous is lifted up, and the Lamb is slain from the foundation of the world; and through faith I am in the bosom of the Father, and behold, Zion is with me."

We are our brother's keeper after all. If we love one another, we are only loving Him.[1509]

As the chorus completed the great hymn of praise I was grateful for the reminder of that Holy Night when Christ was born. We all still kneel before His great presence, for nothing else will adequately show our adoration of Him.[1510] We dare not stand in His presence until His command to "arise."[1511] At the command, a momentary conflict takes place inside you between the inappropriate pride to stand in His presence and the compelling respect for His command. All doubts presently flee. His word is sovereign. It is obedience to His will that lets you stand before Him.

As my group reassembled and left the North Visitor's Center, I was glad we had come. And glad for the great anthem I'd heard from the teenage choir. It was just what I'd hoped to find when we first departed for Temple Square.

The Whole Not the Parts

There are a few important ideas that define my understanding of the Gospel of Jesus Christ as restored by the Lord through the Prophet Joseph Smith. These are the ideas that make the Gospel whole, and not just a group of disconnected thoughts. Until these were part of the core of my understanding, I was left with disconnected dots and no overall harmony from which to orient myself.

First and foremost is that we are not to follow any man or men. No man is worthy of discipleship. Not me, not another. There is

---

[1509] John 13:34 "A new commandment I give unto you, That ye love one another; as I have loved you, that ye also love one another."

[1510] 3 Nephi 11:17 "Hosanna! Blessed be the name of the Most High God! And they did fall down at the feet of Jesus, and did worship him."

[1511] 3 Nephi 11:20 "And the Lord commanded him that he should arise. And he arose and stood before him."

only one who is worth following. He is the way, the truth and the life.[1512] Beside Him there is no other person who can save you.[1513]

This first principle is what has motivated all I have written. It is a mistake to think there is a departure in *Passing the Heavenly Gift* from the topic begun in *The Second Comforter: Conversing With the Lord Through the Veil*. They are both necessary. They do not reflect a change in my testimony or commitment to the truth, only an elaboration on the essential core principle that we are not going to be saved by following men. Rather, you will become "darkened in your mind" (*TPJS,* 237) if you do so.

Second and equally important, it is not the depth of your study that matters, but the quality of your connection with heaven that matters. Expounding doctrine is not only insufficient, it is oftentimes a distraction from what matters. We go from unbelief to belief when we learn truth. Not every source, including institutional sources, can be trusted to tell you the truth. Only the light of Christ, followed by the Holy Ghost is a reliable guide to distinguish between unbelief and belief. We go from belief to faith as we take action consistent with belief in truth. Faith is a principle of power. It will lead you to receive angels who still minister to those of a sound mind, not given to flights of fantasy or unstable behavior.[1514] We are brought from

---

[1512] John 14:16 "And I will pray the Father, and he shall give you another Comforter, that he may abide with you for ever;"

[1513] Mosiah 3:17 "And moreover, I say unto you, that there shall be no other name given nor any other way nor means whereby salvation can come unto the children of men, only in and through the name of Christ, the Lord Omnipotent."

[1514] Moroni 7:30 "For behold, they are subject unto him, to minister according to the word of his command, showing themselves unto them of strong faith and a firm mind in every form of godliness."

faith to knowledge as angels prepare us through their ministry.[1515] Knowledge comes from contact with Jesus Christ.[1516] This is the knowledge that saves, and nothing else.[1517] The idea that knowledge of Christ through His personal appearance to you is now unavailable is an old sectarian notion and is false.[1518]

Third, there is no written record, including the scriptures, which are able to tell you all you must know. You can only know the truth by having it revealed to you from heaven itself.[1519] This is the reason Joseph said if you could gaze into heaven for five minutes you would know more than you would by reading everything that has ever been

---

[1515] Moroni 7:31 "And the office of their ministry is to call men unto repentance, and to fulfil and to do the work of the covenants of the Father, which he hath made unto the children of men, to prepare the way among the children of men, by declaring the word of Christ unto the chosen vessels of the Lord, that they may bear testimony of him."
Moroni 7:25 "Wherefore, by the ministering of angels, and by every word which proceeded forth out of the mouth of God, men began to exercise faith in Christ; and thus by faith, they did lay hold upon every good thing; and thus it was until the coming of Christ."
Alma 32:23 "And now, he imparteth his word by angels unto men, yea, not only men but women also. Now this is not all; little children do have words given unto them many times, which confound the wise and the learned."

[1516] Ether 3:19 "And because of the knowledge of this man he could not be kept from beholding within the veil; and he saw the finger of Jesus, which, when he saw, he fell with fear; for he knew that it was the finger of the Lord; and he had faith no longer, for he knew, nothing doubting."

[1517] John 17:3 "And this is life eternal, that they might know thee the only true God, and Jesus Christ, whom thou hast sent."

[1518] John 14:23 "Jesus answered and said unto him, If a man love me, he will keep my words: and my Father will love him, and we will come unto him, and make our abode with him."
D&C 130:3 "John 14:23—The appearing of the Father and the Son, in that verse, is a personal appearance; and the idea that the Father and the Son dwell in a man's heart is an old sectarian notion, and is false."

[1519] D&C 76:114–118 "But great and marvelous are the works of the Lord, and the mysteries of his kingdom which he showed unto us, which surpass all understanding in glory, and in might, and in dominion; Which he commanded us we should not write while we were yet in the Spirit, and are not lawful for man to utter; Neither is man capable to make them known, for they are only to be seen and understood by the power of the Holy Spirit, which God bestows on those who love him, and purify themselves before him; To whom he grants this privilege of seeing and knowing for themselves; That through the power and manifestation of the Spirit, while in the flesh, they may be able to bear his presence in the world of glory."

written on the subject (*TPJS*, 324). Either you do as James says, and ask of God, or you will forever remain ignorant of the only knowledge which can save a man.[1520]

Fourth, the truth is intended to save us. We should welcome corrections. Too often, however, we are offended and think the truth is a hard thing to endure.[1521] That is a product of pride and arrogance. It is impossible to learn what must be learned unless we are willing to be corrected.[1522] Therefore, only the qualified will arrive at the gates, because the rest are unwilling to take the trip required of them.

Fifth, this is a personal journey which each must take for themselves. It cannot be shared. You must approach the Throne yourself. Joseph was alone when he met the Father and Son. Moses was alone when he ascended the Mount to meet the Lord. Enoch was alone when he was caught up to heaven. Elijah was alone on the mountain when the whirlwind, lightning and earthquake preceded the Lord's own voice. Daniel alone saw the vision of the Lord. Paul alone saw

---

[1520] JS-H 1:13 (referring to James 1:5) "At length I came to the conclusion that I must either remain in darkness and confusion, or else I must do as James directs, that is, ask of God. I at length came to the determination to "ask of God," concluding that if he gave wisdom to them that lacked wisdom, and would give liberally, and not upbraid, I might venture."
James 1:5 "If any of you lack wisdom, let him ask of God, that giveth to all *men* liberally, and upbraideth not; and it shall be given him."

[1521] 1 Nephi 16:1–3 "And now it came to pass that after I, Nephi, had made an end of speaking to my brethren, behold they said unto me: Thou hast declared unto us hard things, more than we are able to bear. And it came to pass that I said unto them that I knew that I had spoken hard things against the wicked, according to the truth; and the righteous have I justified, and testified that they should be lifted up at the last day; wherefore, the guilty taketh the truth to be hard, for it cutteth them to the very center. And now my brethren, if ye were righteous and were willing to hearken to the truth, and give heed unto it, that ye might walk uprightly before God, then ye would not murmur because of the truth, and say: Thou speakest hard things against us."

[1522] Mosiah 3:19 "For the natural man is an enemy to God, and has been from the fall of Adam, and will be, forever and ever, unless he yields to the enticings of the Holy Spirit, and putteth off the natural man and becometh a saint through the atonement of Christ the Lord, and becometh as a child, submissive, meek, humble, patient, full of love, willing to submit to all things which the Lord seeth fit to inflict upon him, even as a child doth submit to his father."

the light. Nephi alone saw his father's vision. Enos was alone in the wilderness in his encounter with God. Abraham was alone when the Lord spoke to him. Jacob slept alone when the ladder to heaven descended for him. You will also be alone should the Lord come to visit you. This cannot be borrowed from another.

These are the core. This core is what faith, repentance, baptism and the Gift of the Holy Ghost are meant to bring about. The religion of heaven always involves heaven. It does not involve men and administration and popularity. It is solitary, between you and God. The proud, however, are content to proclaim their righteousness and sit in judgment of others. They live without God in the world[1523], and their end will be destruction. They think their own imagination is revelation, and they foolishly value only their conceit.[1524]

I will never flatter you. But I will never lie to you, either. My faith in the Gospel is stronger now than the day I was baptized into The Church of Jesus Christ of Latter-day Saints. My fidelity to the church is greater now than it has ever been. It offered me baptism and I gladly accepted. If offered me scriptures, and I gladly accepted. It offered me ordination, laying on hands, washings, anointings, covenants and sacraments, and I gladly accepted them all. It gives me fellowship, and I value it. But my faith is in Christ alone.

Questions:

When a new day dawns, should not a man awaken?

What does it profit a man to awaken if he does not arise?

[1523] Mormon 5:16 "For behold, the Spirit of the Lord hath already ceased to strive with their fathers; and they are without Christ and God in the world; and they are driven about as chaff before the wind."

[1524] Proverbs 26:11–12 "As a dog returneth to his vomit, *so* a fool returneth to his folly. Seest thou a man wise in his own conceit? *there is* more hope of a fool than of him."

Does a man awaken only then to boast in his own conceit that he no longer slumbers, while all around him remain asleep; yet the man arise not from his bed? Where is the benefit in that?

The coming day will burn with heat, and those who remain in their beds, either asleep or awake, will be burned. If shade is offered but not taken, there is no benefit to awakening.

If His servant comes alone, he is rejected for the lack of witnesses. If with a company, he is rejected for having followers. Clothed with the spirit and filled with light, he is rejected as innovating. If he mourns, he is too sorrowful; and if rejoicing, he is too merry. You need only ask, and the Lord will tell you what you need to know.

PRIESTHOOD

Fullness of Priesthood

I received the following in an email:

"As I'm re-reading *The Second Comforter* I'm trying to clarify in
my mind the issue of power in the priesthood and ordination
under God's hand. Our first trip to the veil is when we have
our Calling & Election made sure. Nephi's example (son of
Helaman) indicates that at that time we are given power in the
priesthood—sealing power. This is included in the fullness of
the priesthood. But you have also made the clear arguments
that (1) we do not see the Lord at this time—that is part of
receiving the Second Comforter; (2) the fullness of the priesthood and its inherent powers are only received of God, under
His hand. I'm sure it's possible to be ordained under the hand
of the Lord without seeing Him, but nowhere do I find an
indication that this is what happens at one's C&E—only that
you hear a voice from heaven covenanting and promising. Are
you able to share anything that could clarify this for me? I'm
happy to read it on your blog if you wish."

This is a topic I've never attempted to straighten out. It is marred
by many errors in traditional understanding, and almost impossible
to recover because of the vocabulary we use now. We have become
accustomed to speaking about priesthood using terms we think we

understand. Therefore, when the topic arises the first problem is that we speak about something not well developed, using terms we think we understand, but employing incorrect meanings.

The result is that I've used the term but haven't bothered defining it. The closest I've come to providing anything is the Tenth Parable in *Ten Parables*. I've also used the concluding chapters of *Beloved Enos* to give an overview, without changing the terms we are all accustomed to using.

In the "big picture" there are three levels of priesthood discussed by Joseph Smith. He uses the terms "Aaronic" (which includes Levitical) for one, Melchizedek for another, and Patriarchal for the third. In the D&C, there is a revelation stating the church has two priesthoods.[1525] Since the church claims to possess these two because of Section 107, and since Joseph used the term "Patriarchal Priesthood" to identify a third, I have used this category to explain what is set out in *Beloved Enos*; then used it further to develop the topics in *Passing the Heavenly Gift*.

Forget the nomenclature for a moment (because it is not as important as the underlying reality), and no matter what term you use, recognize there are three levels of priesthood. There are three members of the Godhead. There is a different member of the Godhead associated with three levels of salvation, three levels of Divine ministration, and correspondingly three levels of priesthood. There is a priesthood that belongs to the Telestial order, or the world where we presently live. There is a priesthood that belongs to the Terrestrial order, or this world in its Paradisiacal state during the Millennium. There is a priesthood that belongs to the Celestial order, or the final redeemed state which men hope to inherit in the Father's Kingdom. Read Section 76 and you will see these set out as conditions of glory.

[1525] D&C 107:1 "THERE are, in the church, two priesthoods, namely, the Melchizedek and Aaronic, including the Levitical Priesthood."

Then take the conditions and associate a priesthood with each. If you do that, you have a better grasp of the idea of "fullness of the priesthood."

There are many problems with how we discuss this topic. I have made no attempt to challenge our current vocabulary, or the definitions we use with it. I've just accepted it and tried to set out the things I know to be true using the limited and accepted definitions we currently employ.

The Patriarchal Priesthood is not defined in scripture. We think the office of Patriarch in the church is what is meant by that. Or, alternatively, we teach that when you are sealed in the temple you acquire the Patriarchal Priesthood because you become a father within your family and that is kind of the meaning. Joseph made a remark which referred to finishing the Nauvoo Temple, and then going into the Temple and receiving the Patriarchal Priesthood. I've found it useful to refer to this most poorly understood form of priesthood to name and define it the third level of priesthood. I can make a persuasive argument to do so. I think it offers a rather elegant solution to our current vocabulary problems. But I won't do that in this post.

The most important point is that there is priesthood which exists, but is not contained within or conferred by the church. It comes from one source—the Father. To receive that, read the Tenth Parable and you will have a description of how it unfolds. The Son is necessarily involved. He is the gatekeeper, who alone decides if the person is going to qualify. Then the Son takes it as His work, or His ministry, to bring a person before the Father. However, the ministry of the Son can take many years, and is designed to cure what is wrong, fix all that is broken, remove all that is impure, in the candidate. Only when the Son can vouch for the individual is he brought before the Father. It is the Father who confers and ordains a man to the highest priesthood.

I've left these topics alone because there is something much more important than having me write about them. The first step along the path is to make it through the veil. Not the veil in a Temple, or in a rite offered by men to one another. We must be brought through the veil back into the Lord's presence. That is the step which stops most of our progress. By and large we don't believe it possible. We make no attempt because we think it is not available, or we should not be trying to become more than our leaders, or we are not qualified, or some other false teaching which hedges up our progress. I've focused on that topic alone. If I can bring a person to have faith to approach the Lord, the Lord will tell them all things they need to do thereafter. He will work with them to bring them into possession of all they need for Eternal Lives. That is His ministry. Mine is but to point to Him.

I can testify the Lord continues to have a ministry. I can also testify it includes bringing you to a point of understanding that enables you to repent of your generation's sins and come before the Father. It is happening today, just as anciently.

Joseph Smith's ministry offered mankind an opportunity to have the ancient order restored. Not just a New Testament church. In the beginning there was one, unified priesthood. There were not three. There was one. It was called the Holy Order. Later it got several additive descriptors, including the Holy Order after the Son of God; or Holy Order after the Order of Enoch; or Holy Order after the Order of Melchizedek. We think we have that in the church today. We think that is what we give to Elders when we first ordain them. But Joseph Smith could not confer that on another person. It requires God. Through Joseph we were offered an opportunity to receive it, but we were more interested in having a church than the original Holy Order.

It was always necessary to restore the Holy Order—the original fullness. That must be here before the Second Coming. As soon, however, as the matter is fully set out, men will immediately begin to imitate and pretend to things because of pride, ignorance, or vanity. In fact, the more readily it is explained in detail, the more often there will be those who falsely claim to have power they were never given by God. So I have confined what I've written to the first leg of the journey, and testified to the possible return to the presence of the Son. That is a precaution, and is designed to keep the message focused on saving souls. For the rest, I leave it to the Lord's ministry to inform the disciple of what then must occur.

I believe at some point there will be a more public declaration of the fullness of the priesthood. But at the present, I think the greatest problem lies in connecting men back to angels, then to the Lord. When they have reached that point, the Lord will take them further.

Sealing power is part of higher priesthood, but men suppose God's word alone is enough. No power comes from heaven without faith. There is always an apprenticeship. There is always further sacrifice required of the student. No one comes to the point in an instant, but increases by degrees in their trust with our God. You will find that in every prophet's life.

Show me a man who has entered into the Father's presence and I will testify that he has a fullness. But show me any man, no matter what position or keys he claims to possess, who has not entered into the Father's presence, and I will testify he has not yet received a fullness. No matter what keys he has, he cannot possess the fullness. For that, the Father has a role He is required to fulfill. Hence the saying by Joseph that no man has seen the Father but He has born record of the Son. The question to ponder is what it means for the Father to bear record of the Son. Therein lies a great key.

Follow-up Question

I got another follow-up from the same person asking:

"In your latest post there is some discussion on these two topics which imply that they are different. My wife and I discussed this and what we came up with is that the first step is to have an audience with Christ (Second Comforter), from which point He will undertake to perfect you after which the Father will promise you eternal life (Calling and Election Made Sure). Is that correct? If not could you shed some more light on this?"

These are two different topics. They are related, but are different. I've talked about the Second Comforter extensively. I've not said much about Calling and Election. I think focusing on that topic is a mistake. It will take care of itself if you can get the Second Comforter. Therefore I've remained largely silent on that topic.

There is a tremendous tendency to see things in a linear way and to impose an order into something which does not always follow the time-line pattern we live within. God has before Him information which, for us, remains yet future and hidden. Therefore we tend to want Him to conform to our time-sensitive perceptions, when in fact He does not. All the elements of the pattern will happen. But the order, time-line or sequence can be completely scrambled from our limited perspective inside of time.

If you look at the experience of Enoch, the Lord spoke to him about gifts and power his faith was to produce some time in Enoch's future[1526] as an existing fact.

[1526] Moses 6:34 "Behold my Spirit is upon you, wherefore all thy words will I justify; and the mountains shall flee before you, and the rivers shall turn from their course; and thou shalt abide in me, and I in you; therefore walk with me."

The events which would display these powers were, however, hundreds of years in Enoch's future.[1527] Likewise Joseph Smith beheld the Father and Son in a vision while yet in his youth.[1528] He saw the Father. Therefore Joseph had at that very moment, while still a youth, possession of the highest order of priesthood.[1529] Despite

---

[1527] Moses 7:13–17 "And so great was the faith of Enoch that he led the people of God, and their enemies came to battle against them; and he spake the word of the Lord, and the earth trembled, and the mountains fled, even according to his command; and the rivers of water were turned out of their course; and the roar of the lions was heard out of the wilderness; and all nations feared greatly, so powerful was the word of Enoch, and so great was the power of the language which God had given him. There also came up a land out of the depth of the sea, and so great was the fear of the enemies of the people of God, that they fled and stood afar off and went upon the land which came up out of the depth of the sea. And the giants of the land, also, stood afar off; and there went forth a curse upon all people that fought against God; And from that time forth there were wars and bloodshed among them; but the Lord came and dwelt with his people, and they dwelt in righteousness. The fear of the Lord was upon all nations, so great was the glory of the Lord, which was upon his people. And the Lord blessed the land, and they were blessed upon the mountains, and upon the high places, and did flourish."

[1528] JS–H 1:17–20 "It no sooner appeared than I found myself delivered from the enemy which held me bound. When the light rested upon me I saw two Personages, whose brightness and glory defy all description, standing above me in the air. One of them spake unto me, calling me by name and said, pointing to the other—*This is My Beloved Son. Hear Him!* My object in going to inquire of the Lord was to know which of all the sects was right, that I might know which to join. No sooner, therefore, did I get possession of myself, so as to be able to speak, than I asked the Personages who stood above me in the light, which of all the sects was right (for at this time it had never entered into my heart that all were wrong)—and which I should join. I was answered that I must join none of them, for they were all wrong; and the Personage who addressed me said that all their creeds were an abomination in his sight; that those professors were all corrupt; that: "they draw near to me with their lips, but their hearts are far from me, they teach for doctrines the commandments of men, having a form of godliness, but they deny the power thereof." He again forbade me to join with any of them; and many other things did he say unto me, which I cannot write at this time. When I came to myself again, I found myself lying on my back, looking up into heaven. When the light had departed, I had no strength; but soon recovering in some degree, I went home. And as I leaned up to the fireplace, mother inquired what the matter was. I replied, "Never mind, all is well—I am well enough off." I then said to my mother, "I have learned for myself that Presbyterianism is not true." It seems as though the adversary was aware, at a very early period of my life, that I was destined to prove a disturber and an annoyer of his kingdom; else why should the powers of darkness combine against me? Why the opposition and persecution that arose against me, almost in my infancy?"

[1529] D&C 84:21–22 "And without the ordinances thereof, and the authority of the priesthood, the power of godliness is not manifest unto men in the flesh; For without this no man can see the face of God, even the Father, and live."

this, Joseph would be later ordained by John the Baptist to Aaronic Priesthood.[1530] The Aaronic Priesthood has the keys of ministering angels.[1531] Yet before receiving this form of priesthood, Joseph had

---

[1530] JS–H 1:68–70 "We still continued the work of translation, when, in the ensuing month (May, 1829), we on a certain day went into the woods to pray and inquire of the Lord respecting baptism for the remission of sins, that we found mentioned in the translation of the plates. While we were thus employed, praying and calling upon the Lord, a messenger from heaven descended in a cloud of light, and having laid his hands upon us, he ordained us, saying: *Upon you my fellow servants, in the name of Messiah, I confer the Priesthood of Aaron, which holds the keys of the ministering of angels, and of the gospel of repentance, and of baptism by immersion for the remission of sins; and this shall never be taken again from the earth until the sons of Levi do offer again an offering unto the Lord in righteousness.* He said this Aaronic Priesthood had not the power of laying on hands for the gift of the Holy Ghost, but that this should be conferred on us hereafter; and he commanded us to go and be baptized, and gave us directions that I should baptize Oliver Cowdery, and that afterwards he should baptize me."

[1531] D&C 84:26 "And the lesser priesthood continued, which priesthood holdeth the key of the ministering of angels and the preparatory gospel;"

an angel minister to him.[1532] So before Joseph received "keys" from John the Baptist he was exercising the keys belonging to the priesthood he would receive. I could go on, but these illustrate the point.

[1532] JS–H 1:30–41 "While I was thus in the act of calling upon God, I discovered a light appearing in my room, which continued to increase until the room was lighter than at noonday, when immediately a personage appeared at my bedside, standing in the air, for his feet did not touch the floor. He had on a loose robe of most exquisite whiteness. It was a whiteness beyond anything earthly I had ever seen; nor do I believe that any earthly thing could be made to appear so exceedingly white and brilliant. His hands were naked, and his arms also, a little above the wrist; so, also, were his feet naked, as were his legs, a little above the ankles. His head and neck were also bare. I could discover that he had no other clothing on but this robe, as it was open, so that I could see into his bosom. Not only was his robe exceedingly white, but his whole person was glorious beyond description, and his countenance truly like lightning. The room was exceedingly light, but not so very bright as immediately around his person. When I first looked upon him, I was afraid; but the fear soon left me. He called me by name, and said unto me that he was a messenger sent from the presence of God to me, and that his name was Moroni; that God had a work for me to do; and that my name should be had for good and evil among all nations, kindreds, and tongues, or that it should be both good and evil spoken of among all people. He said there was a book deposited, written upon gold plates, giving an account of the former inhabitants of this continent, and the source from whence they sprang. He also said that the fulness of the everlasting Gospel was contained in it, as delivered by the Savior to the ancient inhabitants; Also, that there were two stones in silver bows—and these stones, fastened to a breastplate, constituted what is called the Urim and Thummim—deposited with the plates; and the possession and use of these stones were what constituted "seers" in ancient or former times; and that God had prepared them for the purpose of translating the book. After telling me these things, he commenced quoting the prophecies of the Old Testament. He first quoted part of the third chapter of Malachi; and he quoted also the fourth or last chapter of the same prophecy, though with a little variation from the way it reads in our Bibles. Instead of quoting the first verse as it reads in our books, he quoted it thus: *For behold, the day cometh that shall burn as an oven, and all the proud, yea, and all that do wickedly shall burn as stubble; for they that come shall burn them, saith the Lord of Hosts, that it shall leave them neither root nor branch.* And again, he quoted the fifth verse thus: *Behold, I will reveal unto you the Priesthood, by the hand of Elijah the prophet, before the coming of the great and dreadful day of the Lord. He also quoted the next verse differently: And he shall plant in the hearts of the children the promises made to the fathers, and the hearts of the children shall turn to their fathers. If it were not so, the whole earth would be utterly wasted at his coming.* In addition to these, he quoted the eleventh chapter of Isaiah, saying that it was about to be fulfilled. He quoted also the third chapter of Acts, twenty-second and twenty-third verses, precisely as they stand in our New Testament. He said that that prophet was Christ; but the day had not yet come when "they who would not hear his voice should be cut off from among the people," but soon would come. He also quoted the second chapter of Joel, from the twenty-eighth verse to the last. He also said that this was not yet fulfilled, but was soon to be. And he further stated that the fulness of the Gentiles was soon to come in. He quoted many other passages of scripture, and offered many explanations which cannot be mentioned here."

Events involving God do not necessarily follow the same time-line as we would expect them to follow. When, however, Joseph received angels, you can know for certain he held priesthood. When he was visited by the Son, you can know he held priesthood and keys for that. When he was visited by the Father, Joseph Smith had priesthood. It was necessarily present and was in him. Don't ever doubt that. Even if you don't quite understand it at present, it is nevertheless true. So also you can receive things from God which are apparently out of sequence with the time-line we live in here.

God is not limited as we are. He lives in a place where all things, past, present and future, are before Him.[1533] Time is not only irrelevant, it is non-existent with God.

So if you're trying to prepare a list, the list can include all the ingredients, but it cannot be linear and progressive in a time-confined progression. God doesn't conform to that kind of list. He will touch all the points, but in His own way. Our difficulties in understanding this kind of matter is further complicated by limitations on language and lack of faith. Therefore Joseph wisely confined his comments to what the Lord required him to say, and left the rest for each person to discover for themselves. To a great degree these things are not explainable in our language. We are two-dimensional, attempting to explain four-dimensional material. There is always a gap.

As a Gospel Dispensation is unfolded, the Lord will always violate rules we think exist involving timing and sequence. He will confer things which apparently belong long into the process, and will do it apparently independent of the established requirements. But His strange act is not ours. He will do as He wills. For us, once an order is established by Him, the order is followed. Joseph may have re-

---

[1533] D&C 130:7 "But they reside in the presence of God, on a globe like a sea of glass and fire, where all things for their glory are manifest, past, present, and future, and are continually before the Lord."

ceived the highest priesthood as a youth, but that still required the ministering of angels and conferral of progressive keys in the process of establishing the dispensation. It also required him to conform to ordinances, including baptism, as the order was re-established on the earth. [Jesus was tutored by angels before His baptism, as well. But He was still required to be baptized.]

Through Joseph the Lord set a system in place which would teach and perpetuate the process, which then became linear and time-sensitive. Once established it respected the order of things in this dimension. But as soon as you begin to project our dimension onto God's, you begin to make mistakes about God. He is not bound, as we are, by time or by timing. [This is a very great—meaning vast—topic. It can only be mentioned here, and not fully developed. But it is nevertheless a very real difference between "gazing into heaven for five minutes" on the one hand, and reading all that has ever been written on the subject on the other. It is only referenced in passing in the scriptures. Therefore don't expect this to become a well developed subject by what some man writes. Look to God for understanding on this topic.] I've dealt with some of this in *Beloved Enos*. You might want to revisit that book with the question in mind because there's information in there that help. But it only "helps" and cannot say all on the topic.

Joseph Smith made a comment about a relationship between the Second Comforter and Calling and Election. I quote it early in *The Second Comforter*, and I think you can read it on the bottom of page 3. (It is a quote taken from *TPJS, 150*). Joseph's description is linear. He talks about proving you're determined to follow God at any cost, and then you have your Calling and Election made sure, and then the Second Comforter comes to you. It is a nice quote. It covers the topic. But any implication in Joseph's statement about a linear progression is belied by Joseph's own experience. For him the events did not take place in a linear way. He started at the top and worked backwards. But his quote suggests an order based upon this estate and our need for orientation here. So it's a good quote and altogether accurate (from our perspective here).

Right now we are all in need of a new dispensation of the Gospel. Some lost (or never completed) components of the work need to be dispensed to us either anew or for the first time. Joseph promised more, and the scriptures predict more, will be given before the Lord's return in glory. An obvious example is the establishment of the New Jerusalem and Zion. It hasn't happened yet. Joseph wanted to see the Lord bring it again, but it didn't happen in his day. When he crossed the river on June 23, 1844 he was headed west to the Rocky Mountains to try and find the remnant and the site of the New Jerusalem. Instead because of criticism about abandoning the flock when it was threatened (accusing him of being a "false shepherd") he returned and surrendered and was killed. Now we all think the New Jerusalem is to be located in Jackson County Missouri. I suppose that's a good thing we all think that. But it may not necessarily be true. There's still some missing information on that topic, I believe.

Well, you proceed just as Joseph did. Inquire of God, who gives to all men liberally and does not upbraid. And if you ask in faith, nothing wavering, He will make the truth known to you. That is what this generation needs to hear. That is where it begins. Once it begins, all things get added thereto. God is patient and understanding of His children's needs. He will never abandon the earnest seeker. So become one of those. Follow what He directs and you will find yourself in possession of life and light and hope and covenants. Not between you and another man, but between you and God. The full answer to your question should be given to you by angels, or the Lord or the Father, and not a man. When men interject themselves into that process they generally create distance between you and your God. They hinder, rather than help.

Having said that, here are the events: Angels minister to you and confer power, light and truth. They prepare you to receive the Lord. He ministers to you and confers promises, administers covenants, takes away your awful shame, and gives you promises. He prepares you to be introduced to the Father. The Father makes you a son by accepting you through His Only Begotten Son. Along the way you will know for yourself the things which occur on the other side of the veil, where God and Christ dwell in glory.

Creation and Death

Of all the powers given to mankind by God, the one most like God Himself is the power to create offspring. The sexual union of the man and woman resulting in children is a power so great it is called God's reward.[1534] God's covenant with Abraham was based upon a numerous posterity.[1535]

Sex involves not only "knowing" (i.e., intercourse) between a man and woman,[1536] but also the woman "conceiving" a child.[1537] Sex also includes the woman bringing forth the child, and the father then nam-

---

[1534] Psalm 127:3 "Lo, children *are* an heritage of the Lord: *and* the fruit of the womb *is* his reward."

[1535] Genesis 22:17 "That in blessing I will bless thee, and in multiplying I will multiply thy seed as the stars of the heaven, and as the sand which *is* upon the sea shore; and thy seed shall possess the gate of his enemies;"

[1536] Genesis 4:1 "And Adam knew Eve his wife; and she conceived, and bare Cain, and said, I have gotten a man from the Lord."

[1537] Ibid.

ing the child.[1538] It includes teaching the child the ways of God.[1539] It extends to a parent's duty to provide care, food, clothing and shelter for the child as well.[1540]

When the child is raised, the child then is obligated to honor and care for the parent.[1541] The cycle binds together generations in care, nurture and honor, altogether a godlike process.[1542]

In a word, sex is life. It is the entirety of life. It produces and provides for generation after generation in a godly connection between man, woman and God.

If sex is separated from the entire scope of the Divine order, and redefined to be nothing more than orgasm, then it ceases to be life and becomes chaos and death. For example, if the ability of a homosexual union to produce physical gratification for the participants is regarded as the same thing, it not only fails to comply with the Divinely ordained order, it results in death. Homosexual unions produce no offspring and the participants go down to the grave childless. Their sexual powers have failed to result in creation, order, or fulfilling the pattern for life to continue.

If sex is separated from the entire scope, then children are born unwanted and are not raised with the care, love and sacrifice of the

---

[1538] Matthew 1:25 "And knew her not till she had brought forth her firstborn son: and he called his name JESUS."

[1539] Deuteronomy 6:6–7 "And these words, which I command thee this day, shall be in thine heart: And thou shalt teach them diligently unto thy children, and shalt talk of them when thou sittest in thine house, and when thou walkest by the way, and when thou liest down, and when thou risest up."

[1540] 1 Timothy 5:8 "But if any provide not for his own, and specially for those of his own house, he hath denied the faith, and is worse than an infidel."

[1541] Deuteronomy 5:16 "Honour thy father and thy mother, as the Lord thy God hath commanded thee; that thy days may be prolonged, and that it may go well with thee, in the land which the Lord thy God giveth thee."

[1542] Enos 1:1 "BEHOLD, it came to pass that I, Enos, knowing my father that he was a just man—for he taught me in his language, and also in the nurture and admonition of the Lord—and blessed be the name of my God for it—"

parents. They are not taught in the ways of God. They become less than what they were intended to be because they have inherited less than God intended for them to inherit.

Our society has largely confined its understanding of sex to nothing more than physical gratification. It is an orgasm and nothing more. Once we loose that single component from the Divine order, we have changed godlike creation into disorder and chaos. Ultimately it is the difference between life and death.

Learning

I do not believe we are under any obligation to be bored in church. I do not believe there is any virtue in sitting in a class without being either edified or taught. Of all the terrible offenses under the claim it is done in Christ's name, taking high school students and asking them to color pictures in a Sunday School class or seminary course seems to me to be a solemn offense to them and the Lord. When we have an audience of young people who are curious and eager to learn, we ought to capture their minds and hearts with the wonder and glory of Christ's Gospel. We owe it to them and to God. It should delight them. I've told my kids it is their duty to leave and study their scriptures rather than waste time coloring, or engaging in any other activity that is a waste of their time. And I trust them to know the difference.

Politics

I'm not very political. Unlike the rabid who believe political salvation is possible for the United States, I believe if the "Elders of Israel" are going to have any effect on the Constitution, it will not be through litigation, legislation or elected office. It will be through preaching the Gospel and converting Americans to the truth. When people agree on fundamental principles, they will elect to office those who reflect those fundamental principles. But you don't elect someone whose values are alien to a corrupt population and thereby "save" the population. If you want to have a lasting effect on the government, preach the truth and convert people. If you want to occupy your time in a temporary effort, then push a single candidate in an election.

I believe it is good for Mormonism to have two LDS candidates running for the Presidency who disagree with and criticize one another. It is good to have the leader of the US Senate be a Democrat. It is good to have radio personality Glen Beck criticize and disagree with Mitt Romney. One of the fears inspired in others by Mormonism is the apparent monolithic appearance of the faith. These public splits among the Saints shows there is intellectual flexibility on political matters, which gives hope to non-Mormons that an LDS leader can be persuaded by something other than their religious affiliation. I believe that is a good thing.

I also believe the church is subject to the government, and not the government subject to the church. Our scriptures declare:

"We believe that governments were instituted of God for the benefit of man[.]" (D&C 134:1)

In the same section,

"We believe that all men are bound to sustain and uphold the respective governments in which they reside, while protected in their inherent and inalienable rights by the laws of such governments; and that sedition and rebellion are unbecoming every citizen thus protected, and should be punished accordingly; and that all governments have a right to enact such laws as in their own judgments are best calculated to secure the public interest[.]" (D&C 134:5)

Perhaps more importantly, we declare as a matter of scripture that government should not have religious influence mingled with political power, nor to benefit one religion over another:

"We do not believe it just to mingle religious influence with civil government, whereby one religious society is fostered and another proscribed in its spiritual privileges, and the individual rights of its members, as citizens, denied." (D&C 134:9)

Also, as an Article of Faith, the church has adopted the following statement:

"We believe in being subject to kings, presidents, rulers, and magistrates, in obeying, honoring, and sustaining the law." (12th Article of Faith.)

This is so absolute a proposition that the church surrendered what it claimed to be a duty imposed by God once the law of the land required it. "Inasmuch as laws have been enacted by Congress forbidding plural marriages, which laws have been pronounced constitutional by the court of last resort, I hereby declare my intention to submit to those laws, and to use my influence with the members of the Church over which I preside to have them do likewise." (*OD* 1: Paragraph 4.) In other words, the rule of law required submission, even in the face of doctrine declaring otherwise. There is no question the US Government commands the LDS Church's submission.

I believe the submission to government to be so doctrinally established, that if a Mormon were elected President of the United States, he would "preside" over the church's President. This is not just a New Testament principle,[1543] but also a matter of Latter-day revelation, as well.[1544] This is so compelling a point that, if there

---

[1543] Titus 3:1 "Put them in mind to be subject to principalities and powers, to obey magistrates, to be ready to every good work"

[1544] D&C 58:21–22 "Let no man break the laws of the land, for he that keepeth the laws of God hath no need to break the laws of the land. Wherefore, be subject to the powers that be, until he reigns whose right it is to reign, and subdues all enemies under his feet."

were a General Conference at which a sitting LDS US President attended, correct doctrine would require the announcement that the US President was "presiding" at that Conference, rather than the church's President. The church's President is "sustained" by the members of the church alone; while the US President is "sustained" by the entire nation to which the church is subject.

Why Here?

I got an inquiry asking: "I am interested in any thought you would be willing to share about why we were willing to sacrifice to come to this earth. I don't think that this earth is the only place in all of creation where one can learn to return to the presence of the Lord, so what is the purpose of the righteous in the preexistence coming here? Why not take an 'easier' route and go to a different terrestrial mortal state?"

Because we saw great benefit in coming. In fact, the opportunity was greeted with shouts of joy.[1545] Perspective from here is not the same as perspective from above.

There is a required opposition in "all things".[1546]

To ascend you must first descend.

[1545] Job 38:4–7 "Where wast thou when I laid the foundations of the earth? declare, if thou hast understanding. Who hath laid the measures thereof, if thou knowest? or who hath stretched the line upon it? Whereupon are the foundations thereof fastened? or who laid the corner stone thereof; When the morning stars sang together, and all the sons of God shouted for joy?"

[1546] 2 Nephi 2:11 "For it must needs be, that there is an opposition in all things. If not so, my first-born in the wilderness, righteousness could not be brought to pass, neither wickedness, neither holiness nor misery, neither good nor bad. Wherefore, all things must needs be a compound in one; wherefore, if it should be one body it must needs remain as dead, having no life neither death, nor corruption nor incorruption, happiness nor misery, neither sense nor insensibility."

The path to the highest state runs through the lowest.[1547]

You will not see the Father and Son[1548] without also seeing the fallen angel cast out for rebellion.[1549]

[1547] Moses 1:18–20 "And again Moses said: I will not cease to call upon God, I have other things to inquire of him: for his glory has been upon me, wherefore I can judge between him and thee. Depart hence, Satan. And now, when Moses had said these words, Satan cried with a loud voice, and ranted upon the earth, and commanded, saying: I am the Only Begotten, worship me. And it came to pass that Moses began to fear exceedingly; and as he began to fear, he saw the bitterness of hell. Nevertheless, calling upon God, he received strength, and he commanded, saying: Depart from me, Satan, for this one God only will I worship, which is the God of glory."
JS-H 1:15–17 "After I had retired to the place where I had previously designed to go, having looked around me, and finding myself alone, I kneeled down and began to offer up the desires of my heart to God. I had scarcely done so, when immediately I was seized upon by some power which entirely overcame me, and had such an astonishing influence over me as to bind my tongue so that I could not speak. Thick darkness gathered around me, and it seemed to me for a time as if I were doomed to sudden destruction. But, exerting all my powers to call upon God to deliver me out of the power of this enemy which had seized upon me, and at the very moment when I was ready to sink into despair and abandon myself to destruction—not to an imaginary ruin, but to the power of some actual being from the unseen world, who had such marvelous power as I had never before felt in any being—just at this moment of great alarm, I saw a pillar of light exactly over my head, above the brightness of the sun, which descended gradually until it fell upon me. It no sooner appeared than I found myself delivered from the enemy which held me bound. When the light rested upon me I saw two Personages, whose brightness and glory defy all description, standing above me in the air. One of them spake unto me, calling me by name and said, pointing to the other—*This is My Beloved Son. Hear Him!*

[1548] D&C 76:20–21 "And we beheld the glory of the Son, on the right hand of the Father, and received of his fulness; And saw the holy angels, and them who are sanctified before his throne, worshiping God, and the Lamb, who worship him forever and ever."

[1549] D&C 76:25–26 "And this we saw also, and bear record, that an angel of God who was in authority in the presence of God, who rebelled against the Only Begotten Son whom the Father loved and who was in the bosom of the Father, was thrust down from the presence of God and the Son, And was called Perdition, for the heavens wept over him—he was Lucifer, a son of the morning."

Nor will you behold the Celestial Kingdom[1550] without also seeing the horror of outer darkness.[1551]

To comprehend you must become acquainted with both glory and darkness. You cannot receive the one without also the other. Joseph put it this way:

"Thy mind, O man! if thou wilt lead a soul unto salvation, must stretch as high as the utmost heavens, and search into and contemplate the darkest abyss, and the broad expanse of eternity—thou must commune with God." (*TPJS*, 137)

You do not get to behold glory without also beholding the darkest abyss. There is a parallel to comprehension, a symmetry to understanding.

You came here to increase your understanding of truth, and to broaden your capacity to appreciate what is good. For that, you

---

[1550] D&C 76:50–58 "And again we bear record—for we saw and heard, and this is the testimony of the gospel of Christ concerning them who shall come forth in the resurrection of the just— They are they who received the testimony of Jesus, and believed on his name and were baptized after the manner of his burial, being buried in the water in his name, and this according to the commandment which he has given— That by keeping the commandments they might be washed and cleansed from all their sins, and receive the Holy Spirit by the laying on of the hands of him who is ordained and sealed unto this power; And who overcome by faith, and are sealed by the Holy Spirit of promise, which the Father sheds forth upon all those who are just and true. They are they who are the church of the Firstborn. They are they into whose hands the Father has given all things— They are they who are priests and kings, who have received of his fulness, and of his glory; And are priests of the Most High, after the order of Melchizedek, which was after the order of Enoch, which was after the order of the Only Begotten Son. Wherefore, as it is written, they are gods, even the sons of God—"

[1551] D&C 76:44–48 "Wherefore, he saves all except them—they shall go away into everlasting punishment, which is endless punishment, which is eternal punishment, to reign with the devil and his angels in eternity, where their worm dieth not, and the fire is not quenched, which is their torment— And the end thereof, neither the place thereof, nor their torment, no man knows; Neither was it revealed, neither is, neither will be revealed unto man, except to them who are made partakers thereof; Nevertheless, I, the Lord, show it by vision unto many, but straightway shut it up again; Wherefore, the end, the width, the height, the depth, and the misery thereof, they understand not, neither any man except those who are ordained unto this condemnation."

wanted and now are receiving, exposure to the brackets which allow your comprehension to expand.

You will eventually leave here. But you will depart with an expanded capacity which could come in no other way.

Read the perils through which Abraham passed, and know this was necessary for him to become the Father of the Righteous. There is no path back to heaven apart from walking through the valley of the shadow of death. Your understanding of eternal life will come from suffering death. Your appreciation of eternal glory will come from having been first composed of the decaying dust of this earth.

You wanted this. You shouted for joy when it was offered.

Marlin Jensen's Release

The church has released Marlin K. Jensen as the Church Historian. I knew him when he practiced law in Ogden, many years ago before he became a General Authority. He was an honorable man then, and has provided a long and honorable service to the church as the Church Historian. The policy of releasing General Authorities and making them emeritus is costing us a valuable resource. I hate to see him go.

Brother Steven Snow, an attorney from St. George and current member of the Seven Presidents of the Seventy will replace him. I wish him well in his new assignment. The Church Historian's job is challenging, to say the least. It would be wonderful if there is a continuation of the Joseph Smith Papers project, a second volume of the Mountain Meadows Massacre work (which was promised when the first came out), and a more open-door policy about our history.

I do not think we have anything to fear by letting more information flow into the public arena from our history. The more the better, in my view. What may be viewed as an embarrassing revelation from one vantage point, may be a hopeful declaration that God's work can be done despite human weaknesses by another. Some of our grandiose claims will necessarily become more modest, but that will only help, not hurt, people of faith.

Some of the greatest figures in the Bible are flawed, craven people. David's triumphs and failures are exposed to full view and we are not the worse for it. Quite the opposite, we are the better for it. Solomon's legendary wisdom sank into a mire of foolishness in old age, and we are blessed to read about it all.

Perhaps if we let our own heroic figures reveal themselves in more a complete and complex light, it would help us de-mythologize the way we treat our living leaders. They might be able to get more done if we let them make mistakes from time to time. When they are forced to defend every action as "truly inspired" we have a much harder time fixing our many problems.

Our history is great, even glorious. It doesn't need to be fiction to be edifying. Scriptural characters like Sampson, Job and Jonah are as valuable to us as Elijah, Nephi and Christ. Who among us would want to hide Aaron's golden-calf building? Who would eliminate Lot's residency in Sodom? When we edit our history to remove the shadows, we lose more than contrast. Sometimes we lose context as well.

I'd like to see the church's history become the thing of wonder it was meant to be, rather than the sometimes plastic imitation we've allowed it to become. It will still be more than enough, even if it is merely the truth.

2 Nephi 2:21–22

I was asked about the application of 2 Nephi 2:21–22[1552] to the fall and man's condition here, in contrast to what would have happened if Adam and Eve had awaited the command to partake of the fruit.

These verses state: "And the days of the children of men were prolonged, according to the will of God, that they might repent while in the flesh; wherefore, their state became a state of probation, and their time was lengthened, according to the commandments which the Lord God gave unto the children of men. For he gave commandment that all men must repent; for he showed unto all men that they were lost, because of the transgression of their parents. And now, behold, if Adam had not transgressed he would not have fallen, but he would have remained in the garden of Eden. And all things which were created must have remained in the same state in which they were after they were created; and they must have remained forever, and had no end."

This explanation by Lehi to his son Jacob focuses on what happened. Adam did transgress. As a consequence he, and his posterity fell. Therefore we find ourselves in the present conditions.

Lehi is not focused on what would have happened if Adam had not transgressed, only what did happen because Adam did transgress. The reference to "all things which were created must have remained in the same state in which they were after they were created," is speaking about the condition prior to the transgression. The explana-

---

[1552] 2 Nephi 2:21–22 "And the days of the children of men were prolonged, according to the will of God, that they might repent while in the flesh; wherefore, their state became a state of probation, and their time was lengthened, according to the commandments which the Lord God gave unto the children of men. For he gave commandment that all men must repent; for he showed unto all men that they were lost, because of the transgression of their parents. And now, behold, if Adam had not transgressed he would not have fallen, but he would have remained in the garden of Eden. And all things which were created must have remained in the same state in which they were after they were created; and they must have remained forever, and had no end."

tion does not focus on what would have happened if, instead of a transgression, Adam partook under a commandment to do so.

Adam needed to partake. Man needed to transition from the Garden. It was never intended for mankind to "remain in the same state in which they were after they were created . . . forever." This world was designed to be a place where mankind would come, experience mortality, and die. This is something done on other worlds, as well. It did not need to be done in transgression, for it is more often done by mankind on other worlds in obedience to a commandment to partake. During the Millennium there will be millions who live in such a world. But Adam was tempted, as was Eve, and together they partook in transgression of a commandment to not partake.

The resulting fall distinguishes this world, as I showed earlier and will not repeat again. We are in the worst place of all the Father's creations.[1553] Here alone, in the worst place, among the worst people of that place, the Son of God came to die. This is the only people who would kill Him.[1554] The sacrifice of the Son was ordained before the foundation of the world. That is one of His names, "the Lamb Slain from the Foundation of the World."[1555]

God was not surprised by Adam's transgression. He always anticipated it. The conditions necessary for Christ's sacrifice could only come about in that way. But foreknowledge does not remove other possibilities. There is *always* choice, and the choice is real. It could be

---

[1553] Moses 7:36 "Wherefore, I can stretch forth mine hands and hold all the creations which I have made; and mine eye can pierce them also, and among all the workmanship of mine hands there has not been so great wickedness as among thy brethren."

[1554] 2 Nephi 10:3 "Wherefore, as I said unto you, it must needs be expedient that Christ—for in the last night the angel spake unto me that this should be his name—should come among the Jews, among those who are the more wicked part of the world; and they shall crucify him—for thus it behooveth our God, and there is none other nation on earth that would crucify their God."

[1555] Revelation 13:8 "And all that dwell upon the earth shall worship him, whose names are not written in the book of life of the Lamb slain from the foundation of the world."

taken. If it could not be taken, then by definition there is no choice. Had the transgression not happened, there would have been a commandment, as in other worlds, to partake. Mortality would have happened, as it does on other worlds.[1556]

Understanding what might have been is far less important than understanding what is. We are faced with a fallen world, into which the Lamb Slain from the Foundation of the World came to rescue us. Adam did transgress. The repair for that will come through and from the Lamb.

Parables

I just got asked for help with the Parables. It was a nice request, so I'm responding here. I'm worried about giving a complete answer. The joy of a parable is the discovery by the reader for herself (himself) of the hidden meanings. I rob you when I take away the discovery from you. Someone asked for some help, and I'm willing to give a few things. You really need to discover for yourself because the exercise is important. It unlocks the scriptures, also. This is the language of the Lord. He gives us parables far more often than we're willing to consider.

For "A Busy Young Man" ask yourself:

Why "busy?" What does it imply? How are "the cares of this world" and "business" connected? What does it mean to be laden with business here? Don't we respect this kind of thing? Aren't we looking to elect someone who understands business to be our next US President, because the current one doesn't do enough to keep us busy in a profitable way?

Why "young man" rather than an elderly one? What is it about relative youth that makes a person more open to consider something

---

[1556] D&C 76:24 "That by him, and through him, and of him, the worlds are and were created, and the inhabitants thereof are begotten sons and daughters unto God."

new? Can anyone be a "young man" even if they are a child? Elderly? What was Christ at 12 when visiting the Temple? Was He a child or a "young man" at the time? Do the words convey something apart from age itself?

What does it mean to be "on his way?" What do we mean when we say someone is "on their way" to the top? If a person is "really on their way" is that economic? Political? Is there a worldliness about the phrase? Why?

When someone is "sitting" what is implied? Why would the person sitting be "beside the road" rather than on it? The road is for movement, and getting somewhere. But here is someone beside the road, almost as if they were rejecting it. Why? Does sitting make them at rest? But here is someone both sitting and busy in their own small way. Why?

What does a tree symbolize? Why would the one sitting be under the tree? How do the images of sitting and being under the tree combine to present an identity for the one there? When we think of a person meditating, where would we expect to find them in relation to nature? In relation to a tree?

Why were there three days in the initial transition? Then why years? Then cycles of seven years? Then enlightenment? Why did the identity, once it was discovered, no longer result in any requests, demands or inquiries? Why was there only contentment?

The tediousness of the activity, and the narrow confinement to the hands of the one who left the road to help the man under the tree suggests something deeply personal and within the grasp of any person. Why is that? Why would the activity be so little, so narrow, possible for anyone with hands to accomplish?

Think about the descriptions of the hands of both the Busy Young Man and the Master. Words convey messages about the person, and the hands are where these individual's souls are on display.

Think of the braiding, and how that conveys an image. How are lives "braided" as they are lived? To whom are you "braided" as you go through your own life? Why? What little things are repeated day-by-day to braid you together with your immediate peers?

Well, this could go on for many pages. But already I'm cheating you. You don't need me, you have the parables.

I like parables. You can accomplish so much with so few words, and you can put so much on display for someone with the eyes to see it.

I'd say the parables are the best writing form to be used if there could only be a single form. Interestingly, they seem to have attracted little attention, except for a handful of quite exceptional people I've encountered. Most people are far more interested in volume and scope, rather than the still, quite intensity possible by meditating on a parable. Too busy. They think they can get further on their way by amassing a great volume of material, rather than pausing to think deeply, sitting beside the way, on short tales containing hidden wisdom. They're probably right. Most people will get a lot more of life's business done if they stay on the road they've already chosen.

LET'S JUST VOTE ON IT

Whose Church Is It?

To whom does The Church of Jesus Christ of Latter-day Saints belong? To us, or to the Lord?

That seems like an easy question, but it isn't. Because to answer it requires a great deal of understanding of both history and doctrine. The Lord told the Nephites a church had to bear His name or it wasn't His.[1557] At the beginning our church was originally called "The Church of Christ." By a vote of a conference on May 3, 1834 the name was changed to "The Church of the Latter-day Saints" (*DHC* 2:62–63). By 1838 the Lord put His name back into the title by revelation, but approved adding our names when the name changed to "The Church of Jesus Christ of Latter-day Saints."[1558] So our name is in the title. The Lord told the Nephites that if named after someone, then it is their church. His name is in our title, but so is ours.

[1557] 3 Nephi 27:8 "And how be it my church save it be called in my name? For if a church be called in Moses' name then it be Moses' church; or if it be called in the name of a man then it be the church of a man; but if it be called in my name then it is my church, if it so be that they are built upon my gospel."

[1558] D&C 115:4 "For thus shall my church be called in the last days, even The Church of Jesus Christ of Latter-day Saints."

If the church belongs to us, then we can do as we like. Our sustaining votes are all that are required to implement any changes we choose to make.

If, on the other hand, the church belongs to the Lord, then we have no right to make any change to it. We conform to what He tells us. We cannot make a change, and must keep what He chooses to give us intact, awaiting His instruction before altering anything.

One of the most remarkable differences between Joseph's era, or the first phase of Mormonism, is the direction we received from the Lord. The outpouring of revelation established not only three new volumes of scripture, but control was in the Lord's hand, not Joseph's nor the church's. Direction came, and we conformed.

The absence of that Divine control since Joseph's passing has been covered over by insistence that keys were given from Joseph to successors, and with those keys the right to direct everything remains intact. So much so that we can vote new "prophets, seers and revelators" and their decisions are God's. God's will is obtained by proxy, decided by councils, and accepted as if it were His.

If this is our church, proxies work fine. We are supposed to carry things on in the absence of Divine direction. Sentiments and feelings that we are going in the right direction is all we need. When good men acting in good faith make a unanimous decision prayerfully, we *should* feel good about it. Is that enough? If it is our church, I think it is.

What if the church is the Lord's, though? I mean what if it is *only* His, and we have no right to implement any alteration? What if it is our obligation to listen, then conform, and only to obey? Do our good faith, honest desires, prayerful discussions, hopeful changes, and best feelings then matter? Do we get the right to change anything if the Lord alone owns the exclusive right?

If someone is His, what does that mean? What does it mean to be "His people?" Can "His people" act independently of Him? Does independent action constitute rebellion or rejection of Him? After all, didn't He tell us it wasn't necessary to command us in all things?[1559] How far does that commandment extend? Because He also warned us to give heed to everything revealed to Joseph Smith.[1560]

What if a church president spends many long hours in the upper room of the temple praying for an answer, and can't get one? The Lord won't even give a "yes" or a "no" despite repeated prayers, for months, even years; what then? Can a decision be made because frustrated church leaders all feel good about going forward? Is "feeling good" about going forward a "revelation" from God?

What does it mean to "take the Lord's name in vain?" Clearly we sustain leaders, follow them, trust them to do what is right, and all have testimonies this is the Lord's great work. How much latitude do we possess?

Who then owns the church? Him or us?

Knowledge and Indifference

Should the study of church history be limited to the superficial, faith-promoting summaries given through the "official" church publications? Doesn't that risk accurate histories being tools used by the critics against the church? Should the church accept members who choose to believe in the restoration of the Gospel through Joseph Smith? Who believe in the Book of Mormon, and other scriptures that came through Joseph? Who believe in God's purposes in start-

---

[1559] D&C 58:26 "For behold, it is not meet that I should command in all things; for he that is compelled in all things, the same is a slothful and not a wise servant; wherefore he receiveth no reward."

[1560] D&C 21:4 "Wherefore, meaning the church, thou shalt give heed unto all his words and commandments which he shall give unto you as he receiveth them, walking in all holiness before me;"
D&C 50:35 "And by giving heed and doing these things which ye have received, and which ye shall hereafter receive—and the kingdom is given you of the Father, and power to overcome all things which are not ordained of him—"

ing a new dispensation of the Gospel? Who also recognize the course the saints pursued in the past and are pursuing at present with the restoration has been neglectful, even harmful?

One of our great non-Mormon friends is Harold Bloom. He has written about Joseph Smith and his authentic revelations. He has heaped praise on Joseph's ability to restore lost ancient, First-Temple era teachings. Yet as an astute observer of Mormonism he has recently written about his complete disappointment with Mormonism, and how badly it has changed in a few short years. He is not being unkind. He has honestly assessed the many radical changes underway with the restored church in the last few years. Since he does not feel any emotional need to defend the church, and is therefore free to give his candid views, his assessment represents an honest way to view the radical alterations currently happening with Mormonism.

If Mormonism is limited to The Church of Jesus Christ of Latter-day Saints (and for the most part it is), then the recent changes and radical innovations are so dramatic that our largest denomination now runs the risk of following in the steps of the second-largest "Mormon" denomination. The Community of Christ (formerly the Reorganized Church of Jesus Christ of Latter-day Saints) is now just another quasi-Protestant faith bearing almost no resemblance to the movement begun through Joseph.

How much study should be given to the history of the restoration? How carefully should Joseph's teachings be preserved, studied and followed? When the Lord commanded us to "give heed to all his [meaning Joseph Smith] words and commandments" to what extent are we justified in forgetting his words and teachings?[1561]

In the commandment, Joseph is identified in these words: "*thou shalt be called a seer, a translator, a prophet, an apostle of Jesus Christ, an elder of the church through the will of God the Father, and the grace of your Lord Jesus Christ[.]*" (*Ibid*, v. 1, emphasis added.) We know Joseph was called "through the will of God the Father, and the grace of your Lord Jesus Christ" because we have the records before us. For example, Joseph witnessed the Father and Son appearing to him in the Spring of 1820.[1562] Again on the 16th of February 1832 Joseph saw the Father and Son.[1563] The description and explanation of why we should "give heed" to Joseph's words are set out in both scripture and history. Therefore it makes perfect sense we should pay careful attention to them. Subsequent office holders had no similar experiences. (I've covered President Brigham Young's state-

---

[1561] D&C 21:1–6 "BEHOLD, there shall be a record kept among you; and in it thou shalt be called a seer, a translator, a prophet, an apostle of Jesus Christ, an elder of the church through the will of God the Father, and the grace of your Lord Jesus Christ, Being inspired of the Holy Ghost to lay the foundation thereof, and to build it up unto the most holy faith. Which church was organized and established in the year of your Lord eighteen hundred and thirty, in the fourth month, and on the sixth day of the month which is called April. Wherefore, meaning the church, thou shalt give heed unto all his words and commandments which he shall give unto you as he receiveth them, walking in all holiness before me; For his word ye shall receive, as if from mine own mouth, in all patience and faith. For by doing these things the gates of hell shall not prevail against you; yea, and the Lord God will disperse the powers of darkness from before you, and cause the heavens to shake for your good, and his name's glory."

[1562] JS–H 1:17 "It no sooner appeared than I found myself delivered from the enemy which held me bound. When the light rested upon me I saw two Personages, whose brightness and glory defy all description, standing above me in the air. One of them spake unto me, calling me by name and said, pointing to the other—*This is My Beloved Son. Hear Him!*"

[1563] D&C 76:20–24 "And we beheld the glory of the Son, on the right hand of the Father, and received of his fulness; And saw the holy angels, and them who are sanctified before his throne, worshiping God, and the Lamb, who worship him forever and ever. And now, after the many testimonies which have been given of him, this is the testimony, last of all, which we give of him: That he lives! For we saw him, even on the right hand of God; and we heard the voice bearing record that he is the Only Begotten of the Father— That by him, and through him, and of him, the worlds are and were created, and the inhabitants thereof are begotten sons and daughters unto God."

ments about never seeing angels or Christ or the Father in my last book. President Grant thought it was dangerous to encounter such spiritual experiences because they might lead to apostasy. Therefore, he never asked for them, and never experienced them.)

On the other hand, current Mormonism as practiced by The Church of Jesus Christ of Latter-day Saints has shied away from its history, abandoned many of Joseph Smith's key teachings, altered some of the most important ordinances restored through him, and so heavily edited the latest study guide on his teachings that the results sometimes contradict what he originally said. I have a friend who has compiled a list of abandoned teachings of Joseph Smith. The list is now nearly two-hundred separate items long. This friend retains his believe in Joseph, the Book of Mormon, other restored scriptures, and in Jesus Christ. But he is alarmed by and alienated from the church. I think his approach in voluntarily withdrawing from fellowship is wrong. I think he has a duty to remain in fellowship with the saints. But what happens as shifting demographics lead to changes such as open acceptance of homosexual marriages? The leadership model implemented during Gordon B. Hinckley's long tenure in leadership (which began long before he was president) uses opinion polling to guide decision-making. Using the current format, the church is helpless to resist changing public opinion trends.

The church draws leadership from successful internal leader-pools. Young bishops become high councilors and stake presidents. Those with wealth and business acumen become mission presidents. Before long a resume of church service attracts higher office and such men are called as a general authorities. These men are drawn from business, law, banking, education and government. Oftentimes their business acumen is the overwhelming forte' and their knowledge of the church's history and doctrine are lacking. In fact, knowledge of doctrine and history is not required for higher church office. (If you study the history and journals, you will find there are those who didn't even believe in the Gospel who were called to be members of the Twelve. They were great businessmen, and the church's many assets and interests required that talent.)

Oftentimes the reality is that leaders know far less about the religion than members who have devoted themselves to studying the Gospel and the church's history. The results are sometimes interesting, because doctrinal or historic errors are made by those we sustain as our leaders. How big an issue this becomes for some very devoted believers is up to each individual. I choose to cover their shortcomings with charity, and to remember how difficult a challenge it is to manage a 14 million-member all-volunteer organization spanning cultures and languages across most of the world. But that does not mean their mistakes go unnoticed, just that I accept human-limitations as inevitable. There is a difference between not knowing something and being indifferent to it. I try to keep that in mind.

Abraham's Gospel

Abraham was in possession of the records going back to Adam. All the records of "the fathers" from the beginning came down to him.[1564] This would have gone back to the time of Adam.[1565] It would also have included the record kept by Enoch which contained a prophecy of all things from the beginning to the end of the

---

[1564] Abraham 1:31 "But the records of the fathers, even the patriarchs, concerning the right of Priesthood, the Lord my God preserved in mine own hands; therefore a knowledge of the beginning of the creation, and also of the planets, and of the stars, as they were made known unto the fathers, have I kept even unto this day, and I shall endeavor to write some of these things upon this record, for the benefit of my posterity that shall come after me."

[1565] Moses 6:5 "And a book of remembrance was kept, in the which was recorded, in the language of Adam, for it was given unto as many as called upon God to write by the spirit of inspiration;"

world.[1566] These are the records he studied to increase his own desire to be a man of greater understanding and to follow greater righteousness and also to possess the singular form of High Priesthood known to the Patriarchs.[1567]

It is a mistake to assume Abraham had less of the Gospel than do we. He had more. We have not yet risen to his level of understanding or priesthood. I reject the idea that Abraham's "Gospel" and priesthood was inferior to ours. He was a peer of Adam, Enoch and Noah in his priesthood and the understanding given to him.

Further, the Lord personally ministered to Abraham and conferred priesthood, sonship, and an everlasting inheritance upon him.[1568]

I think it is a mistake to believe we have more, or even as much, as Abraham did. Reading his record (which is his endowment) it becomes apparent there is an understanding of the heavens, including a

---

[1566] D&C 107:53–57 "Three years previous to the death of Adam, he called Seth, Enos, Cainan, Mahalaleel, Jared, Enoch, and Methuselah, who were all high priests, with the residue of his posterity who were righteous, into the valley of Adam-ondi-Ahman, and there bestowed upon them his last blessing. And the Lord appeared unto them, and they rose up and blessed Adam, and called him Michael, the prince, the archangel. And the Lord administered comfort unto Adam, and said unto him: I have set thee to be at the head; a multitude of nations shall come of thee, and thou art a prince over them forever. And Adam stood up in the midst of the congregation; and, notwithstanding he was bowed down with age, being full of the Holy Ghost, predicted whatsoever should befall his posterity unto the latest generation. These things were all written in the book of Enoch, and are to be testified of in due time."

[1567] Abraham 1:2 "And, finding there was greater happiness and peace and rest for me, I sought for the blessings of the fathers, and the right whereunto I should be ordained to administer the same; having been myself a follower of righteousness, desiring also to be one who possessed great knowledge, and to be a greater follower of righteousness, and to possess a greater knowledge, and to be a father of many nations, a prince of peace, and desiring to receive instructions, and to keep the commandments of God, I became a rightful heir, a High Priest, holding the right belonging to the fathers."

[1568] Abraham 1:17–19 "And this because they have turned their hearts away from me, to worship the god of Elkenah, and the god of Libnah, and the god of Mahmackrah, and the god of Korash, and the god of Pharaoh, king of Egypt; therefore I have come down to visit them, and to destroy him who hath lifted up his hand against thee, Abraham, my son, to take away thy life. Behold, I will lead thee by my hand, and I will take thee, to put upon thee my name, even the Priesthood of thy father, and my power shall be over thee. As it was with Noah so shall it be with thee; but through thy ministry my name shall be known in the earth forever, for I am thy God."

detailed account of the path back to God's presence through the stars, which has yet to be restored to us.

Joseph Smith Quote

I was asked about a quote from Joseph Smith. Thought I'd put it up here, also. It is taken from the journal of Mosiah Hancock, and is Bro. Hancock's recollection of a statement made by Joseph Smith:

> . . . you will travel west until you come to the valley of the Great Salt Lake . . . you will live to see men rise in power in the church who will seek to put down your friends and the friends of our Lord and Savior, Jesus Christ. Many will be hoisted because of their money and the worldly learning which they seem to be in possession of; and many who are the true followers of our Lord and Savior will be cast down because of their poverty. (*Mosiah Hancock Journal*, 19)

The Book of Mormon

There is a presumption that "the Book of Mormon" means the book "Book of Mormon" we have now. That is, the one you can get off the shelf at Deseret Book. That is not the only possible meaning of the words.

Nephi records he made two sets of plates. On one he recorded the "full record" of his people. We do not have that record. On the other he included little history and a summary of his religious teachings and prophecies.[1569] The small plates we have are devoted pri-

---

[1569] 1 Nephi 9:2 "And now, as I have spoken concerning these plates, behold they are not the plates upon which I make a full account of the history of my people; for the plates upon which I make a full account of my people I have given the name of Nephi; wherefore, they are called the plates of Nephi, after mine own name; and these plates also are called the plates of Nephi."

marily to his "ministry."[1570] When Nephi prepared the first, larger plates, he was unaware he would later receive a commandment to make the second, shorter record devoted to only his ministry.[1571]

The commandment to make the second set of plates was not given until after Lehi died in the promised land, and Nephi and those who followed him separated from his older brothers Laman and Lemuel.[1572] This would have been several decades after the events in and around Jerusalem.

Mormon did not use Nephi's "small plates" to abridge in his original book. He used Nephi's large plates, containing "more history part" of the people. But, after finishing his abridgment, he attached the small plates to his abridged record, noting that the small plates he attached contained "this small account" of the prophets from Jacob

---

[1570] 1 Nephi 9:4 "Upon the other plates should be engraven an account of the reign of the kings, and the wars and contentions of my people; wherefore these plates are for the more part of the ministry; and the other plates are for the more part of the reign of the kings and the wars and contentions of my people."

[1571] 1 Nephi 19:1–3 "And it came to pass that the Lord commanded me, wherefore I did make plates of ore that I might engraven upon them the record of my people. And upon the plates which I made I did engraven the record of my father, and also our journeyings in the wilderness, and the prophecies of my father; and also many of mine own prophecies have I engraven upon them. And I knew not at the time when I made them that I should be commanded of the Lord to make these plates; wherefore, the record of my father, and the genealogy of his fathers, and the more part of all our proceedings in the wilderness are engraven upon those first plates of which I have spoken; wherefore, the things which transpired before I made these plates are, of a truth, more particularly made mention upon the first plates. And after I had made these plates by way of commandment, I, Nephi, received a commandment that the ministry and the prophecies, the more plain and precious parts of them, should be written upon these plates; and that the things which were written should be kept for the instruction of my people, who should possess the land, and also for other wise purposes, which purposes are known unto the Lord."

[1572] 2 Nephi 5:30 "And it came to pass that the Lord God said unto me: Make other plates; and thou shalt engraven many things upon them which are good in my sight, for the profit of thy people."

down to King Benjamin.[1573] Within the small plates Mormon explained there were "many of the words of Nephi".[1574] For all of Nephi's words, we would need access to the large plates.

The "Book of Mormon" included: 1) Mormon's summary of the Nephite records, which was based on the larger plates and not the smaller ones, 2) the small plates of Nephi, 3) Moroni's translation of part of the Jaredite records, 4) Some correspondence between Mormon and Moroni, along with Moroni's final warnings, and 5) An extensive, sealed and untranslated record containing information not yet revealed to us.[1575] We no longer have a portion of part 1, it having been lost through Martin Harris' neglect. It was not re-translated after the first version was lost.[1576] Part 5, or the sealed portion of the record, contains a revelation from God of everything from the beginning to the end.[1577]

When "the Book of Mormon" is said to contain the "fullness of the Gospel"[1578] is that referring to what we have now (parts 2, 3, 4)?

[1573] Words of Mormon 1:3 "And now, I speak somewhat concerning that which I have written; for after I had made an abridgment from the plates of Nephi, down to the reign of this king Benjamin, of whom Amaleki spake, I searched among the records which had been delivered into my hands, and I found these plates, which contained this small account of the prophets, from Jacob down to the reign of this king Benjamin, and also many of the words of Nephi."

[1574] Ibid.

[1575] 2 Nephi 27:6–8 "And it shall come to pass that the Lord God shall bring forth unto you the words of a book, and they shall be the words of them which have slumbered. And behold the book shall be sealed; and in the book shall be a revelation from God, from the beginning of the world to the ending thereof. Wherefore, because of the things which are sealed up, the things which are sealed shall not be delivered in the day of the wickedness and abominations of the people. Wherefore the book shall be kept from them."

[1576] D&C 10:30 "Behold, I say unto you, that you shall not translate again those words which have gone forth out of your hands;"

[1577] 2 Nephi 27:7 "And behold the book shall be sealed; and in the book shall be a revelation from God, from the beginning of the world to the ending thereof."

[1578] D&C 42:12 "And again, the elders, priests and teachers of this church shall teach the principles of my gospel, which are in the Bible and the Book of Mormon, in the which is the fulness of the gospel."

Does it or did it also include what was originally included by Mormon, but has been lost to us as a result of Martin Harris (part 1)? Does it include the sealed portion of the record we have never been given (part 5)? Although the traditional discussion presumes what we now have (parts 2, 3, 4) are what is meant by "the Book of Mormon" there are other possible meanings.

False Spirits

Whenever there is an increase in spiritual manifestations, there is always an increase in both true and false spiritual phenomena. You do not get one without the other.

In Kirtland, new converts who were overzealous to participate in the new heavenly manifestations coming as a result of Joseph Smith's claims, opened themselves up to receiving influences they could not understand, and did not test for truthfulness. They were so delighted to have any kind of experience, they trusted anything "spiritual" was from God. As a result, there were many undignified things, degrading conduct, foolish behavior and evil influences which crept in among the saints. Joseph received a revelation in May 1831 concerning this troubling development. In it the Lord cautioned there were "many false spirits deceiving the world."[1579] That Satan wanted to overthrow what the Lord was doing.[1580] The presence of hypocrites and of people harboring secret sins and abominations caused false claims to be accepted.[1581] It is required for all people to proceed in

---

[1579] D&C 50:2 "Behold, verily I say unto you, that there are many spirits which are false spirits, which have gone forth in the earth, deceiving the world."

[1580] D&C 50:3 "And also Satan hath sought to deceive you, that he might overthrow you."

[1581] D&C 50:4, 6–7 "Behold, I, the Lord, have looked upon you, and have seen abominations in the church that profess my name. But wo unto them that are deceivers and hypocrites, for, thus saith the Lord, I will bring them to judgment. Behold, verily I say unto you, there are hypocrites among you, who have deceived some, which has given the adversary power; but behold such shall be reclaimed;"

truth and in righteousness[1582] if they are going to avoid deception. Meaning that unrepentant and unforgiven men will not be able to distinguish between a true and a false spirit.

All spiritual gifts, including distinguishing between true and false spirits, requires the Holy Ghost, given through obedience to the truth, which allows a person to distinguish between truth and error.[1583] The truth is like light, and when you follow the light of truth it grows inside you until you have a "perfect day" in which there is no more darkness,but everything is illuminated by the light of the spirit within you.[1584]

The revelation clarifies that a preacher of truth will become only a servant. He will not claim greatness, but will seek only to give truth; as a result of which false spirits will be subject to him.[1585] But this only comes as a result of repenting of all sin, because the light of a perfect day cannot arise when men harbor evil desires and inappro-

---

[1582] D&C 50:9 "Wherefore, let every man beware lest he do that which is not in truth and righteousness before me."

[1583] D&C 50:17–23 "Verily I say unto you, he that is ordained of me and sent forth to preach the word of truth by the Comforter, in the Spirit of truth, doth he preach it by the Spirit of truth or some other way? And if it be by some other way it is not of God. And again, he that receiveth the word of truth, doth he receive it by the Spirit of truth or some other way? If it be some other way it is not of God. Therefore, why is it that ye cannot understand and know, that he that receiveth the word by the Spirit of truth receiveth it as it is preached by the Spirit of truth? Wherefore, he that preacheth and he that receiveth, understand one another, and both are edified and rejoice together. And that which doth not edify is not of God, and is darkness."

[1584] D&C 50:24 "That which is of God is light; and he that receiveth light, and continueth in God, receiveth more light; and that light groweth brighter and brighter until the perfect day."

[1585] D&C 50:26–27 "He that is ordained of God and sent forth, the same is appointed to be the greatest, notwithstanding he is the least and the servant of all. Wherefore, he is possessor of all things; for all things are subject unto him, both in heaven and on the earth, the life and the light, the Spirit and the power, sent forth by the will of the Father through Jesus Christ, his Son."

priate ambitions within their hearts.[1586] Truth will not leave you confused, but will enlighten your understanding.[1587]

From this you can see how necessary it is for each of us to continually repent, conduct our lives in conformity with such truth as you presently understand, and avoid deliberate wrongdoing in order to be able to distinguish between a true and a false spirit. You must attract light. It is attracted by obedience to such light as you already have. When you proceed forward using the light you already possess to attract more light it will grow in one, consistent and truthful manner from a lesser to a greater light. All of it conforming to the teachings of Jesus Christ.

Ambition in spiritual gifts leads to acceptance of evil influences. As part of the same problem in Kirtland, in September of the previous year, Hiram Page wanted to be like Joseph, and was able to attract a deceiving spirit to communicate with him through a seer stone. But the commandments he received were designed to lead him into error.[1588]

[1586] D&C 50:28–29 "But no man is possessor of all things except he be purified and cleansed from all sin. And if ye are purified and cleansed from all sin, ye shall ask whatsoever you will in the name of Jesus and it shall be done."

[1587] D&C 50:31 "Wherefore, it shall come to pass, that if you behold a spirit manifested that you cannot understand, and you receive not that spirit, ye shall ask of the Father in the name of Jesus; and if he give not unto you that spirit, then you may know that it is not of God."

[1588] D&C 28:11 "And again, thou shalt take thy brother, Hiram Page, between him and thee alone, and tell him that those things which he hath written from that stone are not of me and that Satan deceiveth him;"

Truth will always testify of Christ and lead to repentance. It will lead you to do good, not evil. To serve God and not follow men. To repent and forsake darkness which appeals to the carnal mind.[1589]

Just because you have a "spiritual experience" you cannot trust it will invariably be from God.

True spirits will:

- Testify of Christ.

- Lead to repentance.

- Be consistent with existing scripture.

- Lead you to be submissive to authority in the church.

- Edify and enlighten your mind.

- Be understandable and not cause confusion.

- Cause light to grow within you.

- Turn you toward Christ, not men.

- Never cause pride.

- Make you a better servant.

- Increase your love of your fellow man.

[1589] Moroni 7:12–19 "Wherefore, all things which are good cometh of God; and that which is evil cometh of the devil; for the devil is an enemy unto God, and fighteth against him continually, and inviteth and enticeth to sin, and to do that which is evil continually. But behold, that which is of God inviteth and enticeth to do good continually; wherefore, every thing which inviteth and enticeth to do good, and to love God, and to serve him, is inspired of God. Wherefore, take heed, my beloved brethren, that ye do not judge that which is evil to be of God, or that which is good and of God to be of the devil. For behold, my brethren, it is given unto you to judge, that ye may know good from evil; and the way to judge is as plain, that ye may know with a perfect knowledge, as the daylight is from the dark night. For behold, the Spirit of Christ is given to every man, that he may know good from evil; wherefore, I show unto you the way to judge; for every thing which inviteth to do good, and to persuade to believe in Christ, is sent forth by the power and gift of Christ; wherefore ye may know with a perfect knowledge it is of God. But whatsoever thing persuadeth men to do evil, and believe not in Christ, and deny him, and serve not God, then ye may know with a perfect knowledge it is of the devil; for after this manner doth the devil work, for he persuadeth no man to do good, no, not one; neither do his angels; neither do they who subject themselves unto him. And now, my brethren, seeing that ye know the light by which ye may judge, which light is the light of Christ, see that ye do not judge wrongfully; for with that same judgment which ye judge ye shall also be judged. Wherefore, I beseech of you, brethren, that ye should search diligently in the light of Christ that ye may know good from evil; and if ye will lay hold upon every good thing, and condemn it not, ye certainly will be a child of Christ."

- Clothe you with charity for the failings of others.
- Conform to the true whisperings of the Holy Ghost you previously have received.
- Leave you humble and grateful for God's condescension.
- Make you want to bring others to the light.
- Be grounded in love toward God and all mankind.
- Lead you to rejoice.

False spirits will:
- Deny Christ.
- Cause pride.
- Make you believe you are better because of the experience.
- Contradict the scriptures.
- Appeal to carnality and self-indulgence.
- Lead to rebellion against the church's right to administer ordinances.
- Cause confusion.
- Lead to ambition to control others.
- Make you intolerant of others' failings.
- Seek self fulfillment rather than service.
- Appeal to your vanity and assure you that you are a great person.
- Bring darkness.
- Repulse the Holy Ghost.
- Prevent you from repenting and forsaking sins.
- Interfere with serving others.
- Focus on yourself rather than the needs of others.

Do not think all spiritual experiences can be trusted. There is no difference between the activities of deceiving spirits today and those in Kirtland, as well as those in the New Testament times. If you follow the Lord you must still test the spirits and only follow those which point to Christ.[1590] Even Joseph Smith had to ask God about some of the phenomena going on in Kirtland before he knew which were of God and which were deceiving.

Submission to Church

I was asked about "submission to the church" and "criticism as rebellion." Here is my response:

The church is formed by a mutual agreement between the members and the leaders. The leaders occupy their positions because they are sustained to the offices they hold. When sustained, they are the office holders. No one has the right to preside or conduct church activities other than the regularly constituted church authorities. It is their right.

But if you love the church and want her best interests, it is a mistake to leave her uncriticized for mistakes and blunders. Those who care for her the most will be the most eager to help. Criticism designed to improve, to overcome mistakes or solve dilemmas the church faces is what a person who cares would always do. Only a fool would mistake comments motivated by concern and care as a sign of rejection or rebellion.

The church is struggling. Only about 10% of the converts remain with the church today. Half of the returned missionaries drift into inactivity within two years of returning home. Temple marriages in the U.S. are ending at a rate nearly comparable to national averages, and the fertility rate of Mormons in the U.S. has dropped to nearly the national average. Tithing contributions have dropped. There is a crisis underway at present. If a member cares, they owe it to the church to offer views for discussion.

[1590] 1 John 4:1 "Beloved, believe not every spirit, but try the spirits whether they are of God: because many false prophets are gone out into the world."

I think using professional business consultants to help solve the crisis is what has led to the crisis. They do not, indeed cannot, understand the things of the spirit. It is impossible to treat the Gospel as another commodity and market it like you would soft drinks, cars or office supplies. Businessmen cannot remedy a spiritual illness. The church does not need good marketing. Indeed it grew the most as an overall percentage of growth, when it boldly proclaimed a new doctrine, a new revelation from heaven, and suffered the indignity and criticism of the entire world. While editorial pages were railing against the church, and cartoonists were mocking Joseph Smith, the church went from nothing to tens-of-thousands. That was how the truth should always be spread. Not by aligning with the world and employing its methods, but by proclaiming the truth and rejecting the world.

We've been using more and more of the same failed business marketing approach to try and smooth out the message and deliver it more agreeably to the world. That will NOT attract those seeking the truth. We must not blend in, but must stick out. Doing more of this marketing and social-science driven management will lead to less: Less activity. Less retention. Less tithing. Less membership. Less success. It needs to reverse.

Sooner or later someone who is open to that message will decide the failure has continued long enough and will decide to return to what established the church in the first place against all opposition.

Elective Adultery and Election Ambition

Though I am not political, some moments in the political world spill over into things I do care about. One of them is unfolding at the moment. The disclosure of Newt Gingrich's marital infidelity, and on-going extramarital misconduct resulting in his second divorce and third marriage, is one of those rare moments when the United States has an opportunity to make a significant moral error. It is true we have had past presidents who have engaged in sexual misconduct while in office. Some were discovered only after they left office. President Clinton, of course, was known to have done so while still serving. But the United States has never elected a man whose extra-marital affairs were publicly known *before* the election. Such conduct has always been disqualifying. This is because the United States has always cared about morality as much as about policy.

Apparently many political commentators cannot see the difference between offering an adulterous man whose sins are publicly known before the election as a candidate to the nation's highest office, in contrast to later discovering we've inadvertently elected an adulterous man. [Grover Cleveland was a bachelor and young when he may have fathered a child, not a married adulterer. He paid child support and was never conclusively shown to be the father.] When given the choice beforehand, adultery should always be disqualifying. Yet such "conservative" commentators as Rush Limbaugh and Laura Ingraham have championed Newt Gingrich after the disclosure; even Sarah Palin has defended Mr. Gingrich after it became an issue. Gov. Rick Perry has also endorsed Mr. Gingrich after this moral failing has become public.

Mr. Gingrich is ego-maniacal. He was dishonest and thrown out of Congress for his ethical lapses. His infidelity to his wife is mirrored in his infidelity to high office while serving in Congress. If he betrayed his wife before, and betrayed his public office before, he is unworthy to be trusted again. His very public penitence I view more as public theatre than humble submission to God. He proclaims his God-given forgiveness as a shield against criticism, rather than a matter of private devotion. Such conduct always raises a question about sincerity. He is ambitious, self-centered, now using religion to justify himself, and unworthy of renewed public trust. When someone has been involved in such a troublesome history I would expect they would voluntarily disqualify themselves by never running. I understand and sympathize with failed marriages and moral lapses. They happen. But contrition and ambition are incompatible. Some personal failings are so great they disqualify. At least from the right to hold an office of public trust which was designed to be viewed as much as a "pulpit" of righteousness as a seat of power.

He was careful yesterday to deny wanting an "open marriage" because the definition of the word used in the question does not quite fit his immoral conduct. He was not prepared to welcome his wife joining him in extramarital sexual relations, as "open marriage" implies. He wanted to do that alone. He wanted his wife to "share" him with his paramour. (This loophole allowing the denial was fed to him by Rush Limbaugh.) Therefore he could probably pass a lie-detector test about his denial of wanting an "open marriage." Yet he wants his adulterous companion to be the nation's First Lady, and himself to occupy the high position originally designed for George Washington—the most trusted man of his generation. A man whose morality was beyond question. A man who led by example, freeing his slaves in his will as the example he hoped would end slavery without requiring the nation to be torn apart. Newt Gingrich will bring dishonor to any office he holds because of his inability to look beyond self-interest and personal glorification.

When a person is known to be an adulterer, they are by definition also a liar. Liars and adulterers are by any scriptural definition wicked.

When a nation on this land chooses to uphold a wicked man to head their government, they are ripe for destruction.[1591]

You uphold such a man at the peril of national destruction. His campaign has also exposed the underlying confused morality of some popular political commentators.

Jensen Comments

The interview of Marlin Jensen by USU Professor Phil Barlow is now on the Internet. The statement below is interesting for several reasons:

"The fifteen men [1st Pres. & 12] really do know, and they really care. And they realize that maybe since Kirtland, we never have had a period of, I'll call it apostasy, like we're having right now; largely over these issues [meaning the church's history]. We do have another initiative that we have called, 'Answers to Gospel Questions'. We are trying to figure out exactly what channels to deliver it in and exactly what format to put it in. But we want to have a place where people can go. We have hired someone that's in charge of search engine optimization. We realize that people get their information basically from Google. They don't come to LDS.org. If they get there, it's through Google. So, we are trying to create an offering that will address these issues and be available for the public at large and to the church leaders, because many of them don't have answers either. It can be very disappointing to

---

[1591] Mosiah 29:27 "And if the time comes that the voice of the people doth choose iniquity, then is the time that the judgments of God will come upon you; yea, then is the time he will visit you with great destruction even as he has hitherto visited this land." Alma 10:19 "Yea, well did Mosiah say, who was our last king, when he was about to deliver up the kingdom, having no one to confer it upon, causing that this people should be governed by their own voices—yea, well did he say that if the time should come that the voice of this people should choose iniquity, that is, if the time should come that this people should fall into transgression, they would be ripe for destruction." Helaman 5:2 "For as their laws and their governments were established by the voice of the people, and they who chose evil were more numerous than they who chose good, therefore they were ripening for destruction, for the laws had become corrupted."

church members. And, for people who are losing their faith, or who have lost it, we hope to regain to the church."

Another questioner asked how these fifteen men know. Is it through anecdotal means or from statistics? Elder Jensen said that he has received much information anecdotally and added,

> "The church has a very progressive research and information division, with tremendous public opinion surveyors. And the church is constantly running surveys, and employing consultants that do focus groups on a variety of topics, but especially on the ones that we are talking about right now, that are so sensitive to the faith of members. Where has the prophet laid his emphasis right now? It's on something called 'The Rescue'. And with good reason, because we are suffering a loss; both in terms of our new converts that come in that don't get really established in the church, as well as very faithful members who because of things we're talking about, as well as others, are losing their faith in the process. It is one of our biggest concerns right now."

If I could offer something useful to the "fifteen men" (whom I am certain could care less what I'd have to say), it would be the following:

Standing in an echo chamber and hearing the same things repeated to you is not a conversation. The "crisis" will not be solved by the approach that has precipitated the crisis. This is not at all like the Kirtland Apostasy, other than the vastness of the scope involved. It is because the leadership has lost the confidence of large numbers who simply do not trust them to tell the truth about things. It is being packaged and marketed. That is not cured by "search engine optimization" because it is not believed.

Taking just one incident as an example: Those who study our history know the contemporaneous accounts all fail to mention the "transfiguration of Brigham Young into Joseph Smith" on August 8,

1844. It was not the reason the Nauvoo population voted to sustain the 12. They did NOT sustain Brigham Young separately to anything, nor did Brigham Young ask to be sustained to anything apart from advancing the claims of the 12 to preside. It would be years before Brigham Young sought to be separately sustained to lead. Repeating the false inspirational story of his transfiguration is not useful. It is not inspirational, but evidence of duplicity and dissembling. There are hundreds of other examples which could be given. They are discovered by reading history.

Very progressive research using public opinion surveyors is *not* going to help. After all, Mitt Romney was ahead by a large margin two weeks before his resounding defeat in South Carolina. Today he is behind by more than 10% in Florida, after leading for months. When the vote is taken in a few days he may well win. The shifting sands of opinion are as unstable as water. The Lord warned against establishing a house on such vulnerable sand. We should instead build upon the rock of knowing Christ. Everything I've written is intended to point to that rock. All that is required to vastly shift opinions is more information. Employing consultants who do focus groups on a variety of topics is what has caused the problems now facing the church.

A steady tune of fixed truth, bold declaration of doctrine, even when it fades from popularity, and seeking light from God is what built the church. It is the reason for the church's existence. When it lapses into another well managed business operation whose product is the religion called Mormonism, it ceases to attract men's hearts. Opinion polling and focus groups are not a substitute for revelation.

People want to believe in the restored Gospel. They want to hear truth. They know the Lord spoke to Joseph Smith. We want what was restored through Joseph to be preserved, not to be repackaged and squandered at the feet of popular opinion.

For the first time since Joseph Smith it is possible the restoration may continue without the church. The prophecies declare the work will culminate in establishing Zion. Whether the church chooses to be involved or not, it is coming.

As a final aside, the reason I say the "fifteen men" have no interest in what I have to say is because they use these professionals who conduct opinion polling and focus groups as a substitute for knowing the hearts of the faithful. Someone who is active, doing 100% home teaching and faithfully serving in their callings like myself is viewed as an inappropriate source of information. If my views differ from the leadership's then I am considered to be 'out of harmony' and in error. When they employ non-believing professionals who could care less about the underlying faith (apart from it being the product to be marketed), they are viewed as objective and professional. The result is to prefer the views of the non-believer over the views of the faithful, and to discard, and even question the loyalty of the faithful. The system is broken. You must fix that first. Blaming the members for "apostasy" like Kirtland is incorrect.

The Lord's Witnesses

When the Lord returned from the grave, the first witness He showed Himself to was not one of His apostles. It was Mary.[1592] He appeared to several others throughout the day (which I discuss in detail in *Come, Let Us Adore Him*) before finally appearing to some of

---

[1592] John 20:11–16 "But Mary stood without at the sepulchre weeping: and as she wept, she stooped down, *and looked* into the sepulchre, And seeth two angels in white sitting, the one at the head, and the other at the feet, where the body of Jesus had lain. And they say unto her, Woman, why weepest thou? She saith unto them, Because they have taken away my Lord, and I know not where they have laid him. And when she had thus said, she turned herself back, and saw Jesus standing, and knew not that it was Jesus. Jesus saith unto her, Woman, why weepest thou? whom seekest thou? She, supposing him to be the gardener, saith unto him, Sir, if thou have borne him hence, tell me where thou hast laid him, and I will take him away. Jesus saith unto her, Mary. She turned herself, and saith unto him, Rabboni; which is to say, Master."

His apostles in the evening of the first day of His return to life. When He met with the apostles, He rebuked them for not believing the reports of those with whom He visited earlier in the day.[1593]

It is interesting the first witness was a woman. It is interesting the Lord spent hours walking and talking with two disciples, Cleopas and an unnamed second companion, on a journey to Emmaus. [In *Come, Let Us Adore Him,* I explain why I believe the companion was Luke.] As He walked with them, He spent the time expounding the scriptures and prophets, showing how they testified of His death. He "opened the scriptures unto them."[1594] This is how the risen Lord

---

[1593] Mark 16:14 "Afterward he appeared unto the eleven as they sat at meat, and upbraided them with their unbelief and hardness of heart, because they believed not them which had seen him after he was risen."

[1594] Luke 24:13–32 "And, behold, two of them went that same day to a village called Emmaus, which was from Jerusalem *about* threescore furlongs. And they talked together of all these things which had happened. And it came to pass, that, while they communed *together* and reasoned, Jesus himself drew near, and went with them. But their eyes were holden that they should not know him. And he said unto them, What manner of communications *are* these that ye have one to another, as ye walk, and are sad? And the one of them, whose name was Cleopas, answering said unto him, Art thou only a stranger in Jerusalem, and hast not known the things which are come to pass there in these days? And he said unto them, What things? And they said unto him, Concerning Jesus of Nazareth, which was a prophet mighty in deed and word before God and all the people: And how the chief priests and our rulers delivered him to be condemned to death, and have crucified him. But we trusted that it had been he which should have redeemed Israel: and beside all this, to day is the third day since these things were done. Yea, and certain women also of our company made us astonished, which were early at the sepulchre; And when they found not his body, they came, saying, that they had also seen a vision of angels, which said that he was alive And certain of them which were with us went to the sepulchre, and found *it* even so as the women had said: but him they saw not. Then he said unto them, O fools, and slow of heart to believe all that the prophets have spoken: Ought not Christ to have suffered these things, and to enter into his glory? And beginning at Moses and all the prophets, he expounded unto them in all the scriptures the things concerning himself. And they drew nigh unto the village, whither they went: and he made as though he would have gone further. But they constrained him, saying, Abide with us: for it is toward evening, and the day is far spent. And he went in to tarry with them. And it came to pass, as he sat at meat with them, he took bread, and blessed *it,* and brake, and gave to them. And their eyes were opened, and they knew him; and he vanished out of their sight. And they said one to another, Did not our heart burn within us, while he talked with us by the way, and while he opened to us the scriptures?"

chose to spend the afternoon of the first day of His return to life. (The talk I gave on this walk appears as an appendix to *Eighteen Verses*.)

Again, it is interesting that, after first showing Himself to a woman, He then spent hours walking and talking with two disciples, neither of whom were apostles, expounding doctrine and the scriptures to them.

I've searched the scriptures diligently to try and discover where the Lord ever commanded that we follow a man. I've not found it. Instead, I've found Him warning us to "Follow [Him]".[1595] The phrase "follow the prophet" does not appear anywhere in scripture. It does not appear there because it is an institutional invention designed to reduce resistance to centralized church decision-making. It was implemented deliberately during the administration of David O. McKay in the fourth phase of Mormon history. It is an idea which is altogether alien to the Gospel of Jesus Christ. Instead, what appears in the scriptures is a curse pronounced on those who follow man or put their trust in man's arm.[1596] Nephi's final address warns the gentiles how vulnerable they are to this mistake, and how they will be

---

[1595] Matthew 4:19 "And he saith unto them, Follow me, and I will make you fishers of men."
John 10:27 "My sheep hear my voice, and I know them, and they follow me:"
John 21:22 "Jesus saith unto him, If I will that he tarry till I come, what *is that* to thee? follow thou me."
Luke 5:27 "And after these things he went forth, and saw a publican, named Levi, sitting at the receipt of custom: and he said unto him, Follow me."
Luke 9:59 "And he said unto another, Follow me. But he said, Lord, suffer me first to go and bury my father."
Mark 2:14 "And as he passed by, he saw Levi the *son* of Alphaeus sitting at the receipt of custom, and said unto him, Follow me. And he arose and followed him."

[1596] 2 Nephi 4:34 "O Lord, I have trusted in thee, and I will trust in thee forever. I will not put my trust in the arm of flesh; for I know that cursed is he that putteth his trust in the arm of flesh. Yea, cursed is he that putteth his trust in man or maketh flesh his arm."
2 Nephi 28:31 "Cursed is he that putteth his trust in man, or maketh flesh his arm, or shall hearken unto the precepts of men, save their precepts shall be given by the power of the Holy Ghost."
D&C 1:19 "The weak things of the world shall come forth and break down the mighty and strong ones, that man should not counsel his fellow man, neither trust in the arm of flesh—"

cursed as a consequence. He offers hope, however, conditioned on repentance and return to following the Lord.[1597]

I am grateful for all who serve in The Church of Jesus Christ of Latter-day Saints. From my own Home Teacher to the President. They all have my gratitude, my prayers, my support. I do not challenge the right of any who preside in the church to conduct and to manage the church's affairs.I do not envy them in assuming the burdens they bear. It is an almost impossible responsibility for any man. I am confident they do a better job than I would.

Despite my gratitude to them, I trust my salvation to no man or set of men. For that I rely entirely on my understanding of, acquaintance with, covenants and promises from the Lord. If I can encourage anyone else to pursue the path to know Him, I want to do so. The difference between truth which can save and error which will damn is so fine a line it is sometimes compared to a two-edged sword, cutting both ways. Encouraging people to find that edge and to rightly divide between truth and error oftentimes will offend. It is still the truth. We really ought to fear God and not man.[1598] The One who keeps the gate of salvation is not a man or men, for He alone

---

[1597] 2 Nephi 28:31–32 "Cursed is he that putteth his trust in man, or maketh flesh his arm, or shall hearken unto the precepts of men, save their precepts shall be given by the power of the Holy Ghost. Wo be unto the Gentiles, saith the Lord God of Hosts! For notwithstanding I shall lengthen out mine arm unto them from day to day, they will deny me; nevertheless, I will be merciful unto them, saith the Lord God, if they will repent and come unto me; for mine arm is lengthened out all the day long, saith the Lord God of Hosts."

[1598] D&C 3:7–8 "For, behold, you should not have feared man more than God. Although men set at naught the counsels of God, and despise his words— Yet you should have been faithful; and he would have extended his arm and supported you against all the fiery darts of the adversary; and he would have been with you in every time of trouble."

will open or shut that gate. There is "no servant" employed there.[1599] If you arrive at that gate having been misled regarding your obligation to *Him*, having *"followed the prophets"* you will be among those whose eternal opportunities have been curtailed, no better off than liars and whoremongers.[1600] [If you read those verses from Section 76, you should ponder the difference between "following" and "receiving" a prophet. If you "follow" him, what are you substituting? If you "receive" him, what are you doing? Therein lies a distinction worth pondering.]

Job

I got an email stating:

"Job is not pious fiction. D&C 121:10 reads, 'Thou art not yet as Job; thy friends do not contend against thee, neither charge thee with transgression, as they did Job.'"

I responded: I understand your point. But could it also mean "you are not yet like Little Orphan Annie, you still have a family," or another similar analogy? That is, the Lord refers to the character to

---

[1599] 2 Nephi 9:41 "O then, my beloved brethren, come unto the Lord, the Holy One. Remember that his paths are righteous. Behold, the way for man is narrow, but it lieth in a straight course before him, and the keeper of the gate is the Holy One of Israel; and he employeth no servant there; and there is none other way save it be by the gate; for he cannot be deceived, for the Lord God is his name."

[1600] D&C 76:98–105 "And the glory of the telestial is one, even as the glory of the stars is one; for as one star differs from another star in glory, even so differs one from another in glory in the telestial world; For these are they who are of Paul, and of Apollos, and of Cephas. These are they who say they are some of one and some of another—some of Christ and some of John, and some of Moses, and some of Elias, and some of Esaias, and some of Isaiah, and some of Enoch; But received not the gospel, neither the testimony of Jesus, neither the prophets, neither the everlasting covenant. Last of all, these all are they who will not be gathered with the saints, to be caught up unto the church of the Firstborn, and received into the cloud. These are they who are liars, and sorcerers, and adulterers, and whoremongers, and whosoever loves and makes a lie. These are they who suffer the wrath of God on earth. These are they who suffer the vengeance of eternal fire."

illustrate a circumstance. That would be akin to His use of parables to communicate truth.

The reference in Section 121 does not settle the question of historicity. It merely employs Job as a reference point to console the imprisoned Joseph Smith. That leaves whether or not Job is a real person unresolved.

Job, like many of the Psalms, was borrowed from other surrounding cultures and adopted as part of the Jewish religious text. This has resulted in many scholars concluding that he wasn't a real person, but a character developed to tell a morality tale. I'm not challenging that view, I'm accepting it. If he was a real person, then I suppose one day we will all meet him. In the meantime, his story does help us understand truths about this life.

Book of Mormon as Fiction

I got another email asking:

"If Job is pious fiction, I've read about other folks who think the Book of Mormon is too. What do you think of that?"

I responded: Since Moroni came to and was seen by Joseph Smith, Oliver Cowdery, David Whitmer and Martin Harris we know at least one of the book's characters was a real person. Which implies the others were also. Personally, I think they were all real people.

INTERPRETING
HISTORY

There is an art to interpreting history. No matter what the schools teach, in the end there are judgment calls that are always made in arriving at a final interpretation.

The problems of church history are not evidence that some people are acting in bad faith and others are not. Everyone should be motivated to seek and know the truth. However, even when claiming to seek the truth, various motivations color the results of our interpretation.

When a court case is presented to a jury, both sides are duty bound to tell the truth. All the witnesses are sworn in before they are allowed to tell the jury anything. Then whatever they say is supposed to be the truth. If they lie, they do so under the condition they will be charged with perjury. Despite this, in almost every case the story told by the Plaintiff is completely at odds with the story told by the Defendant. If you believe the Plaintiff's witnesses and arguments, the Plaintiff will win. If you believe the Defendant's witnesses and arguments, the Defendant will win. The jury's responsibility is to decide who to believe.

Sometimes a witness is believable because of their demeanor. Sometimes it is the content of their statements, sometimes the way they appear. Their age, opportunity to observe, self-interest, relationship with the parties, clarity of explanation and other things all play a part. There are intangibles that affect credibility, some so difficult to explain they are reduced to "impressions" or "feelings" about the witness. Their reputation for honesty, or personal history matters. When the case ends the jury deliberates all they've heard and seen, consult their common sense, talk the matter over and reach a consensus. That consensus becomes the verdict. The case is then concluded.

History is no different. The witnesses are evaluated, and what they have to say is considered. But in the end, they are weighed and either believed or not. Orson Hyde arrived back in Nauvoo on August 13th. He was not present on August 8th. Therefore, his two lengthy reminiscences of the transfiguration of Brigham Young on August 8th cannot be believed by me. I suppose *you* could decide to believe Orson Hyde, despite the fact that his story could not possibly be based on what he saw August 8, 1844. But if you decide to believe him, you must show me the courtesy of allowing me to disbelieve him.

The daily diaries of Brigham Young, Heber C. Kimball, Willard Richards and Wilford Woodruff all had entries on August 8, 1844. None of them mention the "transfiguration" of Brigham Young. Nauvoo newspapers, *Times and Seasons* and *Nauvoo Neighbor* both covered the debates on August 8, 1844 and neither one mention the transfiguration. Even Orson Hyde's accounts written in 1844 and 1845 fail to mention the transfiguration. He did not begin to provide his elaborate account of the event until 1869, when he claimed Brigham Young's "words went through [him] like electricity. It was not only the voice of Joseph Smith but there were the features, the gestures and even the stature of Joseph before us in the person of Brigham" (*JD* 13:181, 6 Oct 1869).

So, when I weigh the evidence, I conclude the story is merely faith-promoting, and much like Paul Dunn, bearing something less than an accurate retelling of the truth.

The truth of the restoration does not depend merely upon men's imagination to support it. After all, Joseph produced the Book of Mormon, revelations found in the Doctrine and Covenants, Pearl of Great Price, and other unpublished revelations. He left a body of letters, talks, and ordinances. What Joseph did accomplish is more than enough proof of his stature as a prophet of God.

I am interested in the truth of the restoration. It is not important for me to justify succession, or to defend any office or friends. I do not want to be popular or to have anyone follow me. I hope only to please God and defend the truth. If it causes anyone, including myself, embarrassment I couldn't care less. We have a duty to our Maker to act our part in helping one another to find our way back to Him.

I also don't care if someone chooses to believe otherwise and to weep like a child while retelling the story of Brigham Young being transfigured into Joseph Smith as he pleaded for votes following Joseph's death. I can endure that without insulting them or arguing the point. They are free to believe what I regard as false. But what should not happen is for someone who holds this view to forbid or condemn me for thinking them wrong. I enjoyed Paul Dunn's stories. They were inspiring. If you accept them as inspirational fiction, you can enjoy them too. The likelihood is that Job is pious fiction also. It is part of a category of "Wisdom Literature" written to explain a true principle, but probably not based on an actual person named Job. It is "true" in the sense of teaching principles of truth, not in the sense the characters existed.

I've weighed the evidence in our history, sorted through what I accept and find persuasive, and what I find less than believable. It has involved considerable effort. It is fine with me for others to disagree.

When a disagreement is based on a superficial review of the available record, or on bombast without ever studying the history, then I'd appreciate the courtesy of allowing me to continue in my honest, good faith delusion.

Interpreting History, Part 2

Everyone who contributes to the documentation of history must be evaluated to decide if they are a believable source or a source to be discounted. Even an otherwise unreliable source may be believable on a point. Deciding whether to accept or reject their information is part of your responsibility in interpreting history for yourself. You can't put that responsibility on others. We are each one accountable for what we believe about life's most important topic.

Another standard I use to evaluate a someone's story is also drawn from the law. When a witness admits something contrary to their own position, or contradicts the position they are trying to advance, that should attract your notice. Admissions against personal interests are almost inherently credible. When someone is saying something self-deprecating they are almost always telling the truth, both in the courtroom and in life. For example, throughout John D. Lee's final *Confessions,* he makes a number of admissions of his own failings. He acknowledges his guilt and attempts to set the record straight with members of his family and close friends. These admissions expose his failures. It is not likely he is lying when making such personal admissions of guilt. Therefore, I do not dismiss his material out of hand. Instead, it becomes something to weigh and consider piece by piece. As I do that, I also consider that there are a number of incidents which are distant in time and location that would tax the memory of anyone trying to retell the events. For such things his accounts become useful only in a big-picture. The details are likely to be the product of his imagination rather than his actual memory. So there needs to be other sources consulted before reaching a conclusion about such details.

When Brigham Young makes the same admission multiple times, using almost the same words over a period of decades, I think he is telling the truth. Particularly when the admission is contrary to his own best interests, or they reduce his stature as a religious figure. That is why in *Passing the Heavenly Gift* I quote his repeated admission about never seeing an angel or having contact with heavenly beings. It is an important and believable factor in understanding Brigham Young. When he goes on to explain that God is "duty bound" to support his best decision, we can then know and understand how he led the church. He used his best judgment. He proceeded without angelic guidance and fully expected that the Lord would uphold his decisions.

Put yourself in his shoes and try to understand what pressures that would exert on a normal person. When there were serious mistakes made, like the incident at Battle Creek near Pleasant Grove, there is no time to second-guess the slaughter of the Indians. You just move on. When Blackhawk (a survivor of the slaughter) later leads a war against the saints in retaliation for the event, Brigham Young knew he had created the mess. I read in his reactions a detectable crisis. It was a deep personal loss of confidence. There was a breakdown. For all the bombast we are used to in reading Brigham Young, he was very troubled by some of the things that resulted from decisions he made.

The Reformation he led in the 1850's grew out of his frustration with the hardships and overall failing of the early western movement. He reacted by blaming the saints for their personal impurity and lack of faith. The Reformation was an attempt to have the saints to take their religion more seriously. He thought they needed to repent. God would not be visiting all these troubles on the church if the saints were living their religion. So he started the Reformation, with all its excesses and threats. The Reformation, a terrible moment, now all but forgotten, confirms several things: first, the saints were not doing well as a people; second, Brigham did not think the problem came from the top; third, the members were blamed and then punished because Brigham believed they were not living the religion well enough. (He even cut off the entire church from receiving the sacrament for a period of time.)

Interesting that throughout Brigham Young's Reformation there was never a thought given to the failures in Nauvoo discussed in *Passing the Heavenly Gift*. Instead, the leaders presumed they were right, and God was punishing the unfaithful membership. This approach led to mistakes.

Today, as Elder Jensen discussed, there is a view that the church is undergoing an apostasy comparable to Kirtland. But no thought is being entertained that the church itself has created these problems through leadership decisions at the top. The presumption is that God has been behind all that they've decided in their counsels, and therefore, the problem lies in the membership.

I've already posted about the unfolding disaster of the "raising the bar" program that resulted in preventing many young men from serving who wanted to serve. Eighty percent of the results in the mission field were being produced by 20% of the missionaries. So the church cut back the missionary rolls to purge the ineffective few who required babysitting from the mission presidents. We now have thousands of young men who feel rejected, judged and found unworthy by the church. They bear deep inward resentments as a result of this rejection. They all knew older brothers, or friends of their older brothers, who did as much wrong, or worse things than they had done. But these older brothers and their friends were allowed to serve. Some of them were noble missionaries. Their lives changed while serving. But the "raised bar" kept these younger brothers out of service and stigmatized them. Now we have earnest young men who wanted to serve, were told they weren't good enough who now have to reconcile that rejection by the church.

The missionary who baptized me would not have qualified under the "raised bar." [I hesitate to confess another's sins, but I do not view that acknowledgement as a criticism of him. It reflected his true intent to repent and serve. For that I am eternally grateful.] He was a gift from heaven and a servant of God when I met him. He taught and testified of the truth, and baptized me with authority. He is active and faithful still today. Some of his own conversion happened while serving. I thank God there was no administratively imposed "bar" to his service.

The point is that some, perhaps much, of the church's present malaise is driven by mistakes made at the top. But those mistakes become very difficult to discuss in an atmosphere where every subordinate is expected to testify that God is making the decisions and never question the mistakes as they are made. "It's good Bart did that" is the mantra. [You'd need to have seen the *Treehouse of Horrors* episodes of *The Simpsons* to understand that remark. Get one of your kids to explain it to you.]

At the risk of having some think it is blasphemy, I think the current problems stem largely from top-down mistakes more so than the members being disobedient and unfaithful. I think the people at the bottom want to please God. But they're led that in many instances they err. Not for any lack of good faith on their part, but because there are not enough true principles taught to permit them to govern themselves correctly. There is at a minimum some shared responsibility. Our history prevents leadership from sharing any responsibility because of the fundamentals established in fourth phase Mormonism. The adoration of the president has been co-opted by

Correlation to spread a veil of implied inspiration across everything done at the top. This problematic historical issue leaves us with little choice now but to blame the members for current problems. All the leaders need to do is what Marlin Jensen says they're presently attempting. Just optimize search engine results, direct the public to the church's website where the faith promoting stories are found, and everything will turn out just fine.

All of this arises from our history. All of this fits seamlessly into a continuation of steps begun more than a century ago. The issues run into our past and cannot be adequately understood apart from our history. But a corollary to our history also arises from the present difficulties. History brought us to this moment. There must be answers to be found there. But the 'only-faith-promoting' account of our past does not give an adequate answer. Therefore something is missing. We need to let other views help explain how we arrived here. *Passing the Heavenly Gift* provides a better answer to the questions than the traditional narrative. Even if you decide it is not persuasive, it offers another view to be considered to explain how we got where we are now.

Interpreting History, Part 3

I believe in Mormonism and want it to succeed. I am cheering for our success. I evaluated it as an investigator while taught by missionaries, and received a spiritual impression sufficient to believe in the religion. So I joined. After joining I studied the faith. A spiritual impression was not enough for me. The impression was the beginning, not the end, of the inquiry. Then the new found faith needed to be scoured to find what it offered, what great truths it held, and what mysteries were now available. Therefore, its history needed to become part of my study and inquiry.

Mormonism has an important history that has been little explored even now. Its history should be celebrated, not cautiously guarded. The history contains wonderful lessons that will aid in moving the faith forward. But to do so it must be based on a truthful telling. You cannot create the kingdom of heaven from a foundation of lies. So history must be faced, even if it proves temporarily painful and disorienting while sorting through the errors.

Toward the end of the Jensen interview someone asked him about problems of history and mentioned his own struggle. He explained that new data-points had been disorienting to him. He had to work his way through them to emerge with faith once again. The question was more than illuminating. It was an honest Latter-day Saint who had triumphed in retaining faith in the face of troubling historic truths. This is an issue at two levels.

First, when mistakes are discovered, they require you to adjust what you believe to take into account the new information. This is work. It requires effort to sort out incorrect or false information from the information that is correct. Some ideas about your religion must now be adjusted, adapted or abandoned. It can be painful. But what emerges from the experience is better than what you started with.

Second, and perhaps much more formidable an issue is that you discover the church is not reliable on some important details of its history. You are forced to grapple with the realization that some of the people you've respected, even admired, either did not tell the truth or were ignorant of the truth. Whether they were dishonest or just mistaken, it is painful. No one wants a hero to fall. When the heroes are thought to be God's agents, true prophets, bona-fide revelators, and you discover they didn't know what they were doing the fall leaves a choking cloud of dust behind. You have to emerge from that cloud with your faith in God intact.

When stripping truth from error, we all need to be careful not to throw away perfectly sound truths because of our disgust at the errors. It is better still if you can be compassionate about the errors rather than disgusted. Unfortunately, human nature is such that we tend to start with disgust and only proceed to compassion after we've lived long enough to have failed repeatedly ourselves. Our own humiliating defeats permit us to gain a sense of perspective regarding other people's failings. Compassion grows from our injuries.

Marlin Jensen's questioner was stating his faith while asking about the possibility of broader acceptance of more accurate history by the church itself. The question is now before us all. Whether you study church history or you just see a spreading crisis of faith among your fellow ward members, it is now before you. We are all in the same dreadful mix.

What is to be done? Are we going to adopt an increasingly militant and cloistered defense of our myths? Are we going to purge our ranks so we are left only with a small handful of intensely devoted believers in faith-promoting errors? Will we become the church of Paul Dunn? Or will we allow some to search deeply into the history and reach new conclusions? Will we allow those who have different, and perhaps more well informed conclusions to teach? To defend their understanding? To speak in sacrament meetings and present new ideas to the rest of us? Will we open up general conference to allow discussion openly of the many problems of inaccurate church history? Will we break apart?

Our history is too central a matter for it to be co-opted by a central hierarchy intent on limiting, packaging and controlling the truth rather than revealing the truth. We will save the church and our own souls if we are only interested in knowing truth. There should be an eager openness about it all. The restoration of the Gospel is too wonderful a matter to be reduced to lies. We should all fight against that. It *will* survive. It will be vindicated. God did originate this process. It is His work, and fear does not change that.

I'll return to two great problems with Mormons and our history in Part 4.

Interpreting History, Part 4

Two great obstacles in Mormon history are institutional lying and inner secrets. Both have been built into our faith. When Joseph Smith was confronted with plural marriage in a society that would be scandalized by such a practice, he hid it from public view. We all know the public statements and even scriptural declarations about marriage between a man and one wife were belied by the private practice of Joseph Smith. Therefore, our religion's history starts with a gap in telling the truth. We accept the fact that church leaders, beginning with Joseph Smith, lied to the public. There was an "inside" story and a "public" story. This is a problem for Mormon history.

Second, any Latter-day Saint who has been through the temple is aware there are things we regard as sacred that we just don't talk about. We keep secrets. Our faith reaches its deepest meaning in an atmosphere of secrecy and hidden knowledge.

When these two parts of the faith are present, it creates a challenge to telling our history in a frank, forthright and true manner. You must create filters in your analysis to account for the presence of these two skewing factors. One of the most significant historic disputes between the RLDS (Community of Christ) and the LDS church arises from this very problem. Emma taught Joseph Smith III (and her other children) that their father never practiced plural marriage. So when "young Joseph" came west, he was shocked by the stories and thought (at least initially) that the Utah Mormons were lying. Emma used well known public statements of Joseph denouncing "polygamy" as well as several canonized statements on the subject to support her claim that Joseph never took other wives. To reconcile it all a person must come to grips with the fact that Joseph Smith was not telling the truth to the public. There are echoes of this disparity still today.

Plural marriage caused the hierarchy to lie to the public. They did it when plural marriage was both coming and going. It was practiced in private, shielded from public view and shrouded in lies, both before it was acknowledged in 1853 and after it was publicly abandoned by the Manifesto in 1890. The Manifesto was a public relations document intended to hide the fact the church was continuing the practice. There are too many available sources now in public to claim otherwise. But the adoption of Official Declaration 1 makes it awkward to admit the practice continued. So most church members are unaware that it continued in secret even after the Manifesto.

Oddly, neither Joseph Smith nor the church itself could pass a temple recommend interview. ("Are you honest in your dealings with your fellow man?") Any faithful Latter-day Saint with just a small amount of knowledge about our history knows the church and its leaders have been less than honest in the past to prevent the public from knowing what they were doing.

In saying that I want to be clear. I am not condemning the church. There were sufficient reasons for these public dis-information campaigns, and there has been a theological justification used to defend the practice. The church has pointed out that Abraham said Sarah was his "sister" rather than to candidly acknowledge she was his wife. But the theological implications are not what this line of discussion is about. So I'm leaving that topic unaddressed.

The bottom line is that when you attempt to unravel the church's history, you must contend with the fact that the church has a history of dissembling. They publish lies to prevent embarrassment or prosecution. You must include a filter, or detector, or whatever you want to describe it as, in order to arrive at the underlying truth.

The idea something is "sacred" is also important in understanding our history. It has been used to compensate for missing revelation. At one extreme the leaders are thought to meet regularly (every Thursday) with Jesus Christ in the Temple. Under this happy view, the leaders are never wrong because they're just doing what Jesus says each Thursday. To suggest this may not be the case is so foreign a concept to these people that anyone who does so is weak in the faith and on the road to apostasy. Therefore, you must also account for the mythical elevation of leadership through the "too sacred to discuss" veil which makes honest analysis difficult and emotionally charged.

These are two great challenges to anyone trying to know the truth. Any person seeking to understand our history must account for both as they evaluate the events.

Interpreting History, Part 5

In the search through our history, at some point you must reach conclusions on events. The weight of the evidence accumulates and you reach a conclusion. Your conclusion may be different than mine. Each of us is free to find something persuasive and believe it. But we all must make our minds up about the events.

The evidence you find convincing may be based on what a single person had to say. Even if there are fourteen witnesses saying something else, you may choose to believe a single witness telling a story you are willing to accept as the truth. The reasons for that are personal. For example, your own great-grandmother may have told a story that was handed down within the family and now you cherish that version of the events because it was told to you when you were a child by people you love. Other proof may never convince you otherwise because you have an emotional need to believe that story. For you to think otherwise would feel tantamount to rejection of your own family.

However, suppose you learn that the great-grandmother's story originated with the popular retelling of an earlier event. The actual event was in the 1840's but it was popular to retell it in a much more inspirational way some twenty years after the event, in the 1860's. The push to belong among the saints was so compelling they began to compete with one another to embellish the retelling. As a result the story grew well beyond anything that was recorded contemporaneous with the actual event. Even after learning this, you may still resist changing your view because you worry it makes your great-grandmother a liar. It really does no such thing. Her faith produced a culture. She lived inside that culture. The culture encouraged her to say faith-promoting things like others in the culture. She succumbed to the temptation, joined in the recasting of the event, and it helped secure both her own faith and the beliefs of her children. Your life and your parents' were all enriched by the story.

But when it comes to your understanding of history, something more than traditions ought to at least be considered. If that is impossible for you, then at a minimum you must allow others who do not share your great-grandmother in their genealogy to explore the question and reach their own conclusion. You can believe as you do for the reasons you find convincing, but others should not be required to join you. They do not share your emotional need to believe the retelling, and therefore ought to be free to consider other sources. What we all share, however, is faith in the religion. We all believe this is a true faith restored by God through the Prophet Joseph Smith. I can have tolerance for your view and your needs, but you should permit me to believe as I do. My beliefs should not threaten you. Yours do not threaten me. I freely allow you to hold onto the family tradition, and respect the value that has provided your family. I am a convert. There are no family traditions I need to honor when it comes to Latter-day Saint history. I am not being negative when I think differently than you. Instead I am honestly trying to grapple with the events to reach my own conclusion about the truth. When I read the fourteen other witnesses I may disregard the one you believe.

As people of good faith attempt to retell Mormon history, there will always be events some people view differently than others. For example in Richard Van Wagoner's book *Sidney Rigdon: A Portrait of Religious Excess*, he puts Joseph and Sidney into the underground Danite movement in Missouri. I was surprised he did that. I don't agree and thought he was wrong, but I don't for a minute doubt he believed his conclusion.

Since Sampson Avard's testimony before the Court of Inquiry was not believed by even the hostile anti-Mormon crowd, I discount him as a reliable source. He was trying to save his own skin. He was like a jailhouse snitch who got free for telling a lurid tale about another prisoner. Motivation, background, overall credibility and inconsistency make him an unreliable source to me. Sampson Avard was the primary mover behind the Danite group. He had a great interest in pushing Joseph and Sidney forward and retreating into the shadows. His story did that. I don't believe him.

This issue illustrates how difficult it is to weigh the evidence and reach the right conclusion. When someone as good as Van Wagoner reaches this conclusion, any fair-minded person needs to consider his evidence. I checked his footnotes, considered his arguments, rethought the matter and found I was not persuaded. I kept my view that Joseph Smith was not involved and was the victim of a perjured witness in the Missouri court proceedings. If someone else chooses to believe it, that is up to them. It certainly complicates Joseph Smith's story. It does not utterly compromise it. The primary effect it would have, in my view, is that Joseph learned from the Missouri disaster that a violent response to the church's enemies was a very bad idea. He never did it again. When the next crisis arose in Nauvoo, he surrendered the Nauvoo Legion state arms and surrendered to the authorities. He did not use his army to protect his followers.

So the choice is between what I believe (i.e., that Joseph was already pre-disposed to avoid violent reactions) and Van Wagoner's view (i.e., that Joseph attempted violence through the Danites before learning that violence was not useful). Either way the final lesson is the same. I believe mine is more consistent with Joseph's overall behavior and character, both during Zion's Camp and later in Nauvoo. Van Wagoner has Joseph fluctuating in between. But there is no real meaningful difference to the alternatives.

What this issue illustrates, however, is that the matter has been out there since 1838 and remains unsettled and open for debate and discussion today. The discussion is very interesting. More information will undoubtedly arise as more of the church's archives are made available to read. Hiding the information does not alter the truth, it only temporarily hides it. Those who distrust our leaders, resolve all questions by claiming the failure to open the complete historical records to public view is evidence there will be incriminating things found there. That argument no doubt has some weight to it, but on this point of Joseph Smith's Danite involvement I very much doubt there's a hidden "smoking gun" to be found in unopened archival material.

The Jensen interview ended on a troubling note to me. He explained the Church History Department was a tool for the "fifteen men" and ultimately "the Prophet" to direct. The Department was going to act in conformity with their desires, and would not proceed as an independent source of historical information. That aside puts the problem of candor and motivation back to the fore. It makes absolute sense the Church History Department supports the church's leadership. However, for anyone interested in a full disclosure, you must remember that the Church History Department acts as an agent controlled by a group whose agenda is not always to let history be told in less than a "faith promoting" way. They feel the responsibility of promoting faith. That is natural. They don't want to challenge people's faith by letting out any ugliness. It risks turning the Department into the purveyor of propaganda, rather than history.

This may have worked well in the past, but in the age of the Internet there are leaks. It is all coming out. It will be better for the church to take the initiative than to let it just slip out through inadvertence. If Mitt Romney is the candidate, and even more so if he becomes the President, there will be pressure from the media, perhaps even efforts to pay church employees for copies of previously undisclosed documents. Who knows what will occur in the future to empty the vaults of the hidden materials. The recent dust-up over the *Joseph Smith Papers* draft volume on plural marriage between an apostle and the staff working on the project is now known by a wide group. To their credit both Dallin Oaks and Jeffrey Holland were supportive of the effort. Another member of the twelve was scandalized by it, thinking the church membership was unprepared to read the material. It will all be out there eventually. Those who advocate candor will be respected in the future, and those who insist on secrecy will be less so.

Nothing will remain hidden. Even if the Lord is the one who does it, the day will come when it will all be "shouted from the rooftops" and every hidden thing will be revealed. It will be too late to acquit yourself if you've been one hiding the truth. Better to do it now, before the coming forced confession.

Interpreting History, Part 6

There will always be those who are skeptical about our history. Converting someone to believe (a process I underwent to become LDS), cannot proceed without facing critical examination of the stories. On occasion I think about what would have happened if I were investigating the church's claims today for the first time. Without question I would use the Internet to check what the missionaries were telling me. Given the fact that I would have to decide whether to believe this new faith, and the troubling perception our critics urge that it is being offered by a Fortune 500 corporation, I do not think I would trust anything on the church's own website. I think I would avoid considering that until I had first been convinced of the missionaries' message.

I think my approach would be typical. There's nothing more troubling to someone thinking about changing their religion than the risk of being duped by foolish believers in some nonsensical cult. And like it or not, Mormonism is thought of in those terms. I know. I've been there, but I came aboard in the days of flannel board missionary lessons and computers driven by punch cards. There was no Wikipedia or Google. The world changed. So Mormonism must face down the challenges of widespread information. This information challenges the traditional stories and presents very different views of the events. Missionaries must be able to overcome these many honest questions. I'm certain today I would ask a good deal more than what I asked in 1973. Church members also must become part of the solution.

When a prospective convert comes to hear our lessons, observe our meetings, and talk with our members they come equipped with a body of questions arising from the acidic environment of the Internet. Every omission in our story can become the stumbling block to accepting the challenge to convert. I would never have prayed and

asked God if Mormonism was true until after first inspecting enough
of the Mormons to determine they were sound people. Sound in
their lives, marriages and teaching. The "weirdness gauge" was employed. Any strange, aberrant behavior would have sent the alarm
sounding and I would have been unwilling to proceed further; but I
found the church quite likable. Understand I did *not* want the Mormons to be likable. I wanted to dismiss them, and continue on with
my happy life. However, they satisfied the initial concerns enough
that I was willing to consider it seriously.

Today, when asked about troubling matters, every Mormon
should to be able to show the faith in a positive light. In a very real
way the only progress we can hope to make in today's environment
will come through an educated population of believers. Myths and
half-truths may be "inspirational" and keep immature faith around
for a while, but sooner or later the acid of today's information age
will burn away anything that is not gold. We have tens-of-thousands
of adults now leaving the church after having spent their lives believing Mormonism. They are discovering the information exists to challenge every step of our faith, from Joseph Smith's youth to the 1978
revelation on priesthood. Members are vulnerable and they are leaving. The problem is already well underway. What we've been doing
with our history has not prepared us for what is now happening.

Confining the church's educational efforts to "faith promoting"
stories may have been enough in the 1950's through the year 2000,
but it is absolutely not enough now. If the church insists that this
must continue, then the church will become a tiny organization of
myth believers who cloister together and repeat endlessly a litany
of imaginative stories. That is the course we are on at the moment.
The great apostasy underway is because the environment changed.
The church's opinion polling and focus group testing is not adequate
to adapt to the real challenges. The real challenges are to undergo the

rigors of opening the history up to deal forthrightly with our past. The church needs to undergo a metamorphosis into the most open, most candid, most self-critical and inviting faith on earth. We must allow ideas to be expressed in an environment of tolerance and learning. Militant insistence on following a centrally produced lesson manual as an unyielding standard will not be enough. People are walking out of those classes. Either they are turned off and mentally checking out, or they are physically leaving. This is not their fault. They cannot control the fact they are bored.

What is almost impossible to accomplish has been accomplished by the central planners of Mormonism. The most exciting thing in the world is to learn new truth. Nothing is quite as delightful as finding new truths. *The Gospel contains all truth.* Our lessons and meetings should be celebrations of truth. Instead they have become wary gatherings of fearful people who are on the lookout for unorthodox comments. Some feel Mormon meetings are held inside a police-state. The central planners are fearful of new ideas. They guard against freedom of thought precisely because they are living in a bunker, trying to uphold a dishonest or incomplete history. It will not work. We must openly discuss our history. We must return to delighting in the doctrine. The Gospel is wonderful, not oppressive. It is not mere tradition to be guarded or defended. It is Christ's message of love and hope for all mankind.

Our history has influenced who we call to leadership positions because it has affected what the leaders responsibilities are. They *must* administer a far-flung corporate empire with almost unmanageable human resources challenges. Budgets, staffing, property management, liability management, accounting, banking and legal concerns are overwhelming. These are the realities of the top leadership's job. It is the result of the events in phase 2 and 3, and the explosive growth in phase 4. There aren't many mystics available in our ranks who have enough banking, accounting, legal, business management or personnel competence to occupy the present leadership responsibilities. That is a product of the church's history. But it is also the church's present reality.

The church itself has a great challenge now directly bearing down on it. I sympathize and lend my prayers to its success. The struggle will require perhaps more from it than the church is willing to change. One great advantage grows out of one of the church's apparent weaknesses. We elevate to the highest position a man who is almost always elderly, frail and beyond the age of most unhealthy appetites. Such a man will consider carefully his proximity to the judgments of God, and likely will be willing to do what is right, even if painful.

Interpreting History, Part 7

The topic of our history becomes even more challenging when it is overlaid with emotion and fear. Since the study of Mormonism is also the study of what will save your soul, we associate grave importance to being "right" about things. Therefore, when we make up our mind about a storyline, we defend that story against any challenges offering another view.

As is apparent from the last question posed to Marlin Jensen in the interview referred to previously, there are painful adjustments involved in going back into your belief system, taking part of it down, or adding something new, and then adjusting everything else to accommodate the new data. It is upsetting. We don't like to unsettle what we thought was settled. This is why once a tradition takes hold it is almost impossible to make changes to it.

In the Book of Mormon, the word "tradition" or the phrase "traditions of the fathers" is almost always used in a negative way. Do a word study yourself and see how "tradition" is used. That is one of the Book of Mormon's warnings to us. We have to be very cautious about accepting something as true because it came to us through tradition. *Every one of us needs to be converted to the truth.*

Also, the "converts" in the Book of Mormon were almost always religious apostates. They had been part of the truth and fallen away. Notice how the splinter groups who were converted were almost without exception being re-converted. From the macro-level (with the Lamanites) to the micro-level (with the Zoramites—who were dissenters from the Nephites[1601]), the missionary effort was to bring believers back to the truth. These apostates were religious. They were firm believers in all kinds of religious ideas handed to them through incorrect traditions.

Our story is similar to the Nephite story. It has been marked by traditions that have time and again discarded what we were originally given through Joseph Smith, and are foundational to the restoration. To go into our history is to discover wonderful, exciting things that were once taught, but now are either slowly or quickly being lost. We need to ask why they were lost? If they belonged in the first place, why did we discard them? When Joseph introduced the teachings and claimed they were from God, why did we fail to preserve them? Did we lose them because we heard from God and He said, "don't do that," or "don't believe that anymore?" Was it because we were jarred from our settled places in Kirtland and Nauvoo, and in the forced migrations had a hard enough time retaining part of our religion? Is our forgetfulness perfectly understandable?

To be able to discuss this openly we need to stop reacting with emotion and fear at the thought of the discussion. We can go back and consider what happened and suspend judgment about the correct narrative until we have studied and discussed the matters more fully. It should be fun. It should be wonderful. It should excite us,

---

[1601] Alma 31:8 "Now the Zoramites were dissenters from the Nephites; therefore they had had the word of God preached unto them."

but instead we fear it. That is not healthy and will only preserve a continuing dwindling tradition of the faith. The process of Correlation has enshrined the process of dwindling. Go to the Book of Mormon and look up "unbelief" and you'll find it almost invariably associated with "dwindling." That is, the apostates of the Book of Mormon got out of line with the Lord because they "dwindled in unbelief." They lost truths they were supposed to have remembered. Look at the word "remember" in the Book of Mormon and you'll also find it is a very important principle. How can we ever avoid dwindling and be able to remember if we fear a close scrutiny of our history? They go hand in hand. Once again the Book of Mormon proves to be the "keystone of our religion" because it bravely faces the very problems we are currently struggling with but are afraid to discuss openly. We fear what the Book of Mormon expects us to discuss.

If you love your faith, you will allow it to inform you. You will not fight against it and only look at part of it. If you insist it can only conform to your present notions, then you do not really believe the religion at all. You only want to hold to your traditions. You are like the Book of Mormon apostates who have dwindled in unbelief because they refused to remember the original faith given to them by the Lord. None of us should want that. Open discussion should not threaten Latter-day Saints. Nor should those who are willing to engage in the discussion be called apostates or wolves in sheep's clothing. That only ensures we will continue to ignore problems, and as a result of ignoring see a collapse in church membership.

We should be open to discussing our history in our church meetings. We should not be afraid. The discussion itself is healthy even if nothing changes in the lives of most saints. It will leave them better informed and allow those who are struggling a safe place to voice concerns and help find answers. At present, our church meetings are pretty hostile to the whole history discussion. We tolerate only centrally approved propaganda which some good-hearted people have found to be more fiction than fact. The people who view it as fiction shouldn't be renounced for their honest questions. Instead they deserve answers from a friendly, open church.

Interpreting History, Part 8

When you come to understand something in our history as an actual event then you need to understand the event. What are its details? How important are differing accounts? If there are contradictions among witnesses, how are they harmonized? When you've sorted through the material and arrived at the most accurate version, what does the incident mean? If you change the details does the meaning change?

In the King Follett Discourse, for example, there were several note-takers who left accounts of the sermon. Most people are acquainted with this talk through *The Teachings of the Prophet Joseph Smith*. That version is an amalgamation of the various notes of those who were present. In compiling the consolidated version, some of the trimming and harmonizing left details out of the final transcript that may be important. Almost all of the notes from that day have been gathered by Andrew Ehat and Lyndon Cook in their book *The Words of Joseph Smith*. That very valuable book allows you compare what one person preserved of the talk with what another person preserved. The contrasts are important and make actual doctrinal differences.

If you are content with the *TPJS* version and have developed some of your religious views based on it, then discovering that it may have omitted details from Joseph's talk may alarm you. You must decide whether you want to know what Joseph actually said, and perhaps what he actually meant, or if you are only interested in keeping what you already believe.

Many people "feel" the truth. They determine what they believe by how it makes them feel. Their "truth detector" is not rational, but intuitive. I've been involved in litigation for long enough to realize there is an irrational component to every conclusion we make. Despite the effort to be rational, we always have our personal filters and our hidden biases. Humans are rational, but not entirely so. Therefore this "feel" for truth happens in us all. Malcom Gladwell has written several books exploring this trait.

The challenge is to control your impulse to come to a conclusion about something before you let all the available information develop. You may come to a conclusion that you can defend rationally and emotionally, but it may not be true. If, instead, you suspend your impulse to decide something and let information expand, you may still reach the same conclusion, but it will be deeper, richer and more complete.

I've found that since my conversion, the simple stories told in 1973 have remained basically intact. But they are now much more complex, more nuanced, poignant, and wonderful. Sometimes it has been painful to approach a new and expanded account of familiar events. D. Michael Quinn's work has sometimes left me wondering how he could make such mistakes. But I've never doubted the impressive, even amazing capacity he has for gathering information and adding new sources to tell the stories of our history. He is valuable and almost irreplaceable as a pioneer in moving our understanding of Mormon history forward. I still disagree with some of his conclusions, but I respect and admire his work. Some of what I originally thought were mistakes by him I now find I accept and believe to be true.

It made me nervous to read some of Quinn's work at first. I was afraid I would encounter something that would break my heart and show there was nothing to this faith I had adopted as my own. That would be difficult for me. I stared down that dark corridor and decided to proceed anyway. As I did there were painful moments, and anxiety-filled nights. I know the bitterness expressed by some of the people who have fallen away from our faith and now are vocal critics. If Mormonism is a fraud and I was certain of it I would also probably express a vocal opposition to it. Therefore, if that is their conclusion, they are coping with their sense of loss by venting. I understand it. I was willing to risk it too. But my faith has remained intact.

I still believe God spoke to young Joseph Smith, and that Oliver Cowdery, David Whitmer and Martin Harris saw the angel Moroni and the gold plates. I've also very much appreciated the "apostasy" of both Cowdery and Whitmer and their post-church affiliation writings. They remained true to their testimony as witnesses of the Book of Mormon, even if they left the church. That enhances their credibility in my view. In my opinion, if they hadn't seen the plates and the angel, they would have denounced Joseph as a fraud after they were disaffected toward him.

These three witnesses make a formidable obstacle to dismissing Joseph Smith. As a result, there have been efforts to diminish the significance of their testimony. I think the best summary of the reasons to question their testimony can be found in Grant Palmer's book *An Insider's View of Mormon Origins*. He does a good job of putting together the best way to disregard the Three Witnesses' Testimony. But his work is entirely derivative from other critics and therefore you need to begin with Palmer and work your way back through the footnotes to the earlier stuff to arrive at the point of departure. In the case of his book, I was already acquainted with his sources and therefore found nothing new in it. The approach is basically to discount the idea of "second sight" and to "spiritualize" away the event. For me it was not a problem. I've seen angels. I've been taught by them. I know what the experience is like. Therefore, I know what the challenge is to convert the otherworldly into this-worldly. That other world is more real and even more concrete than this. But it isn't here. It is more tangible, but not the same as what we experience here. Joseph taught about "shaking an angel's hand"[1602] so you can know it is possible to touch and feel them. They are tangible. But if you're quickened and they are quickened then it is not like this place. So how do you make it possible for someone else to understand. Paul says "whether in the body or out I cannot tell"[1603] and that's a pretty good way to put it. He just couldn't tell. Because it is concrete even if you want to say you saw it with "spiritual eyes." So Grant Palmer takes those statements and turns them into the ephemeral, then into imagination, and dismisses the Testimony of the Three Witnesses. In that way he hoped to evade the Book of Mormon by turning it into a work of fiction. None of that persuaded me. I know better. Not only do I have experience in studying history, and the lives of Cowdery, Whitmer and Harris, but also in comparing other scriptures and experiences of Paul, Daniel, Joseph, Abraham, Enoch, Moses, and so many others. In addition to all the rest I have personal experience.

On the matter of "feeling" things to be true and right, we should not be hasty about closing the door on additional information. New information may change your view dramatically, and then with the new insights you will "feel" right about another, better informed view. When you deal with less information you may think in your heart that everything is just as you believe it to be; only to later find that good-faith belief was sadly under-informed or misinformed. You can only proceed on the basis of what you know, and never on the basis of what you do not know. This is why our good-faith critics

---

[1602] D&C 129:4–5 "When a messenger comes saying he has a message from God, offer him your hand and request him to shake hands with you. If he be an angel he will do so, and you will feel his hand."

[1603] 2 Corinthians 12:3 "And I knew such a man, (whether in the body, or out of the body, I cannot tell: God knoweth;)"

who advance honest objections are not evil. They even raise questions we should ask ourselves and try to provide an honest answer.

I do not believe it is possible to acquire the faith necessary to arrive at the truth unless you are willing to know the truth. I believe that history is intended to be a test of faith and we bar ourselves from heaven and heavenly messengers through our fears. Fear is the opposite of faith.

All I've written has been done in the hope I can increase faith in others. I understand why I have been denounced, accused of being apostate, and had claims that I'm disrespectful of the church authorities. It is always easy to allow your fears to interpret my motives. But I can tell you that I hope to save souls. The way I write is intended to accomplish that end. If it were possible to do it in any other way I would do it differently. But I don't intend to be popular. I only want the Lord to approve what I've been able to do with what I've been given.

Interpreting History, Part 9

History and doctrine are linked. To alter history is to alter doctrine. You can see the links throughout scripture. Just one example from the New Testament illustrates the point:

Jesus was confronted by the Pharisee lawyers and accused of breaking the law. He and His disciples had taken plucked wheat (labor of harvesting), then rubbed them in their hands (threshing), and eaten it on the Sabbath. (Luke 6:1–2.) As His explanation Jesus reminded the accusers of an earlier incident involving King David and his men. They had eaten the showbread which, under the law, was forbidden to be eaten by any but a priest. (Luke 6:3–4.) This incident involving David was the precedent Jesus pointed to as justification. (1 Samuel 21:1–6.) The law said only Aaron and his descendants could eat this bread. (Leviticus 24:5–9.) However, Jesus relied on an incident from history to justify His and the disciples' conduct. If the history showed it could be done, then Jesus questioned the "righteousness" of complaining about the matter.

There are hundreds of other examples to draw from, but this illustrates the point. History is the mill whose grist is the stuff from which we construct doctrine. It matters. If we do not comprehend it, we cannot sort through the dangling statements that get tossed about unanchored. We do not understand their original real meaning. One of the problems of fourth phase Mormonism is the apparent corruption of our vocabulary. We use the same words as the first phase, but we have adopted altogether different meanings for them. Meaning arises from context. Context comes from history.

Joseph gazed into heaven for more than five minutes. He knew more than if you had read everything that had ever been written on the subject (*TPJS*, 324). He was succeeded by Brigham Young, who lamented he had never seen an angel or entertained a heavenly being. Therefore, it is important to study Brigham Young's qualifications in contrast to Joseph Smith's qualifications. If you understand Joseph had the heavens opened to him a number of times, including several audiences with both the Father and Son, you put Joseph's remarks into one category. If you understand that Brigham Young never had a similar experience, then you put Brigham Young's into another category. When Joseph is contradicted by Brigham, the first effort should be to reconcile or attempt to harmonize the two men's statements. If you cannot reconcile them with one another, you can use the knowledge you have about each of them to choose which one you will rely on. The same would also be true of others. We study the history to learn what the qualifications are/were for any of God's chosen leaders, what God showed to them, whether the heavens have opened to them, and exactly what they knew, or did not know when they contradict Joseph.

History must be true to be useful. If it is inaccurate or incomplete we can reach one conclusion only to find we have made a mistake because there was much more (or less) to the event. The events on August 8, 1844 are critical. If there was a transfiguration of Brigham Young on that day, then we can assume God was directly involved in solving the succession dilemma. If there was no transfiguration of Brigham, then God was not directly involved, and the outcome is a product of our common consent and still binding on the saints. Although binding, if the transfiguration did not happen, then the "precedent" is administrative and voluntary, and not a sign of God's desire to have the precedent followed forever thereafter. It is nothing more than an agreement among the saints on how to proceed.

This is important. Before June 27, 1844, the question of who would succeed Joseph Smith as the church president was known. Joseph's successor would be Hyrum Smith, but Hyrum died with Joseph. Before June 27th, the question of what was to be done upon the death of both Joseph and Hyrum was never contemplated. There was no answer to the question.

In the debates of August 8th no one urged the provisions of Section 107 as a revealed outcome for succession. The language of that revelation has since become the scriptural basis for how we proceed, but it was not thought to be relevant in the first debate over succession. Section 107 is anything but a definite answer to the question. If you adopt our system, and then use 107 to justify our system, it seems to fit, but there is another, more relevant solution found elsewhere. D&C 43:3–4 was used to appoint Hyrum Smith to succeed Joseph.[1604] The appointment was made by revelation in Section

---

[1604] D&C 43:3–4 "And this ye shall know assuredly—that there is none other appointed unto you to receive commandments and revelations until he be taken, if he abide in me. But verily, verily, I say unto you, that none else shall be appointed unto this gift except it be through him; for if it be taken from him he shall not have power except to appoint another in his stead."

124.[1605] This was the scriptural pattern, and the pattern followed in the case of Hyrum.

Brigham Young's arguments at the time were not as clear about succession as we have made them by our adopting the method of apostolic succession based on seniority. Brigham Young admitted that Joseph Smith's sons had a right to be the church's leader and he was only a caretaker awaiting their development. He explained that since they had never converted to the church, they were not able to lead, and so he served in their absence.

History and the scriptures allow for a different method for succession. In the final analysis it is nothing more than the common consent of the church that has elected Brigham Young and all his successors to the offices they have held. Our last descendant of Hyrum Smith, occupying the office of Patriarch to the Church, is now 105 years old, emeritus, and not likely to be succeeded when he passes. The Smith Family male line will be out of the top level of the hierarchy. Of course, there are female line descendants who are there, including Elder Ballard. But direct male line descendants are gone or will be when the Patriarch Emeritus passes on.

Does that matter? What was the point of having that office? Was it important to the church's organization? Why was Hyrum the successor to Joseph? Why did Brigham Young expect a son of Joseph to come and preside over the church? Does history shed any light on these questions? Do they even matter? What purpose was originally served and does that purpose remain today? Why was the Patriarch sustained as a "prophet, seer and revelator" in general conference

---

[1605] D&C 124:94–95 "And from this time forth I appoint unto him that he may be a prophet, and a seer, and a revelator unto my church, as well as my servant Joseph; That he may act in concert also with my servant Joseph; and that he shall receive counsel from my servant Joseph, who shall show unto him the keys whereby he may ask and receive, and be crowned with the same blessing, and glory, and honor, and priesthood, and gifts of the priesthood, that once were put upon him that was my servant Oliver Cowdery;"

right up until he was made emeritus? Could a general conference sustain him as the church's president, or does the system presently preclude anyone other than the nominees of the sitting president from being considered? Why did the local congregations once choose their own bishops? When did that change? Why did it change? Does the original history matter? Once we give common consent to what is done, are we accountable for the changes that occur?

There are a lot of interesting history-based questions that could be explored. But the questions themselves require us to study something that no longer even gets mentioned.

Interpreting History, Part 10 Conclusion

Seriously studying history allows us to recognize unresolved issues or to fix our errors. With a superficial knowledge of our history we risk making presumptions and missing the mark, or risk not even recognizing there are errors to what we believe today. Isn't the subject of our religion and its beginnings important enough to want to carefully examine it?

The mission of Elijah is so important to the wrapping up of God's strange act that the prophecy about his return before the great and dreadful day of the Lord appears in every volume of scripture. From the Old Testament to the Pearl of Great Price, it is mentioned repeatedly.

When we discover Joseph Smith speaking of Elijah's return as a future event in 1844, we get our first hint that our current doctrine on the subject may need further examination. However, if we only know the popular story borne out of Orson Pratt's analysis in the *Deseret Evening News* of D&C 110 when it was found and first published, then raising the issue seems unnecessary. Since you think you know the truth already, a reexamination seems stupid. Do you look into the matter, and risk discovering there have been historic, and therefore, doctrinal errors made for 160 years on Elijah's mission? Do you think this is important enough to study it again?

We are the subject and object of many Book of Mormon prophecies. Some of them hold us up in a rather negative light. They seem to suggest we are riddled with mistakes and errors. That we have gone far astray, and are being led to err in many instances. Those prophecies do not trouble us, however, if we accept the self-vindicating narrative that we've been headed in the right direction all along.

One of the things that helps orient an historical analysis is the language of scripture. If the scriptures warn us against thinking all is well in our version of Zion, and tells us to never resist hearing more of the word of God, and further tells us (repeatedly) not to trust the arm of flesh, what does this mean? We have a popular account of events that more or less suggests all is well. We are God's chosen. We have the power to save ourselves. We have a great body of revelation to guide us and don't need much revelation anymore. And some of what Joseph Smith talked about we don't really know much about and aren't sure we believe anyway. We are safe, and the odds are we'll all be exalted. Those ideas are the polar opposite of what the Book of Mormon says about us. Should the Book of Mormon provide us the themes to apply to our history, or do they not matter at all? If we allow the Book of Mormon to inform the dialogue, then do we reconcile the disparity between our claims and the prophetic text by re-looking at our history, or instead merely by trusting we are led that in no instance do we currently err?

People of good faith, who believe in Mormonism, can differ in their conclusions about matters. Those differences are not signs of apostasy or evil. They are, in fact, healthy. They ought to be the source from which stimulating discussion and deep thought comes. An unexamined and superficial belief system is always vulnerable to collapse. A thoughtful and reflective believer does not fly to pieces when something new is told to them. They are already acquainted with the idea and practice of prayerfully and through personal revelation considering and reconsidering their faith. New ideas do not cause despair, but become part of the normal process for them. They consider, suspend judgment, study, reflect, pray and then reach a careful conclusion. The conclusion is put into the larger framework and any necessary adjustments are considered, adapted or corrected, and faith improves. This process is allowed to work over and over as they explore their faith more deeply.

The environment of Mormonism is not conducive to healthy discussion at the moment. Correlation and the need for central control has preempted the kind of healthy intellectual inquiry that is needed to solve the present crisis of apostasy. History should be allowed to be merely our true, unembellished, unprotected history. Not a tool for propaganda used by central planners to accomplish a desired end. Using it that way in an information-based society invites the disaster presently unfolding.

I believe in Mormonism. I cherish the faith. It is vibrant and resilient. It does not need institutional protection—borne out of fear. Efforts to protect have, in fact, injured the faith and discredited this approach.

History matters. May we allow it to become the source of truth informing our open discussions, rather than a tool to be manipulate and manage people. Managing people is a dark enterprise. Inform them and allow them the freedom to choose to govern themselves. That is what the Prophet Joseph Smith did. The mere ambition to control people is the beginning of a dark trail that leads to the imprisonment of souls. Not just those who are the targets, but more importantly the souls of those with the ambition. It should be repugnant to anyone claiming to be a saint to allow anyone to control them. Unless they are willing to retain for themselves their right to choose, and then exercise their choice in a responsible and well informed way, they deceive themselves. Saints are made of sterner stuff. They do not recoil from the obligation, difficulty, pain and work necessary to have their minds mirror the mind of God. Surrendering to other men the responsibility devolving on yourself will never happen. But, then again, mankind rarely produces a saint.

Vanity and pride are no substitute for sainthood. Arrogance and flattery from leaders will not produce a saint either. It comes from man reaching up to God, and God answering the honest petition of the humble soul, reaching down to him. Contact with God will inevitably lead to sainthood. False ideas and incomplete or misleading history will prevent that contact from happening.

IT WAS ALREADY LIKE THIS WHEN WE FOUND IT...

Marlin Jensen's Last Answer

The last question put to Marlin Jensen began with the questioner retelling his own struggle to adjust his beliefs after discovering new information in our history. The "new data points" required him to change his understanding. He was asking for a more broadminded approach that would allow open discussion of troubling history in church meetings.

The answer given by Marlin Jensen was very interesting and raises another matter about current church decision-making. When the idea of broadmindedness was raised in the context of church history, Bro. Jensen responded by speaking about homosexuality. Church history was gone, and instead his mind turned to the need for tolerance—and that meant homosexuals. It was almost a complete disconnect of topics, but quite important to understanding the internal discussion underway at the top of the church presently.

This apparent change-of-subject shows how important the present "tolerance of homosexuality" discussion has become. When Pres.

Packer's comments about homosexuality as sinful behavior in a general conference talk are edited before they appear in the conference issue of the *Ensign*, you can know there is a great deal of internal discussion underway. Editing Bro. Poelman's talk is one thing, but editing a talk given by the President of the Quorum of the Twelve is altogether another.

Jim Dabakis is the Chairman of the Utah Democratic Party. He was a radio personality at KTKK when I did a call-in radio show for seven years during the 1980's. He is an articulate, affable and intelligent man. He is also openly homosexual and an advocate for increased legal protection for the homosexual community. His negotiation successes include persuading the LDS Church to speak in favor of Salt Lake City's recently adopted anti-discrimination ordinance. This ordinance protects a homosexual's rights to housing and employment in Salt Lake. The City Council would not have voted in favor of the ordinance if the church had not spoken in favor of it. And the church would not have done so if Jim Dabakis had not successfully advocated and persuaded them to do so.

The success in persuading the church to go from Proposition 8 opposition in California, to advocating adoption of a gay-rights ordinance in Salt Lake City in just a few short months is not possible without the leadership of church at the highest level actively discussing and troubling over the issue.

When Marlin Jensen's mind goes from a question about troubling history and tolerance of differing views of our past, immediately to tolerance of homosexuality, that is not so bizarre a jump as you might think. It is a reflection of the current discussion underway at the very top of the church.

Public opinion is shifting. Particularly among the younger Americans. The trends all suggest that acceptance of homosexual conduct as normal will be shared by the majority of Americans. Those holding contrary views are aging and dying, and those who hold the more open and accepting view are replacing them. Unless opinions change this is the inevitable result.

Any organization that is sensitive to survey's and polling to determine public opinion on the topic of homosexuality will discover growing demographic evidence of inevitable majority acceptance. Therefore, if you are going to make decisions on the basis of public opinions, you are going to respond to this shifting view.

Given Bro. Jensen's immediate response to the trigger word "tolerance" by introducing homosexuality into the conversation, it is apparent the church is quite actively discussing this issue. Additionally, given the censorship of the talk given by President Packer (the current President of the Quorum of the Twelve) in general conference on the subject, it appears there is an unmistakable alignment of the leadership's inclinations with public opinion.

It will be interesting to watch this issue unfold. For those who believe the practice of homosexuality is wrong because it frustrates the Divine order, and is desolating to humanity because it ends the continuation of family life through the union of the sexes, the idea of church approval for such relations is unthinkable. For more socially progressive Mormons who wish to be aligned with popular opinion, it is a relief to have another divisive issue excised from the principles of Mormon religion.

When an abomination that renders sexual relations desolate (they don't produce offspring) occurs in the holy place, you can know the promised destruction is soon at hand. Christ said those living in that day would live to see the end of the world.[1606] The way to decide when the virtue of tolerance becomes the wickedness of permissiveness can only be done by those who treasure up His (Christ's) words.[1607] For those few willing to do so, the Lord will send angels to gather them.[1608]

Some say it is good to be popular. It is better to not care. It is best to have an eye single to the word of the Lord.

"Some of Christ"

I was asked in an email what the words "some of Christ" means in D&C 76. The verse reads:

"These are they who say they are some of one and some of another—some of Christ and some of John, and some of Moses, and some of Elias, and some of Esaias, and some of Isaiah, and some of Enoch[.]" (D&C 76:100)

[1606] JS–M 1:32–36 "And again shall the abomination of desolation, spoken of by Daniel the prophet, be fulfilled. And immediately after the tribulation of those days, the sun shall be darkened, and the moon shall not give her light, and the stars shall fall from heaven, and the powers of heaven shall be shaken. Verily, I say unto you, this generation, in which these things shall be shown forth, shall not pass away until all I have told you shall be fulfilled. Although, the days will come, that heaven and earth shall pass away; yet my words shall not pass away, but all shall be fulfilled. And, as I said before, after the tribulation of those days, and the powers of the heavens shall be shaken, then shall appear the sign of the Son of Man in heaven, and then shall all the tribes of the earth mourn; and they shall see the Son of Man coming in the clouds of heaven, with power and great glory;"

[1607] JS–M 1:37 "And whoso treasureth up my word, shall not be deceived, for the Son of Man shall come, and he shall send his angels before him with the great sound of a trumpet, and they shall gather together the remainder of his elect from the four winds, from one end of heaven to the other."

[1608] Ibid. See also D&C 77:11 "Q. What are we to understand by sealing the one hundred and forty-four thousand, out of all the tribes of Israel—twelve thousand out of every tribe?
A. We are to understand that those who are sealed are high priests, ordained unto the holy order of God, to administer the everlasting gospel; for they are they who are ordained out of every nation, kindred, tongue, and people, by the angels to whom is given power over the nations of the earth, to bring as many as will come to the church of the Firstborn."

This verse occurs in a larger explanation of those who are damned because of their false religious beliefs (or more correctly, their unbelief). The larger explanation is in verse 97 through 107.[1609]

The context of these verses about false religion makes it clear those who practice it accept messengers who have been actually sent by the Lord with a warning from Him. The names of John, Moses, Elias, Isaiah and Enoch, for example, are names of those who were known to the Lord and entrusted by Him with a message of repentance from Him. However, despite the truthfulness of the messenger and the authentic origin of their message, the recipients have gone astray. They imagine their claim to follow the man is a substitute for receiving the message of repentance. They take pride in their status as followers of true messengers while neglecting the message to repent.

In the case of Christ, it is no different. They claim to be "of Christ" by associating His name with their brand of unbelief. They use His name in vain, however, because their practices and hearts are not inclined to follow His teachings, to endure His cross, to suffer

---

[1609] D&C 76:97–107 "And the glory of the terrestrial is one, even as the glory of the moon is one. And the glory of the telestial is one, even as the glory of the stars is one; for as one star differs from another star in glory, even so differs one from another in glory in the telestial world; For these are they who are of Paul, and of Apollos, and of Cephas. These are they who say they are some of one and some of another—some of Christ and some of John, and some of Moses, and some of Elias, and some of Esaias, and some of Isaiah, and some of Enoch; But received not the gospel, neither the testimony of Jesus, neither the prophets, neither the everlasting covenant. Last of all, these all are they who will not be gathered with the saints, to be caught up unto the church of the Firstborn, and received into the cloud. These are they who are liars, and sorcerers, and adulterers, and whoremongers, and whosoever loves and makes a lie. These are they who suffer the wrath of God on earth. These are they who suffer the vengeance of eternal fire. These are they who are cast down to hell and suffer the wrath of Almighty God, until the fulness of times, when Christ shall have subdued all enemies under his feet, and shall have perfected his work; When he shall deliver up the kingdom, and present it unto the Father, spotless, saying: I have overcome and have trodden the wine-press alone, even the wine-press of the fierceness of the wrath of Almighty God."

the rejection which comes from this world and the worldly, and to give up honor, friends and family to follow Him.[1610]

The crux of their defect is set out in this verse:

"But received not the gospel, neither the testimony of Jesus, neither the prophets, neither the everlasting covenant." (D&C 76:101)

These are four things:

1. *The Gospel.* You need to know that that term really means. If you do not, then you have not received it. You have claimed, like these others, to be "of Christ" without ever comprehending what His Gospel includes and does not include.

2. *The "testimony of Jesus."* Do you know what that term means? Do you imagine it is something you state or something you declare? Have you considered Jesus may have His own testimony which He will give to you? Have you imagined you can receive His testimony without ever entering His presence? What would Jesus' testimony necessarily include?

3. *The failure to receive "the prophets."* This is something different than merely following the prophet, because we saw in the earlier verses the hosts who claim to follow the prophets John, Moses, Isaiah, Enoch, etc. were damned. To receive is different than to follow. But implicit in the phrase, also, is the ability to actually discern when a prophet is sent.

[1610] Luke 12:51–53 "Suppose ye that I am come to give peace on earth? I tell you, Nay; but rather division: For from henceforth there shall be five in one house divided, three against two, and two against three. The father shall be divided against the son, and the son against the father; the mother against the daughter, and the daughter against the mother; the mother in law against her daughter in law, and the daughter in law against her mother in law."
Mark 10:29–30 "And Jesus answered and said, Verily I say unto you, There is no man that hath left house, or brethren, or sisters, or father, or mother, or wife, or children, or lands, for my sake, and the gospel's, But he shall receive an hundredfold now in this time, houses, and brethren, and sisters, and mothers, and children, and lands, with persecutions; and in the world to come eternal life."

4. The failure to receive "the everlasting covenant." This, also, may not be what you imagine. Joseph Smith spoke often about the everlasting covenant. It is worth a good deal of study if you have interest in knowing about those things.

To claim to be "of Christ" without having received His Gospel, heard from Him His own testimony, recognized and received the message to repent from a prophet, not just to say but to do, and to thereby receive the everlasting covenant from heaven, these are the meaningless claims which will damn. Those who fail to do so but still claim to be "of Christ" will be like the liars and thieves who are left suffering until the final resurrection. They will suffer the wrath of God. Their pride will be burned away by the things they suffer. Then will they lament, "O that we had repented in the day that the word of the Lord came unto us." (See Helaman 13:36.) Such people are religious, in fact very much so. They are eager to claim the status of a follower of the prophets. They boast they follow them. They think themselves better than others precisely because they claim to worship true prophets who will save them.

But without the Gospel, they are damned. Without the testimony from Jesus they are damned. Without receiving the prophetic message to repent, awake and arise, they are damned. And without these first three they are unable to receive the everlasting covenant. Therefore, they depart this world proudly, filled with unbelief and foolish pride from their false religion, and enter into their suffering.

Standing Up to History

LDS scholar Dan Peterson has written an article in the Deseret News on February 9th titled The Restoration Stands Up to History. His notion is that there are three levels to church history following an Hegelian model of thesis, antithesis and synthesis. Although this puts a happy face and familiar intellectual language on the subject, I respectfully disagree.

The first level is what could be described using any of the following terms, some favorable and some insulting:

- Faith Promoting
- Sunday School's version
- General Conferencesque
- Faithful
- Testimony Building
- Sanitized
- Limited
- Burning-in-the-bosom inspiring
- True
- Incomplete
- Propaganda
- One-sided
- Censored
- Correlated
- Official
- Entirely Trustworthy
- Missing Important Details
- (many others)

These descriptors reflect the point of view of the one using them. Depending on the person's vantage point, they describe the view a certain way. Interestingly, there are people of great faith who would feel comfortable using some of the more pejorative terms.

The second level could be described in any of the following e-qually contradictory terms:

- Critical
- Historically Accurate
- The Full Story

- Anti-Mormon
- Faith Destroying
- Sanitized
- Incomplete
- Propaganda
- One-Sided
- Faithless
- More Trustworthy
- Candid
- Including Important Details
- Unofficial
- Not Allowed in Sunday School
- Forbidden
- True
- Uncensored
- (many others)

These descriptors overlap with the first and begin to show the problem of the first two category approach (thesis/antithesis). Once again, despite the fact some are unflattering, these second level descriptors could be used by people of faith who strongly believe in the Restoration.

This leads to the final level where Bro. Peterson proposes it is possible to return to something akin to the first level, but with "a richer and more complicated version of history." This is the happy ending of the process.

This kind of orderly progression is becoming more difficult by the day. The Internet has introduced a new world. The result of that explosion in available information has made the first level an island of isolated views. Anyone participating in such lessons can return home (or even sit in class), go on-line and look further into anything said by the instructor or manual. What was once "Fantasy Island" is now just a peninsula being besieged. It cannot thrive any longer in pretended isolation. The barbarians are already inside the gate.

If the church persists in imposing the first level as its stock-in-trade, the "apostasy" Bro. Marlin Jensen speaks about will continue. The first level cannot sustain a day long shelf life anymore. We need to drop the pretense of having all antiseptic characters, living or dead. History needs to unfold. It *will* still be faith promoting. But the faith it will promote will be more hearty, robust, realistic and enduring. We will become acquainted with characters who at times made serious mistakes, were struggling, befuddled, headed in the wrong direction, but suffered for their mistakes and came to peace with faith despite the pain of this mortal realm.

The basic argument of Bro. Peterson is absolutely correct. The Restoration *will* stand up to history. In a much more marvelous way than it does in the first level of wasted effort. That may have been good in an era of limited information, and may still be good for the Primary children. By the time they are age 12, the complications of life and the failures of mortals should be introduced and discussed.

Why hide George Albert Smith's mental illness? Why avoid the origins of his mental instability? Why not let those who suffer from similar maladies know there has been a church president with such serious problems? Why use the pedestal to support a fictional character? Why not let him emerge as the frail, likable man he was?

Why not take the initiative as saints to go to the third level voluntarily? Why not acknowledge, face and discuss the very matters that are costing people their faith right now? Why let them discover the problems from hostile sources instead of from friendly sources? Why not strengthen one another in our faithful search for the truth, rather than let those who dispense historical events from a perspective which challenges faith get the first chance to tell our children and our converts? When they do that they gain credibility and we lose it.

Valentine's Day

We have a few thanks to dispense for Valentine's Day:

- Rome, for killing Christians.
- Roman Catholicism for honoring the killed Christians.
- Pope Gelasius I for designating the Feast of St. Valentine. His decision would be rescinded by Pope Paul VI, but by then it was too late to undo the celebration.
- Valentine (there may have been three of them sharing the same name) for giving his (their) life as a martyr(s) to a hostile Rome.
- Chaucer for turning the day into something romantic.
- Hallmark for dramatically pushing the commercial opportunity in the day.
- Wall Street, candy makers, jewelry sellers, teddy-bear companies, and the detritus of commercialism that exploits the relationship between those who care for one another for preying on insecurities and using it to lever us into purchasing stuff.
- Commercial television, radio, the Internet, newspapers and outdoor advertising for their contributions to the selling and buying frenzy now associated with the day.
- And last and least of all me—for reminding you who bother to come to this blog today or tomorrow that tomorrow is Valentine's Day and you ought to do something to note the event. In homage to Chaucer, that ought to be romantic, but in rebellion against the commercialism of our day, make it an act or write a poem (or if you're incapable of that then a letter), or show some kindness instead of making a purchase.

Now, I gotta figure something out myself . . . because I really do love her and want that idea to be clear in her mind. And the commercialism of the event makes it clear is *must* be observed.

Bishop Whitney's Revelation to Joseph Smith

Years after the revelation (after the problems in Kirtland) informing Oliver Cowdery that it was inappropriate for him to command Joseph Smith because Joseph was at the head of the church[1611] Bishop Whitney sent a note to Joseph Smith:[1612]

"Thus saith the voice of the spirit to me, if thy Brother Joseph Smith will attend the feast at thy house this day (at 12 o'cl) they poor & lame will rejoice at his presence & also think themselves honored.

"Yours in friendship & Love,

"NKW"

Joseph responded by immediately canceling the Hebrew school that day and attending with his wife, father and mother the feast for the poor offered by Bishop Whitney.

Clearly, the idea that another person could receive revelation that involved even the church president was not an apostate idea during Joseph's day as it is in ours. Bishop Whitney was not rebuked by Joseph. Instead he and his revelation were honored by Joseph responding, attending the feast and being grateful for the invitation.

Since Joseph Smith received the early revelations setting the order for the church, and yet responded to Bishop Whitney's revelation to him, it suggests our current view of limits on who can get revelation may not be the same as Joseph understood them.

It is another interesting topic worth studying in our history to help us understand how the Lord really operates. We should be careful about adopting formulas as the solution to something when the

---

[1611] D&C 28:6 "And thou shalt not command him who is at thy head, and at the head of the church;"

[1612] Dean Jesse, *The Papers of Joseph Smith*, 2:130–131.

conduct of the Prophet through whom the revelation came did not apply it consistently the same way we do today.

First Impression

The interview I did for *Mormon Stories* has an introductory title designed to grab attention and get the followers of that site to listen to the interview. I presume most of that audience is unacquainted with what I've written. I know John Dehlin had not read any of the books I've written before interviewing me. He did read some of the posts on this blog, but has not completed reading any book I've written and has a copy of only one of them. He had limited information from which to conduct the interview.

The impetus for doing the interview came from recommendations John Dehlin received from others who had read some of my writings. He followed up on the recommendation, and persuaded me to participate.

In some of the reactions to the interview, his audience has presumed the headline title to the podcast is an accurate representation of what I'm all about. It's rather attention grabbing to say that someone "Claims to Have Seen Christ." That was a deliberate attempt on John Dehlin's part to get someone who knows nothing about me and knows nothing about my work to listen to the podcast. It gives the impression to a stranger that I wear that claim on my sleeve. That I am a braggart. Worse still, that I have little regard for the sacred and tend to profane deeply personal experiences and to parade them about as if it made me noteworthy. If that were true, I would think such a person would be unbelievable. Therefore, when the listener's reaction is indignation, I can understand that. It is reasonable.

On the other hand, if someone had actually read my writings, they would find there is almost nothing of me in them. I write about doctrine, history and scriptural exegesis. Even *The Second Comforter* is a book about the reader, not the writer. It gets inside the person reading it and causes them to reflect on their own relationship with God. To the extent that I am mentioned, it is in the context of my failings, shortcomings and mistakes. The reader is walked through the process of overcoming their own failings, following a path, and undoing their mistakes. At the end the reader should be better acquainted with their own deepest desires, and regard me as little more than a flawed, but believing fellow-sojourner in this challenging predicament of mortality.

I am not bothered by the first impression given by the title. The best reaction I can think of to what I've written would be this: "I can't stand Denver Snuffer; but what he has written is of value to me." That reaction will do two things: First, it will establish a proper view of my irrelevance. Second, it will focus on the ideas advanced, which are in my view, a reflection of the Lord's plan to rescue us all from our fallen condition.

Those who collect their first impression of me from John Dehlin's headline will be quite disappointed to find there is very little of me in anything written. Or, perhaps not disappointed, but rather relieved. Either way, I am not responsible for the way he has titled the matter and have no complaints about the way he did. After all, he came into the interview without an adequate basis to know anything about the work I've been doing. Knowing almost nothing about that work, I thought he did an admirable job of asking critical, important and relevant questions. As a composer of headlines, I suppose he displays a flair for that, as well.

Priesthood Authority: Pres. Packer's Remarks

In the Worldwide Leadership Conference this month President Packer made this interesting statement:

"Any elder holds as much priesthood as does the President of the Church or as I do as an Apostle—different offices. But the priesthood is not delegated out and parceled a little here and a little there. It is given all at once. In the ordinance where ordinations take place, the priesthood is conferred, and then the office is conferred. So a young man as young as 18 planning to go on a mission has this ordinance, and they first say, "We confer upon you the Melchizedek Priesthood" and then ordain you to the office of elder in that priesthood." (See Priesthood Power in the Home.)

This statement is interesting in its implications. All the more so because of President Grant's alteration of the practice. He discontinued conferring the priesthood. Instead he had the church ordaining to an office in the church, which he said was enough. There was no need to confer priesthood, only to ordain to an office. On the point raised by President Packer, we have an earlier statement of President Jos. F. Smith dealing with a slightly different issue. These two statements, however, can be considered together:

"Then again, if it were necessary, though I do not expect the necessity will ever arise, and there was no man left on the earth holding the Melchizedek Priesthood, except an elder— that elder, by the inspiration of the Spirit of God and by the direction of the Almighty, could proceed, and should proceed, to organize the Church of Jesus Christ in all its perfection, because he holds the Melchizedek Priesthood." (*Gospel Doctrine*, 148)

These explanations of the "whole" being present in the conferral to anyone of the Melchizedek Priesthood has profound doctrinal implications regarding the subject of "keys" and their application. Brigham Young claimed possession of keys through his ordination to the apostleship (1835). He would later adopt Elder Pratt's position that the relevant keys came in the 1836 Kirtland Temple appearances.

This topic of how authority is preserved or passed is also quite interesting and worth pondering, I think. Something about which many claims are made, but the underlying mechanics are not well understood.

Clearly, if it was important for angels to individually appear to Joseph (and Oliver or Sidney), then it raises the question of how widely that gets spread about, and how any surviving Elder could organize the church "in all its perfection." Then again, what does Jos. F. Smith's reference to "the inspiration of the Spirit of God and by the direction of the Almighty" include?

President Packer's teaching that any elder in the church holds as much priesthood as does the church president or any of the apostles is, however, a very valid point. I agree with President Packer on that score.

Groups

An observation about discussion groups:

The greatest mischief of discussion groups lies in the mistaken impression that collective effort will help the individual in their personal journey. The path to God is solitary. It is between the individual and the Lord. Groups create an artificial environment. The stage erected lets the group appear to occupy center stage moving the Lord into the wings.

It would be better to spend the same hours pondering or praying. Any person doing that would be better served than they are by devoting time to arguing, debate or the convincing of others.

When you learn a new idea and that is followed up with questions or uncertainties about how to make it fit together with current belief or understanding, pondering and praying is more useful. Groups debate. They argue over how to fit it together. How you fit it into your understanding will be different than how another does. The group may not share your background or have studied what you have. Therefore, a group discussion may not even address the difficulties you are contemplating.

In a group discussion there is more contention than harmony. Contention is dark and invites errors. It would be far better to contemplate, meditate, study scriptural passages, to look into related statements from prior patriarchs, prophets and apostles than to debate with others. New information can open the mind. Contentious debate will close it.

When the Lord appeared to Paul on the Road to Damascus, there were others with Paul. But the interview was between Paul and the Lord. The same is true of Joseph in the Grove, Nephi on the mountain, Moses on the mountain, the Brother of Jared, Enoch, Abraham, These and the many other times the Lord spoke with or appeared to His followers came in solitary interviews. (There are of course exceptions. There were two disciples on the Road to Emmaus. The appearance at Bountiful involved twenty-five hundred. But these exceptions are just that—exceptions. On the Road, the two disciples had previously been acquainted with and taught by Him. They were prepared. It was the very day of His resurrection. He was looking to establish a body of witnesses. The same is true of Bountiful. As I discuss in *The Second Comforter*, those witnesses were carefully prepared and self-selecting.)

Another problem with discussion groups, or even valued teachers, is the tendency to take attention that belongs to the Lord and give it to a man. No man is supposed to be the focus of your adoration. That belongs to the Lord alone. Men who seek to become the focus or to "win" a debate are likely to draw attention to themselves, rather than to place the focus where it belongs.

If even one member of a discussion group is unprepared, the Lord will withhold from everyone the greater light. If you tie yourself to others, you may find it hinders, rather than helps your progress. Since no two people are similarly situated, there will be hinderances for some participants.

The scriptures are a gold standard for parsing the mysteries. They contain a great deal of undiscovered truth. Unlocking those mysteries is almost always done in study, contemplation, prayer and solitary reflection apart from the world. Discussion groups become part of the world as soon as they deteriorate into contention. Take a look at discussion boards. How often are they wholesome and free of contention? The "comments" on this blog were disabled because of the deterioration that took place here.

No one can help you find your way back to God. Ideas and doctrines will; men will not. They are a poor substitute for truth, careful study, individual prayer and meditation, pondering and parsing the scriptures and developing your mind. If someone has something to teach, let them teach. Then go your way and ponder upon it. But debating and arguing is valueless or worse.

A Contrast

Two dialogues:

Jehovah: Abraham, take thy son, thine only son whom thou lovest, and offer him as a sacrifice unto me.

Abraham: Thy will be done.

— — —

Jehovah: Pharisaint, take thy son, thine only son whom thou lovest, and offer him as a sacrifice unto me.

Pharisaint: I don't feel good about that. That is neither tender nor merciful. I doubt God would ever ask such a thing.

Lucifer: Take thy son and anoint him, call him blessed, and keep him in thy care.

Pharisaint: Now that is tender!

Lucifer: Sacrifice is not needed, for I intend to save all mankind so that not one soul will be lost. The odds are you shall be exalted.

Pharisaint: Now that is merciful!

Lucifer: Yes, I am the god of this world, worship me and there will be nothing but reward to follow.

Pharisaint: Who was that other one asking for sacrifice?

Lucifer: He has been my opponent from the beginning. He has opposed my ever mercy, my ever tenderness, and he pretends to displace me as the god of this world.

Pharisaint: How can such a being, demanding cruel effort, who does not offer tender mercies as you do, ever hope to be worshiped?

Lucifer: He is not. There are some who pretend to do so, but there are none among my chosen, holy Pharisaints who do.

Interview by My Wife

My wife looks at links to the blog, and also searches other sites to review discussions. As a result, she has posed the following questions and asked I answer them:

1. Why do you refer to the church presidents as "modern popes" in your new book?

A: That is not my term, but a term borrowed from President J. Reuben Clark, a respected counselor in the First Presidency. I use it because he used it. I assume he meant no disrespect. I certainly did not.

2. Why did you refer to the First Presidency and Quorum of the Twelve as "the fifteen men" on your blog?

A: That is not my term, but a term used by Church Historian Marlin Jensen, a respected member of the Seventy. I use it because he used it. I assume he meant no disrespect. I certainly did not.

3. Why do you refer people to your books in answers you give in the Mormon Stories interview? Are you trying to market a product?

A: The interview actually started and stopped with my first answer. When John Dehlin heard me answer his first question, he stopped the interview and told me I had to let him control the flow and keep the answers short. He explained that long answers would make for a poor interview and we could not get it done, and I needed to trust him. So we started over again and what is on the podcast is the "take two" version involving short answers.

Questions that ask about a topic I've written 180,000 words to carefully explain cannot be done in a brief oral response. Therefore, I attempted to be clear by referring to what I've written rather than leaving a listener with the impression all I had to say was what was included in a brief oral response. I couldn't care less if someone actually reads my books. I provide them as an explanation of what I believe and why, but it requires someone to take the trouble to find them, buy them and read them. That is a barrier I assume few will overcome, but those who do will have the full answer rather than a sound-bite response.

Since my livelihood is practicing law, if I were attempting to promote something of economic value to me it would need to be my law practice. I do not do that. Apart from giving free copies to friends, there are very few members of my own ward who even know I've written a book. In my stake, there can't be more than a handful. I've never spoken of them while serving in any capacity in the church. But it is actually amusing to think a niche market like Mormon doctrine and history is a money-making audience to begin with. When you add to that the fact nothing I write is advertised, and we've declined two approaches from Deseret Book to have them carry copies, it becomes even less of a money-making venture. The books are not for everyone. They are difficult to obtain and not widely distributed because I know they are not meant for everyone. I mention them on *my* blog, but that is because if someone is interested in reading the blog they should have become acquainted with what I've written first. That is purely voluntary. I don't want everyone reading what I write.

4. Why do you think it appropriate to call Joseph Smith "bone-headed" in your Mormon Stories interview?

A: Joseph called himself foolish. The Lord rebuked him for his carnal desires, boasting and fearing man more than God. These are both Joseph's[1613] and the Lord's[1614] characterizations of him. Therefore, I mean no disrespect, but believe the term is a modern descriptor which reflects what both Joseph himself and the Lord have stated about him. It does not lessen him in my estimation.

[1613] JS–H 1:28 "During the space of time which intervened between the time I had the vision and the year eighteen hundred and twenty-three—having been forbidden to join any of the religious sects of the day, and being of very tender years, and persecuted by those who ought to have been my friends and to have treated me kindly, and if they supposed me to be deluded to have endeavored in a proper and affectionate manner to have reclaimed me—I was left to all kinds of temptations; and, mingling with all kinds of society, I frequently fell into many foolish errors, and displayed the weakness of youth, and the foibles of human nature; which, I am sorry to say, led me into divers temptations, offensive in the sight of God. In making this confession, no one need suppose me guilty of any great or malignant sins. A disposition to commit such was never in my nature. But I was guilty of levity, and sometimes associated with jovial company, etc., not consistent with that character which ought to be maintained by one who was called of God as I had been. But this will not seem very strange to any one who recollects my youth, and is acquainted with my native cheery temperament."

[1614] D&C 3:4–7 "For although a man may have many revelations, and have power to do many mighty works, yet if he boasts in his own strength, and sets at naught the counsels of God, and follows after the dictates of his own will and carnal desires, he must fall and incur the vengeance of a just God upon him. Behold, you have been entrusted with these things, but how strict were your commandments; and remember also the promises which were made to you, if you did not transgress them. And behold, how oft you have transgressed the commandments and the laws of God, and have gone on in the persuasions of men. For, behold, you should not have feared man more than God. Although men set at naught the counsels of God, and despise his words—"

5. Do you believe the church leaders today are comparable to the Jewish leaders at the time of Christ, specifically do you compare Thomas S. Monson to Caiphus?

A: No. I did not do that in the interview and do not believe that is true. I used the reference Christ made to supporting the clearly wicked leaders of His day to illustrate how great a deference is owed. If those wicked men were deserving respect, then good men trying hard to perform a difficult job deserve all the more respect and deference. In fact, if you listen carefully to the words used you will find that comparison was not made in the interview, but instead the contrast was made.

6. Do you lead a following?

A: Not as far as I am aware. I tell all who either listen to what I say or read what I write not to follow me. All should remain active and faithful as Latter-day Saints. The church leaders alone have the right to preside over the church's affairs. I believe we all have a duty arising from baptism to mourn with those who mourn, and to serve one another, which is best done inside the church.

7. Have you said the Correlation movement has led the church into apostasy?

A: No. I only quote President David O. McKay's statement that he believed it would have that result. Everyone is free to decide for themselves the results of the Correlation process.

8. You must have extremely good balance in order to walk the razor's edge: pride; membership; priestcraft; discipleship. How do you do it? What lessons have been afforded you, allowing you to remain objective?

A: I'm not sure I understand the question, but I disagree with the premise. I fail in every respect. I suffer for my failings. I will continue to suffer for many things because the failings continue. I do not believe it is possible to be perfect and mortal, but I do believe a mortal can have a perfect intent. God appears to weigh our intent far more than our actions. He knows the desire of the heart motivating the conduct, and can look beyond the errors and foolishness displayed to the underlying desire to serve and honor Him. Christ repeatedly said this was the case. The rich Pharisee was contrasted to the widow. He certainly gave more. She clearly gave much less. But her heart willed to give all. His did not. Her sacrifice was accepted, his pride was rejected. This is how God views us all. He is not handicapped as we are.

9. Do you think the temple keys are lost?

A: Church presidents have frequently said the keys to perform plural marriages have been taken from the earth. The 1990 changes to the endowment removed some of what had previously been regarded as keys to salvation. However, anti-Mormon crusaders Jerald and Sandra Tanner have preserved them and make them available on the Internet. So, if they are in fact keys, and if they need to be known, then they have not been lost but merely removed from the temple and put onto the Tanner's website. If someone believes they need them, they can still be had and cannot be said to have been lost. Beyond that, I leave it to each person to decide how important such things are to their relationship with God. I'm of the view that the temple rites are not the real thing, but are instruction and an invitation to receive the real thing.

10. Why do you believe it appropriate to speak about something so sacred as an appearance to you by the Lord ?

A: Anyone who has had the Lord appear to them should testify as a witness to that fact. That is paramount. It is important for witnesses to declare He lives. That they have seen Him. That His life did not end on a Roman cross in Judea. That He rose from the grave and all of us have hope through

Him for our own rescue from death. That is critical. What is not appropriate for disclosure are details that go beyond what the Lord has chosen to make public already through the scriptures or ordinances. He controls that. Though He may reveal much to a person, and place them under a different standard than what is given openly to mankind, that is His decision. Until He commands, the line is drawn between witnessing He lives—which is required, and disclosing what He alone reserves for Himself to reveal—which is forbidden. I have said and I do believe our Lord has a continuing ministry. But that is His, not mine. Like any Latter-day Saint with a testimony of the Lord, I testify to help my fellow Saint increase in faith in Jesus Christ. I have an obligation to do so. We all do.

11. Have you ever been criticized by church leaders?

A: No. I've never been criticized nor asked to stop writing by any church leader. Not from my bishop, stake president, nor any higher authority. I have had some contacts, but they have been private, and encouraging me to continue. There have been a number of people who have returned to church activity because of what I've written. Those results are viewed with some support. The criticism I am aware of, some of which has been quite harsh, has come from overanxious church members who have not read the things I've written.

12. Have you singled out President Boyd K. Packer for criticism?

A: No. In fact he is the single most often quoted living authority in my writings. I have a great regard for him and have never criticized him, but have often defended or quoted from him. His *"Candle of the Lord"* sermon was a milestone talk. When Pres. Monson and Pres. Packer die, that will mark the first time there will be no apostles in the Quorum of the Twelve who were there when I joined the church. He represents a symbolic transition point for me, and I will very much mourn his passing which I hope is many years from now.

13. Why do you criticize the church if you are a faithful member?

A: I do not believe I criticize the church. I believe I respond to criticism by providing an explanation of the issues which are alive and driving people away from activity or membership. If everything I had written disappeared this instant, that would not stop the issues from being discussed. The real critics are studying ways to undermine faith and developing new arguments against the church all the time. They do not need to lie about the church to undermine faith. They only need to tell truths which we have hidden. The best thing we can do is to tell the truth first, and do it from the vantage point of faith. If we still believe, and we know about the problems, then we are best situated to disclose and address them. Being angry with a faithful member for being honest is a futile act. Hiding from the truth is equally futile. The truth is going to be told. Better us than the antagonists to tell it.

14. Do you admit some of Joseph Smith's sexual activities were sinful or immoral?

A: That is not as easy a question as it may appear. You would need to know about the ancient kingship, and the king's duties to begin to answer. That is a topic so foreign to current culture that I'm not even going to undertake an answer. Under American social, cultural and religious mores of the 1800's Joseph Smith was immoral. Under the traditional Christian values of both his and our day, he was immoral. Under an ancient form of kingship, that is a great deal less clear. So the conclusion on the question must ultimately await several things:

First, a determination if Joseph Smith was being placed in a very ancient form of conduct by the commandment of God. I happen to believe he was. But that is not a topic that can be answered in passing. Second, was Joseph Smith's conduct justified under that ancient standard? Again, that depends on Joseph's role and God's command. Third, does this have anything to do with current practices? Clearly it does not. We've long since lost track of those things and perhaps we are the better for it. When Joseph was crowned a "King and Priest" (Melek and Zadok) he was confirming a peculiar and ancient tradition. The tradition does not belong inside a democratic republic like the United States, and the rules governing the conduct of such a person are completely foreign and quite distasteful to modern sensibilities. So we are left with a standard which would condemn him, and the possibility of another standard which would justify him. One of the requisites of this ancient office required the death of the king. Not merely in ritual, though later imitators would substitute a surrogate to kill in the renewal of kingship. The original required the actual sacrifice of the king himself. Joseph did that, as well. In that sense he was perhaps an authentic return of the ancient order at more than one level. As one learned friend of mine has characterized Joseph, "he was a Divine King and a Divine Victim." There is only one of those at a time. And his death by sacrifice is required as one of the incidents of the ancient office. But those ideas hardly belong to our day. Just alluding to it will confuse most people. There are probably only a handful of people who could speak intelligently about the topic. Yet, if you know what you're seeing, it is all over in the Old Testament.

So let me reduce it to this: Based on our standards and based on social and religious standards in his day, Joseph Smith was sinful and immoral. Whether God viewed him as such is a different question. That would need to be taken up with Him rather than me. I would hesitate to reach a conclusion on that question, however, unless you know a great deal more than most people know today, and even then not before receiving the Lord's judgment on the question.

15. Why do you say the restoration through Joseph Smith was intended to being back something more ancient than the New Testament Church?

A: Because that is what Christ taught. He did not say we would return to conditions like His day. He said when He returned the conditions would be like the days of Noah. Noah's day is to be mirrored in ours. That day is pre-New Testament. I think Christ knew what He was talking about. Even the restoration itself is an imitation of the more ancient family of Abraham. Abraham, Isaac and Jacob are the three great patriarchs. The Twelve Sons of Israel are the next tier of patriarchs. There were seventy descendants of Israel who went into Egypt.[1615] The church structure imitates the patriarchal family. We will be going back there before the Lord's return. You don't live as "one" when you are inside a hierarchy. You live as "one" when you are a family having all things in common. The family was the "church" in the day of Noah. That is where it is headed. We've just temporarily frozen the process. It will resume again.

16. Why do you ignore the church's claim that the Nauvoo Temple was completed and the fullness was retained by the church?

A: I don't ignore the claim. I explain it. It is called "the traditional narrative" and is set out in my last book. The church's position is essentially that completing the baptismal font is all that was required, and Joseph conveyed the fullness above his red brick store. That position leaves many questions unanswered:

Why did the Lord state the fullness could only come in the temple if the red brick store was sufficient? Is it correct to conflate baptism for the dead with fullness? Why did Brigham Young, upon his return to Nauvoo in August, abruptly change his mind and teach that completing the temple was essential? What about the ultimate failure to finish the structure? Did it matter that in 1847 the structure was not complete, even though it had been "regarded as sufficiently complete" to be

---

[1615] Exodus 1:5 "And all the souls that came out of the loins of Jacob were seventy souls: for Joseph was in Egypt *already.*"

dedicated? What about the revealed warnings? Were the saints driven out of Nauvoo, or planted and protected there? Did that matter? Were the saints put through judgments and buffetings rather than being protected and blessed? Did that matter? What reason is there for the Lord to state He had taken the fullness away in 1841? Does the church's traditional narrative answer all the questions, or start from the conclusion and reason backward? If you begin with the conclusion that it was successful, and then string together whatever is needed to justify the conclusion, is that a faithful retelling of events? These and many other questions deserve at least careful consideration.

I set out the church's position or the traditional narrative, then give some careful consideration to the obvious questions which remain worth asking and grappling to resolve. If the traditional narrative is correct, then much of the language in Section 124 is a "bluff" by the Lord, apparently only to motivate the saints to engage in the drudgery of a public works building. But He apparently did not really intend to discipline them, drive them out of Nauvoo, put them through suffering and buffeting, and stir them up to repentance. Therefore, the events in Nauvoo belong inside a narrative of success, blessing, glory and vindication by the faithfulness of those involved. Their bickering, ambition, and even Brigham Young's condemnation of the those receiving their endowments as being "thieves" because they stole the temple garments intended to be used by others reflects only credit on these faithful saints. It is puzzling to me, but perhaps it is not to others.

If the traditional narrative answers all the questions of the faithful, active saints today, it does not do so for other reasonably-minded people. I'm trying to have it make sense to them. So, in a way, those who only want to consider the traditional narrative really don't need to read the book or to consider the difficult questions I raise. But for this question, I maintain I have not ignored the traditional narrative, but have responded to it with a reasonable discussion told in an objective way. I hoped it would be matter-of-fact and dispassionate. It was not written to be any kind of "hit piece" but instead a rational discussion of reasonable historic events holding some importance for those who believe, as I do, in the Lord's involvement in the history of the Latter-day Saints.

17. Do you love your wife?

A: Beyond all reason and forevermore. Apart from the Lord, there is no friend or other companion whose company I long to retain for all eternity than hers.

Faithful History

Is "faithful history" required to be accurate? Is it better if there is an effort to improve the facts by adding details drawn from the writer's imagination? Is it our responsibility to be faithful to the truth or to promote faith? Because a "faithful history" could be either of those.

As an example, the sacrifices of those who built the Kirtland Temple were a living testimony of their conversion to the restored Gospel. They literally suffered to build the Temple. They endured poverty to make it possible for the building to be completed. Some went without food, because they were not always paid for their labors. Their heroism is beyond question.

For some reason, however, we aren't willing to retell their great sacrifices without fanciful embellishment. We insist on improving the story by adding a fake overlay about the women donating their best china to be ground up and put into the exterior plaster. LDS Church History researcher, employed by the Church History Department, Mark Staker researched the topic and found the story of the women donating china originated in the 1930's. The story was such good fodder for "faith promotion" that it soon found its way into official versions of Kirtland history.

There was china ground up into the exterior plaster, but it came from a community dump where such things were discarded. Kirtland, like all other communities, had a broken china dump from which the children retrieved scraps to use in the building process.

When the truth of the sacrifices are then overlain with a fictional story about the best china sacrifices/donations, we run the risk of having our members find out about the exaggeration later. Then upon learning this "faithful history" is nothing more than "faith promoting fiction" we risk having them disbelieve everything about the church's history. What is true and what is exaggeration? What is left of the stories we retell? If we'll add this fake account of the sacrifices, does that mean there really weren't sacrifices made?

We invite the crisis of faith when we turn from "faithful retelling" and offer "faith promoting fiction" as our Sunday School fare. We could get away with that once. We can't now.

Similarly, a recently converted Willard Richards visited Kirtland after the Temple had been built. He observed this about the city: "Sectarians build their own houses first, then, if ever, a house for their Gods. The Latter Day Saints first build the Lord a house & now he is giving them an opportunity to build their own dwellings." (Willard Richards letter to his sister Jan. 30, 1837.) This was the example in Kirtland. It was not repeated in Nauvoo, where the brick mansions we have restored today bear testimony to the priority change from Kirtland to Nauvoo. In Nauvoo the brick mansions were all built and completed before the Temple was completed. Indeed, there were no more mansions being built (because the city was then abandoned) while the Temple was being completed. The Nauvoo Temple attic was used from November 1845–February 1846 by Brigham Young and the Twelve to perform ordinances in the incomplete

Temple. The first wave of refugees left in February, the day following the last endowment rites performed in the unfinished structure. The Temple was not considered complete enough to dedicate until April of 1846, but even then was not finished. A year following the dedication a Palmyra newspaper editor visited the building in 1847 and remarked on its incomplete condition. He speculated about how grand it might have been had it ever been completed.

We have a tendency to "know" what we want to have other people believe or conclude. Then we adapt our story to support our conclusion. That is not history. It is an approach that invites us to tell faith promoting but unfaithful history. We ought to confine ourselves to a faithful retelling. No matter how poorly that reflects on our history, it reflects credit upon us.

Zion

I do not think Zion will initially be where people think it will.

I do not think Zion will be at all what people think it will be.

Nor do I think people are at all ready in our current circumstances to begin to learn what Zion will require; what standards of conduct will be required; what covenants will need to be assumed to establish Zion.

I do not think Zion will be an institutional enterprise. The angels will be the ones responsible for that gathering.[1616] This presents an apparent impediment to those who either don't believe angels minister to mankind, or who believe they only minister to church leaders,

---

[1616] D&C 77:11 "Q. What are we to understand by sealing the one hundred and forty-four thousand, out of all the tribes of Israel—twelve thousand out of every tribe?
A. We are to understand that those who are sealed are high priests, ordained unto the holy order of God, to administer the everlasting gospel; for they are they who are ordained out of every nation, kindred, tongue, and people, by the angels to whom is given power over the nations of the earth, to bring as many as will come to the church of the Firstborn."
Mark 13:27 "And then shall he send his angels, and shall gather together his elect from the four winds, from the uttermost part of the earth to the uttermost part of heaven."

or who think them possible, but have never been administered personally by them.

In the Mark 13 text, the repeated "and then" language of the KJV is not chronological or sequential. It is referring to the generation living at the time it starts, who will live to see it all occur. Meaning "in that day" or more precisely, "among the generation then living."

When there is an abomination that renders desolate in the Temple, you will also see afflictions. You will see those who claim they are Christ, or they are Christ's true living prophet—though they are not. You will see signs and wonders, including great building projects and the astonishing ability to speak in every language across the world in a single time, but that will not deceive those who take the Holy Spirit for their guide. They will be able to distinguish between the truth and error. Heaven will be shaken. Angels will gather those who follow Christ rather than trust the arm of flesh, and ultimately Christ will return and the world will be wasted at His coming. Though there will be some fragment, like the days of Noah, there will be those who have been gathered by the angels. Those few will be preserved.

Ezra Booth was among the first to hear the original four missionaries sent out at the very beginning of the restoration. He wrote about what Oliver Cowdery told him of the original mission. It was to include identifying the location for the New Jerusalem. Ezra Booth explained:

> "This is the person commissioned by the Lord to proceed to the western wilds, and as he himself stated, 'to the place where the foot of a white man never trod,' to rear up a pillar for a witness, where the temple of God shall be built, in the glorious New Jerusalem. But alas! he was arrested by man in his course, and by the breath of man the mighty undertaking was blown into the air, and Cowdery was thrown back among the Gentiles, to await for the spirit to devise some new plans in the place of those which had been frustrated. But as the

city and temple must be built, and as every avenue leading to the Indians was closed against the Mormonites, it was thought that they should be built among the Gentiles, which is in direct opposition to the original plan." (Ezra Booth, Letter IX, originally published in the *Ohio Star* in 1831. It has since been reprinted in numerous places and can be found on-line as well.)

This is referring to the charge given to Oliver Cowdery, and the other 3 missionaries to find the place where the New Jerusalem would be located. That effort was aborted when the Federal Indian Agents threatened to arrest them if they didn't go back across the line separating the whites and Indians from each other. That line was at Independence, Missouri. So Independence was as close as they could get at the time. By default Independence became the location for the New Jerusalem.

It has remained the location in popular understanding ever since then. Subsequent revelations seem to confirm that as the site.

When Joseph Smith fled Nauvoo on June 22, 1844, and crossed the Mississippi headed west, he explained his purpose was based on revelation. "The Lord warned him to flee to the Rocky Mountains to save his life," according to his brother Hyrum. (*DHC* Vol. 6, p. 547.) It was there he hoped to locate the Book of Mormon remnant who have the prophetic responsibility to build the New Jerusalem. It will not be built without their involvement.

If the first missionary assignment for this purpose (finding the location for the New Jerusalem to be built before the Lord's return) was directed to the distant west, beyond Missouri, and Joseph's ambition was westward toward the Rocky Mountains, there is reason to suspect that our presumption that the New Jerusalem will be in Independence Missouri is somewhat misplaced. I am persuaded it will not be there until after the Lord's return. There will be a location elsewhere, in the Rocky Mountains, where the preliminary gathering to a Holy City to be built will occur before the Lord's return. Then, following His return, activities will also involve Jackson County.

What precedes His return may be diminutive, but that didn't matter in the case of Noah, so it won't matter in the coming days *like* the time of Noah. It will be interesting to see how the Lord fulfills His prophecies, promises and warnings, because He does tend to fulfill the prophecies He speaks. Oftentimes not in the way we imagine. Then we will understand the saying "the boundaries of the everlasting hills shall tremble at their presence."[1617] The initial gathering before the Lord's return will be in the Rocky Mountains.

This gathering will require a kind of social order we are unprepared to live. We cannot be "one" in the sense required for Zion in our present social, political, economic and educational systems. It requires a kind of inter-dependence and cooperation we find repulsive. Even those in the commune on Isaac Morely's farm, after converting to Mormonism, couldn't live the united order and have all things in common. It was this experience, prior to conversion, that led to the revelations about the united order. It fell apart. We've never had a successful long-term experience trying to live within that kind of system.

Question on Priesthood/Monarch

I received the following question:

"I was reviewing the audio version of *Teaching of the Prophet Joseph Smith*, and came across the part where Joseph makes the comment that High Priests are to administer in Spiritual things and hold communion with God. But not to 'exercise monarchical government', or appoint meetings with out the approval of the Elders. Considering the limited comment you

---

[1617] D&C 133:31 "And the boundaries of the everlasting hills shall tremble at their presence."

recently made on your blog regarding the divine right of kings, but also considering the invitation found in the temple to be both a priest and a king, I wondered how these thoughts reconciled and was interested to hear your thoughts."

My response:

The object of the Lord's return is governmental. More specifically, Monarchical. He will return to be a "King of kings" and a "Lord of lords."[1618] To be a King who presides over "kings" requires the existence of other kings. To be a Lord over other "lords" requires the existence of other lords. But the church's High Priests are not qualified to be that, and therefore cannot exercise such a monarchical form of government. To do that is a revolutionary act inside the United States of America. That is one reason the Lord has decreed there will be a full end to all nations.[1619] He will institute a new form of government that will not be compatible with other national interests.

The Lord's plans are quite different than we sometimes presume them to be. Joseph Smith was apparently tuned in to that in a surprisingly revolutionary way. It is no wonder he was killed. He represented a new era where old things were to be thrown down and a new order established.

Joseph represented an opportunity; but we weren't interested in it. Ultimately it was the Saints themselves who complained and got him to return and surrender. He remarked that if his life was of no value to his friends, it was of no value to him. He realized the Saints

---

[1618] Revelation 19:16 "And he hath on *his* vesture and on his thigh a name written, KING OF KINGS, AND LORD OF LORDS."

[1619] D&C 87:6 "And thus, with the sword and by bloodshed the inhabitants of the earth shall mourn; and with famine, and plague, and earthquake, and the thunder of heaven, and the fierce and vivid lightning also, shall the inhabitants of the earth be made to feel the wrath, and indignation, and chastening hand of an Almighty God, until the consumption decreed hath made a full end of all nations;"

were unwilling to follow into the kind of remaking of the world his ministry offered.

I doubt Joseph Smith would be any more welcome today than he was in his own time. I think we'd treat him like a crank, who entertained delusional ideas and offered a foolish, magical view of the world unworthy of serious consideration.

Kingship is tied to the promise of land, as we see in the case of Abraham, Isaac and Jacob, and Lehi and Nephi, among many others. When the land is given to the Lord's "king and priest" it comes from the Lord by His word and is everlasting. It is received by covenant, and when received the king *is* the land in a very real sense. He and it are connected by the covenant, and what goes on thereafter is a reflection of how the king (or his descendants) honor or dishonor the covenant.

Although the Melchizedek priesthood cannot exercise monarchical government (a form of government involving Patriarchal rule), there will be a return of this kind of order before the Lord returns. The remnant will build Zion. There will be an Ephraimite with the authorization there to "crown" those kings and lords who will rule with Christ at His return.[1620] Everything will happen as foretold. But we can't and aren't supposed to be able to see it beforehand. We are only supposed to witness it unfold before us. We cannot comprehend God's strange act. Those who take the Spirit for their guide will not be deceived or hewn down.[1621] This was the original form of priestly order from the beginning of time. It will return at the end of the

---

[1620] D&C 133:32 "And there shall they fall down and be crowned with glory, even in Zion, by the hands of the servants of the Lord, even the children of Ephraim."

[1621] Mark 13:5–6 "And Jesus answering them began to say, Take heed lest any *man* deceive you: For many shall come in my name, saying, I am *Christ;* and shall deceive many."
D&C 45:57 "For they that are wise and have received the truth, and have taken the Holy Spirit for their guide, and have not been deceived—verily I say unto you, they shall not be hewn down and cast into the fire, but shall abide the day."

world again.[1622] This priestly order is what allowed a small group to gather at Adam-Ondi-Ahman where the Lord visited with them and comforted Adam.[1623] That scene, involving Adam and seven who held this same priesthood will be re-enacted again at the end. We are working our way back in a great chiasm of history as the Lord counts us back to the beginning and we draw to the end. He calls it His "strange act".[1624] Joseph's ministry took us back to an earlier time. The Lord intends to return us back further.

But, again, these are things Joseph understood and began to put in place. Now we have only a tattered remainder of that original purpose and an ambition to become something more modern, like the other faiths. Today we have no capacity for monarchical government under the present organization of things. That might be a good thing. We get into less trouble that way.

Ambition for these things will not accomplish a thing. It will be the Lord's doing or it will not happen at all. He always tells us em-

---

[1622] Moses 6:7 "Now this same Priesthood, which was in the beginning, shall be in the end of the world also."

[1623] D&C 107:53–55 "Three years previous to the death of Adam, he called Seth, Enos, Cainan, Mahalaleel, Jared, Enoch, and Methuselah, who were all high priests, with the residue of his posterity who were righteous, into the valley of Adam-ondi-Ahman, and there bestowed upon them his last blessing. And the Lord appeared unto them, and they rose up and blessed Adam, and called him Michael, the prince, the archangel. And the Lord administered comfort unto Adam, and said unto him: I have set thee to be at the head; a multitude of nations shall come of thee, and thou art a prince over them forever."

[1624] D&C 101:95 "That I may proceed to bring to pass my act, my strange act, and perform my work, my strange work, that men may discern between the righteous and the wicked, saith your God."
Isaiah 28:21 "For the Lord shall rise up as *in* mount Perazim, he shall be wroth as *in* the valley of Gibeon, that he may do his work, his strange work; and bring to pass his act, his strange act."

phatically that it will be *Him* who brings again Zion, not us.[1625] Our ambition will not bring it to pass. Only His will can do so. The challenge, of course, is to be among those invited by the angels to participate rather than to be left among the residue who will be hewn down.

More Ancient than the New Testament

Someone made this comment: "I was listening to an interview in which you were talking about the current LDS church being like the New Testament church, as opposed to being like a much older patriarchal religion. I don't see the difference between the two. On my mission, a woman related the following story: Her brother had served his mission in Italy and on a p-day, while participating in some tourism activities, they toured an ancient Roman Catholic cathedral which had some fascinating murals on the walls. This missionary was amazed by the murals, took pictures, and she showed me copies. I requested copies of the pictures which she gave to me. They were pictures of paintings of people wearing robes which were unmistakably temple robes, the most amazing painting was depicting the veil in a temple. The temple robes were different from what we wear today in some respects, but with enough similarities there was no mistaking them. They had similar hats to what the men wear and

---

[1625] 3 Nephi 16:8 "But wo, saith the Father, unto the unbelieving of the Gentiles—for notwithstanding they have come forth upon the face of this land, and have scattered my people who are of the house of Israel; and my people who are of the house of Israel have been cast out from among them, and have been trodden under feet by them;"

Mosiah 12:22 "Thy watchmen shall lift up the voice; with the voice together shall they sing; for they shall see eye to eye when the Lord shall bring again Zion;"

Isaiah 52:8 "Thy watchmen shall lift up the voice; with the voice together shall they sing: for they shall see eye to eye, when the Lord shall bring again Zion."

D&C 84:99 "The Lord hath brought again Zion;
    The Lord hath redeemed his people, Israel,
    According to the election of grace,
    Which was brought to pass by the faith
    And covenant of their fathers."

they had the fig shaped aprons and most tellingly, they had symbols of the compass and the square. The painting of the temple depicted several posts covered by the veil between the posts. One of the posts had a little mallet hanging down and a hand sticking out between the curtain and the post. According to the story, the missionary asked the priest about the paintings and the priest could tell him nothing other than they were old paintings. The missionary knew better, as did I and anyone else who had ever been inside a modern temple."

My response: Read Nibley's book *Temple and Cosmos* and you'll probably see these ancient paintings, murals and mosaics. He has gathered together some interesting material. Val Brinkerhoff's two volume set *The Day Star* also gathers together a good deal of photographic material showing the antiquity of the temple themes and ceremonies. There is no question there are temple rites restored through Joseph Smith that relate to antiquity, and not merely to updating and correcting Masonic-inspired innovations. There was a liturgical return to antiquity in the post-New Testament era which many believe was grounded either in secret teachings of Christ during His ministry, or developed in His post-resurrection forty-day ministry.

However, in the case of the Restoration, had Joseph finished his work, there was something more coming. That is the issue I was referring to in the podcast. Look at Facsimile No. 2, explanatory notes numbers 9–21. You'll see there was more to come. Take a look at the *TPJS*, also, and you will find Joseph intended for something more than the New Testament era religion. His work was intended to bring back the very religion of the first man. This was to be more than merely a church, but "this is a new and an everlasting covenant, even that which was from the beginning."[1626]

[1626] D&C 22:1 "BEHOLD, I say unto you that all old covenants have I caused to be done away in this thing; and this is a new and an everlasting covenant, even that which was from the beginning."

You can also look at Margaret Barker's work such as *The Older Testament, The Great High Priest, The Great Angel, Temple Theology, The Lost Prophet, Hidden Tradition,* and *Temple Mysticism* and you will find a Protestant scholar whose thesis is that Christ was restoring the older faith, not creating a new one. Her work has so impressed Mormon scholars that she has been invited and spoken at BYU, in addition to presenting at the Smithsonian Conference on the Bicentennial of Joseph Smith.

Margaret Barker's writings suggest there was some very ancient covenant, along with an ancient priesthood that Christ was returning to the earth through His ministry. The New Testament church was not the objective of either Christ or Joseph Smith. Both were engaged in returning "that which was from the beginning."

Joseph's restored Temple rites are set in Eden. The quest to find God runs through the earliest contact between God and man involving the experience of the first man, Adam and his wife, Eve. They lived in God's presence at the beginning and the Temple message is that we must return there. Our quest is not to stop with a partial return, but a complete return to the beginning.

We tend to think we "have it all" and we got it from Joseph Smith. We have a New Testament church which is by far better than any other form of Christian organization, Catholic or Protestant. We tend to think that was the object the Lord had in mind when Joseph was spoken to from heaven. Then we claim to have preserved it perfectly from then until now. I'm suggesting two things: First, Joseph may not have given us everything because he died before the Nauvoo Temple was completed. The Lord's planned visit there did not happen. We got a lot, to be sure. Whether we have "that which was from the beginning" in the full panoply of what may have been received had the Lord come to restore the fullness in the completed Nauvoo Temple remains an interesting matter worth at least contemplating.

Second, we may not have perfectly preserved what we were given. After the November 1845 to February 1846 endowments ended, the endowment was not performed again until 1855. It was not reduced to writing until the 1870's. Several of the church leaders remarked at how surprised they were at how much Brigham Young could remember. That does not mean it was perfectly preserved, only that the volume of recalled material was surprising to them.

You are free to believe as you choose. You can presume the restoration was intended to deliver a replica of the New Testament church. We got that. If that was the objective, I would not dispute it was accomplished. However, I ask the question of whether the purpose was to reach back much further, and has yet to be accomplished. Will the time come when the restoration will have a look and feel rather more like the days of Noah than like the New Testament? I think if Christ knew what He was talking about then this is likely to be the case. I am of the view that there are many great and important things pertaining to the Kingdom of Heaven which He has yet to reveal.[1627]

I think the path to God will run back to the very beginning. It will involve a return to the the original, paradisiacal glory which was Eden. Zion is connected to that very return.[1628]

This is why I made the remark. It is my view, and certainly not the view of many others. You are in very good company if you think otherwise. We are, after all, allowed to believe according to the dic-

---

[1627] Article of Faith 9 "We believe all that God has revealed, all that He does now reveal, and we believe that He will yet reveal many great and important things pertaining to the Kingdom of God."

[1628] Article of Faith 10 "We believe in the literal gathering of Israel and in the restoration of the Ten Tribes; that Zion (the New Jerusalem) will be built upon the American continent; that Christ will reign personally upon the earth; and, that the earth will be renewed and receive its paradisiacal glory."

tates of our own conscience, and are free to exercise that privilege according to how we each understand God's will and intentions.[1629]

I like the idea that if an idea troubles you, then set it aside. It is either true or not true, and you are not yet in a position to comprehend it. Either way, it is not for you. Since we are all in the search to find our salvation before God, I trust God will deal with each of us in His patient, benign way and the truth will unfold before each sincere seeker. Until God in His wisdom makes a matter clear, no one should presume they can rush another person into accepting it.

I also believe the Lord will not leave the sincere seeker uninformed. He will not answer one person and deny another if they both ask and do so in sincerity willing to accept the answer. Any person who comes before God acknowledging He is a God of truth and cannot lie will learn the truth from Him.[1630] That also means if you are not willing to accept truth from Him, but require Him to meet you standard then there is really no point for Him to clarify things for you.

I am personally satisfied that the objective of returning to the most ancient, original faith, both was and is the purpose of Joseph Smith's calling. And that objective remains an unfinished work. It will finish, I think coincidentally with establishing Zion.

Ether's Reference to Christ as Father

Here is a question taken from the Book of Ether. The question:

"Explain Ether 4:12 where the Lord says: 'he that will not believe me will not believe the Father who sent me. For behold, I am the Father . . . ' I understand that the Father and

---

[1629] Article of Faith 11 "We claim the privilege of worshiping Almighty God according to the dictates of our own conscience, and allow all men the same privilege, let them worship how, where, or what they may."

[1630] Ether 3:12 "And he answered: Yea, Lord, I know that thou speakest the truth, for thou art a God of truth, and canst not lie."

Son are unified in everything and I understand that the Son is the Father because he has begotten us through the atonement and that He was also the creator. How would you explain that verse to someone just reading it for the first time? It sounds like a description of the trinity as many Christian religions view that the Father and Son are literally one being."

Response: Foremost in this creation is the reality of Christ. He lived. He died, voluntarily, as a sacrifice. His death was unmerited.[1631] He died because of other's sins, not because of His own.[1632] He did so to make an offering to appease the ends of the law.[1633]

Law has one purpose: It establishes required conduct that when violated requires a punishment to be imposed. Without punishment there is no law.[1634] We came here to live in a fallen state where we are subject to law and knowing when violate the law the result would

---

[1631] 1 Peter 2:22 "Who did no sin, neither was guile found in his mouth:"
Alma 22:13–14 "And Aaron did expound unto him the scriptures from the creation of Adam, laying the fall of man before him, and their carnal state and also the plan of redemption, which was prepared from the foundation of the world, through Christ, for all whosoever would believe on his name. And since man had fallen he could not merit anything of himself; but the sufferings and death of Christ atone for their sins, through faith and repentance, and so forth; and that he breaketh the bands of death, that the grave shall have no victory, and that the sting of death should be swallowed up in the hopes of glory; and Aaron did expound all these things unto the king."

[1632] 1 Peter 2:21–23 "For even hereunto were ye called: because Christ also suffered for us, leaving us an example, that ye should follow his steps: Who did no sin, neither was guile found in his mouth: Who, when he was reviled, reviled not again; when he suffered, he threatened not; but committed *himself* to him that judgeth righteously:"

[1633] 2 Nephi 2:6–7 "Wherefore, redemption cometh in and through the Holy Messiah; for he is full of grace and truth. Behold, he offereth himself a sacrifice for sin, to answer the ends of the law, unto all those who have a broken heart and a contrite spirit; and unto none else can the ends of the law be answered."

[1634] Alma 42:22 "But there is a law given, and a punishment affixed, and a repentance granted; which repentance, mercy claimeth; otherwise, justice claimeth the creature and executeth the law, and the law inflicteth the punishment; if not so, the works of justice would be destroyed, and God would cease to be God."

inevitably require punishment.[1635]   Christ came to suffer that punishment.[1636]

Overarching all else in this creation are the acts of two parties. Adam fell.[1637] Christ arose.[1638] Adam introduced death. Christ overcame it.[1639] Through Christ the law was made unjust because death could make no claim upon Him, but He willingly died to suffer the punishment He did not merit. That forever satisfied death's claim.[1640] Once it had claimed the life of one who did not deserve to die, it could no longer make claim on Him or those He came to redeem. His punishment was infinite, because His sacrifice was infinite. If He did not merit death then death took from Him what was infinite and would have no end.[1641] He submitted. His death satisfied the need for dying.

[1635] Alma 42:18 "Now, there was a punishment affixed, and a just law given, which brought remorse of conscience unto man."

[1636] 1 Peter 3:18 "For Christ also hath once suffered for sins, the just for the unjust, that he might bring us to God, being put to death in the flesh, but quickened by the Spirit:"

[1637] Moses 6:48 "And he said unto them: Because that Adam fell, we are; and by his fall came death; and we are made partakers of misery and woe."

[1638] Alma 11:42 "Now, there is a death which is called a temporal death; and the death of Christ shall loose the bands of this temporal death, that all shall be raised from this temporal death."

[1639] Mosiah 16:8 "But there is a resurrection, therefore the grave hath no victory, and the sting of death is swallowed up in Christ."

[1640] Mosiah 15:9 "Having ascended into heaven, having the bowels of mercy; being filled with compassion towards the children of men; standing betwixt them and justice; having broken the bands of death, taken upon himself their iniquity and their transgressions, having redeemed them, and satisfied the demands of justice."

[1641] Hebrews 4:15 "For we have not an high priest which cannot be touched with the feeling of our infirmities; but was in all points tempted like as *we are, yet* without sin."

Mankind still die. That is just; but after their death, Christ's sacrifice makes it possible to live again, just as He did.[1642] But you know all this already.

The "Father" of your eternal life will be Christ.[1643] He is your Father who is in heaven, because your continuation after the grave will come through His sacrifice. He will literally provide you with the resurrected body you will inherit. This makes Him the Father.[1644]

Secondly, they are His teachings which will provide you with more than just resurrection. He will provide the further possibility of glory to you on the conditions He has made possible through obedience to Him. The one you follow, whose teachings you accept, whose ordinances you accept, is also your Father.[1645] The role of the Father is to raise His seed in righteousness. Christ's teachings are given in His capacity of a Father to all who will follow Him. Through His teachings you can have a new life here and now. You can be "born again" as His seed.[1646] To do that you must first accept His role as your Father/guide. Then you must further accept His role as Father/Redeemer. When you do that, He gives you a new life by His teachings and new life by His ordinances.

[1642] Jacob 6:4 "And how merciful is our God unto us, for he remembereth the house of Israel, both roots and branches; and he stretches forth his hands unto them all the day long; and they are a stiffnecked and a gainsaying people; but as many as will not harden their hearts shall be saved in the kingdom of God."

[1643] D&C 35:2 "I am Jesus Christ, the Son of God, who was crucified for the sins of the world, even as many as will believe on my name, that they may become the sons of God, even one in me as I am one in the Father, as the Father is one in me, that we may be one."

[1644] Mosiah 5:7 "And now, because of the covenant which ye have made ye shall be called the children of Christ, his sons, and his daughters; for behold, this day he hath spiritually begotten you; for ye say that your hearts are changed through faith on his name; therefore, ye are born of him and have become his sons and his daughters."

[1645] 1 Corinthians 4:15 "For though ye have ten thousand instructors in Christ, yet have ye not many fathers: for in Christ Jesus I have begotten you through the gospel."

[1646] 1 Peter 1:23 "Being born again, not of corruptible seed, but of incorruptible, by the word of God, which liveth and abideth for ever."

Here, excluded from the presence of Heavenly Father Ahman[1647], we have no way back except through Christ.[1648] He must become our Father to bring us back again into the Ahman's presence. Christ visits here. Christ labored here, lived among us, ministers still among us, and though resurrected still walked alongside two of His disciples. He appeared in an upper room, cooked and ate fish on the lake's shore, and appeared to many. He will come to dwell here again. The Father Ahman, however, only appears in a state of glory, has not stood here since the Fall of Adam, and awaits the completion of the work of Christ before He will again take up His abode here.

Christ is not the same person as Father Ahman. Christ becomes the Father of all who are redeemed through Him. Therefore, by redeeming you Christ has become your Father in Heaven. You will have many fathers, including Christ, Adam, Noah, Abraham, Isaac, Jacob, and in our dispensation, Joseph Smith as well. And all these will also be children of Father Ahman.

Question on Sealing

Someone asked about sealing power. This is something that I'm not going to be able to answer on the blog. It would require too much, even for a multi-part posting as I have done on the Remnant and on Interpreting History. On the subject there are three chapters at the end of *Beloved Enos*, written from a perspective that accepts the church's claims to this authority. All the first seven books, to the extent the issue arises, accept the church's claim. In *Passing the Heavenly Gift,* the history is viewed from another perspective, but the ques-

---

[1647] D&C 78:20 "Wherefore, do the things which I have commanded you, saith your Redeemer, even the Son Ahman, who prepareth all things before he taketh you;"

[1648] Mosiah 3:12 "But wo, wo unto him who knoweth that he rebelleth against God! For salvation cometh to none such except it be through repentance and faith on the Lord Jesus Christ."

tion of whether this perspective is better than the traditional narrative is left to the reader to decide.

The closest thing to a direct discussion of how the Father seals someone His is found in the last parable in *Ten Parables*. Even there, however, the story is focused on the interplay between heaven and mankind, not those ordinances that exist in the unexplained events happening in the background.

Because of the importance of the subject and the many scriptures and important details which bear on the topic, it cannot be adequately explained without significant effort to marshall together the critical information. That is not appropriate for a blog. Nor are blog readers necessarily even going to understand the posts if they are unfamiliar with why the question would be asked.

I've pointed out that our ordinances contemplate a further ratification from heaven. In D&C 121:36–37 the power of heaven must ratify priestly power, or it is nonexistent.[1649] This is the same principle Joseph wrote about in Liberty Jail.[1650] In D&C 132:26 the ratification through the "Holy Spirit of Promise" must confirm a sealing for it to become eternal.[1651] Then in D&C 132:7 we learn it is possible for this to be conferred "on but one on the earth at a time"

[1649] D&C 121:36–37 "That the rights of the priesthood are inseparably connected with the powers of heaven, and that the powers of heaven cannot be controlled nor handled only upon the principles of righteousness. That they may be conferred upon us, it is true; but when we undertake to cover our sins, or to gratify our pride, our vain ambition, or to exercise control or dominion or compulsion upon the souls of the children of men, in any degree of unrighteousness, behold, the heavens withdraw themselves; the Spirit of the Lord is grieved; and when it is withdrawn, Amen to the priesthood or the authority of that man."

[1650] Ibid.

[1651] D&C 132:26 "Verily, verily, I say unto you, if a man marry a wife according to my word, and they are sealed by the Holy Spirit of promise, according to mine appointment, and he or she shall commit any sin or transgression of the new and everlasting covenant whatever, and all manner of blasphemies, and if they commit no murder wherein they shed innocent blood, yet they shall come forth in the first resurrection, and enter into their exaltation; but they shall be destroyed in the flesh, and shall be delivered unto the buffetings of Satan unto the day of redemption, saith the Lord God."

which made it possible for Joseph Smith to seal up to eternal life.[1652] In effect, Joseph became the Holy Spirit of Promise through operation of the Divine appointment to hold the right. That term "Holy Spirit of Promise" we use without adequate appreciation that it can be an office held by Divine appointment. The office is held by more than just a single mortal man at one time, and includes others who minister here as well. These, at a minimum, are the Lord, John the Beloved, the Three Nephite Disciples, Elijah, other angelic ministers, as well as potentially others about whom we know nothing.[1653] There is also the meaning of limiting it to one man "on the earth at a time" when it comes to widely separated people without any probability of contact during their lifetimes. An example would be when the Lord in His post-resurrection ministry appointed Apostles in Palestine and Disciples in the New World. He also may have had others in other locations during His many appearances in that season, all of whom were given similar authority to seal. Were they so geographically separated they could be said to be on different earths for all practical purposes? Or is there an exception undiscussed in Section 132 because the world has become smaller and more integrated since the Meridian of Time? I take no position on that, only pose the question.

The Missing Virtue focuses on the love between the man and woman. That love is what attracts the notice of angels, the approval

---

[1652] D&C 132:7 "And verily I say unto you, that the conditions of this law are these: All covenants, contracts, bonds, obligations, oaths, vows, performances, connections, associations, or expectations, that are not made and entered into and sealed by the Holy Spirit of promise, of him who is anointed, both as well for time and for all eternity, and that too most holy, by revelation and commandment through the medium of mine anointed, whom I have appointed on the earth to hold this power (and I have appointed unto my servant Joseph to hold this power in the last days, and there is never but one on the earth at a time on whom this power and the keys of this priesthood are conferred), are of no efficacy, virtue, or force in and after the resurrection from the dead; for all contracts that are not made unto this end have an end when men are dead."

[1653] D&C 49:8 "Wherefore, I will that all men shall repent, for all are under sin, except those which I have reserved unto myself, holy men that ye know not of."

of the Lord and the effort by heaven to bring the couple to salvation. They become fruit worth laying up against the season. Therefore, the work assigned by the Lord to the angels was to repair what was lacking in the man so as to preserve them against the day of the harvest. The underlying reason, the driving force, the preservative justifying heavenly attention in the story is the love between the man and woman which the angels recognize fits the pattern of heaven.

John said "God is love".[1654] Of all the power in earth and heaven, the greatest form of power is love. It is the power of creation, and motivation of God, the reason for existence and the purpose behind all we see here. It is the harmonizing attribute between man and woman, man and fellow-man, God and man, our descendants and ancestors. Our love motivates the highest aspirations, causes our greatest anxieties, moves us to action and summons our greatest will. This is godlike.

The ordinances matter a great deal. They are the physical manifestation of our love for God. They are important and symbolize everything we hope for, and all we desire to be in God's eyes. Our service to our ancestors through Temple work matters. It is the way we show our love for those who went before, even if we do not know a thing about them. The devotion and service we render does not go unnoticed by heaven.

God will preserve our love above everything else. It is in that attribute we find ourselves most like Him. Or, in other words, most like Them. Heaven is a community. The General Assembly and Church of the Firstborn are all elevated by their love for one another and love for their posterity, and are able to live in peace because they are given over to love.

Beyond ordinances and rites there is a power by which God governs. It is the power which creates, and which binds together as noth-

---

[1654] 1 John 4:8 "He that loveth not knoweth not God; for God is love."

ing else in the universe. The ordinances point to it, but you must become love for the Lord to pour power into the things you hope to have preserved.

No act of service will go unnoticed. No act of devotion is meaningless. Our ordinances matter a great deal. When done with love they have power. But the power to seal should be viewed as related to this great power, not as an administrative authorization or a corporate franchise. That view is so skewed and divorced from heaven that it almost always results in abuse, ambition, and perversion of men's hearts. When that happens, amen to the priesthood or authority of that man. If used to favor friends or to control and exercise dominion over others, it is political power, not priesthood power. But you have the revelations before you so you should already know that.

If I were to recommend any answer to someone troubled by the issue I would suggest first, it is a matter between you and heaven, not you and another man. The Lord has ample means to seal you up to eternal life whether you live in the most remote location on earth or in downtown Salt Lake City. That is irrelevant. Second, the greatest preservative is your love of God and your love of your fellow-man.[1655] This matters a great deal more than your calling, your connections, your income, your social status, age, genealogy or education.

More Ado about Church History and Race

We have yet another pronouncement concerning the church's past ban on priesthood for blacks. This is the most recent church statement:

[1655] Matthew 22:36–40 "Master, which *is* the great commandment in the law? Jesus said unto him, Thou shalt love the Lord thy God with all thy heart, and with all thy soul, and with all thy mind. This is the first and great commandment. And the second *is* like unto it, Thou shalt love thy neighbour as thyself. On these two commandments hang all the law and the prophets."

"The Church unequivocally condemns racism, including any and all past racism by individuals both inside and outside the Church. In 2006, then Church president Gordon B. Hinckley declared that 'no man who makes disparaging remarks concerning those of another race can consider himself a true disciple of Christ. Nor can he consider himself to be in harmony with the teachings of the Church. Let us all recognize that each of us is a son or daughter of our Father in Heaven, who loves all of His children.' Recently, the Church has also made the following statement on this subject: 'The origins of priesthood availability are not entirely clear. Some explanations with respect to this matter were made in the absence of direct revelation and references to these explanations are sometimes cited in publications. These previous personal statements do not represent Church doctrine.'"

If this is altogether accepted as a carefully considered, inspired and accurate statement of the truth, it raises some interesting questions about the church today and in the past:

President Hinckley's statement, reiterated again today, is that "no man who makes disparaging remarks concerning those of another race can consider himself a true disciple of Christ." If this is correct, how are we to now regard Brigham Young?

["In the preisthood I will tell you what it will do. Where the children of God to mingle there seed with the seed of Cain it would not only bring the curse of being deprived of the power of the preisthood upon themselves but they entail it upon their children after them, and they cannot get rid of it. If a man in an ungaurded moment should commit such a transgression, if he would walk up and say cut off my head, and kill man woman and child it would do a great deal towards atoning for the sin . . . It is a great blessing to the seed of Adam to have the seed of Cain for servants . . . Let this Church which is called the kingdom of God on the earth; we will sommons the first presidency, the twelve, the high counsel, the Bishoprick, and all the elders of Isreal, suppose we summons them to apear here, and here declare that it is right to mingle our seed, with the black race of Cain, that they shall come in with with us and be pertakers with us of all the blessings God has given to us. On that very day, and hour we should do so, the priesthood is taken from this Church and kingdom and God leaves us to our fate. The moment we consent to mingle with the seed of Cain the Church must go to desstruction . . . " (*Address to the Legislature* by LDS Church President and Territorial Governor Brigham Young, Feb. 5, 1852, spellings not corrected.)]

John Taylor?

["Why is it, in fact, that we should have a devil? Why did not the Lord kill him long ago? . . . He needed the devil and great many of those who do his bidding just to keep . . . our dependence upon God, . . . When he destroyed the inhabitants of the antediluvian world, he suffered a descendant of Cain to come through the flood in order that he [the devil] might be properly represented upon the earth (*Journal of Discourses*, vol. 23, Oct. 29. 1882, p. 336)].

Many others, even President J. Reuben Clark who objected to pictures in the Deseret News showing black and white children mingling together, made disparaging remarks. What of them? Are we now to regard them as not true disciples of Christ? If so, then what does that do for the church's status? Did the church pass through a lengthy era of being led by those who were not true disciples of Christ and yet retain all of our blessings, entitlements, power and priesthood? How did that operate? Can a non-true disciple of Christ pass along priesthood authority? Or is President Hinckley's declaration an overstatement because it proves too much? Does any of this raise the possibility that church leaders can in fact "lead us astray?" Or instead is it that we are never led astray, but they can make mistakes?

If so, how are we to distinguish between mistakes, and errors so serious they cannot be regarded as "true disciples of Christ" and yet
preclude leading us astray? Doesn't something have to give? Were the
church members who opposed the ban "true disciples" even though
they were out of harmony with their leaders? If that is the case, how
can we know where "true disciples" are to be found, if there is a
possibility for the lesser, dissident members who are out of harmony
with those leaders to be "true disciples of Christ?" Does it mean we
can have "true disciples" led by those who err in teaching for doctrine the commandments of men? Isn't this the problem the Lord
intended to solve in His opening statement to Joseph Smith? Are
there some leaders now serving who are "not true disciples of
Christ?" How do we distinguish between those who will be regarded
as "not true disciples of Christ" at some future point but who are
now serving in leadership? When do we know we are being taught
for doctrine the commandments of men?

These are very interesting questions. What a great opportunity
this presents for more study and careful contemplation by us
all. Should I agree with President Hinckley and think the worse of
earlier leaders? It seems harsh to think them "no true disciple of
Christ" on the one hand, but on the other their remarks are quite
disparaging of those of another race. Actually, disparaging of one specific race, not other races generally. Should culture bend a "prophet's
voice" or does a "prophet's voice" require culture to bend? Were they
originally just reflecting social values when speaking disparagingly
about the race, and are they doing the same now there is widespread
antipathy for racism? If that is the case, then do we really need anything more than popular opinion to guide us then and now?

If these church leaders spoke "in the absence of revelation" how
were they "revelators?" Or weren't they? If they were sustained as
"revelators" but spoke in the absence of revelation and were wrong,

how often has that happened? How often does it happen? How do we tell the difference between truth and teaching for doctrine the commandments of men? Aren't we told essentially everything coming out of the hierarchy is entitled to respect as if it were the Lord speaking? Does that apply when they speak "in the absence of revelation?" What a fascinating assortment of issues the church has now given us to ponder.

Does our eternal salvation require us to resolve these things correctly?

There are so many more questions I can think of now that the church has given this new announcement. I wonder why they weren't addressed in the latest announcement.

Fullness of the Gospel Among Gentiles

I've written about the issue of the "fullness of the Gospel" being rejected by the Gentiles on this blog in connection with a discussion of the Book of Mormon remnant and 3 Nephi 16:10. There is another mention made of this matter by the Lord in a prophecy He spoke to His Apostles at Jerusalem. That prophecy was restored by revelation through Joseph Smith.

The Lord explained to His Apostles that:

- Men's love to one another would wane.
- Iniquity would increase.
- The Times of the Gentiles would come in and the Gospel light would be restored to them.
- The Gentiles would not be willing to receive it, however.
- They would turn their hearts away from Christ.
- They would prefer the precepts of men.
- Then, because the Gentiles refused to accept His fullness, the Times of the Gentiles would be fulfilled.

- Nevertheless, there would be a few disciples who would stand in holy places and not be moved by the overflowing scourge poured out.[1656]

In the prophecy, the Lord returned to His parable of the Ten Virgins. For those who would take the Holy Spirit for their guide, and because of that "have not been deceived" they will abide the day and not be hewn down by the judgments to be poured out.[1657]

This revelation to Joseph Smith was in March 1831. It anticipated more would be given as the scriptures were revised. Matthew Chapter 24 was translated later that same year and appears in The Pearl of Great Price, as "Joseph Smith-Matthew." The latter-day tribulations begin with verse 31. There the warning again refers to the widespread latter-day deception. Even His "elect" will be vulnerable to being misled. However, before His return His ministering angels will preserve and gather those few who "treasureth up [His] word."[1658]

The Lord's prophecy focuses on two things His elect will have to rely on: Angels and the Holy Spirit. These two are the last days source through which His elect will find safety. Conspicuously absent are men, or perhaps more accurately, the arm of man.

[1656] D&C 45:27–32 "And the love of men shall wax cold, and iniquity shall abound. And when the times of the Gentiles is come in, a light shall break forth among them that sit in darkness, and it shall be the fulness of my gospel; But they receive it not; for they perceive not the light, and they turn their hearts from me because of the precepts of men. And in that generation shall the times of the Gentiles be fulfilled. And there shall be men standing in that generation, that shall not pass until they shall see an overflowing scourge; for a desolating sickness shall cover the land. But my disciples shall stand in holy places, and shall not be moved; but among the wicked, men shall lift up their voices and curse God and die."

[1657] D&C 45:56–57 "And at that day, when I shall come in my glory, shall the parable be fulfilled which I spake concerning the ten virgins. For they that are wise and have received the truth, and have taken the Holy Spirit for their guide, and have not been deceived—verily I say unto you, they shall not be hewn down and cast into the fire, but shall abide the day."

[1658] JS-Matthew 1:37 "And whoso treasureth up my word, shall not be deceived, for the Son of Man shall come, and he shall send his angels before him with the great sound of a trumpet, and they shall gather together the remainder of his elect from the four winds, from one end of heaven to the other."

Interestingly, the elect will be able to see this as it unfolds.[1659] They will recognize it is like the time of Noah.[1660] Then again, if those who thought themselves wise actually knew when the thief was coming in the night to overtake them, they would not have remained asleep.[1661]

Taken in aggregate, it appears the Gentiles do have a fair chance given to them. We can understand the Lord's lament, "what more could I have done?" Still, there is always a difference between saying, "I am of Christ," and "receiving the testimony of Christ."[1662]

The Importance of Scriptures

As a sign of the Lord's keen interest in the scriptures He pointed out to the Nephites they had neglected to include Samuel the Lamanite's prophecy in their records. He admonished them to "search the prophets" who had testified of Him.[1663] Samuel the Lamanite was an outsider, whose ethnic identity was with the largely apostate enemies of the Nephites. His genealogy was not kept among the Nephites. He did not live among them. Where he came from and

---

1659 JS–Matthew 1:39 "So likewise, mine elect, when they shall see all these things, they shall know that he is near, even at the doors;"

1660 JS–Matthew 1:41–42 "But as it was in the days of Noah, so it shall be also at the coming of the Son of Man; For it shall be with them, as it was in the days which were before the flood; for until the day that Noah entered into the ark they were eating and drinking, marrying and giving in marriage;"

1661 JS–Matthew 1:47 "But know this, if the good man of the house had known in what watch the thief would come, he would have watched, and would not have suffered his house to have been broken up, but would have been ready."

1662 D&C 76:100–101 "These are they who say they are some of one and some of another—some of Christ and some of John, and some of Moses, and some of Elias, and some of Esaias, and some of Isaiah, and some of Enoch; But received not the gospel, neither the testimony of Jesus, neither the prophets, neither the everlasting covenant."

1663 3 Nephi 23:5 "And whosoever will hearken unto my words and repenteth and is baptized, the same shall be saved. Search the prophets, for many there be that testify of these things."

where he went afterwards was apparently unknown to the Nephites. None of that mattered to the Lord, because the Lord sent him.

Samuel had no Nephite credentials. Everything necessary to assess his relevance is summed up by the Lord: "Verily, I say unto you, I commanded my servant Samuel, the Lamanite, that he should testify unto this people[.]"[1664]

When he spoke, Samuel modestly stated his credential: "Behold, I, Samuel, a Lamanite, do speak the words of the Lord which he doth put into my heart[.]"[1665] And, "behold, an angel of the Lord hath declared it unto me[.]"[1666]

Samuel warned them they were condemned because of their love of riches.[1667] This love caused them to be filled with "great pride, unto boasting, and unto great swelling, envyings, strifes, malice, per-

---

[1664] 3 Nephi 23:9 "Verily I say unto you, I commanded my servant Samuel, the Lamanite, that he should testify unto this people, that at the day that the Father should glorify his name in me that there were many saints who should arise from the dead, and should appear unto many, and should minister unto them. And he said unto them: Was it not so?"

[1665] Helaman 13:5 "And he said unto them: Behold, I, Samuel, a Lamanite, do speak the words of the Lord which he doth put into my heart; and behold he hath put it into my heart to say unto this people that the sword of justice hangeth over this people; and four hundred years pass not away save the sword of justice falleth upon this people."

[1666] Helaman 13:7 "And behold, an angel of the Lord hath declared it unto me, and he did bring glad tidings to my soul. And behold, I was sent unto you to declare it unto you also, that ye might have glad tidings; but behold ye would not receive me."

[1667] Helaman 13:20–22 "And the day shall come that they shall hide up their treasures, because they have set their hearts upon riches; and because they have set their hearts upon their riches, and will hide up their treasures when they shall flee before their enemies; because they will not hide them up unto me, cursed be they and also their treasures; and in that day shall they be smitten, saith the Lord. Behold ye, the people of this great city, and hearken unto my words; yea, hearken unto the words which the Lord saith; for behold, he saith that ye are cursed because of your riches, and also are your riches cursed because ye have set your hearts upon them, and have not hearkened unto the words of him who gave them unto you. Ye do not remember the Lord your God in the things with which he hath blessed you, but ye do always remember your riches, not to thank the Lord your God for them; yea, your hearts are not drawn out unto the Lord, but they do swell with great pride, unto boasting, and unto great swelling, envyings, strifes, malice, persecutions, and murders, and all manner of iniquities."

secutions, and murders, and all manner of iniquities."[1668] Samuel warned them they boast they would have accepted the true prophets and not persecuted them[1669], but they were worse than their predecessors because "if a prophet come among you and declareth unto you the word of the Lord, which testifieth of your sins and iniquities, ye are angry with him, and cast him out and seek all manner of ways to destroy him; yea, you will say that he is a false prophet, and that he is a sinner, and of the devil, because he testifieth that your deeds are evil."[1670]

In contrast, when a man comes to declare the people are righteous, and do not need to repent, but all is well with them, such a man "ye will receive him, and say that he is a prophet. Yea, ye will lift him up, and ye will give unto him of your substance; ye will give unto him of your gold, and of your silver, and ye will clothe him with costly apparel; and because he speaketh flattering words unto you, and he saith that all is well, then ye will not find fault with him."[1671]

[1668] Helaman 13:22 "Ye do not remember the Lord your God in the things with which he hath blessed you, but ye do always remember your riches, not to thank the Lord your God for them; yea, your hearts are not drawn out unto the Lord, but they do swell with great pride, unto boasting, and unto great swelling, envyings, strifes, malice, persecutions, and murders, and all manner of iniquities.

[1669] Helaman 13:25 "And now when ye talk, ye say: If our days had been in the days of our fathers of old, we would not have slain the prophets; we would not have stoned them, and cast them out."

[1670] Helaman 13:26 "Behold ye are worse than they; for as the Lord liveth, if a prophet come among you and declareth unto you the word of the Lord, which testifieth of your sins and iniquities, ye are angry with him, and cast him out and seek all manner of ways to destroy him; yea, you will say that he is a false prophet, and that he is a sinner, and of the devil, because he testifieth that your deeds are evil."

[1671] Helaman 13:27–28 "But behold, if a man shall come among you and shall say: Do this, and there is no iniquity; do that and ye shall not suffer; yea, he will say: Walk after the pride of your own hearts; yea, walk after the pride of your eyes, and do whatsoever your heart desireth—and if a man shall come among you and say this, ye will receive him, and say that he is a prophet. Yea, ye will lift him up, and ye will give unto him of your substance; ye will give unto him of your gold, and of your silver, and ye will clothe him with costly apparel; and because he speaketh flattering words unto you, and he saith that all is well, then ye will not find fault with him."

Though the Nephites rejected him, and he fled from among them, when the Lord came He acknowledged He had sent Samuel. He criticized the Nephite records for neglecting to include the full extent of Samuel's prophecy, asking "How is it that ye have not written this thing[?]"[1672] The content of scriptures should always reflect the Lord's words, no matter the source He elects to speak them.

This example from the Book of Mormon is a clear warning intended for our day. Christ's admonition to "Search the prophets" is just as important an admonition now as it was then. So the challenge remains to keep ourselves ready, and listen to the words of the Prophets. It is our common misconception, however, that there will never be another Samuel the Lamanite who is an outsider and without credentials to be given a message for us by the Lord. We expect that if there is a message for our day it will come from the head of the church, not some obscure outsider, like Samuel. We imagine it is always safe to disregard such characters. It is curious, however, that the Book of Mormon, which is the "most correct book" includes this odd departure as an example. It is odd the Nephites never figured out our system. It is so much better than theirs was. We really are a royal generation, the most blessed of all who have ever lived! We never face such a test, because we imagine we have an authorized source of truth, an institutional charisma that can never fail, and through which we can never be led astray. The Lord has made it so much easier for us in our day. It somehow makes sense to us, but leaves me wondering if the Lord ought not apologize to the Nephites for making it so much harder for them. Then there is that unfortunate recent announcement by the church a few days ago about church leaders speaking "in the absence of revelation" which complicates these questions.

[1672] 3 Nephi 23:11 "And Jesus said unto them: How be it that ye have not written this thing, that many saints did arise and appear unto many and did minister unto them?"

It makes me wonder if our eternal salvation depends on sorting out the truth from error. Or, alternatively, if it matters in the more immediate unfolding history preliminary to the Second Coming and the whole earth being cursed if we get it wrong.

Cake: Shadow Stabbing

Cake's lyrical prose sometimes strikes a chord of truth. I've puzzled over why they aren't recognized for their musical genius by more folks.

> "Adjectives on the typewriter
> He moves his words like a prizefighter
> The frenzied pace of the mind inside the cell . . .
> Outside, outside the world
> Out there you don't hear the echoes and calls
> But the steel eye, tight jaw,
> Say it all, say it all
> But the white paint, plastic saints
> Say it all, say it all, say it all . . .
> Say somebody's got to say it all
> Somebody's got to say it all . . . " (*Cake: Shadow Stabbing*)

How much wasted time is devoted on the umbilical keyboards of the Internet ranting over things that have no value, giving the misimpression of accomplishing something important? In the din of opinion, we gather that the truth no longer has an independent existence. It is all opinion. If you should sway it then you've done something godlike, because in the polling and measuring what people think really matters.

Outside there is still God. Even if we don't hear the echoes and calls of the flood engulfing mankind when we turn to Him. There, apart, outside the world, if you should encounter God you will find yourself with a steel eye and tight jaw, and no longer able to look upon the white paint and plastic saints where the world continues to adore and worship.

Somebody's got to say it all . . .

Not to please others, but to just speak what desperately needs to be said. Somebody's got to speak it.

I am a Latter-day Saint. But that is merely a congregation. It doesn't matter much, really. Within that congregation there are those who want to control what I think. They are waging a losing battle. To win they must persuade, not condemn and intimidate. Show me the errors and I will gladly abandon them. Demand I walk away from truth and I will die first. This is why truth can only ever be spread by gentleness and meekness, by persuasion and kindness. It cannot be dictated.[1673]

When all you have left is a hollow cry that you have authority, you've lost the argument. *You* (no matter who "you" are) don't have any authority. Only heaven has that.[1674] And it isn't sharing it with the proud, vain, ambitious and controlling.[1675]

Quoting someone in a position of "authority" who is not in possession of the truth should not persuade anyone, and certainly does

---

[1673] D&C 121:41–42 "No power or influence can or ought to be maintained by virtue of the priesthood, only by persuasion, by long-suffering, by gentleness and meekness, and by love unfeigned; By kindness, and pure knowledge, which shall greatly enlarge the soul without hypocrisy, and without guile—"

[1674] D&C 121:35–36 "Because their hearts are set so much upon the things of this world, and aspire to the honors of men, that they do not learn this one lesson— That the rights of the priesthood are inseparably connected with the powers of heaven, and that the powers of heaven cannot be controlled nor handled only upon the principles of righteousness."

[1675] D&C 121:37 "That they may be conferred upon us, it is true; but when we undertake to cover our sins, or to gratify our pride, our vain ambition, or to exercise control or dominion or compulsion upon the souls of the children of men, in any degree of unrighteousness, behold, the heavens withdraw themselves; the Spirit of the Lord is grieved; and when it is withdrawn, Amen to the priesthood or the authority of that man."

not persuade me. Those echoes and calls can't even be heard once you've gone outside the world.

Ignorance can be put on stilts and equipped with a bullhorn, requiring everyone to notice it. But it remains unworthy of the time it takes from you.

It would be better to know God than to please men. I doubt many men who know God ever do please men again. Instead they look with pity at the white paint and plastic saints. It would be good to reach them, but it is only necessary to let God reach you.

It Will Be Again

As it was once, it will be again. Adam was born again and received the Record of Heaven, or in other words the Holy Ghost.[1676] Adam was born of the Spirit and quickened in the inner man.[1677] Through this he was after the Order of the Father.[1678] This same Order will return again at the end of the world.[1679] The end of the

---

[1676] Moses 6:66 "And he heard a voice out of heaven, saying: Thou art baptized with fire, and with the Holy Ghost. This is the record of the Father, and the Son, from henceforth and forever;"

[1677] Moses 6:65 "And thus he was baptized, and the Spirit of God descended upon him, and thus he was born of the Spirit, and became quickened in the inner man."

[1678] Moses 6:67 "And thou art after the order of him who was without beginning of days or end of years, from all eternity to all eternity."

[1679] Moses 6:7 "Now this same Priesthood, which was in the beginning, shall be in the end of the world also."

world is the destruction of the wicked[1680] to happen at the Lord's return.[1681]

This same Order is connected with surviving the day of His return. "There are, in the church, two priesthoods."[1682] "There are three grand orders of priesthood referred to [in the Epistle to the Hebrews]" (*TPJS*, 22–23; *DHC* 5:554–55).

God, who presides over this process, created Adam in His likeness and image. The image of God's body consists of both the male and female, and they together are called Adam.[1683] Through it, the man and woman called Adam begat a son named Seth.[1684] From this we can see the procreative power, which produces offspring, is possible only through the man and woman called Adam, because together they possess this godlike attribute. Apart they are not in God's

---

[1680] JS-Matt. 1:4 "And Jesus left them, and went upon the Mount of Olives. And as he sat upon the Mount of Olives, the disciples came unto him privately, saying: Tell us when shall these things be which thou hast said concerning the destruction of the temple, and the Jews; and what is the sign of thy coming, and of the end of the world, or the destruction of the wicked, which is the end of the world?"

[1681] Matthew 13:38–40 "The field is the world; the good seed are the children of the kingdom; but the tares are the children of the wicked *one;* The enemy that sowed them is the devil; the harvest is the end of the world; and the reapers are the angels. As therefore the tares are gathered and burned in the fire; so shall it be in the end of this world."

[1682] D&C 107:1 "THERE are, in the church, two priesthoods, namely, the Melchizedek and Aaronic, including the Levitical Priesthood."

[1683] Moses 6:9 "In the image of his own body, male and female, created he them, and blessed them, and called their name Adam, in the day when they were created and became living souls in the land upon the footstool of God."

[1684] Moses 6:10 "And Adam lived one hundred and thirty years, and begat a son in his own likeness, after his own image, and called his name Seth."

image. Their seed continues, which is what God does.[1685] The return of this Order, that was from the beginning, requires the man and woman who have had God's Spirit poured on them, and have been quickened. It is promised to return again before the end of the world.

We do not inherit these things by imposing our views on God, but by allowing ourselves to become converted to His views. His are as far above ours as the heavens are above the earth.[1686] We must receive counsel from Him, not give it.[1687] God alone makes us a son of God.[1688] Enoch was also a son of God.[1689]

[1685] D&C 132:19–20 "And again, verily I say unto you, if a man marry a wife by my word, which is my law, and by the new and everlasting covenant, and it is sealed unto them by the Holy Spirit of promise, by him who is anointed, unto whom I have appointed this power and the keys of this priesthood; and it shall be said unto them—Ye shall come forth in the first resurrection; and if it be after the first resurrection, in the next resurrection; and shall inherit thrones, kingdoms, principalities, and powers, dominions, all heights and depths—then shall it be written in the Lamb's Book of Life, that he shall commit no murder whereby to shed innocent blood, and if ye abide in my covenant, and commit no murder whereby to shed innocent blood, it shall be done unto them in all things whatsoever my servant hath put upon them, in time, and through all eternity; and shall be of full force when they are out of the world; and they shall pass by the angels, and the gods, which are set there, to their exaltation and glory in all things, as hath been sealed upon their heads, which glory shall be a fulness and a continuation of the seeds forever and ever. Then shall they be gods, because they have no end; therefore shall they be from everlasting to everlasting, because they continue; then shall they be above all, because all things are subject unto them. Then shall they be gods, because they have all power, and the angels are subject unto them."

[1686] Isaiah 55:9 "For as the heavens are higher than the earth, so are my ways higher than your ways, and my thoughts than your thoughts."

[1687] D&C 22:4 "Wherefore, enter ye in at the gate, as I have commanded, and seek not to counsel your God. Amen."

[1688] Moses 6:68 "Behold, thou art one in me, a son of God; and thus may all become my sons. Amen."

[1689] Moses 6:27 "And he heard a voice from heaven, saying: Enoch, my son, prophesy unto this people, and say unto them—Repent, for thus saith the Lord: I am angry with this people, and my fierce anger is kindled against them; for their hearts have waxed hard, and their ears are dull of hearing, and their eyes cannot see afar off;"

Noah, whose days are like the Coming of the Son, was ordained to this same Order by God.[1690] Noah called upon men to repent, but men did not listen to him.[1691] Moses told them to repent and follow Jesus Christ, receive the Spirit and be taught by heaven which will reveal all things; but the people did not listen.[1692]

When they refused to repent, God destroyed all flesh because of their corruption and violence.[1693] "But as it was in the days of Noah, so it shall be also at the coming of the Son of Man" (JS–Matthew 1:41). The good news is that this Order will return. There will be the opportunity to repent. God intends to make sons again. This promise should make us all search the matter and freely repent of our sins, using the Spirit as our guide to find God's will. Then we should have the courage to conform to it. This is good news, as long as we are willing to heed it.

Discarding and Staying Aloft

You can throw things out of the hot air balloon to try to stay aloft. But eventually, you will run out of things to discard and will descend anyway.

[1690] Moses 8:19 "And the Lord ordained Noah after his own order, and commanded him that he should go forth and declare his Gospel unto the children of men, even as it was given unto Enoch."

[1691] Moses 8:20 "And it came to pass that Noah called upon the children of men that they should repent; but they hearkened not unto his words;"

[1692] Moses 8:24 "Believe and repent of your sins and be baptized in the name of Jesus Christ, the Son of God, even as our fathers, and ye shall receive the Holy Ghost, that ye may have all things made manifest; and if ye do not this, the floods will come in upon you; nevertheless they hearkened not."

[1693] Moses 8:28–30 "The earth was corrupt before God, and it was filled with violence. And God looked upon the earth, and, behold, it was corrupt, for all flesh had corrupted its way upon the earth. And God said unto Noah: The end of all flesh is come before me, for the earth is filled with violence, and behold I will destroy all flesh from off the earth."

There is only one real solution to staying aloft: You must return to what got you lighter than air in the first place. There must be more fire.

You can't fake such a fire. Your claims to have fire will accomplish nothing. You will continue to descend, even if there are momentary jumps from throwing something weighty overboard. Rhetoric is powerless to curb the fall.

Repentance

I received a question: "Knowing that the local church leaders sometimes misjudge the repentance process and sometimes struggle to know what the individual truly needs. Is it possible to properly repent for serious sins and have the repentance process be between just you and the Lord, without confessing your sins to your bishop? On many occasions, we read in the scriptures that repentance was done by confession to the Lord alone. If you truly had a change of heart and had abandon the sin, wouldn't it be ok for you and I to do the same today, as recorded in the scriptures, without confessing to church authorities?"

This question is a reflection of just how "institutional" our orientation has become. The church is powerless to forgive sins. Christ forgave sins during His mortal ministry.[1694] Christ forgives sins in His current ministry.[1695]

Christ may allow men to possess the power to forgive sins as in the case of Joseph Smith,[1696] but that has definite limits. Men are given such power because they will **never** use it *independently* of the Lord's will.[1697]. Even those who will be allowed to "judge" others in the final judgment, will not have independent reign, but must announce Christ's judgment, not their own.[1698]

[1694] Mark 2:5–12 "When Jesus saw their faith, he said unto the sick of the palsy, Son, thy sins be forgiven thee. But there were certain of the scribes sitting there, and reasoning in their hearts, Why doth this *man* thus speak blasphemies? who can forgive sins but God only? And immediately when Jesus perceived in his spirit that they so reasoned within themselves, he said unto them, Why reason ye these things in your hearts? Whether is it easier to say to the sick of the palsy, *Thy* sins be forgiven thee; or to say, Arise, and take up thy bed, and walk? But that ye may know that the Son of man hath power on earth to forgive sins, (he saith to the sick of the palsy,) I say unto thee, Arise, and take up thy bed, and go thy way into thine house. And immediately he arose, took up the bed, and went forth before them all; insomuch that they were all amazed, and glorified God, saying, We never saw it on this fashion."

[1695] D&C 61:2 "Behold, verily thus saith the Lord unto you, O ye elders of my church, who are assembled upon this spot, whose sins are now forgiven you, for I, the Lord, forgive sins, and am merciful unto those who confess their sins with humble hearts;"

[1696] D&C 132:46 "And verily, verily, I say unto you, that whatsoever you seal on earth shall be sealed in heaven; and whatsoever you bind on earth, in my name and by my word, saith the Lord, it shall be eternally bound in the heavens; and whosoever sins you remit on earth shall be remitted eternally in the heavens; and whosoever sins you retain on earth shall be retained in heaven."

[1697] Helaman 10:5 "And now, because thou hast done this with such unwearyingness, behold, I will bless thee forever; and I will make thee mighty in word and in deed, in faith and in works; yea, even that all things shall be done unto thee according to thy word, for thou shalt not ask that which is contrary to my will."

[1698] 3 Nephi 27:27 "And know ye that ye shall be judges of this people, according to the judgment which I shall give unto you, which shall be just. Therefore, what manner of men ought ye to be? Verily I say unto you, even as I am."

The only one who can forgive sin is Christ. He requires us to forgive one another, but will Himself determine whose sins He will forgive.[1699] He is the only gatekeeper for forgiveness.[1700]

If you think the church leader is attuned to the Lord's voice and can give you comfort, encouragement to come to Christ, and help guide you in the path, then counseling with such a man is very worthwhile, but he cannot forgive sins, for that you are required to look to the Lord.

[1699] D&C 64:10 "I, the Lord, will forgive whom I will forgive, but of you it is required to forgive all men."

[1700] 2 Nephi 9:41 "O then, my beloved brethren, come unto the Lord, the Holy One. Remember that his paths are righteous. Behold, the way for man is narrow, but it lieth in a straight course before him, and the keeper of the gate is the Holy One of Israel; and he employeth no servant there; and there is none other way save it be by the gate; for he cannot be deceived, for the Lord God is his name."

Nephi's Brother Jacob

The first words from Jacob, Nephi's brother, are marvelous. He begins his public ministry among the people of Nephi with these words:

"I, Jacob, having been called of God, and ordained after the manner of his holy order, and having been consecrated by my brother Nephi," (2 Nephi 6:2.)

Jacob was "called of God." He was also "ordained after the manner of his holy order," meaning that his ordination came from God. He was like Melchizedek. The manner of this ordination is described as follows:

"[H]aving been approved of God, he was ordained an high priest after the order of the covenant which God made with Enoch, It being after the order of the Son of God; which order came, not by man, nor the will of man; neither by father nor mother; neither by beginning of days nor end of years; but of God; And it was delivered unto men by the calling of his own voice, according to his own will, unto as many as believed on his name." (JST–Genesis 14:27–29)

This was the holy order to which Jacob was called by God.

In the restoration of the Gospel, the first time this appeared in the church was in June, 1831 on Isaac Morley's farm. As Joseph Smith recorded it in his history:

" . . . the authority of the Melchizedek Priesthood was manifested and conferred for the first time upon several of the Elders. It was clearly evident that the Lord gave us power in proportion to the work to be done, and strength according to the race set before us, and grace and help as our needs required." (*DHC* 1:175–177)

To understand this statement of Joseph you would need to recognize there is a great difference between being "an Elder in the church"—an office held by operation of the church's organization, much like a Relief Society President or a Sunday School President— and the Melchizedek Priesthood. Today there is no appreciation of that distinction. That is because we have little understanding of the history of the church or the scriptures.

In any event, Jacob was ordained by God to "his holy order" or, in other words, received the same High Priesthood as Melchizedek in the only way it can be received: "It [is] delivered unto men by the calling of His own voice." Jacob was one of those.

Despite this, Jacob's right to be a teacher among the people of Nephi reckoned from his brother's presiding authority. Although Jacob was in possession of this calling from God, in order to minister to the people he needed to also be "consecrated by my brother, Nephi." It was Nephi who was the presiding authority. Therefore, to preach to the congregation Jacob needed to be called and authorized. Nephi did this, and Jacob became a recognized, sustained teacher.

Without both, Jacob could have preached, taught and expounded, but he would not be able to speak in an organized meeting of the church over which Nephi presided. From this we see the order of things. The church and God's authority do not necessarily overlap. But, in his wisdom, Nephi used the very man who God had empowered to be a minister of righteousness within the church over which Nephi presided. Nephi did not envy his younger brother's calling, but supported and advanced him in it. Of course Nephi held the same calling, but that does not matter. Somehow men can find it within them to be jealous of others even if they are called themselves. After all, Lucifer *was* a son of the morning.

Joseph Smith, by revelation in January, 1841, was told that his brother Hyrum was to become "a prophet, and a seer, and a revelator unto my church."[1701] Joseph did not envy his brother this calling, but immediately ordained him to the office of Assistant President; in an almost identical manner as had Nephi with his brother Jacob.

From the first phrase out of Jacob's mouth, we encounter doctrine so very meaningful to understanding the way of God. What a great book we have in the Book of Mormon. I do think a man can get closer to God by abiding its precepts than from any other book!

Nephi's Brother Jacob, Part 2

Jacob's first *recorded* sermon is not his **first** sermon. Quite the contrary. He admits he was given to a lot of preaching. Jacob records this:

> "ye know that I have spoken unto you exceedingly many things. Nevertheless, I speak unto you again; for I am desirous for the welfare of your souls. Yea, mine anxiety is great for you; and ye yourselves know that it ever has been. For I have exhorted you with all diligence; and I have taught you the words of my father; and I have spoken unto you concerning all things which are written, from the creation of the world." (2 Nephi 6:2–3)

[1701] D&C 124:94 "And from this time forth I appoint unto him that he may be a prophet, and a seer, and a revelator unto my church, as well as my servant Joseph;"

Jacob's preaching was plentiful, and always based on two things: First, the words of Lehi. Second, the scriptures. In other words, he was not an innovator. He was a custodian of truth. He wanted to preserve the revelations entrusted to the Nephites; not to add to them, or stray from them.

It is interesting he had this strict orientation in his teaching, because give his background, he could have ventured into a great many other thing. We know his knowledge reached beyond the veil. As Nephi put it: "[Isaiah] verily saw my Redeemer, even as I have seen him. And my brother, Jacob, also has seen him as I have seen him" (2 Nephi 11:2–3). In their knowledge of the Redeemer, Isaiah, Nephi and Jacob were peers. Notice how distinct they were from one another in what they revealed. Although Nephi revealed some of what he learned, he used Isaiah as the primary source for his prophetic teaching. Jacob was even more discreet in how he ministered. Isaiah, on the other hand, wrote an extensive prophecy about all of history.

In his earliest recorded sermon Jacob reminds the audience how strictly he confined himself to the two categories above. Then, after Nephi's death, when he took over as the primary prophetic leader of the Nephites, he still displayed the same caution about the text he took for his material. He told the people to come to the Temple and he would prophesy to them.[1702] Then in his sermon he quoted at length an allegory from the Prophet Zenos (in Jacob 5). When he finished the lengthy quote he added his prophecy:

> "as I said unto you that I would prophesy, behold, this is my prophecy—that the things which this prophet Zenos spake, concerning the house of Israel, in the which he likened them unto a tame olive tree, must surely come to pass." (Jacob 6:1)

[1702] Jacob 2:2 "Now, my beloved brethren, I, Jacob, according to the responsibility which I am under to God, to magnify mine office with soberness, and that I might rid my garments of your sins, I come up into the temple this day that I might declare unto you the word of God."

It goes by quickly, but there it is. Jacob's prophecy is that what he read, the account Zenos wrote, was true. Jacob knew it was true. He had seen it, just like Isaiah had seen it, just like Nephi had seen it, and could tell you that Zenos also saw it and recorded the truth concerning the Lord's unfolding work among the chosen house of Israel.

There is so much about Nephi's younger brother which is a model of the true prophet. His ministry reflects the very things which we should expect to see from a messenger sent by the Lord.

Nephi's Brother Jacob, Part 3

When Nephi composed his small plate account, it was approximately 40 years after they left Jerusalem. He included his visionary experiences, but stopped short of giving a full account.[1703] As he prophesied about the coming of a Messiah to his brothers, they challenged Nephi's teaching of a future Messiah. In that context, he resorted to quoting Isaiah "that I might more fully persuade them to believe in the Lord their Redeemer" (1 Nephi 19:23). Nephi's use of Isaiah in his first book is limited to the single topic of whether the scriptures confirmed his *own prophesy* that there would be a Redeemer (see 1 Nephi 20 and 21.)

The next quote of Isaiah occurs in Nephi's second book. There the material is quoted by Nephi's younger brother Jacob in his first recorded sermon. In Jacob's use of Isaiah, the scope expands dramatically. Jacob uses it to cover the history, the scattering and regathering of Israel, the latter-day Zion, and then he preaches and expounds on these materials to give context to the Nephite experience (see 2 Nephi 6–10.)

[1703] 1 Nephi 14:25 "But the things which thou shalt see hereafter thou shalt not write; for the Lord God hath ordained the apostle of the Lamb of God that he should write them."

It is Jacob's more expansive use of Isaiah that seems to have inspired Nephi to turn to the Isaiah materials to complete his own record. When Jacob's sermon is finished, Nephi then adds 14 additional chapters of Isaiah material to complete his record. Then, to end his message Nephi takes Isaiah's themes and gives his final lessons in an American setting, elaborating on the Isaiah themes.

These transcripts raise the possibility that it was Jacob, rather than Nephi, who saw the fit between Isaiah's materials and the Nephite/latter-day Americas. Nephi no doubt used the Isaiah material first, but confined it to the promise of a Messiah. He used it defensively to respond to his older brothers' criticism. Jacob, on the other hand, uses it expansively.

If Nephi was giving credit to Jacob for this expansion (as his two books seem to indicate), then it tells us a great deal about Jacob, and even more about Nephi. For Jacob, we can know:

- He was a careful student of scripture.
- He saw what was possible, not only what was evident on the surface.
- He could apply Isaiah prophetically into the distant future.
- He could put his life and his people's position in history into a prophetic context.
- He was more concerned with the future than with the past.
- He saw their time as important, but not the end of times.

What it would tell us about Nephi is that:

- He was meek.
- He gave credit to his younger brother.
- He allowed truth from the younger brother to instruct even him, the elder brother.
- He refused to fall into his own older brother's jealousy and resentments.
- He was a ready student of Jacob's—the younger brother.

- He recognized inspired truths.

- He wanted others to rejoice in the truth, even if he took a step back in allowing them to be presented.

- He rejoiced in the learning of others.

There is a great deal about the interplay between these two brothers that ought to inform our own approach to authority, truth, learning, "presiding" and recognizing inspiration in others. The Book of Mormon is a treasury of lessons applicable to us. We do not adequately appreciate them.

Nephi's Brother Jacob, Part 4

Jacob's first recorded sermon identifies what concerns him. It is the "welfare of souls"[1704] and "things which are, and which are to come".[1705] The definition of truth is knowledge of things which are, which were, and which are to come.[1706] Jacob is interested in teaching truth. But the truth he wants to focus on is the present and future of his people.

He identifies Isaiah as speaking "concerning all the house of Israel"[1707] and therefore they can be likened to the Nephites. Then he turns to the Gentiles and places them in the future role of "bringing

---

[1704] 2 Nephi 6:3 "Nevertheless, I speak unto you again; for I am desirous for the welfare of your souls. Yea, mine anxiety is great for you; and ye yourselves know that it ever has been. For I have exhorted you with all diligence; and I have taught you the words of my father; and I have spoken unto you concerning all things which are written, from the creation of the world."

[1705] 2 Nephi 6:4 "And now, behold, I would speak unto you concerning things which are, and which are to come; wherefore, I will read you the words of Isaiah. And they are the words which my brother has desired that I should speak unto you. And I speak unto you for your sakes, that ye may learn and glorify the name of your God."

[1706] D&C 93:24 "And truth is knowledge of things as they are, and as they were, and as they are to come."

[1707] 2 Nephi 6:5 "And now, the words which I shall read are they which Isaiah spake concerning all the house of Israel; wherefore, they may be likened unto you, for ye are of the house of Israel. And there are many things which have been spoken by Isaiah which may be likened unto you, because ye are of the house of Israel."

thy sons in their arms, and thy daughters shall be carried upon their shoulders."[1708] In the dismal future of Nephite destruction by the Gentiles, there is still a more distant day when Gentile efforts will become helpful, not destructive. When that happens, the Gentile fortunes are reversed, and they will "bow down to [the Nephite remnant] with their faces towards the earth, and lick up the dust of [Nephite] feet."[1709] So the cataclysm which befalls the Nephites will also befall their Gentile vanquishers. They will be brought down to the dust as well.

Jacob also reports to his audience "the Lord has shown unto me that those who were at Jerusalem, from whence we came, have been slain and carried away captive."[1710] Jacob must have asked to be shown. He asked and was shown, and therefore he knew his family had left Jerusalem in time to avert death or captivity. Jacob was born after they left Jerusalem; but he knew about it, inquired to know, and was shown their destruction.

This reaffirms how the departure by Lehi and the destruction of Jerusalem was inter-related. The Lord uses 'just-in-time' scheduling of events more often than not. There is no need to flee until the moment when the destruction is about to begin. Nor is there a need to begin the rainfall before the ark is completed. Nor is there a need to send down fire to consume the offering until the altar is built, the

---

[1708] 2 Nephi 6:6 "And now, these are the words: Thus saith the Lord God: Behold, I will lift up mine hand to the Gentiles, and set up my standard to the people; and they shall bring thy sons in their arms, and thy daughters shall be carried upon their shoulders."

[1709] 2 Nephi 6:7 "And kings shall be thy nursing fathers, and their queens thy nursing mothers; they shall bow down to thee with their faces towards the earth, and lick up the dust of thy feet; and thou shalt know that I am the Lord; for they shall not be ashamed that wait for me."

[1710] 2 Nephi 6:8 "And now I, Jacob, would speak somewhat concerning these words. For behold, the Lord has shown me that those who were at Jerusalem, from whence we came, have been slain and carried away captive."

sacrifice offered, the water poured on the offering, and the prayer completed.[1711] Timing is always the Lord's.

Jacob also leaves nothing to the imagination of his audience. He tells them the Messiah will come to Jerusalem, will be scourged there, and will be crucified by them. Jacob knows this "according to the words of the angel who spake it unto me."[1712] From this we see Jacob's pre-sermon preparation does not consist of gathering together thoughts and quotes from poets or philosophers. He consults with angels and dispenses information from heaven. Here is a source which is to be trusted. When speaking of Jerusalem's destruction, it comes from the Lord's showing him, and of the Messiah's mission. It comes from the angel's speaking to him.

We think it an odd thing to have a man speak with the Lord and be ministered to by angels. Yet in the example of Jacob, it is almost matter-of-fact. As if he wouldn't dream of speaking about such things without consulting with heaven.

[1711] 1 Kings 18:31–38 "And Elijah took twelve stones, according to the number of the tribes of the sons of Jacob, unto whom the word of the Lord came, saying, Israel shall be thy name: And with the stones he built an altar in the name of the Lord: and he made a trench about the altar, as great as would contain two measures of seed. And he put the wood in order, and cut the bullock in pieces, and laid *him* on the wood, and said, Fill four barrels with water, and pour *it* on the burnt sacrifice, and on the wood. And he said, Do *it* the second time. And they did *it* the second time. And he said, Do *it* the third time. And they did *it* the third time. And the water ran round about the altar; and he filled the trench also with water. And it came to pass at *the time of* the offering of the *evening* sacrifice, that Elijah the prophet came near, and said, Lord God of Abraham, Isaac, and of Israel, let it be known this day that thou *art* God in Israel, and *that* I *am* thy servant, and *that* I have done all these things at thy word. Hear me, O Lord, hear me, that this people may know that thou *art* the Lord God, and *that* thou hast turned their heart back again. Then the fire of the Lord fell, and consumed the burnt sacrifice, and the wood, and the stones, and the dust, and licked up the water that *was* in the trench."

[1712] 2 Nephi 6:9 "Nevertheless, the Lord has shown unto me that they should return again. And he also has shown unto me that the Lord God, the Holy One of Israel, should manifest himself unto them in the flesh; and after he should manifest himself they should scourge him and crucify him, according to the words of the angel who spake it unto me."

Nephi's brother Jacob is among the great figures in all of sacred scripture. The critical differences between him and his teaching, and other men giving what they regard as inspirational thought, should not pass by unnoticed. I'm growing to respect this man Jacob.

Nephi's Brother Jacob, Part 5

Jacob has some relevant instruction for us. He reports:

"And blessed are the Gentiles, they of whom the prophet has written; for behold, if it so be that they shall repent and fight not against Zion, and do not unite themselves to that great and abominable church, they shall be saved; for the Lord God will fulfil his covenants which he has made unto his children; and for this cause the prophet has written these things." (2 Nephi 6:12)

Some of the Gentiles will be preserved, as well. It will be those who:

1. Are among those of whom the prophet has written. Interesting condition. These are already the topic of revelation. That requires us to study the revelations to know something of the Gentiles "of whom the prophet has written." That is no small topic in its own right.

2. Are repentant. Of course, that requires the recognition of the need for repentance. Most of the Gentiles are unaware of their need to do so. Some because they are not religious. Others because they are overly religious and fail to understand that their religion condemns them. It does not justify them.

3. Fight not against Zion. Here is "Zion" which will come into being at some point. Not today, but by and by. When it does, there will be Gentile opposition to it. Those who aren't initially invited will find the idea of Zion without them offensive. Their response should be to repent (as in 2, above). Instead, because of their blindness and jealousy, they will "fight against Zion."

4. Do not unite with the great and abominable church. This is not a single congregation. It is the world itself. The entire world is divided into two: One is the church of the Lamb of God. The other is everything else.[1713] This is a bigger problem than it may first appear. Inasmuch as there are endless ways to belong to the great and abominable church, but a single way to avoid the great and abominable church, the odds are Gentiles will not find Zion. Instead they will fight against her and join the worldly minions who are opposed to her.

Most of the Gentiles will not meet these four conditions. Consequently, they will be so reduced they will "lick up the dust of their feet" who are in Zion.[1714] For those few Gentiles who give heed to Jacob's teaching, there is good news.

Despite all the Gentiles have done to disappoint the Lord, He will "set himself again the second time to recover them."[1715] Jacob will elaborate on this future in his own book. Chapter 5 of his book contains an allegory describing all the Lord's efforts to produce fruit suitable to be preserved against the harvest. Jacob was well qualified to know what he was teaching. His brief confirmation that the allegory is true is so modest, so plain, so direct that it speaks of the man's confidence. It is unadorned by rhetoric. The starkness of it suggests Jacob is a man of few words because they aren't necessary.

[1713] 1 Nephi 14:10 "And he said unto me: Behold there are save two churches only; the one is the church of the Lamb of God, and the other is the church of the devil; wherefore, whoso belongeth not to the church of the Lamb of God belongeth to that great church, which is the mother of abominations; and she is the whore of all the earth."

[1714] 2 Nephi 6:13 "Wherefore, they that fight against Zion and the covenant people of the Lord shall lick up the dust of their feet; and the people of the Lord shall not be ashamed. For the people of the Lord are they who wait for him; for they still wait for the coming of the Messiah."

[1715] 2 Nephi 6:14 "And behold, according to the words of the prophet, the Messiah will set himself again the second time to recover them; wherefore, he will manifest himself unto them in power and great glory, unto the destruction of their enemies, when that day cometh when they shall believe in him; and none will he destroy that believe in him."

Jacob bears close study. Unlike the later writers (beginning with Mosiah), Jacob carved his book onto the small plates of Nephi himself.

Nephi's Brother Jacob, Part 6

Jacob makes a startling promise for those who live when the destruction begins preliminary to the cleansing of the world before the Lord returns. He says "none will he destroy that believe in him. And they that believe not in him shall be destroyed, both by fire, quakes, and by bloodsheds, and by pestilence, and by famine" (2 Nephi 6:14–15).

This amazing promise is predicated on "believing in Him." This requires us to understand what the word "believe" means in the parlance of the Book of Mormon. Those who believe in Him know and accept correct doctrine, or the truth about Him. Those who do not know and will not accept correct doctrine or the truth have dwindled in unbelief. They do not believe in Him. They may have religion, may belong to churches, may be active in all their observances, but they are not in possession of belief in Him. Instead they accept for doctrines the commandments of men, and their hearts are far from Him. They teach false and vain things. As a result they neither enter into the kingdom nor suffer those who are entering to go in. This includes those who, though they are humble followers of Christ, are nevertheless led that in many instances they do err in doctrine.[1716]

There will be many who are destroyed who will be quite surprised by it. They will complain that they have prophesied in Christ's name, and in His name cast out devils, and done many wonderful works,

---

[1716] 2 Nephi 28:14 "They wear stiff necks and high heads; yea, and because of pride, and wickedness, and abominations, and whoredoms, they have all gone astray save it be a few, who are the humble followers of Christ; nevertheless, they are led, that in many instances they do err because they are taught by the precepts of men."

but they do not know Christ, and therefore never did believe in Him.[1717]

If you are one of those who believe in Him, and who will not dwindle in unbelief, will not accept the commandments of men as doctrine, but will take the Spirit for your guide, then Jacob promises that Christ will not destroy you. The rest He will destroy.

Fire will upset the order of things and make societal collapse inevitable. Men's self-inflicted woes will not be the only sign of Divine disapproval. The earth will quake to signal God's disapproval. Interruptions of social order and control will be followed by self-inflicted violence. Bloodshed will be widespread among the survivors. Disease and pestilence will be one of the results of the lack of social order. Air and water will be contaminated. Neglected hygiene will lead to the promised pestilence. As the downward spiral continues, food production and distribution will be inadequate to prevent widespread, global famine. It is as if Jacob could see the sequence of events and gave us the list of how it would unfold, step by step, as the unbelieving are wiped from the earth.

Survival during this bleak time depends on the qualification of "believing in Him." Suddenly, if you think Jacob knew what he was talking about then our doctrines take on terrible significance. What we believe matters. Not just in the distant after-life, but for the preservation of our present lives. Jacob does make a powerful case for studying the Gospel a good deal more carefully than we can accomplish in a 40-minute class discussion, with an approved "discussion leader," using Correlated materials, rather than a teacher declaring and testifying of true doctrine.

[1717] Matthew 7:22–24 "Many will say to me in that day, Lord, Lord, have we not prophesied in thy name? and in thy name have cast out devils? and in thy name done many wonderful works? And then will I profess unto them, I never knew you: depart from me, ye that work iniquity. Therefore whosoever heareth these sayings of mine, and doeth them, I will liken him unto a wise man, which built his house upon a rock."

I'm pretty sure Jacob would be a very marginalized Mormon, if he were among us today.

Nephi's Brother Jacob, Part 7

The problem with war is it arouses the instinct for killing. As men adapt to war, they become predatory, seeking to destroy those they view as the enemy. They study and train to trade life for death.

Zion will not possess those skills. They won't learn them and will not need them. Zion will be a place of peace, where those who are unwilling to take up arms against others will flee.[1718] Though peaceful, the glory of the Lord will strike such fear among the wicked they will not dare come up against that place.[1719] As unlikely as this seems, it is true.

When mankind has degenerated to the point of looking at one another as prey, the Lord will not allow *His people* to become prey to the terrible and the mighty. As Jacob (borrowing from Isaiah) explained,

> "For shall the prey be taken from the mighty, or the lawful captive delivered? But thus saith the Lord: Even the captives of the mighty shall be taken away, and the prey of the terrible shall be delivered; for the Mighty God shall deliver his covenant people. For thus saith the Lord: I will contend with them that contend with thee." (2 Nephi 6:16–17)

[1718] D&C 45:66–69 "And it shall be called the New Jerusalem, a land of peace, a city of refuge, a place of safety for the saints of the Most High God; And the glory of the Lord shall be there, and the terror of the Lord also shall be there, insomuch that the wicked will not come unto it, and it shall be called Zion. And it shall come to pass among the wicked, that every man that will not take his sword against his neighbor must needs flee unto Zion for safety. And there shall be gathered unto it out of every nation under heaven; and it shall be the only people that shall not be at war one with another."

[1719] D&C 45:70 "And it shall be said among the wicked: Let us not go up to battle against Zion, for the inhabitants of Zion are terrible; wherefore we cannot stand."

The Lord intends to establish His covenant among those who take the Spirit as their guide, who reject the doctrines of men as truth, who do not trust in the arm of flesh, and who have not dwindled in unbelief.

Those who qualify, and who are in a covenant with Him, will see the destruction of those oppressors who threaten them. The armies and mobs who think they can overtake Zion will learn to their dismay that the Lord intends to protect them in such unmistakable acts they will be compelled to confess He is God and Zion is His people. As Jacob put it:

> "And I will feed them that oppress thee, with their own flesh; and they shall be drunken with their own blood as with sweet wine; and all flesh shall know that I the Lord am thy Savior and thy Redeemer, the Mighty One of Jacob." (2 Nephi 6:18)

The Lord has two contradictory persona's in scripture. He is the Lamb of God, and He is the Lion of Judah. Those two personas appear in widely separated passages of scripture. They merge together in one passage of scripture written by the Apostle John. It was John who shared Nephi's vision and who was permitted to write of it. Nephi deferred to him. John uses both titles in succession when describing the Lord's role in loosing the seven seals, calling the Lord both "the Lion of the Tribe of Juda" and "a Lamb as it had been slain."[1720] He is the Lion of Judah to those who seek to prey upon His covenant people. He is the Lamb of God to His own.

[1720] Revelation 5:5–6 "And one of the elders saith unto me, Weep not: behold, the Lion of the tribe of Juda, the Root of David, hath prevailed to open the book, and to loose the seven seals thereof. And I beheld, and, lo, in the midst of the throne and of the four beasts, and in the midst of the elders, stood a Lamb as it had been slain, having seven horns and seven eyes, which are the seven Spirits of God sent forth into all the earth."

When you see the Lamb and the Lion lie down together, you may know the Day of Judgment is at hand. It will be both great and terrible to the righteous and wicked.

Jacob knew this. Jacob saw these things before they happened, so he could write his testimony as a warning to those who live in the last days. He was a prophet more for our day than for his own. Provided, of course, we have the eyes and faith to see it.

Jacob's skill in expounding doctrine is not limited to his commentary. It includes the careful selections from Isaiah chosen to illustrate his points and clarify his views. Since he saw the Lord and was ministered to by Him, Jacob becomes adept in recognizing and expounding truth in a way which is trustworthy, and reflects his knowledge of the Lord's great work to save the souls of men.

Nephi's Brother Jacob, Part 8

Jacob uses Isaiah Chapter 50 to establish the reality of a coming Messiah, in addition the centrality of Israel to the Lord's plans. Israel is forever backsliding and wayward. Yet the decision to "divorce" Israel is the Lord's and He refuses to do so.[1721] It was always in His mind to preserve a remnant of Israel as His "fruit" or the product of His mission and ministry. Jacob will return to this theme in his own book. We will look at that later. Here we are just becoming acquainted with Jacob as a teacher.

Even at the end of days, the Lord will continue to focus on redeeming Israel. The "rock" from which they were hewn was Abra-

---

[1721] 2 Nephi 7:1 "Yea, for thus saith the Lord: Have I put thee away, or have I cast thee off forever? For thus saith the Lord: Where is the bill of your mother's divorcement? To whom have I put thee away, or to which of my creditors have I sold you? Yea, to whom have I sold you? Behold, for your iniquities have ye sold yourselves, and for your transgressions is your mother put away."

ham and Sarah, the father of the righteous and his beloved wife.[1722]
The problem with Israel is the slumber that keeps them from awakening to their awful situation and repenting of their sins. Jacob sees
the end of time, and Israel still slumbers and cannot establish Zion
because of their deep sleep. They must awake, put on the strength of
salvation or priesthood, shed their filth for beautiful garments, and
cease association with the unclean and uncircumcised.[1723] Zion will
not otherwise come to pass.

Zion will never emerge from those who slumber in the dust,
whose necks are bound with iron.[1724]

Zion evades those who desire it because they are too ill-educated,
thinking their scholarship has merit and the Holy Spirit does not.[1725]
They are rich, and think it a good thing rather than a hindrance.[1726]
They will not hear, and therefore are as good as deaf. This form of
deafness prevents them from hearing the warning and so they will
perish in their ignorance of the truth.[1727] They are also deliberately
blind, refusing to see the truth when it is presented to them.[1728] They

---

[1722] 2 Nephi 8:1–2 "Hearken unto me, ye that follow after righteousness. Look unto the
rock from whence ye are hewn, and to the hole of the pit from whence ye are digged.
Look unto Abraham, your father, and unto Sarah, she that bare you; for I called him
alone, and blessed him."

[1723] 2 Nephi 8:24 "Awake, awake, put on thy strength, O Zion; put on thy beautiful
garments, O Jerusalem, the holy city; for henceforth there shall no more come into
thee the uncircumcised and the unclean."

[1724] 2 Nephi 8:25 "Shake thyself from the dust; arise, sit down, O Jerusalem; loose
thyself from the bands of thy neck, O captive daughter of Zion."

[1725] 2 Nephi 9:29 "But to be learned is good if they hearken unto the counsels of God."

[1726] 2 Nephi 9:30 "But wo unto the rich, who are rich as to the things of the world. For
because they are rich they despise the poor, and they persecute the meek, and their
hearts are upon their treasures; wherefore, their treasure is their god. And behold, their
treasure shall perish with them also."

[1727] 2 Nephi 9:31 "And wo unto the deaf that will not hear; for they shall perish."

[1728] 2 Nephi 9:32 "Wo unto the blind that will not see; for they shall perish also."

are uncircumcised, liars, whoring after other gods, and worshiping idols.[1729]

It is Jacob who testifies the "keeper of the gate is the Holy One of Israel" and "he employeth no servant there."[1730] Jacob entered through that gate and met the Gatekeeper. He reminds us that He "cannot be deceived, for the Lord God is his name."[1731]

Jacob then reminds us of his role—the prophet's role: "Would I harrow up your souls if your minds were pure? Would I be plain unto you according to the plainness of the truth if you were free from sin?"[1732] The prophet's role is *always* to cry repentance. Priests may preside, and kings may rule, but the prophet's voice is always crying repentance. Prophets have almost never *presided* over a congregation (other than occasionally a small inner-circle). They always speak from the sidelines crying for a return to God's ways. Even when there were cities who repented in response to the message of repentance, the prophets who gathered them taught repentance and left it to the assembly to govern themselves. So it was with Enoch, and Melchizedek, and similarly Joseph attempted to teach repentance to his people. Enoch and Melchizedek were able to teach the people who wanted so desperately to repent (and did so) that they had angels and the Lord come dwell among them. Joseph sought to accomplish the same, but the Lord never dwelt among the Saints of this dispensation. Ja-

---

[1729] 2 Nephi 9:33–37 "Wo unto the uncircumcised of heart, for a knowledge of their iniquities shall smite them at the last day. Wo unto the liar, for he shall be thrust down to hell. Wo unto the murderer who deliberately killeth, for he shall die. Wo unto them who commit whoredoms, for they shall be thrust down to hell. Yea, wo unto those that worship idols, for the devil of all devils delighteth in them."

[1730] 2 Nephi 9:41 "O then, my beloved brethren, come unto the Lord, the Holy One. Remember that his paths are righteous. Behold, the way for man is narrow, but it lieth in a straight course before him, and the keeper of the gate is the Holy One of Israel; and he employeth no servant there; and there is none other way save it be by the gate; for he cannot be deceived, for the Lord God is his name."

[1731] Ibid.

[1732] See 2 Nephi chapter 47.

cob bids his brethren and us to repent, hoping his teaching will eventually lead to a latter-day Zion. Apparently there will be a small group who will eventually repent and qualify for the Lord to come dwell among them. It remains a distant possibility, without any concrete progress underway as yet.

Nephi's Brother Jacob, Part 9

Jacob remarked about the great holiness of God: "O how great the holiness of our God!"[1733] He makes this exclamation after explaining the "mercy of our God, the Holy One of Israel!" Jacob is taken by the enormity of God's mercy. It is proven beyond any dispute in that "he delivereth his saints from that awful monster the devil, and death, and hell, and that lake of fire and brimstone, which is endless torment."[1734] Having seen what awaits the unrepentant, Jacob marvels at God's great mercy. The Lord's "saints" will be spared this torment.

In contrast, Jacob points out that there is nothing but woes awaiting the unrepentant. "But wo unto the rich, who are rich as to the things of the world. For because they are rich they despise the poor, and they persecute the meek, and their hearts are upon their treasures; wherefore, their treasure is their god. And behold their treasure shall perish with them also."[1735] It is a marvel we can read these verses and have no concern for the multi-billion dollar church renovation project underway in downtown Salt Lake City. Upscale hous-

---

[1733] 2 Nephi 9:20 "O how great the holiness of our God! For he knoweth all things, and there is not anything save he knows it."

[1734] 2 Nephi 9:19 "O the greatness of the mercy of our God, the Holy One of Israel! For he delivereth his saints from that awful monster the devil, and death, and hell, and that lake of fire and brimstone, which is endless torment."

[1735] 2 Nephi 9:30 "But wo unto the rich, who are rich as to the things of the world. For because they are rich they despise the poor, and they persecute the meek, and their hearts are upon their treasures; wherefore, their treasure is their god. And behold, their treasure shall perish with them also."

ing, retail and office space are being built to stimulate investment in the downtown economy. This is all under the supervision of the Presiding Bishop and First Presidency, using a for-profit corporation. Though Jacob seems to speak about individuals, it leaves us wondering if the same might be said of institutions as well.

Jacob said, "Yea, who unto those that worship idols, for the devil of all devils delighteth in them."[1736] That is why we are never to allow any man or group of men to get between us and God. God alone is worthy of worship. If you put another man or institution between you and God, you are the delight of the devil of all devils, for he has made you his. You will suffer the wrath of God,[1737] and not qualify for the mercy which Jacob taught proved God's holiness.

Jacob anticipated there would be those who would reject, even become angry by what he taught. But he cautioned them:

> "Do not say that I have spoken hard things against you, for if ye do, ye will revile against the truth; for I have spoken the words of your Maker. I know that the words of truth are hard against all uncleanness; but the righteous fear them not, for they love the truth and are not shaken." (2 Nephi 9:40)

This is another proof we are reading the words of an actual prophet. They speak the truth. They cry repentance. They point to the Holy One of Israel. Prophets do not fear the anger which others will hold toward them. They know they speak what the Lord would have said.

Jacob observes "if ye were holy I would speak unto you of holiness; but as ye are not holy, and ye look upon me as a teacher, it must

---

[1736] 2 Nephi 9:38 "And, in fine, wo unto all those who die in their sins; for they shall return to God, and behold his face, and remain in their sins."

[1737] D&C 76:104–106 "These are they who suffer the wrath of God on earth. These are they who suffer the vengeance of eternal fire. These are they who are cast down to hell and suffer the wrath of Almighty God, until the fulness of times, when Christ shall have subdued all enemies under his feet, and shall have perfected his work;"

needs be expedient that I teach you the consequences of sin."[1738] How marvelous it would be if Jacob had been freed up to speak only of holiness. What great things might this prophet-teacher have given us? How might he who stood in Christ's presence have taught us if we were holy and not in need of repentance?

With almost every new revelation from heaven, mankind learns first and foremost that there is more work to be done to tear down false tradition and error in doctrine. Building Zion will never begin until the errors of teaching for commandments the doctrines of men has been subdued. Jacob is a reminder that great things must be preceded by repentance, and repentance must be preceded by an awakening to the awful situation in which we find ourselves.

Nephi's Brother Jacob, Conclusion

There is a great deal more to Jacob than we have touched on here. This is only intended to lay the groundwork to appreciate the topic I'm turning to next. I want to discuss the meaning of Jacob's 5th chapter. Before doing so however, I wanted to touch briefly on Jacob's sound understanding and heavenly qualification to teach the truth. He was in command of the truth and knew what he was teaching.

In his initial sermon, he includes another explanation of how he knew his teachings were sound:

> "It must needs be expedient that Christ—for in the last night the angel spake unto me that this should be his name—should come among the Jews, among those who are the more wicked part of the world; and they shall crucify him—for thus it behooveth our God, and there is none other nation on earth that would crucify their God." (2 Nephi 10:3)

[1738] 2 Nephi 9:48 "Behold, if ye were holy I would speak unto you of holiness; but as ye are not holy, and ye look upon me as a teacher, it must needs be expedient that I teach you the consequences of sin."

This scripture tells us:

- Jacob was ministered to by angels, and taught as he was taught from above.
- Jacob was given the Lord's name centuries before His birth.
- Jacob foresaw the Lord's crucifixion.
- Jacob knew this was necessary for God to perform.
- Only a religious people like the Jews would crucify their God.

The irony of a group of religious people, claiming to follow God, killing Christ is set out matter-of-factly by Jacob. Jacob knew it was the very religious who would resist the truth. It was the very religious who fight against God. They think they are following Him when they persecute the prophets. They believe they are doing God a favor when they urge worship of idols, and seek to kill the Son of God.

Despite man's failure to repent and to worship the true God, Jacob foresaw the ultimate triumph of Zion. When it begins, Jacob promises, "he that fighteth against Zion shall perish, saith God" (2 Nephi 10:13). To make the point even more clear he adds:

> "Wherefore, he that fighteth against Zion, both Jew and Gentile, both bond and free, both male and female, shall perish; for they are they who are the whore of all the earth; or they who are not for me are against me, saith our God." (2 Nephi 10:16)

Once again Jacob carves the world into two: One small group whom God will protect and guide, and who will be brought into Zion; and then everyone else. The groups are disproportionate. There is no comparison between the diminutive Zion and the world. It is the world that will be destroyed. The small Zion will be protected and defended by God. Everything else will be gathered in bundles and burned.

With this introduction, we turn to Jacob chapter 5.

JACOB 5

Of all the material Jacob could have adopted as his prophecy, his selection of Zenos' allegory of the Olive Tree is telling. The account is a journey through various dispensations of the Gospel, tracking a bloodline of chosen people. To Jacob's credit, he realized the work of salvation was devoted primarily to rescuing the descendants of a chosen line beginning with Abraham.

The allegory is a family story. The use of the olive tree is a deliberate symbol of a family, and of the tree whose value was beyond question in the culture from which the allegory sprung. To understand the story, it is necessary to settle on meanings.

The tree is a family line belonging to the "house of Israel".[1739] The work of the Lord of the vineyard and his fellow laborers is designed to cause the chosen family line to produce fruit worthy of preservation. The "fruit" is people, or more correctly, children raised in righteousness who comprehend and accept the Gospel and abide by its teachings. The name "Israel" is the new name given to Jacob. Jacob was renamed by the Lord because the Lord took him into His own family. Naming signifies Fatherhood over Jacob, and the name Israel signifies the Family of God.

[1739] Jacob 5:3 "For behold, thus saith the Lord, I will liken thee, O house of Israel, like unto a tame olive-tree, which a man took and nourished in his vineyard; and it grew, and waxed old, and began to decay."

Not every descendant of Jacob is also a descendant of Israel. Blood is one thing, adoption into the Family of God is another. The allegory should be read with the proper context. It is about preserving the Family of Israel, or in other words, the Family of God.

To correct and instruct the chosen family, it was necessary for the Lord of the vineyard, in a desperate attempt to cause the family to produce fruit worthy of preservation, to disburse the children, scatter them throughout the vineyard, graft wild branches into the roots and tame branches into wild roots. In one sense the failure of the chosen family is to the world's great blessing. In the end, the world overcomes the chosen family and all those grafted into it, and in the final effort the work returns to the original roots and the original branches in a desperate final attempt to salvage something from the vineyard before it is burned.

Choosing this allegory as the great central theme of Jacob's book shows his comprehension of sacred history and prophecy, and his knowledge of the future. Unlike Nephi, whose muse was Isaiah, the fully mature prophet Jacob turned to Zenos to act as "second witness" to his prophecy. We have in Jacob Chapter 5 the great explanation of how we got where we are today, and what will unfold before the Lord's return to burn the vineyard. It is odd we spend so little time with the material. It is the central theme of all man's history (from God's point of view).

The family is scattered into several different parts of the vineyard:

First, the location of the original tree.

Second, an undisclosed number of "nethermost parts of the vineyard."[1740]

[1740] Jacob 5:14 "And it came to pass that the Lord of the vineyard went his way, and hid the natural branches of the tame olive-tree in the nethermost parts of the vineyard, some in one and some in another, according to his will and pleasure."

Third, a "poorest spot."[1741]

Fourth, a "poorer spot than the first."[1742]

Fifth, a "good spot."[1743]

However, there is no attempt to quantify the number of spots because the allegory is intended to convey meaning apart from numbers. You can cross check the other prophecies from Nephi[1744] and Christ[1745] and find there is no definitive number given of how many separate groups are included in the "nethermost parts of the vineyard" where Israel was scattered.

What should leap out to you from this allegory is the nature of the Gospel and God's work among mankind. It was and is related to preserving a single family line. The "God of Israel" is concerned with preserving the chosen line of heirs. The Gospel was and is a family matter, and the target of the Lord's work is now and always has been the preservation of a specific group He intends to preserve.

This is an image we have trouble with in our current multiculturalism. We tend to view all mankind as the beneficiaries of God's plans to save mankind. They are to some extent. After all, He provides

---

[1741] Jacob 5:21 "And it came to pass that the servant said unto his master: How comest thou hither to plant this tree, or this branch of the tree? For behold, it was the poorest spot in all the land of thy vineyard."

[1742] Jacob 5:23 "And it came to pass that the Lord of the vineyard said unto his servant: Look hither; behold I have planted another branch of the tree also; and thou knowest that this spot of ground was poorer than the first. But, behold the tree. I have nourished it this long time, and it hath brought forth much fruit; therefore, gather it, and lay it up against the season, that I may preserve it unto mine own self."

[1743] Jacob 5:25 "And he said unto the servant: Look hither and behold the last. Behold, this have I planted in a good spot of ground; and I have nourished it this long time, and only a part of the tree hath brought forth tame fruit, and the other part of the tree hath brought forth wild fruit; behold, I have nourished this tree like unto the others."

[1744] 2 Nephi 29:3 "And because my words shall hiss forth—many of the Gentiles shall say: A Bible! A Bible! We have got a Bible, and there cannot be any more Bible."

[1745] 3 Nephi 17:4 "But now I go unto the Father, and also to show myself unto the lost tribes of Israel, for they are not lost unto the Father, for he knoweth whither he hath taken them."

the sun and rain to everyone regardless of their ethnicity.[1746] And every people are given according to His mercy some portion of truth calculated to benefit them.[1747] However, Zenos and Jacob agree the Lord's primary effort has been directed at preserving one family, and the world has been the incidental beneficiaries of this global effort to preserve them.

We will look at the history of this family as told through the allegory of the Olive tree.

Jacob 5:3–6

Israel was and is the only family which will be saved. It is the "tame olive tree" that the Lord "took and nourished in his vineyard."[1748] Despite all the Lord's efforts, however, the actual family tree "waxed old, and began to decay."[1749] It lost its vitality. It tired of the Lord. His desire and "nourishment" was not able to overcome the tree's indifference to what He offered them. It began to decay.

The Lord was unwilling to abandon His tree even when there was no productivity in it. He intended to continue to create the Family of God, despite the failure by the family to respond to His invitation. He initially set about to "prune it" (that is, to cast away from the Family of God or Israel, those who failed to live worthily) and to "dig

---

[1746] Matthew 5:45 "That ye may be the children of your Father which is in heaven: for he maketh his sun to rise on the evil and on the good, and sendeth rain on the just and on the unjust."

[1747] Alma 29:8 "For behold, the Lord doth grant unto all nations, of their own nation and tongue, to teach his word, yea, in wisdom, all that he seeth fit that they should have; therefore we see that the Lord doth counsel in wisdom, according to that which is just and true."

[1748] Jacob 5:3 "For behold, thus saith the Lord, I will liken thee, O house of Israel, like unto a tame olive-tree, which a man took and nourished in his vineyard; and it grew, and waxed old, and began to decay."

[1749] Ibid.

about it" and then to "nourish it." In the initial work it is the Lord directly who does the work. He does not send a servant to perform the labor.[1750]

"Pruning" involves cutting away. It destroys. The goal is ultimately to bring about vigor and life. But the initial work requires destroying to clear away and make the growth possible. The result is harsh and violent in the short run, but there is something important going on in the work of "pruning" away. The larger purpose is what the Lord has in mind. The short term sacrifices and difficulties are unavoidable and necessary. They must be endured.

"Digging about" the tree is also violent. It is threatening, and imposes upset and difficulties. The Lord's benign intent is not understood when the pruning and digging are measured against short term standards. They must take a longer view.

The Lord's purpose is to "perhaps" produce "young and tender branches."[1751] It is "perhaps" because the Lord grants the tree agency to respond, not compulsion to force compliance. The Lord can coax, but the tree must grow.

The older branches are not intended to be preserved. They bear nothing but bad fruit. The young and tender branches are the goal. These, however, will not yield fruit for some time. They must have an opportunity to develop.

This description of ancient Israel shows how the Lord's work was always purposeful and designed to preserve the tree and continue to create sons and daughters of God. However, despite all He did, the "little, young and tender branches" were comparatively small in the

---

[1750] Jacob 5:4–5 "And it came to pass that the master of the vineyard went forth, and he saw that his olive-tree began to decay; and he said: I will prune it, and dig about it, and nourish it, that perhaps it may shoot forth young and tender branches, and it perish not. And it came to pass that he pruned it, and digged about it, and nourished it according to his word."

[1751] Jacob 5:5 "And it came to pass that he pruned it, and digged about it, and nourished it according to his word.

scheme of things. As to the "main top thereof" it "began to perish."[1752]

The infrastructure, the hierarchy, the temple, the priestly class, the learned Rabbis and the schools of thought were rotting. They were nothing like what would be required to produce fruit. They were religious but heretical. They were devoted, but not His sons and daughters. The family line was broken. They needed to be adopted back again, because they lacked the power to remain connected.

This is an odd juxtaposition: The "main top" is corrupt. The "young tender branches" are nothing like the great growth overshadowing them. Yet the Lord sees in the young growth what He seeks. As to the "main top" there is nothing but "perishing" and decay.

Israel is so often in this predicament. They despise the truth, but respond warmly to flattery telling them they are righteous.[1753] When someone is sent by the Lord of the vineyard calling for repentance, Israel rejects him, says he is a sinner and a false prophet.[1754] Ultimately, however, for the bloodline of Jacob to rise up and become fruit worthy of preservation, there must be a change from blood

---

[1752] Jacob 5:6 "And it came to pass that after many days it began to put forth somewhat a little, young and tender branches; but behold, the main top thereof began to perish."

[1753] Helaman 13:27–28 "But behold, if a man shall come among you and shall say: Do this, and there is no iniquity; do that and ye shall not suffer; yea, he will say: Walk after the pride of your own hearts; yea, walk after the pride of your eyes, and do whatsoever your heart desireth—and if a man shall come among you and say this, ye will receive him, and say that he is a prophet. Yea, ye will lift him up, and ye will give unto him of your substance; ye will give unto him of your gold, and of your silver, and ye will clothe him with costly apparel; and because he speaketh flattering words unto you, and he saith that all is well, then ye will not find fault with him."

[1754] Helaman 13:25–26 "And now when ye talk, ye say: If our days had been in the days of our fathers of old, we would not have slain the prophets; we would not have stoned them, and cast them out. Behold ye are worse than they; for as the Lord liveth, if a prophet come among you and declareth unto you the word of the Lord, which testifieth of your sins and iniquities, ye are angry with him, and cast him out and seek all manner of ways to destroy him; yea, you will say that he is a false prophet, and that he is a sinner, and of the devil, because he testifieth that your deeds are evil."

connection to Jacob to an adoption into Israel. Then they become sons and daughters of God, and fruit worthy of preservation.[1755]

Jacob 5:7–9

As Israel decays, the Lord of the vineyard takes the dramatic step of cutting away the "main branches" or in other words the leading families, the recognized genealogical well-breds, or the families of rank and distinction. They were to be "burned" rather than further cultivated.[1756] Their pride and arrogance disqualified them from preservation or further work. They were riddled with "decay" and unworthy of further effort. They were to be destroyed by fire. Fire is always a symbol of the Lord's judgments designed to cleanse or purge. Killing the decayed and corrupt leading families was cleansing the tree of the decay that had taken hold in the lofty, inner-circles of the people of Israel.

Men may have respected, even admired the success and status of these "main branches" of the Israelites, but that was nothing to the Lord. All their great rank, position, support structure and apparent security were nothing once the Lord decreed they were to be burned. Invading conquerors would target these specific social leaders for removal as a precaution against further loyalty. These would have to be removed for the outside ruler from a foreign power to succeed. The very thing which made them *secure* was the reason they were targeted to be killed. In a natural political purge the "main branches"

[1755] Mosiah 27:25 "And the Lord said unto me: Marvel not that all mankind, yea, men and women, all nations, kindreds, tongues and people, must be born again; yea, born of God, changed from their carnal and fallen state, to a state of righteousness, being redeemed of God, becoming his sons and daughters;"

[1756] Jacob 5:7 "And it came to pass that the master of the vineyard saw it, and he said unto his servant: It grieveth me that I should lose this tree; wherefore, go and pluck the branches from a wild olive-tree, and bring them hither unto me; and we will pluck off those main branches which are beginning to wither away, and we will cast them into the fire that they may be burned."

who seemed forever entrenched to rule were swept away. No more would they "cumber the ground of [His] vineyard."[1757]

To replace the notable families of distinction, the Lord determined to bring in "wild olive tree" branches, or those who have no distinction, or even family connections with the roots of Israel.[1758] There would be new blood brought in by the conquerors with resultant intermarriages.

Unlike the main branches, there were "young and tender branches" which were not to be destroyed, but were instead to be transplanted. From Assyria or Babylon, these dislocated tribes would be spread into the nethermost part of the vineyard, or in the words of the Lord of the vineyard: "I will graft them whithersoever I will."[1759]

With the mixing of foreign blood in the remaining "root" of the tree, and grafting of the "young and tender branches" into "wild" trees throughout the vineyard, the Israelite bloodlines become fragmented, scattered and no longer purely either Jacobian (by blood) or Israelite (by adoption). It would not matter if you look to the main root, or to the many scattered branches, they were all mingled with the "wild" gentile stock to produce a hybrid people. The corruption of the family was too deeply entrenched. They would not be able to repent any longer because their arrogance and ignorance prevented them from seeing their true condition. They thought themselves so highly favored of God they could not fall. Therefore, it was altogether necessary for them to fall. Without such a traumatic message

---

[1757] Jacob 5:9 "Take thou the branches of the wild olive-tree, and graft them in, in the stead thereof; and these which I have plucked off I will cast into the fire and burn them, that they may not cumber the ground of my vineyard."

[1758] Ibid.

[1759] Jacob 5:8 "And behold, saith the Lord of the vineyard, I take away many of these young and tender branches, and I will graft them whithersoever I will; and it mattereth not that if it so be that the root of this tree will perish, I may preserve the fruit thereof unto myself; wherefore, I will take these young and tender branches, and I will graft them whithersoever I will."

delivered to the entire family, they would continue to presume safety meant they were justified. Any sign of prosperity was interpreted to mean they were right with God.

The family of Jacob needed this trauma for the covenant with Israel to be preserved. They were dying and not noticing it. Though it was terrible to endure, the Lord of the vineyard had the ultimate best interests of the entire tree in mind. He did what was needed to restore health and vigor. The covenant had been broken anyway, and this would make possible a renewal of the covenant and restoration from scattered Jacob the Family of Israel.

Jacob 5:10–13

The Lord caused his "servant" to perform all He determined to do for the vineyard.[1760] The wild branches were grafted in and the covenant was suspended. The lines were broken. It would require a restoration of the covenant and adoption for the "natural fruit" to reappear.[1761]

Labor was required from the Lord's servant as well as the Lord Himself. The vineyard required "digging about" and "pruning" and "nourishing" in an attempt to preserve the "root" to which it would be possible to one day to return.[1762] These words tell us how constant the care has been, while scattered and wild remnants have apparently lay fallow without any fruit. Though the people have fallen, the Lord labors on.

[1760] Jacob 5:10 "And it came to pass that the servant of the Lord of the vineyard did according to the word of the Lord of the vineyard, and grafted in the branches of the wild olive-tree."

[1761] Ibid.

[1762] Jacob 5:11 "And the Lord of the vineyard caused that it should be digged about, and pruned, and nourished, saying unto his servant: It grieveth me that I should lose this tree; wherefore, that perhaps I might preserve the roots thereof that they perish not, that I might preserve them unto myself, I have done this thing."

Even when the digging, pruning and nourishing have been finished, and while the results are unknown, the Lord of the vineyard directs His servants to "watch" carefully, and to provide yet further "nourishment" when the damaged tree requires it.[1763] Throughout, it is all done by the Lord's "words." He is not absent. He is diligent; ever watchful. He owns the vineyard and everything that is located there. Because it is His, He wants the best for it.

As to the young branches He wants to preserve, so it may be possible at last to return to producing good fruit, He decided to move them "to the nethermost part of my vineyard."[1764] This allegory contradicts the idea of Jehovah as Lord of Israel alone. The Lord claims the entire vineyard, the world itself, as His. The notion of Jehovah being only a local Deity, as is thought by many scholars to be the prevalent idea at the time of Zenos' prophecy, is destroyed by this assertion of ownership over the entire vineyard. Even "the nethermost part" of the world belongs to the Lord of the vineyard.

Even as He relocates His people throughout the vineyard, He continues to view the scattered branches as part of the same, single "tree" He hoped to preserve. He explains: "[I]t grieveth me that I should lose this tree and the fruit thereof."[1765] His intent is to continue to have covenant people, part of His Family, His own sons and daughters. Even though they are unable to continue in that relationship during the scattering, it is hoped ultimately it will allow Him to yet "lay up fruit thereof against the season."[1766]

[1763] Jacob 5:12 "Wherefore, go thy way; watch the tree, and nourish it, according to my words."

[1764] Jacob 5:13 "And these will I place in the nethermost part of my vineyard, whithersoever I will, it mattereth not unto thee; and I do it that I may preserve unto myself the natural branches of the tree; and also, that I may lay up fruit thereof against the season, unto myself; for it grieveth me that I should lose this tree and the fruit thereof."

[1765] Ibid.

[1766] Ibid.

This purposeful and attentive effort was reassuring to Jacob's people. Though they were long separated from Jerusalem, and although the rising generation had never been there, this allegory assures them of God's watchful eye. The covenant of Jehovah with Israel continued to be with the scattered branches though they had been transplanted across an ocean and were living in an island of the sea.[1767]

The history of the world is the history of Israel. The events are supervised by a Lord whose purpose is to lay up fruit against the season of the harvest. As we grow ever closer to the season of harvest, the plan will need to result in the appearance of natural fruit again. Otherwise, the entire vineyard will be gathered in bundles and burned.

Jacob 5:14–18

When the Lord scattered Israel, He "hid" them "in the nethermost parts of the vineyard."[1768] The word "hid" suggests the deliberate concealment of the people, their true origin, their blood relation to Jacob, their destiny to become part of the covenant Family of Israel, and their loss from the record of history and even their own memory of the earlier connections. The Lord of the vineyard intended for this part of His plan to remain concealed. He knew what He was doing. He was acting on a plan designed to produce preserv-

---

[1767] 2 Nephi 10:20 "And now, my beloved brethren, seeing that our merciful God has given us so great knowledge concerning these things, let us remember him, and lay aside our sins, and not hang down our heads, for we are not cast off; nevertheless, we have been driven out of the land of our inheritance; but we have been led to a better land, for the Lord has made the sea our path, and we are upon an isle of the sea."

[1768] Jacob 5:14 "And it came to pass that the Lord of the vineyard went his way, and hid the natural branches of the tame olive-tree in the nethermost parts of the vineyard, some in one and some in another, according to his will and pleasure."

able fruit, but mankind would be oblivious to His methods. His ways are not always shared or understood by man.[1769]

The places are not numbered, but described as "nethermost." Nor is the design identified other than "some in one and some in another, according to his will and pleasure." This is an order which He keeps to Himself, but we are told it reflects His "will" and His "pleasure."

The Lord left the vineyard to continue in the ordinary course "that a long time passed away."[1770] There is no haste involved. Men come and go across generations while the design of God unfolds. We are impatient and want to see God's plan unfold completely within our lifetime here, but His work is ageless and spans generations. Rarely does He promise a single generation will witness promised events.[1771]

When a "long time" had passed away, the Lord no longer stood watch, but took His servant and "went down" to "labor in the vineyard."[1772] His presence and ministry among men took a more direct effort. He "went down into the vineyard to labor" for the souls of men. Behold the condescension of God, indeed!

The underlying "root" was able to give "nourishment" to the hybrid people living when the Lord came. The surviving prophetic

---

[1769] Isaiah 55:8–9 "For my thoughts *are* not your thoughts, neither *are* your ways my ways, saith the Lord. For *as* the heavens are higher than the earth, so are my ways higher than your ways, and my thoughts than your thoughts."

[1770] Jacob 5:15 "And it came to pass that a long time passed away, and the Lord of the vineyard said unto his servant: Come, let us go down into the vineyard, that we may labor in the vineyard."

[1771] JS–Matthew 1:32–34 "And again shall the abomination of desolation, spoken of by Daniel the prophet, be fulfilled. And immediately after the tribulation of those days, the sun shall be darkened, and the moon shall not give her light, and the stars shall fall from heaven, and the powers of heaven shall be shaken. Verily, I say unto you, this generation, in which these things shall be shown forth, shall not pass away until all I have told you shall be fulfilled."

[1772] Jacob 5:15 "And it came to pass that a long time passed away, and the Lord of the vineyard said unto his servant: Come, let us go down into the vineyard, that we may labor in the vineyard."

warnings and limited practices supported this new Dispensation, making it a field white, already to harvest.[1773]

There He found among those grafted into the natural root disciples willing to follow Him. Among them were those who were "good" and "like unto the natural fruit"—which would make them candidates to be adopted as sons and daughters of God, as the Family of Israel. The Lord rejoiced because He realized He could "lay up much fruit, which the tree thereof hath brought forth; and the fruit thereof I shall lay up against the season, unto mine own self."[1774]

The Lord's personal ministry resulted in a great harvest of souls. There were many willing to accept His mission, respond to Him, and go through the process of changing into covenant Israel again. Sons and daughters of God returned to the earth by adoption into the Family of God.[1775]

Jacob 5:19–26

[1773] Jacob 5:17–18 "And it came to pass that the Lord of the vineyard looked and beheld the tree in the which the wild olive branches had been grafted; and it had sprung forth and begun to bear fruit. And he beheld that it was good; and the fruit thereof was like unto the natural fruit. And he said unto the servant: Behold, the branches of the wild tree have taken hold of the moisture of the root thereof, that the root thereof hath brought forth much strength; and because of the much strength of the root thereof the wild branches have brought forth tame fruit. Now, if we had not grafted in these branches, the tree thereof would have perished. And now, behold, I shall lay up much fruit, which the tree thereof hath brought forth; and the fruit thereof I shall lay up against the season, unto mine own self."

[1774] Ibid.

[1775] Romans 8:16–17 "The Spirit itself beareth witness with our spirit, that we are the children of God: And if children, then heirs; heirs of God, and joint-heirs with Christ; if so be that we suffer with *him,* that we may be also glorified together."
Ephesians 1:5 "Having predestinated us unto the adoption of children by Jesus Christ to himself, according to the good pleasure of his will,"
Ephesians 2:19 "Now therefore ye are no more strangers and foreigners, but fellowcitizens with the saints, and of the household of God;"
1 John 3:2 "Beloved, now are we the sons of God, and it doth not yet appear what we shall be: but we know that, when he shall appear, we shall be like him; for we shall see him as he is."

After establishing good fruit in the original root, the Lord of the vineyard visited the scattered branches in "the nethermost part of the vineyard."[1776] The Lord of the vineyard was satisfied that in each of the places where the natural branches were scattered, good fruit had returned.[1777]

Whether it was the "poorest spot in all the land of the vineyard" or another place "poorer than the first" it did not matter. The result

---

[1776] Jacob 5:19–20 "And it came to pass that the Lord of the vineyard said unto the servant: Come, let us go to the nethermost part of the vineyard, and behold if the natural branches of the tree have not brought forth much fruit also, that I may lay up of the fruit thereof against the season, unto mine own self. And it came to pass that they went forth whither the master had hid the natural branches of the tree, and he said unto the servant: Behold these; and he beheld the first that it had brought forth much fruit; and he beheld also that it was good. And he said unto the servant: Take of the fruit thereof, and lay it up against the season, that I may preserve it unto mine own self; for behold, said he, this long time have I nourished it, and it hath brought forth much fruit."

3 Nephi 16:1–3 "And verily, verily, I say unto you that I have other sheep, which are not of this land, neither of the land of Jerusalem, neither in any parts of that land round about whither I have been to minister. For they of whom I speak are they who have not as yet heard my voice; neither have I at any time manifested myself unto them. But I have received a commandment of the Father that I shall go unto them, and that they shall hear my voice, and shall be numbered among my sheep, that there may be one fold and one shepherd; therefore I go to show myself unto them."

[1777] Jacob 5:20 "And it came to pass that they went forth whither the master had hid the natural branches of the tree, and he said unto the servant: Behold these; and he beheld the first that it had brought forth much fruit; and he beheld also that it was good. And he said unto the servant: Take of the fruit thereof, and lay it up against the season, that I may preserve it unto mine own self; for behold, said he, this long time have I nourished it, and it hath brought forth much fruit."

2 Nephi 29:12 "For behold, I shall speak unto the Jews and they shall write it; and I shall also speak unto the Nephites and they shall write it; and I shall also speak unto the other tribes of the house of Israel, which I have led away, and they shall write it; and I shall also speak unto all nations of the earth and they shall write it."

was good fruit.[1778] The servant was dismayed at the locations to which the Lord had taken the scattered branches. In perplexity he inquired: "How comest thou hither to plant this tree, or this branch of the tree? For behold, it was the poorest spot . . . ?"[1779] The servant was surprised to know the Lord of the vineyard would go to visit these poor places. It seemed beneath the Lord to have ministered in such humble, far flung lands, among such woe-begotten peoples. But the Lord has "descended below them all"[1780] and found no indignity in visiting with such humble people in diminished circumstances. It may well have been because of the difficulty of the circumstances that fruit was produced.[1781]

[1778] Jacob 5:20–21, 23 "And it came to pass that they went forth whither the master had hid the natural branches of the tree, and he said unto the servant: Behold these; and he beheld the first that it had brought forth much fruit; and he beheld also that it was good. And he said unto the servant: Take of the fruit thereof, and lay it up against the season, that I may preserve it unto mine own self; for behold, said he, this long time have I nourished it, and it hath brought forth much fruit. And it came to pass that the servant said unto his master: How comest thou hither to plant this tree, or this branch of the tree? For behold, it was the poorest spot in all the land of thy vineyard. And it came to pass that the Lord of the vineyard said unto his servant: Look hither; behold I have planted another branch of the tree also; and thou knowest that this spot of ground was poorer than the first. But, behold the tree. I have nourished it this long time, and it hath brought forth much fruit; therefore, gather it, and lay it up against the season, that I may preserve it unto mine own self."

[1779] Jacob 5:21 "And it came to pass that the servant said unto his master: How comest thou hither to plant this tree, or this branch of the tree? For behold, it was the poorest spot in all the land of thy vineyard."

[1780] D&C 122:7–8 "And if thou shouldst be cast into the pit, or into the hands of murderers, and the sentence of death passed upon thee; if thou be cast into the deep; if the billowing surge conspire against thee; if fierce winds become thine enemy; if the heavens gather blackness, and all the elements combine to hedge up the way; and above all, if the very jaws of hell shall gape open the mouth wide after thee, know thou, my son, that all these things shall give thee experience, and shall be for thy good. The Son of Man hath descended below them all. Art thou greater than he?"

[1781] Alma 32:12–13 "I say unto you, it is well that ye are cast out of your synagogues, that ye may be humble, and that ye may learn wisdom; for it is necessary that ye should learn wisdom; for it is because that ye are cast out, that ye are despised of your brethren because of your exceeding poverty, that ye are brought to a lowliness of heart; for ye are necessarily brought to be humble. And now, because ye are compelled to be humble blessed are ye; for a man sometimes, if he is compelled to be humble, seeketh repentance; and now surely, whosoever repenteth shall find mercy; and he that findeth mercy and endureth to the end the same shall be saved."

As if to confirm that difficulties are a blessing to His vine, when they get to the "good spot of ground," the transplanted branches have produced conflicting fruit. In this most chosen land of all, the brothers were divided, and fought in continual ethnic-cultural-religious warfare for generations between themselves. Part of these branches produced good fruit, but part was corrupt and wild.[1782] Although this was the best spot in the vineyard, and although the Lord of the vineyard had "nourished this tree like unto the others" it was still half corrupt.[1783] This tree required pruning.

The Lord decided to "Pluck off the branches that have not brought forth good fruit, and cast them into the fire."[1784] Accordingly, nature itself removed the branches:

> "And thus the face of the whole earth became deformed, because of the tempests, and the thunderings, and the lightnings, and the quaking of the earth. And behold, the rocks were rent in twain; they were broken up upon the face of the whole earth, insomuch that they were found in broken fragments, and in seams and in cracks, upon all the face of the land. And it came to pass that when the thunderings, and the lightnings, and the storm, and the tempest, and the quakings of the earth did cease—for behold, they did last for about the space of three hours; and it was said by some that the time was greater; nevertheless, all these great and terrible things were done in about the space of three hours—and then behold, there was darkness upon the face of the land." (3 Nephi 8:17–19)

[1782] Jacob 5:25 "And he said unto the servant: Look hither and behold the last. Behold, this have I planted in a good spot of ground; and I have nourished it this long time, and only a part of the tree hath brought forth tame fruit, and the other part of the tree hath brought forth wild fruit; behold, I have nourished this tree like unto the others."

[1783] Ibid.

[1784] Jacob 5:26 "And it came to pass that the Lord of the vineyard said unto the servant: Pluck off the branches that have not brought forth good fruit, and cast them into the fire."

The pruning then, like the Lord of the vineyard's pruning at any time, was targeted and specific. It is designed to remove *only the branches worthy of destruction.* The righteous do not need to fear. Those who reject the prophets sent to them, reject the prophets' message, and give no heed to the prophets, need to fear.[1785] The message of Jacob comes full circle. He returns to his earlier theme, when he promised the righteous they would be spared.[1786] He is consistent.

An Interruption of Jacob

Jacob 5 discussion will resume. This is a current-events comment:

The City Creek multi-billion dollar project has excited a lot of criticism. The result has been dismay by many faithful Latter-day Saints. Their anxiety over the project has become the subject of many conversations on the Internet.

To grapple with this outpouring of criticism and in some cases disgust, the church has paid employees and volunteers who post on-line responses using personas, or anonymous identities to beat back those who express concern. Many of the multiple personas are put up by the same church employee.

The arguments advanced by those who are concerned about the investment in the City Creek shopping center most often cite scrip-

---

[1785] 3 Nephi 10:12–14 "And it was the more righteous part of the people who were saved, and it was they who received the prophets and stoned them not; and it was they who had not shed the blood of the saints, who were spared— And they were spared and were not sunk and buried up in the earth; and they were not drowned in the depths of the sea; and they were not burned by fire, neither were they fallen upon and crushed to death; and they were not carried away in the whirlwind; neither were they overpowered by the vapor of smoke and of darkness. And now, whoso readeth, let him understand; he that hath the scriptures, let him search them, and see and behold if all these deaths and destructions by fire, and by smoke, and by tempests, and by whirlwinds, and by the opening of the earth to receive them, and all these things are not unto the fulfilling of the prophecies of many of the holy prophets."

[1786] 2 Nephi 6:18 "And I will feed them that oppress thee, with their own flesh; and they shall be drunken with their own blood as with sweet wine; and all flesh shall know that I the Lord am thy Savior and thy Redeemer, the Mighty One of Jacob."

ture. Their observations are based on sincere belief, supported by positions taken from scripture study, and reflect honest concern. The defense is based on the concept of supporting the leadership, sustaining the church's prophet, and uses comments taken from church talks, sermons, etc.

The gulf between these two positions is one of the great divisions in the church today. The numbers of those holding these two positions are not equal, however. The one is held by sincere, believing members of the church who honestly disagree with the use of these funds for this elaborate, costly project. The other is advanced for the most part by paid employees or volunteers who are doing so using multiple personas to justify the church's conduct.

In the realm of political debate, the production of artificial arguments by personas has been termed "astroturf" because it is not real. The artificial "astroturf" is in contrast to the grassroots movement of people. When enough "astroturf" has been sent out by the political machines, the grassroots will often respond. What began as fiction, or hope, turns into actual public opinion. The political parties and big business employ these techniques all the time now.

Interestingly, there are those inside the church's organized effort who do not believe the arguments they are advancing. Some of them have been persuaded the church's position is in fact wrong. They continue to make the arguments. It is their job. But they do not believe in the position they advance.

It is a fascinating moment to watch. It will be equally interesting to see if conference visitors from around the United States and the world visit the City Creek project and return dismayed, or return home gratified to see this expensive investment by the church.

I'd like readers to note I've not taken a position in this post. It does not deal with anything other than the events unfolding and how the reactions are being advanced and defended. Nothing more.

Jacob 5:27–33

The servant agreed with the pruning done by the Lord, but wanted to take the remaining branches after the pruning and to "nourish it a little longer, that perhaps it may bring forth good fruit."[1787] The Lord then visited with the remaining tree branches, established His covenant with them, and made it possible for them to reconnect with covenant Israel and the Family of God.[1788]

[1787] Jacob 5:27 "But behold, the servant said unto him: Let us prune it, and dig about it, and nourish it a little longer, that perhaps it may bring forth good fruit unto thee, that thou canst lay it up against the season."

[1788] 3 Nephi 11:8–17 "And it came to pass, as they understood they cast their eyes up again towards heaven; and behold, they saw a Man descending out of heaven; and he was clothed in a white robe; and he came down and stood in the midst of them; and the eyes of the whole multitude were turned upon him, and they durst not open their mouths, even one to another, and wist not what it meant, for they thought it was an angel that had appeared unto them. And it came to pass that he stretched forth his hand and spake unto the people, saying: Behold, I am Jesus Christ, whom the prophets testified shall come into the world. And behold, I am the light and the life of the world; and I have drunk out of that bitter cup which the Father hath given me, and have glorified the Father in taking upon me the sins of the world, in the which I have suffered the will of the Father in all things from the beginning. And it came to pass that when Jesus had spoken these words the whole multitude fell to the earth; for they remembered that it had been prophesied among them that Christ should show himself unto them after his ascension into heaven. And it came to pass that the Lord spake unto them saying: Arise and come forth unto me, that ye may thrust your hands into my side, and also that ye may feel the prints of the nails in my hands and in my feet, that ye may know that I am the God of Israel, and the God of the whole earth, and have been slain for the sins of the world. And it came to pass that the multitude went forth, and thrust their hands into his side, and did feel the prints of the nails in his hands and in his feet; and this they did do, going forth one by one until they had all gone forth, and did see with their eyes and did feel with their hands, and did know of a surety and did bear record, that it was he, of whom it was written by the prophets, that should come. And when they had all gone forth and had witnessed for themselves, they did cry out with one accord, saying: Hosanna! Blessed be the name of the Most High God! And they did fall down at the feet of Jesus, and did worship him."

This ministry succeeded in establishing fruit-bearing in that and several succeeding generations.[1789]

In each of the places the Lord put the scattered branches, the Lord and His servants visited and labored.[1790] This was a global post-resurrection ministry. He told the Nephites[1791] and Jacob's older brother, Nephi about it.[1792] All of these places in the vineyard began to bear fruit.

Another "long time had passed away" in the vineyard. The end was drawing near, and so it was necessary to recheck the vineyard. The momentum of the Lord's prior ministry needed to be checked again. When the natural tree root, with its grafted branches was checked, there was "all sorts of fruit" that "did cumber the tree".[1793]

[1789] I gave a talk on the Nephite years of fruit-bearing which someone recorded and still distributes. I am not involved with that, having only given consent to allow it to happen. The CD's are sold for a modest amount, and the proceeds are used for supporting missionaries (I don't even handle any of the money). It is the "*Zion*" CD (I don't recall the actual title used) and I think you can get it from Confetti Bookstore in Spanish Fork. I won't repeat that information again, but mention it because it is relevant to the subject of the Nephite people producing fruit for the Lord of the vineyard.

[1790] Jacob 5:28 "And it came to pass that the Lord of the vineyard and the servant of the Lord of the vineyard did nourish all the fruit of the vineyard."

[1791] 3 Nephi 16:1–3 "And verily, verily, I say unto you that I have other sheep, which are not of this land, neither of the land of Jerusalem, neither in any parts of that land round about whither I have been to minister. For they of whom I speak are they who have not as yet heard my voice; neither have I at any time manifested myself unto them. But I have received a commandment of the Father that I shall go unto them, and that they shall hear my voice, and shall be numbered among my sheep, that there may be one fold and one shepherd; therefore I go to show myself unto them."

[1792] 2 Nephi 29:12–13 "For behold, I shall speak unto the Jews and they shall write it; and I shall also speak unto the Nephites and they shall write it; and I shall also speak unto the other tribes of the house of Israel, which I have led away, and they shall write it; and I shall also speak unto all nations of the earth and they shall write it. And it shall come to pass that the Jews shall have the words of the Nephites, and the Nephites shall have the words of the Jews; and the Nephites and the Jews shall have the words of the lost tribes of Israel; and the lost tribes of Israel shall have the words of the Nephites and the Jews."

[1793] Jacob 5:30 "And it came to pass that the Lord of the vineyard and the servant went down into the vineyard; and they came to the tree whose natural branches had been broken off, and the wild branches had been grafted in; and behold all sorts of fruit did cumber the tree."

There were Catholics, Orthodox, Lutherans, Presbyterians, Methodists, Baptists, Campbellites, and an hundred other sorts of fruit on the tree root's branches. But when the Lord "tasted the fruit"[1794]. He found that "none of it was good."[1795]

There was nothing left of the Family of Israel in the original root and its associated branches:

> "they were all wrong; and the Personage who addressed me said that all their creeds were an abomination in his sight; that those professors were all corrupt; that: 'they draw near to me with their lips, but their hearts are far from me, they teach for doctrines the commandments of men, having a form of godliness, but they deny the power thereof.'" (JS–H 1:19)

The Lord's reaction is telling. He immediately wondered "What shall we do unto the tree, that I may preserve again good fruit thereof unto my own self?"[1796] The Lord is neither an optimist nor a pessimist. He is a pragmatic laborer. It is not about blame, only about taking the required next step to rehabilitate the cumbered and unprofitable tree. God's ways are indeed higher.[1797]

[1794] Jacob 5:31 "And it came to pass that the Lord of the vineyard did taste of the fruit, every sort according to its number. And the Lord of the vineyard said: Behold, this long time have we nourished this tree, and I have laid up unto myself against the season much fruit."

[1795] Jacob 5:32 "But behold, this time it hath brought forth much fruit, and there is none of it which is good. And behold, there are all kinds of bad fruit; and it profiteth me nothing, notwithstanding all our labor; and now it grieveth me that I should lose this tree."

[1796] Jacob 5:33 "And the Lord of the vineyard said unto the servant: What shall we do unto the tree, that I may preserve again good fruit thereof unto mine own self?"

[1797] Isaiah 55:9 "For *as* the heavens are higher than the earth, so are my ways higher than your ways, and my thoughts than your thoughts."

Jacob 5:34–37

The servant observes that the original group of people have been preserved by the efforts of the Lord. There is still a "root" which "have not perished."[1798] The bloodline remains. The covenant can be renewed with them. While it would require work, the potential for reviving the failed family remains possible.

Despite the potential, the Lord of the vineyard has a more practical objective in mind. There must be actual saved souls, part of the Family of God, for the work of preserving souls to matter. "The tree profiteth me nothing, and the roots thereof profit me nothing so long as it shall bring forth evil fruit."[1799]

They have been preserved to allow for the possibility for a return of covenant Israel.[1800] However, it must result in an **actual return**, the living tree bringing forth good fruit, children of promise, raised in righteousness, schooled by parents who will raise them to keep the ways of God as His people, for the effort to have been worthwhile.[1801]

The root, and all the various manner of fruit which sprang from it, have "overrun the roots thereof" and only "evil fruit" was left.[1802]

[1798] Jacob 5:34 "And the servant said unto his master: Behold, because thou didst graft in the branches of the wild olive-tree they have nourished the roots, that they are alive and they have not perished; wherefore thou beholdest that they are yet good."

[1799] Jacob 5:35 "And it came to pass that the Lord of the vineyard said unto his servant: The tree profiteth me nothing, and the roots thereof profit me nothing so long as it shall bring forth evil fruit."

[1800] Jacob 5:36 "Nevertheless, I know that the roots are good, and for mine own purpose I have preserved them; and because of their much strength they have hitherto brought forth, from the wild branches, good fruit."

[1801] Ibid.

[1802] Jacob 5:37 "But behold, the wild branches have grown and have overrun the roots thereof; and because that the wild branches have overcome the roots thereof it hath brought forth much evil fruit; and because that it hath brought forth so much evil fruit thou beholdest that it beginneth to perish; and it will soon become ripened, that it may be cast into the fire, except we should do something for it to preserve it."

Not just evil fruit, but "much evil fruit" was the result of this long apostasy from the original.[1803] The overwhelming production of this vile product has overtaken the "root" so that the entire tree appears to "perish" and "it will soon become ripened, that it may be cast into the fire, unless" the Lord does something to alter the course it was following.[1804]

Christianity failed in its original purpose. No one was being saved when the Lord considered His vineyard. Left to its own, the result would be universal destruction at His coming. He would burn the vineyard and remove all the various Christian offshoots claiming to have originated in the New Testament stock.

This allegory shows the need to separate ourselves from Historic Christianity. If we are part of it, then we are nothing worthy of being preserved. Like them, we should be gathered into bundles and cast into the fire.

When the Lord declared that "they were all wrong" and "that all their creeds were an abomination in his sight" and "that those professors were all corrupt".[1805] He was confirming the allegory of Zenos and the prophecy of Jacob. This was the condition of the vineyard.

We should view the ambition of being considered part of that "abomination" and "wrong" "corruption" as an unworthy ambition. We are *not* (or at least should not) be part of the Historic Christian tradition. It is riddled with "much evil fruit" and the people who profess their creeds are "all corrupt." Not in the sense that their hearts

---

[1803] Ibid.

[1804] Ibid.

[1805] JS–H 1:19 "I was answered that I must join none of them, for they were all wrong; and the Personage who addressed me said that all their creeds were an abomination in his sight; that those professors were all corrupt; that: "they draw near to me with their lips, but their hearts are far from me, they teach for doctrines the commandments of men, having a form of godliness, but they deny the power thereof."

are vile, but in the sense that they do not comprehend what it means to be part of the Family of God, much less even occupy that association with Him. They are orphans, unconnected with the "living vine."[1806] Unless they occupy a family relationship with God, they are not His and will be gathered and burned at His coming.

Jacob 5:38–41

The Lord's inspection of the vineyard was global. Even the "nethermost parts of the vineyard" were examined for fruit.[1807] Despite the opportunities given to the vineyard, "the fruit of the natural branches" which belonged to the original root and should have been able to bear fruit "had become corrupt also."[1808] No matter where you looked, "the first and the second and also the last; . . . they had all become corrupt."[1809] The apostasy was now universal. It was not possible for the Lord to find fruit worth preserving anywhere in His vineyard. The ordinances were changed. The covenant was broken.[1810]

Apostasy is always marked by a change of ordinances and breaking of the covenant. Then everything can continue to mimic the

---

[1806] John 15:4–6 "Abide in me, and I in you. As the branch cannot bear fruit of itself, except it abide in the vine; no more can ye, except ye abide in me. I am the vine, ye *are* the branches: He that abideth in me, and I in him, the same bringeth forth much fruit: for without me ye can do nothing. If a man abide not in me, he is cast forth as a branch, and is withered; and men gather them, and cast *them* into the fire, and they are burned."

[1807] Jacob 5:38 "And it came to pass that the Lord of the vineyard said unto his servant: Let us go down into the nethermost parts of the vineyard, and behold if the natural branches have also brought forth evil fruit."

[1808] Jacob 5:39 "And it came to pass that they went down into the nethermost parts of the vineyard. And it came to pass that they beheld that the fruit of the natural branches had become corrupt also; yea, the first and the second and also the last; and they had all become corrupt."

[1809] Ibid.

[1810] Isaiah 24:5 "The earth also is defiled under the inhabitants thereof; because they have transgressed the laws, changed the ordinance, broken the everlasting covenant."

truth, but there can be no fruit. The apostates can keep the vocabulary, claim to have the truth and worship the God of Israel, use the same scriptures as were written by those who were in and kept the covenant, and assume they are either in or headed toward Zion and that "all is well" even as they are covered in chains and bound for hell.[1811] Then the apostasy can rule from the rivers to the ends of the earth, but no-one is capable of telling them to be afraid. While in Satan's power, they think themselves blessed.

The "fruit" to be "laid up against the season" is highly specific. It is God's own family. Those who are bound to Him directly, in an unbroken covenant of adoption, where He recognizes them as His "sons and daughters" and has told them so in an unbreakable bond.[1812] Those who receive Him receive this oath from Him. And through it, He covenants with them, in a bond which He cannot break, that they are His sons and His daughters and heirs to all the Father has.[1813] It will not be an imitation, which does not create "fruit" but it will be Him and His covenant. For "all they who receive

---

[1811] 2 Nephi 28:23–25 "Yea, they are grasped with death, and hell; and death, and hell, and the devil, and all that have been seized therewith must stand before the throne of God, and be judged according to their works, from whence they must go into the place prepared for them, even a lake of fire and brimstone, which is endless torment. Therefore, wo be unto him that is at ease in Zion! Wo be unto him that crieth: All is well!"

[1812] Mosiah 27:25 "And the Lord said unto me: Marvel not that all mankind, yea, men and women, all nations, kindreds, tongues and people, must be born again; yea, born of God, changed from their carnal and fallen state, to a state of righteousness, being redeemed of God, becoming his sons and daughters;"

[1813] D&C 84:35–40 "And also all they who receive this priesthood receive me, saith the Lord; For he that receiveth my servants receiveth me; And he that receiveth me receiveth my Father; And he that receiveth my Father receiveth my Father's kingdom; therefore all that my Father hath shall be given unto him. And this is according to the oath and covenant which belongeth to the priesthood. Therefore, all those who receive the priesthood, receive this oath and covenant of my Father, which he cannot break, neither can it be moved."

this priesthood receive me, saith the Lord."[1814] He will come to and "comfort" those with this covenant.[1815] This is not by proxy, or through an appearance "in the heart" through some feeling, but is an actual appearance leading to an actual bond that cannot be broken, and therefore comforts the sojourner in this lone and dreary world.[1816]

Because there were no longer any who remained in the vineyard with this covenant, or who were adopted into the Family of God, or who were suitable to be preserved through the burning of the vineyard, the entire vineyard, from the first to the last, "had all become corrupt."[1817] Even in the best spot in the vineyard, "the wild fruit of the last had overcome that part of the tree which brought forth good fruit, even that the branch had withered away and died."[1818] The Nephite fall was complete. Nothing remained. All was wild and unsuitable, entirely corrupt.

[1814] D&C 88:35 "That which breaketh a law, and abideth not by law, but seeketh to become a law unto itself, and willeth to abide in sin, and altogether abideth in sin, cannot be sanctified by law, neither by mercy, justice, nor judgment. Therefore, they must remain filthy still."

[1815] John 14:18 "I will not leave you comfortless: I will come to you."

[1816] John 14:23 "Jesus answered and said unto him, If a man love me, he will keep my words: and my Father will love him, and we will come unto him, and make our abode with him."
D&C 130:3 "John 14:23—The appearing of the Father and the Son, in that verse, is a personal appearance; and the idea that the Father and the Son dwell in a man's heart is an old sectarian notion, and is false."

[1817] Jacob 5:39 "And it came to pass that they went down into the nethermost parts of the vineyard. And it came to pass that they beheld that the fruit of the natural branches had become corrupt also; yea, the first and the second and also the last; and they had all become corrupt."

[1818] Jacob 5:40 "And the wild fruit of the last had overcome that part of the tree which brought forth good fruit, even that the branch had withered away and died."

At this terrible state of man "the Lord of the vineyard wept."[1819] The Lord's work and glory is to produce fruit from His vineyard.[1820] The Lord of the vineyard is not able to withhold His tears at our dreadful plight. He is moved with compassion for us.[1821]

As the Lord looked at the complete failure of the entire vineyard, He reflected with sorrow: "What could I have done more for my vineyard?"[1822] The Lord does not fault us. He examines Himself. He begins His inventory of what went wrong with His own actions, not ours. We who rebel against Him are not faulted by Him. But He wonders how He might have been the better Lord. It ought to cause us to weep to realize who He really is, and what He really thinks.

Jacob 5:42–47

There was no fruit being produced anywhere in the vineyard. The Lord recognized that. The separated branches that He had visited were able to produce covenant sons and daughters of God, only to fail to keep the covenant alive. "[N]ow all the trees of [the] vineyard are good for nothing save it be to be hewn down and cast into the fire."[1823] That does not mean they aren't going to be preserved. They will, but they will suffer the wrath of God. Then they will come

---

[1819] Jacob 5:41 "And it came to pass that the Lord of the vineyard wept, and said unto the servant: What could I have done more for my vineyard?"

[1820] Moses 1:39 "For behold, this is my work and my glory—to bring to pass the immortality and eternal life of man."

[1821] Hebrews 4:15 "For we have not an high priest which cannot be touched with the feeling of our infirmities; but was in all points tempted like as *we are, yet* without sin." Matthew 14:14 "And Jesus went forth, and saw a great multitude, and was moved with compassion toward them, and he healed their sick."

[1822] Jacob 5:41 "And it came to pass that the Lord of the vineyard wept, and said unto the servant: What could I have done more for my vineyard?"

[1823] Jacob 5:42 "Behold, I knew that all the fruit of the vineyard, save it were these, had become corrupted. And now these which have once brought forth good fruit have also become corrupted; and now all the trees of my vineyard are good for nothing save it be to be hewn down and cast into the fire."

forth at the end of the season, and be placed in a position of Telestial Glory to dwell in the same condition as this fallen world.[1824] From the Lord's perspective, that is undesirable. It is failure. It is tragic. This is the native condition this vineyard repeatedly lapses into, even with the Lord and His servant's continuing care. What more could He do, indeed! How often would He have gathered us, but we refuse.[1825]

Even when the Lord bestows peculiar advantages on the branches of His vineyard, the results are not dissimilar to what goes on elsewhere. Highly favored and greatly blessed people seem as indifferent to their salvation as those who inherit challenges and difficulties.[1826] The Lord "cut down that which cumbered this spot of ground, that I might plant this tree in the stead thereof."[1827] He provided the best spot in the vineyard by destroying the people inhabiting it. Then, as we shall see, He destroys the branches brought there once they also fail to produce suitable fruit.

[1824] D&C 76:81–85 "And again, we saw the glory of the telestial, which glory is that of the lesser, even as the glory of the stars differs from that of the glory of the moon in the firmament. These are they who received not the gospel of Christ, neither the testimony of Jesus. These are they who deny not the Holy Spirit. These are they who are thrust down to hell. These are they who shall not be redeemed from the devil until the last resurrection, until the Lord, even Christ the Lamb, shall have finished his work."

[1825] 3 Nephi 10:5 "And again, how oft would I have gathered you as a hen gathereth her chickens under her wings, yea, O ye people of the house of Israel, who have fallen; yea, O ye people of the house of Israel, ye that dwell at Jerusalem, as ye that have fallen; yea, how oft would I have gathered you as a hen gathereth her chickens, and ye would not."

[1826] Jacob 5:43 "And behold this last, whose branch hath withered away, I did plant in a good spot of ground; yea, even that which was choice unto me above all other parts of the land of my vineyard."

[1827] Jacob 5:44 "And thou beheldest that I also cut down that which cumbered this spot of ground, that I might plant this tree in the stead thereof."
Ether 13:1 "And now I, Moroni, proceed to finish my record concerning the destruction of the people of whom I have been writing."

The good spot was cleansed of the bad branches, yet the bad still overcame the good.[1828] The Nephite civilization was, in the end, entirely overcome and destroyed because it failed to produce any more sons and daughters of God.

As the Lord surveyed the entire vineyard, He saw nothing but universal failure. There was no fruit able to be preserved against the coming season of judgment. The whole earth was worthy of destruction, because there were none whose hearts were sealed to the fathers in heaven, members of the Family of God, who could endure His presence at His return. In other words, there was no righteous branch living on the earth. All manner of fruit claimed to be good. All kinds of pretenders were claiming they were of God. They clamored "lo here!" and "lo, there!" and claimed they could deliver souls from hell. Yet no one was able to bring the living into contact with God, which was required in order for them to receive the "testimony of Jesus" promising them eternal life.[1829] The Lord needed to begin over again. The vineyard was void of fruit-bearing trees. Despite this, the Lord reflected "it grieveth me that I should lose

---

[1828] Jacob 5:45 "And thou beheldest that a part thereof brought forth good fruit, and a part thereof brought forth wild fruit; and because I plucked not the branches thereof and cast them into the fire, behold, they have overcome the good branch that it hath withered away."

[1829] D&C 76:51–55 "They are they who received the testimony of Jesus, and believed on his name and were baptized after the manner of his burial, being buried in the water in his name, and this according to the commandment which he has given— That by keeping the commandments they might be washed and cleansed from all their sins, and receive the Holy Spirit by the laying on of the hands of him who is ordained and sealed unto this power; And who overcome by faith, and are sealed by the Holy Spirit of promise, which the Father sheds forth upon all those who are just and true. They are they who are the church of the Firstborn. They are they into whose hands the Father has given all things—"

them."[1830] The Lord takes the salvation of mankind seriously. It is His work. And when they fail, He grieves.

The Lord lists all He does to try to provoke His "tree" to bear fruit. He does not "slacken his hand" nor does he fail to "nourish" it. [1831]He "digged," and He "pruned," and He "dunged" the tree. These efforts include sending the Light of Christ, the Holy Ghost, scriptures, prophets, angels, visions, dreams and signs in the heavens above and the earth beneath. He has done this continually for His vineyard. But these many gifts from God, and the great work He has done have failed to produce fruit. At last He poses the question to His servant: "Who is it that has corrupted my vineyard?"[1832] A worthy question, indeed. The answer is surprising, because it does not require a devil to be involved.

Jacob 5:48–51

The vineyard fails continually because of "the loftiness of the vineyard."[1833] That is, the pride and arrogance of Israel itself is the cause of continual failure. They run faster then they are able, reach-

---

[1830] Jacob 5:46 "And now, behold, notwithstanding all the care which we have taken of my vineyard, the trees thereof have become corrupted, that they bring forth no good fruit; and these I had hoped to preserve, to have laid up fruit thereof against the season, unto mine own self. But, behold, they have become like unto the wild olive-tree, and they are of no worth but to be hewn down and cast into the fire; and it grieveth me that I should lose them."

[1831] Jacob 5:47 "But what could I have done more in my vineyard? Have I slackened mine hand, that I have not nourished it? Nay, I have nourished it, and I have digged about it, and I have pruned it, and I have dunged it; and I have stretched forth mine hand almost all the day long, and the end draweth nigh. And it grieveth me that I should hew down all the trees of my vineyard, and cast them into the fire that they should be burned. Who is it that has corrupted my vineyard?"

[1832] Ibid.

[1833] Jacob 5:48 "And it came to pass that the servant said unto his master: Is it not the loftiness of thy vineyard—have not the branches thereof overcome the roots which are good? And because the branches have overcome the roots thereof, behold they grew faster than the strength of the roots, taking strength unto themselves. Behold, I say, is not this the cause that the trees of thy vineyard have become corrupted?"

ing what they cannot attain, claiming to have what they do not have, and relying on their conceit rather than the Lord. As a result, the branches overcome the roots. They grew faster than could be accommodated, and took strength to themselves, which always defeats fruit production.[1834]

The Lord's exasperation with this complete failure results in the announcement that He was going to return to the vineyard, "hew down the trees" and then "cast them into the fire" so they no longer cumbered the land.[1835] It was time to return and destroy everything. Or, to use a phrase from Malachi, to "smite the whole earth with a curse."[1836] We see in this that the Lord does actually consider smiting the entire earth. The allegory reveals it. It is indeed possible for the Lord to consider that as an option.

The only way to prevent it is for the "vineyard" to again bring forth fruit worth laying up against the season of the harvest. It failed. There was a universal apostasy. The Lord announced it was His intention to destroy all the people of the earth.[1837] But it was the "servant" who pleaded for the Lord to "spare it a little longer."[1838] In Zenos' allegory, the Lord is the one wanting to destroy the vineyard. When He was in His mortal ministry, the Lord reversed these roles.

[1834] Ibid.

[1835] Jacob 5:49 "And it came to pass that the Lord of the vineyard said unto the servant: Let us go to and hew down the trees of the vineyard and cast them into the fire, that they shall not cumber the ground of my vineyard, for I have done all. What could I have done more for my vineyard?"

[1836] Malachi 4:6 "And he shall turn the heart of the fathers to the children, and the heart of the children to their fathers, lest I come and smite the earth with a curse."

[1837] Jacob 5:49 "And it came to pass that the Lord of the vineyard said unto the servant: Let us go to and hew down the trees of the vineyard and cast them into the fire, that they shall not cumber the ground of my vineyard, for I have done all. What could I have done more for my vineyard?"

[1838] Ibid.

He had the angels wanting to destroy, and the Lord being patient.[1839] In both, the judgment is postponed until something worthy of preserving can be brought into the harvest. The Lord agrees to spare the vineyard despite the universal failure to bring about "fruit" because it "grieveth" Him to see such a loss, so great a waste.[1840]

Now all of this is about history. It has already happened. Zenos wrote in the unified kingdom, before the division into the Northern Kingdom, or Kingdom of Israel, and the Southern Kingdom, or Kingdom of Judah. He wrote before Isaiah, and before Jeremiah. His prophecy became a benchmark from which other, later prophets would draw in fashioning their own prophecies.

Using these allegorical themes and images (tree, branches, transplanting, grafting, laboring, gathering, burning, trimming, pruning, etc.), we can see what happened historically with the scattering of Israel. Now, however, we have reached a point in the allegory where the events are either current or future. They are underway. This part of the allegory relates to us. It is meant to warn us about the time we live.

We think we've gotten the benefit of the Lord's hand in the effort now underway. However, there is nothing going on at this time in the vineyard that should make us think we can relax. There is more pruning, gathering and yet more labor, before we yield fruit.

As we continue from this point forward, we must pay more attention. It is a blueprint for how the Lord is dealing with us. We should

---

[1839] Matthew 13:28–30 "He said unto them, An enemy hath done this. The servants said unto him, Wilt thou then that we go and gather them up? But he said, Nay; lest while ye gather up the tares, ye root up also the wheat with them. Let both grow together until the harvest: and in the time of harvest I will say to the reapers, Gather ye together first the tares, and bind them in bundles to burn them: but gather the wheat into my barn."

[1840] Jacob 5:51 "And the Lord said: Yea, I will spare it a little longer, for it grieveth me that I should lose the trees of my vineyard."

take every opportunity to consider how the prophecy may be intended to warn us against our own "loftiness" and ultimate failure.

Easter

Tomorrow is Easter, April 8th. The Lord rose from the borrowed tomb while it was dark on that morning approximately two millennia ago.

The assortment of thoughts that run through my mind wanders from past to present to the future. He dominates the landscape no matter where the thoughts run on this approaching Easter:

What are these wounds on your hands and feet?

"Those I suffered in the house of my friends."

How is it possible?

"By the power given unto me from the Father I have overcome all things."

Did not our hearts burn within us?

He is dressed in red, coming in judgment, to reward those who waited on Him and to punish and remove the wicked.

The Lamb slain from the foundation of the world. The Lion of Judah. The Son of David. The Scepter of Judah. The Slain. The Risen. The Redeemer.

So we might understand who He is and have faith in Him, He declared in meekness: "I am greater than them all," and "I am more intelligent than them all." And again, "I am the light and the life of the world. I have drunk out of that bitter cup which the Father hath given me, and have glorified the Father in taking upon me the sins of the world, in the which I have suffered the will of the Father in all things from the beginning."

"What I call 'clean' call thou not 'unclean.'"

"Therefore I command you to repent—repent, lest I smite you by the rod of my mouth, and by my wrath, and by my anger, and your sufferings be sore—how sore you know not, how exquisite you know not, yea, how hard to bear you know not. For behold, I, God, have suffered these things for all that they might not suffer if they would repent; but if they would not repent they must suffer even as I; which suffering caused myself, even God, the greatest of all, to tremble because of pain, and to bleed at every pore, and to suffer both body and spirit—and would that I might not drink the bitter cup, and shrink—Nevertheless, glory be to the Father, and I partook and finished my preparations unto the children of men."

Why is it "preparations" Lord?

"It is given unto you to choose. I can prepare, but you must choose to repent. I call upon all men to repent and come unto Me."

Seeing, they do not understand, hearing, they do not listen. They have lost the desire for knowledge and they have fallen away. Isaiah said we would change the ordinances, break the covenant, but Christ tells us to pray continually: Thy will be done, thy kingdom come . . .

To rescue a broken and fallen people, we have His light and the life He gave for us. Look unto Him and live. We have hope in Christ Jesus.

The Glorious One. The Father of the saved. The Firstborn. The Son of God. Jehovah.

An Important Quote

"That which can be destroyed by truth should be."
—P.C. Hodgell

Source of Information about Tithing

In response to a question about the source of information regarding the church's tithing investment system, I have confirmed that information from three sources in the church offices, therefore put it up because it was accurate. But I keep confidences, and sources are not disclosed unless they want to be disclosed.

Jacob 5:52

We reach our day. In it the Lord of the vineyard has a highly specific intention. He will take the various scattered branches, the far-flung and long lost descendants of Jacob who are in "the nethermost parts of [His] vineyard" and will "graft them into the tree from whence they came."[1841] This is the work Joseph Smith identified as the most critical work of the restoration of the Gospel. This is the only thing that will prevent the earth from being "utterly wasted" at the Lord's coming.[1842]

The manner of this gathering involves connecting the "children" who are disassociated with the House of Israel—and have altogether lost their status in that family back through an adoption by God into His House. In other words, to make them members of the Family of God again. The "fathers" to whom they are to connect are not their ancestors. Their ancestors will require vicarious work to be saved. Connecting to them in their fallen, disconnected condition will not save "the children."

Joseph taught the way this connection is to be accomplished. I would refer you again to the Elijah Talk which is available for download. I won't repeat it again. You can read it for yourself.

This leads to several side issues, including: Who are the gentiles and how do they fit into the plan of regrafting? Who are the rem-

---

[1841] Jacob 5:52 "Wherefore, let us take of the branches of these which I have planted in the nethermost parts of my vineyard, and let us graft them into the tree from whence they came; and let us pluck from the tree those branches whose fruit is most bitter, and graft in the natural branches of the tree in the stead thereof."

[1842] D&C 2:3 "If it were not so, the whole earth would be utterly wasted at his coming." JS–H 1:39 "He also quoted the next verse differently: *And he shall plant in the hearts of the children the promises made to the fathers, and the hearts of the children shall turn to their fathers. If it were not so, the whole earth would be utterly wasted at his coming.*"

nant, and how do they fit into the regrafting? Who are the Jews and how do they fit into the latter-day scheme? What about the latter-day saint practice of identifying a Tribe of Israel in the patriarchal blessings and the effect that has on regrafting?

These questions require a specific reference point from which to answer. The Book of Mormon and Doctrine and Covenants provide answers. In the vocabulary of both, the "gentiles" are the members of The Church of Jesus Christ of Latter-day Saints, and the unconverted European residents of "this land." You should be able to see that for yourself just by reading the material. As a quick example, Nephi explains who the "gentiles" are in 1 Nephi 13:14.[1843] Moroni explains who they are in the Title Page of the Book of Mormon written by him.[1844] Joseph Smith identifies the church as "gentiles" by identity.[1845] We, the latter-day saints to whom the Book of Mormon was given, and who are among the very few readers of the text, are the "gentiles" of prophecy. Notwithstanding that status,

---

[1843] 1 Nephi 13:14 "And it came to pass that I beheld many multitudes of the Gentiles upon the land of promise; and I beheld the wrath of God, that it was upon the seed of my brethren; and they were scattered before the Gentiles and were smitten."

[1844] An Account Written by the Hand of Mormon upon Plates Taken from the Plates of Nephi. "Wherefore, it is an abridgment of the record of the people of Nephi, and also of the Lamanites—Written to the Lamanites, who are a remnant of the house of Israel; and also to Jew and Gentile—Written by way of commandment, and also by the spirit of prophecy and of revelation—Written and sealed up, and hid up unto the Lord, that they might not be destroyed—To come forth by the gift and power of God unto the interpretation thereof—Sealed by the hand of Moroni, and hid up unto the Lord, to come forth in due time by way of the Gentile—The interpretation thereof by the gift of God. An abridgment taken from the Book of Ether also, which is a record of the people of Jared, who were scattered at the time the Lord confounded the language of the people, when they were building a tower to get to heaven—Which is to show unto the remnant of the house of Israel what great things the Lord hath done for their fathers; and that they may know the covenants of the Lord, that they are not cast off forever—And also to the convincing of the Jew and Gentile that Jesus is the Christ, the Eternal God, manifesting himself unto all nations—And now, if there are faults they are the mistakes of men; wherefore, condemn not the things of God, that ye may be found spotless at the judgment-seat of Christ."

[1845] D&C 109:60 "Now these words, O Lord, we have spoken before thee, concerning the revelations and commandments which thou hast given unto us, who are identified with the Gentiles."

there are many among the "gentiles" who have blood of Jacob in them. They are potentially candidates for restoration to the House of Israel. They are the intended targets of the restoration, but their restoration will not be completed until they are adopted back to the line of "the fathers" who are able to save them from the coming harvest.

The "remnant" are those who are descended from Lehi. They are still identifiable (to the Lord) as Nephites, Jacobites, Josephites, Lamanites, Lemuelites, and so forth.[1846] They are known to Him, and are still here, but are without knowledge to save themselves. For that, they also must come to the knowledge of the truth and be restored.[1847]

The Jews are those from Jacob who have retained their original identification with Jacob, but who are also lost as members of the House of Israel, or members of the Family of God. Remember, the vineyard is utterly corrupt no matter which group the Lord considers.[1848] The status alone will not restore good fruit to the vine.

[1846] D&C 3:16–20 "Nevertheless, my work shall go forth, for inasmuch as the knowledge of a Savior has come unto the world, through the testimony of the Jews, even so shall the knowledge of a Savior come unto my people— And to the Nephites, and the Jacobites, and the Josephites, and the Zoramites, through the testimony of their fathers— And this testimony shall come to the knowledge of the Lamanites, and the Lemuelites, and the Ishmaelites, who dwindled in unbelief because of the iniquity of their fathers, whom the Lord has suffered to destroy their brethren the Nephites, because of their iniquities and their abominations. And for this very purpose are these plates preserved, which contain these records—that the promises of the Lord might be fulfilled, which he made to his people; And that the Lamanites might come to the knowledge of their fathers, and that they might know the promises of the Lord, and that they may believe the gospel and rely upon the merits of Jesus Christ, and be glorified through faith in his name, and that through their repentance they might be saved. Amen."

[1847] D&C 3:20 "And that the Lamanites might come to the knowledge of their fathers, and that they might know the promises of the Lord, and that they may believe the gospel and rely upon the merits of Jesus Christ, and be glorified through faith in his name, and that through their repentance they might be saved. Amen."
3 Nephi 5:23 "Yea, and surely shall he again bring a remnant of the seed of Joseph to the knowledge of the Lord their God."

[1848] Jacob 5:39 "And it came to pass that they went down into the nethermost parts of the vineyard. And it came to pass that they beheld that the fruit of the natural branches had become corrupt also; yea, the first and the second and also the last; and they had all become corrupt."

There must be a direct connection, through "the fathers" by adoption into the Family of God, restoring them to "the living vine."[1849]

The identification of a Tribe of Israel in the latter-day saint patriarchal blessings does not restore the covenant, nor does it connect you to the "living vine," nor does it alter the status of being "gentile" by identification. There is another group who are not identified as "gentile," nor as "Jew," nor as the "remnant" who are considered "heathen." These people are "remembered" by the Lord.[1850] Their inheritance is to come forth in the "first resurrection" where "it shall be tolerable for them."[1851] But these other people are not the target of the regrafting. The intended audience and the covenant people to be restored are the "scattered branches" who are unable to bear fruit because they have lost their identification with the original "root" or the "fathers in heaven" as Joseph explained it.[1852]

The Lord of the vineyard has a plan. It is His. He knows all of us and cares more about each of us than we can even understand. However, His ways are His and are reckoned from the vantage point of the one who owns the vineyard, and who has every intention of providing the highest and most exalted outcome for His vineyard. We would be much better off if we took counsel from Him instead of resisting and rejecting it. As Jacob, whose book we are now con-

---

[1849] John 15:4–5 "Abide in me, and I in you. As the branch cannot bear fruit of itself, except it abide in the vine; no more can ye, except ye abide in me. I am the vine, ye *are* the branches: He that abideth in me, and I in him, the same bringeth forth much fruit: for without me ye can do nothing."

[1850] 2 Nephi 26:33 "For none of these iniquities come of the Lord; for he doeth that which is good among the children of men; and he doeth nothing save it be plain unto the children of men; and he inviteth them all to come unto him and partake of his goodness; and he denieth none that come unto him, black and white, bond and free, male and female; and he remembereth the heathen; and all are alike unto God, both Jew and Gentile."

[1851] D&C 45:54 "And then shall the heathen nations be redeemed, and they that knew no law shall have part in the first resurrection; and it shall be tolerable for them."

[1852] See my paper on "Elijah".

sidering, put it: "Wherefore, brethren, seek not to counsel the Lord, but to take counsel from his hand. For behold, ye yourselves know that he counseleth in wisdom, and in justice, and in great mercy, over all his works."[1853]

Jacob 5:53–56

The Lord is quite realistic about salvaging something from the vineyard. He does not state He can produce fruit again, only that "perhaps, I may preserve unto myself the roots thereof."[1854] The vineyard must respond. He respects our agency. He can encourage, invite and entice us, but we are always free to choose.[1855] It is that freedom to choose that results in the vineyard being condemned. They could have responded to the Lord's invitation, but decided not to.[1856]

So this final dispensation is not a guaranteed success. Notwithstanding the optimism of many of our revelations, the Lord of the vineyard knows success (fruit reappearing) will only "perhaps" occur.

The bloodlines are still here. Though they are separated, mixed and disbursed throughout the nethermost parts of the vineyard, they

---

[1853] Jacob 4:10 "Wherefore, brethren, seek not to counsel the Lord, but to take counsel from his hand. For behold, ye yourselves know that he counseleth in wisdom, and in justice, and in great mercy, over all his works."

[1854] Jacob 5:53 "And this will I do that the tree may not perish, that, perhaps, I may preserve unto myself the roots thereof for mine own purpose."

[1855] Moroni 7:13 "But behold, that which is of God inviteth and enticeth to do good continually; wherefore, every thing which inviteth and enticeth to do good, and to love God, and to serve him, is inspired of God."

[1856] D&C 101:78 "That every man may act in doctrine and principle pertaining to futurity, according to the moral agency which I have given unto him, that every man may be accountable for his own sins in the day of judgment."

are "yet still alive."[1857] The Lord has determined, and is now taking the steps, to graft back together the branches to the root in hopes of producing "fruit" again.[1858] Notice it is not the restoration of the link, the regrafting of the branches, or the successful return of the Lord's husbandry to the vineyard that matters. Despite all the coaxing and work, and even the regrafting of branch to root, the purpose is not fulfilled until there is "fruit" produced. The organizational structure of the reassembled tree is nothing. It is the "fruit" and the "fruit" alone which is the object of the effort. *A Divine reconnection of branch and root is not and never has been the object of the Lord of the vineyard.* Bragging about how you are part of a "restored branch" distracts you from the fact you are still unworthy to be laid up against the season. Lacking fruit, you are only worthy to be gathered in bundles and burned.

This restoration of branch to root does not bear and was never expected to bear any fruit at first. It was the preliminary step, intended to lead to a time when the restored branch takes its opportunity seriously and repents, finally returning to Him. "[T]hat when they shall be sufficiently strong perhaps they may bring forth good fruit unto me."[1859] It was always expected to take time. Generations, in fact, before there would be "fruit" in the vineyard." No matter how millennial the first generation of the saints expected their faith to prove, no matter what prophecies and patriarchal blessings the first generation of latter-day saints shared with one another, and no

---

[1857] Jacob 5:54 "And, behold, the roots of the natural branches of the tree which I planted whithersoever I would are yet alive; wherefore, that I may preserve them also for mine own purpose, I will take of the branches of this tree, and I will graft them in unto them. Yea, I will graft in unto them the branches of their mother tree, that I may preserve the roots also unto mine own self, that when they shall be sufficiently strong perhaps they may bring forth good fruit unto me, and I may yet have glory in the fruit of my vineyard."

[1858] Ibid.

[1859] Ibid.

matter what promises Joseph Smith obtained—everything was contingent on producing "fruit" which the Lord of the vineyard could lay up against the season. I've written the last book about the obvious conclusions we ought to reach regarding the beginning of the restoration. It is my effort to explain where we are and how we got here. It is also intended to help us now produce "fruit" in the vineyard.

The Lord began the process.[1860] He and His servants took the wild branches and regrafted them. The potential covenant was restored. He returned again the pattern of covenant-making, the ordinances which testify to us of Christ's Atonement, the ritual return through the veil to the Lord's presence, and the ideas of a priesthood which is inseparably connected with heaven. He gave us the warning that when we undertake to assert the right to compel others to follow the priesthood, then we forfeit it. No power and no influence can or does exist by "virtue" or by reason of the priesthood. It exists because someone has humbled themselves, repented, come into the presence of Christ, and thereby been redeemed from the fall.[1861]

The Lord of the vineyard and His servants did the work. The graft was begun. Now it remains to see if it will bear fruit.

The Lord knows the end from the beginning.[1862] Everything He revealed to Zenos about the past has happened. We ought to respect that enough to allow the prophecy to inform our present and future.

[1860] Jacob 5:55–56 "And it came to pass that they took from the natural tree which had become wild, and grafted in unto the natural trees, which also had become wild. And they also took of the natural trees which had become wild, and grafted into their mother tree."

[1861] Ether 3:13 "And when he had said these words, behold, the Lord showed himself unto him, and said: Because thou knowest these things ye are redeemed from the fall; therefore ye are brought back into my presence; therefore I show myself unto you."
D&C 84:35 "And also all they who receive this priesthood receive me, saith the Lord;"

[1862] Abraham 2:8 "My name is Jehovah, and I know the end from the beginning; therefore my hand shall be over thee."

Jacob 5:57–59

The restoration begins with an amalgamation of old and new. The only things removed are the bare essentials that are required to begin the transplanting or grafting. "Pluck not the wild branches from the trees, save it be those which are most bitter; and in them ye shall graft according to that which I have said."[1863] The restoration was not a wholesale affair at the start. There was and were a lot of wild, unredeemed and unredeemable participants in the work underway. There is a great deal of "loftiness" and "bitter fruit" left to be trimmed away.

As becomes apparent from the incidents in Nauvoo, Joseph Smith's death was as much a result of internal conspiracies to get him into the hands of the Illinois civil authorities as it was the result of outside fear and hatred. He could have left on June 22nd and never returned. When he lamented "if my life is of no value to my friends, it is of no value to me" he clarified the reason for his return. The accusation that he was a false shepherd because he was "fleeing" when "the flock was in danger" was enough to bring him back, surrender to arrest and incarceration, and ultimately be killed. It wasn't the mob that made the accusations which brought it about. It was the saints, his inner circle, his trusted friends.

So when we reflect on how the restoration was interrupted in its beginning states by the death of Joseph, we cannot lay the blame entirely on the mob that ultimately killed him. It began inside the church itself. If we are partly to blame, as I believe the record shows, then killing Joseph was not just an act of violence *against* the church, but also an act of treachery from *within* the church. Such things generally provoke a reaction from heaven which requires a third and

---

[1863] Jacob 5:57 "And the Lord of the vineyard said unto the servant: Pluck not the wild branches from the trees, save it be those which are most bitter; and in them ye shall graft according to that which I have said."

fourth generation to pass away before the Lord of the vineyard begins anew to cultivate, water, dig and dung His tree again. That would make it about now when the Lord's work would resume.

The work required to begin the restoration was not to produce fruit. It was to make it possible for fruit again to return to the vineyard. To that end, the work to "trim up the branches" and then to "pluck from the trees those branches which are ripened, that must perish" will be an ongoing process once the work begins.[1864] There will be trauma. There will be casting away. There will be those who are "plucked" or removed. The patience required will endure for generations, as the Lord rids the tree of the many wild, unfruitful and unworthy growth found in the undisciplined, wild tree.

The Lord's commitment and understanding allows Him to foresee the possibility it will yet result in worthy fruit. He does this "that, perhaps, the roots thereof may take strength because of their goodness; and because of the change of the branches, that the good may overcome the evil."[1865] It is still a "perhaps" proposition. The tree has its own independence. It will need to respond.

Joseph Smith was attempting to explain some of this process when he taught:

> "The Holy Ghost has no other effect than pure intelligence. It is more powerful in expanding the mind, enlightening the understanding, and storing the intellect with present knowledge, of a man who is of the literal seed of Abraham, than one that is a Gentile, though it may not have half as much visible effect upon the body; for as the Holy Ghost falls upon one of the literal seed of Abraham, it is calm and serene; and his whole

---

[1864] Jacob 5:58 "And we will nourish again the trees of the vineyard, and we will trim up the branches thereof; and we will pluck from the trees those branches which are ripened, that must perish, and cast them into the fire."

[1865] Jacob 5:59 "And this I do that, perhaps, the roots thereof may take strength because of their goodness; and because of the change of the branches, that the good may overcome the evil."

soul and body are only exercised by the pure spirit of intelligence; while the effect of the Holy Ghost upon a Gentile, is to purge out the old blood, and make him actually of the seed of Abraham. That man that has none of the blood of Abraham (naturally) must have a new creation by the Holy Ghost. In such a case, there may be more of a powerful effect upon the body, and visible to the eye, than upon an Israelite, while the Israelite at first might be far before the Gentile in pure intelligence." (*TPJS*, 149–150)

There is so much Joseph spoke about we no longer understand, but in the case of restoring the potential for "fruit" to return, the blood of Jacob matters. Even there, each individual is free to respond to the Lord.

There may be "goodness" left in the individual from his birthright, but even the literal seed of Abraham must do the works of Abraham before they are able to produce fruit.

Jacob 5:60–63

The Lord of the vineyard wants to "have joy again in the fruit of my vineyard."[1866] This is an interesting connection by the Lord of "joy" in His "fruit" or joy in His posterity; for the redeemed are the children of God and He dwells in them.[1867] The purpose of having children is to have "joy" with them. In this instance, the Lord of the vineyard is describing not only His "work and glory"[1868] but also

---

[1866] Jacob 5:60 "And because that I have preserved the natural branches and the roots thereof, and that I have grafted in the natural branches again into their mother tree, and have preserved the roots of their mother tree, that, perhaps, the trees of my vineyard may bring forth again good fruit; and that I may have joy again in the fruit of my vineyard, and, perhaps, that I may rejoice exceedingly that I have preserved the roots and the branches of the first fruit—"

[1867] 1 John 4:4 "Ye are of God, little children, and have overcome them: because greater is he that is in you, than he that is in the world."

[1868] Moses 1:39 "For behold, this is my work and my glory—to bring to pass the immortality and eternal life of man."

what pleases Him most. He explains that producing such fruit worthy of preserving would be so "that I may rejoice exceedingly that I have preserved" these souls.[1869] It is a compelling thought: A Lord who would "rejoice exceedingly" at our success!

The effort required to accomplish this is not inconsequential. There will be many "servants" called to labor in the vineyard. It will require some to descend without disclosing their true identities and to "labor diligently with our might in the vineyard" to bring about the potential for fruit.[1870] Servants sent into the Telestial condition to labor in the vineyard with their might is a careful description, I think. Perhaps it is worth careful thought to consider how such servants might come among us to do the labor needed to rescue us from the coming harvest.

The effort is to "prepare the way" for the vineyard to be able to "bring forth again the natural fruit" of the original, natural tree. The effort is the return of covenant, adopted Israel sealed to the fathers and able to endure the return of the Lord. Such a people are not only "good" but also "the most precious above all other fruit."[1871] This is because such people are not merely mortal, but also immortal, even infinite because they have no end.[1872] It is through such rare

---

[1869] Jacob 5:60 "And because that I have preserved the natural branches and the roots thereof, and that I have grafted in the natural branches again into their mother tree, and have preserved the roots of their mother tree, that, perhaps, the trees of my vineyard may bring forth again good fruit; and that I may have joy again in the fruit of my vineyard, and, perhaps, that I may rejoice exceedingly that I have preserved the roots and the branches of the first fruit—"

[1870] Jacob 5:61 "Wherefore, go to, and call servants, that we may labor diligently with our might in the vineyard, that we may prepare the way, that I may bring forth again the natural fruit, which natural fruit is good and the most precious above all other fruit."

[1871] Ibid.

[1872] D&C 132:20 "Then shall they be gods, because they have no end; therefore shall they be from everlasting to everlasting, because they continue; then shall they be above all, because all things are subject unto them. Then shall they be gods, because they have all power, and the angels are subject unto them."

"most precious above all other fruit" that the universe itself expands. The infinite itself grows.

The Lord, however, acknowledges that both He and His servants must "labor with our might this last time" to salvage some few. (5:62.) What an image comes to mind when you consider the Lord of the vineyard laboring with "His might" to bring again some natural fruit in His vineyard. How great an undertaking! How foolish it is for the saints to believe ourselves chosen. How foolish to think that our careless church activities will save us. How arrogant a proposition it is for the saints to point with pride at our institutions and think it reflects credit upon us. It is, in a word, fruitless.

Because the living must be redeemed for the dead to be saved, the labor begins with the last and goes to the first. The work begins with the living, who are last in the vineyard.[1873] They must be grafted back to the fathers who are in heaven.[1874] God's children living today must be sealed to those who now sit upon thrones in the heavens. Then the deceased ancestors may be sealed to the living so the whole earth is not smitten with a curse at the return of the Lord.

Joseph's instruction about adoption to the "fathers in heaven" was short lived. As I pointed out in *Passing the Heavenly Gift*, many of the surviving church leaders who were taught this by Joseph didn't believe it when he said it. Brigham Young said he never understood it. The allegory of Zenos makes it apparent that there must be a

---

[1873] Jacob 5:63 "Graft in the branches; begin at the last that they may be first, and that the first may be last, and dig about the trees, both old and young, the first and the last; and the last and the first, that all may be nourished once again for the last time."

[1874] D&C 132:29, 37 "Abraham received all things, whatsoever he received, by revelation and commandment, by my word, saith the Lord, and hath entered into his exaltation and sitteth upon his throne. Abraham received concubines, and they bore him children; and it was accounted unto him for righteousness, because they were given unto him, and he abode in my law; as Isaac also and Jacob did none other things than that which they were commanded; and because they did none other things than that which they were commanded, they have entered into their exaltation, according to the promises, and sit upon thrones, and are not angels but are gods."

connection, and that connection must produce natural fruit. The thing that will be saved will be the "fruit" and not the roots, trees and branches. There must be children born into the covenant, raised in righteousness who will live an order that can bring to pass the Savior's great petition in prayer. The Lord's prayer instructed us how to pray and what to pray for: "Our Father who art in heaven, Hallowed be thy name. Thy kingdom come. Thy will be done in earth, as it is in heaven."[1875] Zion will return.

How can fruit be harvested and laid up against the day if we cannot endure His presence at His return?

Jacob 5:64–65

When the regrafting begins there is still more work to be done. In addition to the initiation of the regrafting, there is also the need to "dig" about the tree.[1876] There will be disturbance. The tree and the grafts will also need to be "pruned" because fruit will not come unless some considerable growth is cast away.[1877] The Lord is interested in His "fruit" and not in the tree, mind you. Worshiping the tree, celebrating the tree and idolizing the tree are distractions. The result has always been focused on the "fruit" alone. But, of course, you cannot produce fruit if you lack a tree. Elder Hallstrom's talk was correct. There is a difference between the Gospel and the church, but you do not produce, protect or preserve the Gospel without the church. It is the church that preserves and publishes the Book of

---

[1875] Matthew 6:9–10 "After this manner therefore pray ye: Our Father which art in heaven, Hallowed be thy name. Thy kingdom come. Thy will be done in earth, as *it is* in heaven."

[1876] Jacob 5:64 "Wherefore, dig about them, and prune them, and dung them once more, for the last time, for the end draweth nigh. And if it be so that these last grafts shall grow, and bring forth the natural fruit, then shall ye prepare the way for them, that they may grow."

[1877] Ibid.

Mormon (the very text we are now considering). It is the church where we assemble together to edify and instruct one another. It is in the church we offer service, receive ordinances, fellowship, offer our tithes and offerings, bear testimony and discharge our obligations to God and one another. The tree is essential. But the tree can exist for a long time without producing fruit. And the Lord of the vineyard will destroy the tree if it fails to produce fruit, because it is then "good for nothing."[1878]

The Lord also provides "dung" or nourishment for the tree. Soil gets tired and its nutrients depleted, and therefore He must introduce more vitality to the environment of the tree to stimulate growth and vigor. This is designed to provoke the right kind of effort by the tree.

The Lord and His servants watch over the "grafts" to see whether they "shall grow, and bring forth the natural fruit."[1879] This is a careful, deliberate work.

Though it may take some time, eventually the great initial effort to restore the tree should result in some signs of life in the grafts. "And as they begin to grow ye shall clear away the branches which bring forth bitter fruit."[1880] There will be trauma to the tree and to the grafts. Much of what remains after the initial restoration will still bring about "bitter fruit."

[1878] Jacob 5:42 "Behold, I knew that all the fruit of the vineyard, save it were these, had become corrupted. And now these which have once brought forth good fruit have also become corrupted; and now all the trees of my vineyard are good for nothing save it be to be hewn down and cast into the fire."

[1879] Jacob 5:64 "Wherefore, dig about them, and prune them, and dung them once more, for the last time, for the end draweth nigh. And if it be so that these last grafts shall grow, and bring forth the natural fruit, then shall ye prepare the way for them, that they may grow."

[1880] Jacob 5:65 "And as they begin to grow ye shall clear away the branches which bring forth bitter fruit, according to the strength of the good and the size thereof; and ye shall not clear away the bad thereof all at once, lest the roots thereof should be too strong for the graft, and the graft thereof shall perish, and I lose the trees of my vineyard."

Paul wrote a letter about the difference between fruit coming from above, and the bitterness of the flesh:

"This I say then, Walk in the Spirit, and ye shall not fulfil the lust of the flesh. For the flesh lusteth against the Spirit, and the Spirit against the flesh: and these are contrary the one to the other: so that ye cannot do the things that ye would. But if ye be led of the Spirit, ye are not under the law. Now the works of the flesh are manifest, which are these; Adultery, fornication, uncleanness, lasciviousness, Idolatry, witchcraft, hatred, variance, emulations, wrath, strife, seditions, heresies, Envyings, murders, drunkenness, revellings, and such like: of the which I tell you before, as I have also told you in time past, that they which do such things shall not inherit the kingdom of God. But the fruit of the Spirit is love, joy, peace, long-suffering, gentleness, goodness, faith, Meekness, temperance: against such there is no law."[1881]

It is a matter of survival that we avoid the bitterness of these sins, and produce the kinds of things that will make us suitable for adoption as God's sons and daughters. At a minimum, this will require us to possess love, peace, long-suffering, gentleness, goodness, meekness and, in a word, to become godlike.

The patient work of the last days will not result in the Lord "clearing away the bad thereof all at once."[1882] There will be bad,

---

[1881] Galatians 5:16–23 "*This* I say then, Walk in the Spirit, and ye shall not fulfil the lust of the flesh. For the flesh lusteth against the Spirit, and the Spirit against the flesh: and these are contrary the one to the other: so that ye cannot do the things that ye would. But if ye be led of the Spirit, ye are not under the law. Now the works of the flesh are manifest, which are *these;* Adultery, fornication, uncleanness, lasciviousness, Idolatry, witchcraft, hatred, variance, emulations, wrath, strife, seditions, heresies, Envyings, murders, drunkenness, revellings, and such like: of the which I tell you before, as I have also told *you* in time past, that they which do such things shall not inherit the kingdom of God. But the fruit of the Spirit is love, joy, peace, longsuffering, gentleness, goodness, faith, Meekness, temperance: against such there is no law."

[1882] Jacob 5:65 "And as they begin to grow ye shall clear away the branches which bring forth bitter fruit, according to the strength of the good and the size thereof; and ye shall not clear away the bad thereof all at once, lest the roots thereof should be too strong for the graft, and the graft thereof shall perish, and I lose the trees of my vineyard."

bitter fruit in the restoration. Generations will need to be removed from the vineyard before it will be possible for the natural fruit to return. If it were all corrected at once "the roots thereof should be too strong for the graft, and the graft thereof shall perish."[1883] The doctrine Joseph was attempting to restore was confusing and offensive to many in the church. It seems a difficult thing even today, with generations entrenched in the traditions in which they were raised. The doctrinal roots of Mormonism are overwhelming, and even now tend to choke the grafts who find our beginnings riddled with difficult, challenging and offensive teachings. We have not humbly, meekly, faithfully or joyfully reexamined what was originally offered us. My last book attempts to discuss that origin and how it has fared in our history. The reaction to that retelling of our history has been hatred, wrath, strife, and anger.

The allegory suggests we have a good deal of work to do if we want to produce fruit. That work will necessarily require us to not only endure the roots of our faith, but to accept the nourishment which flows from it.

Jacob 5:66–70

In order to develop and grow the tree, the Lord requires there to be good fruit growing before cutting away the bad.[1884] The pruning and trimming away the bad will accelerate as good continues to grow. The good growth cannot be threatened by the bad, because the Lord will cut off, cut down, and discard the bad as the good develops.

[1883] Ibid.

[1884] Jacob 5:66 "For it grieveth me that I should lose the trees of my vineyard; wherefore ye shall clear away the bad according as the good shall grow, that the root and the top may be equal in strength, until the good shall overcome the bad, and the bad be hewn down and cast into the fire, that they cumber not the ground of my vineyard; and thus will I sweep away the bad out of my vineyard."

Ultimately, the purpose is to have the good overwhelm the bad. When that happens, the bad will be cut down, thrown in the fire, and burned.[1885] They will not be allowed to overcome the good, or "cumber the ground" of the Lord's vineyard.[1886]

It does not matter if the bad occupy positions of authority, or have been "called of God" into the lofty positions of the tree. They will be struck down when they attempt to overcome the good growth.[1887] The intention of the Lord, and His prophetic promise is that His house will be set in order.[1888] This, however, is still future.

The natural branches are to return to the natural tree[1889] to produce the natural fruit again.[1890] That is the original doctrine, the covenant of adoption to God's family, the return of covenant Israel. Children suitable for Zion are the Lord's agenda. It hasn't changed. He will bring it to pass, and we cannot claim any credit when it

---

[1885] Ibid.

[1886] Ibid.

[1887] D&C 85:7 "And it shall come to pass that I, the Lord God, will send one mighty and strong, holding the scepter of power in his hand, clothed with light for a covering, whose mouth shall utter words, eternal words; while his bowels shall be a fountain of truth, to set in order the house of God, and to arrange by lot the inheritances of the saints whose names are found, and the names of their fathers, and of their children, enrolled in the book of the law of God;"

[1888] Ibid.

[1889] Jacob 5:67 "And the branches of the natural tree will I graft in again into the natural tree;"

[1890] Jacob 5:68 "And the branches of the natural tree will I graft into the natural branches of the tree; and thus will I bring them together again, that they shall bring forth the natural fruit, and they shall be one."

comes, for it is the Lord alone who will "bring again Zion."[1891] This is His work, after all. We get to participate in it, but the work is His.

Those who falsely claim to be the Lord's will be "cast away" from the tree, because they can never bring again the natural fruit.[1892] This great last work, which will unfold over generations and result in a restored tree, will be the last time He will work in His vineyard.[1893]

The Lord sent His servant to labor. There were to be others. But the numbers of the servants who would be sent were disproportionately small. The servant went, and there were "other servants; and they were few."[1894]

We do not get to choose who the Lord sends. He does. When He sends a servant we have the rare and infrequent opportunity to be invited back to the roots of the restoration again. There is no point in insisting that we are doing things right, and that we have no need to repent and return. We must respond, repent, regain whatever was offered, reconnect with the fathers, or risk being utterly wasted at His coming.

[1891] 3 Nephi 16:18 "And it shall come to pass that I, the Lord God, will send one mighty and strong, holding the scepter of power in his hand, clothed with light for a covering, whose mouth shall utter words, eternal words; while his bowels shall be a fountain of truth, to set in order the house of God, and to arrange by lot the inheritances of the saints whose names are found, and the names of their fathers, and of their children, enrolled in the book of the law of God;"
Mosiah 12:22 "Thy watchmen shall lift up the voice; with the voice together shall they sing; for they shall see eye to eye when the Lord shall bring again Zion;"
Mosiah 15:29 "Yea, Lord, thy watchmen shall lift up their voice; with the voice together shall they sing; for they shall see eye to eye, when the Lord shall bring again Zion."
D&C 84:99 "The Lord hath brought again Zion; The Lord hath redeemed his people, Israel, According to the election of grace, Which was brought to pass by the faith And covenant of their fathers."
Isaiah 52:8 "Thy watchmen shall lift up the voice; with the voice together shall they sing: for they shall see eye to eye, when the Lord shall bring again Zion."

[1892] Jacob 5:69 "And the bad shall be cast away, yea, even out of all the land of my vineyard; for behold, only this once will I prune my vineyard."

[1893] Ibid.

[1894] Jacob 5:70 "And it came to pass that the Lord of the vineyard sent his servant; and the servant went and did as the Lord had commanded him, and brought other servants; and they were few."

I think the proposition is self-evident that this will always be in or near the church. The numbers may not be large in comparison to the world, but the work of the Lord has never created a great harvest. The last days vineyard is either filled with bad branches requiring trimming and burning, or in the Lord's parable, always mingled with tares needing gathering and burning.[1895] The field is always to be burned.[1896]

Remember, however, that any fruit produced is infinite, eternal, and will produce forever in His House.[1897] Even if there were only one couple saved, from that single source there would be worlds without end, and seed like the sand of the sea or as the stars in heaven for their number.[1898] Therefore, from this vantage point, you cannot look upon the harvest as meager. From the vantage point of the Lord in His vineyard it is infinite and eternal. Even if the harvest produced but one, how great would be the joy in heaven over that one.[1899] And if there were one, how much greater would it be if

---

[1895] Matthew 13:30 "Let both grow together until the harvest: and in the time of harvest I will say to the reapers, Gather ye together first the tares, and bind them in bundles to burn them: but gather the wheat into my barn."
D&C 86:7 "Therefore, let the wheat and the tares grow together until the harvest is fully ripe; then ye shall first gather out the wheat from among the tares, and after the gathering of the wheat, behold and lo, the tares are bound in bundles, and the field remaineth to be burned."

[1896] Ibid.

[1897] D&C 132:20 "Then shall they be gods, because they have no end; therefore shall they be from everlasting to everlasting, because they continue; then shall they be above all, because all things are subject unto them. Then shall they be gods, because they have all power, and the angels are subject unto them."

[1898] Genesis 22:17 "That in blessing I will bless thee, and in multiplying I will multiply thy seed as the stars of the heaven, and as the sand which is upon the sea shore; and thy seed shall possess the gate of his enemies;"

[1899] D&C 18:15 "And if it so be that you should labor all your days in crying repentance unto this people, and bring, save it be one soul unto me, how great shall be your joy with him in the kingdom of my Father!"

there were as great a number as seven?[1900] Remember the first Zion was made of seven patriarchs and their families.[1901]

The labor to produce fruit is great. The amount of humility and meekness required to repent and return is almost beyond the tolerance of mankind. Even those who learn a little think they know much more than they do. We tend to gather together, speak reassuring words to one another, and stop up our repentance by the mutual praise we lavish on each other. We interfere with our own repentance.

I've often reflected on our presumption that we can apply the words of scripture that were originally given when Joseph Smith was the church's presiding officer to all later times and individuals. Joseph, of course, stood in the presence of God the Father and His Son Jesus Christ. Therefore, the revelations to him—about him—have their veracity derived from that standing. Can we now apply statements to him, or about him to every situation we've encountered since then? Do we have the right to do that without some further revelation giving us that right? Is God's promise about His protection of the church from error, given while Joseph was living, still applicable when we have lost the man who communed with Jehovah? Are we to expect all successors to also act as if they too hold the keys to the mysteries and sealed truths[1902] even when some have told us they have never received any audience with angels or the Lord? Are we allowed to presume the Lord invariably "sends another" when we

---

[1900] D&C 18:16 "And now, if your joy will be great with one soul that you have brought unto me into the kingdom of my Father, how great will be your joy if you should bring many souls unto me!"

[1901] D&C 107:53 "Three years previous to the death of Adam, he called Seth, Enos, Cainan, Mahalaleel, Jared, Enoch, and Methuselah, who were all high priests, with the residue of his posterity who were righteous, into the valley of Adam-ondi-Ahman, and there bestowed upon them his last blessing."

[1902] D&C 28:7 "For I have given him the keys of the mysteries, and the revelations which are sealed, until I shall appoint unto them another in his stead."

vote to fill Joseph's former office?[1903] Our traditions gives us an answer that we heard again in last General Conference through President Eyring's Priesthood Session talk.[1904] That talk was reassuring indeed. I hope it is altogether correct. I hope it answers this question.

Jacob 5:71–73

Once the decision is made to recover fruit from the vineyard, the Lord and His servants set to work, although there were only "few" sent. The laborers were told to work "with your might" because the "time which will soon come" will harvest only the suitable fruit. This will be "the last time" for such labor before that day of harvest.[1905]

When the servants appeared within the vineyard to labor, they "did go and labor with their mights" because this is serious work, not to be idled away with distractions.[1906] They will relentlessly seek to reclaim souls, preach repentance and faith in Jesus Christ. They have no time to set themselves up for a light, nor to practice priestcrafts.[1907] Getting gain, engaging in commerce, diverting attention from the Lord, becoming the object of adoration; all these things cannot distract the true servants. Their only labor, which involves all their might, is to provide sufficient for their needs and then seek only the

---

[1903] Ibid.

[1904] Eyring, "Families Under Covenant", April 2012.

[1905] Jacob 5:71 "And the Lord of the vineyard said unto them: Go to, and labor in the vineyard, with your might. For behold, this is the last time that I shall nourish my vineyard; for the end is nigh at hand, and the season speedily cometh; and if ye labor with your might with me ye shall have joy in the fruit which I shall lay up unto myself against the time which will soon come."

[1906] Jacob 5:72 "And it came to pass that the servants did go and labor with their mights; and the Lord of the vineyard labored also with them; and they did obey the commandments of the Lord of the vineyard in all things."

[1907] 2 Nephi 26:9 "But the Son of righteousness shall appear unto them; and he shall heal them, and they shall have peace with him, until three generations shall have passed away, and many of the fourth generation shall have passed away in righteousness."

welfare of Zion. Zion's welfare, of course, consists primarily in quali-fying people to be called to Zion. That is no small feat.

The laboring servants are not left comfortless. The Lord of the vineyard "labored also with them."[1908] They will not be confused about whether He is laboring alongside them. He will, of course, take up His abode with them.[1909] The Lord of the vineyard cannot "labor also with them" if He does not return to assist the laborers directly. He will not be an absentee landlord. He will be with them.

This process is not immediate. It is not automatic, nor is the out-come guaranteed. It may be generations before the work results in any fruit. But, at length, "there began to be the natural fruit again in the vineyard."[1910] We will see this. There will yet be sons of God, daughters of God, and a people who are "natural" and within the adopted family of God. They are coming. But, as they return, the first appearance is so small a matter that the only thing which can be said of them is they "began" to return.

These beginnings will be marked by something "peculiar" indeed.[1911] The idea of a "royal priesthood" is apt. It captures the idea of nobility, or royalty, or, in other words, a connection with the Family of God. And the co-extensive proposition is that it will nec-

---

[1908] Jacob 5:72 "And it came to pass that the servants did go and labor with their mights; and the Lord of the vineyard labored also with them; and they did obey the commandments of the Lord of the vineyard in all things."

[1909] John 14:23 "Jesus answered and said unto him, If a man love me, he will keep my words: and my Father will love him, and we will come unto him, and make our abode with him."

[1910] Jacob 5:73 "And there began to be the natural fruit again in the vineyard; and the natural branches began to grow and thrive exceedingly; and the wild branches began to be plucked off and to be cast away; and they did keep the root and the top thereof equal, according to the strength thereof."

[1911] 1 Peter 2:9 "But ye *are* a chosen generation, a royal priesthood, an holy nation, a peculiar people; that ye should shew forth the praises of him who hath called you out of darkness into his marvellous light:"

essarily involve "priesthood" also. This is because one cannot receive the Lord without also receiving priesthood.[1912]

When the Lord bestows this royalty on the individual, it is through His own voice.[1913] This happened in the days of Joseph Smith.[1914] This continued to be the case through March 1835, because the revelation reported there was yet Melchizedek Priesthood in the church at that time.[1915] By January 1841, the fullness of that authority was taken away.[1916] The Lord offered to restore it again, as discussed in *Passing the Heavenly Gift*. I won't repeat that again here.

What is clear from the allegory is that no matter what labor is required, the servants who are sent will labor with their mights to bring again some start to the return of "natural fruit." They will gather those who are born to parents who have received the covenant, been sealed by the Lord, have a lively and warranted expectations of inheriting eternal life, and are acquainted with He whom they serve.[1917]

When it begins, there will be no going back. The appearance of the "natural fruit" signals the beginning of pruning away the wild branches. As the one appears, the other begins to be destroyed, re-

---

[1912] D&C 84:35 "And also all they who receive this priesthood receive me, saith the Lord;"

[1913] JST–Genesis 14:29 "*And it was delivered unto men by the calling of his own voice, according to his own will, unto as many as believed on his name.*"

[1914] See, e.g., D&C 52, when Joseph reported the Melchizedek Priesthood first appeared in the church.

[1915] D&C 107:1 "THERE are, in the church, two priesthoods, namely, the Melchizedek and Aaronic, including the Levitical Priesthood."

[1916] D&C 124:28 "For there is not a place found on earth that he may come to and restore again that which was lost unto you, or which he hath taken away, even the fulness of the priesthood."

[1917] D&C 93:1 "VERILY, thus saith the Lord: It shall come to pass that every soul who forsaketh his sins and cometh unto me, and calleth on my name, and obeyeth my voice, and keepeth my commandments, shall see my face and know that I am;"

moved, plucked off and cast away.[1918] The Lord is interested in preserving, producing and cultivating the branches producing natural fruit. For the rest, they will be destroyed because they cumber the ground and do not (indeed cannot) produce fruit. You cannot have Zion without qualified residents, and Zion must exist on the mountains before the Lord's return. So the focal point of the Lord's labors will shift from the initial cultivation, and grafting to those places where the natural fruit appears.

Jacob 5:74–75

When the final work in the vineyard begins, and the natural fruit reappears, the process of casting the bad branches producing bitter fruit accelerates. The bad is cleared away to make room for the good. [1919]The remaining gentiles will be swept away and their cities will be inhabited again. This time they will be swept away by the natural fruit, to whom the land belongs.[1920]

Though there are two gatherings in the last days, when the natural fruit returns it will be to both. Servants will minister to both. They will all be gathered in, and Israel will gather together in Zion and the long dispersed of Judah will also be given their land in peace.[1921] The

---

[1918] Jacob 5:73 "And there began to be the natural fruit again in the vineyard; and the natural branches began to grow and thrive exceedingly; and the wild branches began to be plucked off and to be cast away; and they did keep the root and the top thereof equal, according to the strength thereof."

[1919] Jacob 5:74 "And thus they labored, with all diligence, according to the commandments of the Lord of the vineyard, even until the bad had been cast away out of the vineyard, and the Lord had preserved unto himself that the trees had become again the natural fruit; and they became like unto one body; and the fruits were equal; and the Lord of the vineyard had preserved unto himself the natural fruit, which was most precious unto him from the beginning."

[1920] 3 Nephi 22:3 "For thou shalt break forth on the right hand and on the left, and thy seed shall inherit the Gentiles and make the desolate cities to be inhabited."

[1921] Isaiah 11:12 "And he shall set up an ensign for the nations, and shall assemble the outcasts of Israel, and gather together the dispersed of Judah from the four corners of the earth."

Lord will hasten His work when the natural fruit reappears.[1922] Some will say it is like before and everything continues from day to day uninterrupted and the Lord delays His coming.[1923] Some will think the Lord will allow everything to be destroyed and still not return.[1924]

Then will be the time when "they became like unto one body" though gathered in both Zion and Jerusalem.[1925] Zion will have her kings[1926] and Judah will have her prophets.[1927]

It begins with the regrafting. Joseph Smith began that process. The purpose was to establish a relationship where it is possible for

---

[1922] D&C 88:73 "Behold, I will hasten my work in its time."

[1923] Luke 12:45 "But and if that servant say in his heart, My lord delayeth his coming; and shall begin to beat the menservants and maidens, and to eat and drink, and to be drunken;"

[1924] D&C 45:26 "And in that day shall be heard of wars and rumors of wars, and the whole earth shall be in commotion, and men's hearts shall fail them, and they shall say that Christ delayeth his coming until the end of the earth."

[1925] Jacob 5:74 "And thus they labored, with all diligence, according to the commandments of the Lord of the vineyard, even until the bad had been cast away out of the vineyard, and the Lord had preserved unto himself that the trees had become again the natural fruit; and they became like unto one body; and the fruits were equal; and the Lord of the vineyard had preserved unto himself the natural fruit, which was most precious unto him from the beginning."

[1926] D&C 133:32 "And there shall they fall down and be crowned with glory, even in Zion, by the hands of the servants of the Lord, even the children of Ephraim."

[1927] Revelation 11:3 "And I will give *power* unto my two witnesses, and they shall prophesy a thousand two hundred *and* threescore days, clothed in sackcloth."
D&C 77:15 "Q. What is to be understood by the two witnesses, in the eleventh chapter of Revelation? A. They are two prophets that are to be raised up to the Jewish nation in the last days, at the time of the restoration, and to prophesy to the Jews after they are gathered and have built the city of Jerusalem in the land of their fathers."
Isaiah 51:19–20 "These two *things* are come unto thee; who shall be sorry for thee? desolation, and destruction, and the famine, and the sword: by whom shall I comfort thee? Thy sons have fainted, they lie at the head of all the streets, as a wild bull in a net: they are full of the fury of the Lord, the rebuke of thy God."
Zechariah 4:11–14 "Then answered I, and said unto him, What *are* these two olive trees upon the right *side* of the candlestick and upon the left *side* thereof? And I answered again, and said unto him, What *be these* two olive branches which through the two golden pipes empty the golden *oil* out of themselves? And he answered me and said, Knowest thou not what these *be?* And I said, No, my lord. Then said he, These *are* the two anointed ones, that stand by the Lord of the whole earth."

natural fruit to return. It would take generations before the natural fruit would reappear.

In the work to reestablish the natural fruit, the Lord of the vineyard would send both servants, like Joseph Smith, and He would work alongside them. In other words He would appear to them.[1928] The Lord will be present for the work of producing natural fruit in the last days. He will appear to them, and both He and the Father will take up their abode with them.[1929] These will be those who are the natural branches, capable of producing the fruit for the final harvest.[1930] This is the culmination of the final chapter in the vineyard. His work and glory is to bring this about. He knows the end from the beginning. His work has always pointed to this great, final labor.

Those who will be gathered will not need to tell one another to "know ye the Lord" for those who remain will all know Him, from

---

[1928] JS–H 1:17–19 "It no sooner appeared than I found myself delivered from the enemy which held me bound. When the light rested upon me I saw two Personages, whose brightness and glory defy all description, standing above me in the air. One of them spake unto me, calling me by name and said, pointing to the other—*This is My Beloved Son. Hear Him!* My object in going to inquire of the Lord was to know which of all the sects was right, that I might know which to join. No sooner, therefore, did I get possession of myself, so as to be able to speak, than I asked the Personages who stood above me in the light, which of all the sects was right (for at this time it had never entered into my heart that all were wrong)—and which I should join. I was answered that I must join none of them, for they were all wrong; and the Personage who addressed me said that all their creeds were an abomination in his sight; that those professors were all corrupt; that: "they draw near to me with their lips, but their hearts are far from me, they teach for doctrines the commandments of men, having a form of godliness, but they deny the power thereof.""
D&C 84:35 "And also all they who receive this priesthood receive me, saith the Lord;"
D&C 93:1 "VERILY, thus saith the Lord: It shall come to pass that every soul who forsaketh his sins and cometh unto me, and calleth on my name, and obeyeth my voice, and keepeth my commandments, shall see my face and know that I am;"

[1929] John 14:23 "Jesus answered and said unto him, If a man love me, he will keep my words: and my Father will love him, and we will come unto him, and make our abode with him.""

[1930] John 15:4–5 "Abide in me, and I in you. As the branch cannot bear fruit of itself, except it abide in the vine; no more can ye, except ye abide in me. I am the vine, ye *are* the branches: He that abideth in me, and I in him, the same bringeth forth much fruit: for without me ye can do nothing.""

the least to the greatest.[1931] These are those who have been re-deemed from the fall, for they have been back into His presence.[1932] These are those who receive a testimony from Christ that they are saved.[1933] Those who claim to follow prophets, but have not received the testimony of Christ that they have part with Him will be burned at His coming and appointed their place in sorrow and suffering.[1934]

There will be no lukewarm saints allowed to stand in that day. If they have received and followed the truth, they will be saved. If they have not, they will be gathered in bundles and burned. The result will be an era of peace in which the entire vineyard, as if one body, pro-

---

[1931] Jeremiah 31:34 "And they shall teach no more every man his neighbour, and every man his brother, saying, Know the Lord: for they shall all know me, from the least of them unto the greatest of them, saith the Lord: for I will forgive their iniquity, and I will remember their sin no more."
D&C 84:98 "Until all shall know me, who remain, even from the least unto the greatest, and shall be filled with the knowledge of the Lord, and shall see eye to eye, and shall lift up their voice, and with the voice together sing this new song,"

[1932] Ether 3:13 "And when he had said these words, behold, the Lord showed himself unto him, and said: Because thou knowest these things ye are redeemed from the fall; therefore ye are brought back into my presence; therefore I show myself unto you."

[1933] D&C 76:51 "They are they who received the testimony of Jesus, and believed on his name and were baptized after the manner of his burial, being buried in the water in his name, and this according to the commandment which he has given—"

[1934] D&C 76:98–106 "And the glory of the telestial is one, even as the glory of the stars is one; for as one star differs from another star in glory, even so differs one from another in glory in the telestial world; For these are they who are of Paul, and of Apollos, and of Cephas. These are they who say they are some of one and some of another—some of Christ and some of John, and some of Moses, and some of Elias, and some of Esaias, and some of Isaiah, and some of Enoch; But received not the gospel, neither the testimony of Jesus, neither the prophets, neither the everlasting covenant. Last of all, these all are they who will not be gathered with the saints, to be caught up unto the church of the Firstborn, and received into the cloud. These are they who are liars, and sorcerers, and adulterers, and whoremongers, and whosoever loves and makes a lie. These are they who suffer the wrath of God on earth. These are they who suffer the vengeance of eternal fire. These are they who are cast down to hell and suffer the wrath of Almighty God, until the fulness of times, when Christ shall have subdued all enemies under his feet, and shall have perfected his work;"

duces again natural fruit.[1935] There will be joy at that day. The Lord
and His servants will rejoice, and the Lord will give praise to those
servants who labored with Him.[1936] When He could take credit, instead He shares it. And He promises to those servants: "behold ye
shall have joy with me because of the fruit of my vineyard."[1937]

Jacob 5:76–77

Zenos wrote at the time of a united Kingdom, before the days of
Isaiah, and in another dispensation than John. However, when it
comes to the prophetic destiny of the vineyard, Zenos and John tell
the same story, using different images to tell the tale.

The allegory has a "long time" in which the vineyard produces
natural fruit.[1938] This peaceful and productive era is Paradisiacal.[1939]
The vineyard will allow the Lord to "lay up the fruit of [His] vine-

---

[1935] Jacob 5:75 "And it came to pass that when the Lord of the vineyard saw that his
fruit was good, and that his vineyard was no more corrupt, he called up his servants,
and said unto them: Behold, for this last time have we nourished my vineyard; and thou
beholdest that I have done according to my will; and I have preserved the natural fruit,
that it is good, even like as it was in the beginning. And blessed art thou; for because ye
have been diligent in laboring with me in my vineyard, and have kept my commandments, and have brought unto me again the natural fruit, that my vineyard is no more
corrupted, and the bad is cast away, behold ye shall have joy with me because of the
fruit of my vineyard."

[1936] Ibid.

[1937] Ibid.

[1938] Jacob 5:76 "For behold, for a long time will I lay up of the fruit of my vineyard
unto mine own self against the season, which speedily cometh; and for the last time
have I nourished my vineyard, and pruned it, and dug about it, and dunged it; wherefore I will lay up unto mine own self of the fruit, for a long time, according to that
which I have spoken."

[1939] Article of Faith 10 "We believe in the literal gathering of Israel and in the restoration of the Ten Tribes; that Zion (the New Jerusalem) will be built upon the American
continent; that Christ will reign personally upon the earth; and, that the earth will be
renewed and receive its paradisiacal glory."

yard" because there will be an end to this era of the vineyard.[1940] There will come a time for final accounting. The vineyard will need to be re-created, and a new one brought in its place. But before that day the vineyard will produce "for a long time, according to that which I have spoken."[1941] During that time Satan is bound and children grow up without sin.

The story of the end of this creation culminates in the last, great day, when Satan is loosed again for a season: "But when the time cometh that evil fruit shall again come into my vineyard" will happen after the period of Paradise. In the allegory, it is when "evil fruit" returns. In John's vision it is when "the thousand years are expired." [1942]John describes how "Satan shall be loosed out of his prison" at that time.[1943] When he is, he "shall go out to deceive the nations which are in the four quarters of the earth."[1944]

Despite all the Lord of the vineyard has done for His trees, the accuser will still find fault. The things of God will again be challenged, criticized, debated, accused and maligned. The Lord's motives will be questioned, and His means will be derided. Why so little natural fruit? What right is there to discard the bitter fruit? Is not the worth of each soul great enough the Lord of the vineyard should have done more? Why should so much of the fruit have been gathered

---

[1940] Jacob 5:76 "For behold, for a long time will I lay up of the fruit of my vineyard unto mine own self against the season, which speedily cometh; and for the last time have I nourished my vineyard, and pruned it, and dug about it, and dunged it; wherefore I will lay up unto mine own self of the fruit, for a long time, according to that which I have spoken."

[1941] Ibid.

[1942] Revelation 20:7 "And when the thousand years are expired, Satan shall be loosed out of his prison,"

[1943] Ibid.

[1944] Revelation 20:8 "And shall go out to deceive the nations which are in the four quarters of the earth, Gog and Magog, to gather them together to battle: the number of whom is as the sand of the sea."

and burned? How can the Lord have the best interests of the vineyard in mind when there were so many who have not been gathered as natural fruit? What of those who came into the vineyard and were produced through wild branches, how can it be fair to leave them for the burning when they were given an unfair challenge? Their plight is not of their own making, and the Lord of the vineyard is unfair!

You see it is one thing to claim you believe in and follow the Lord when in your mistaken arrogance you assume His plan requires nothing from you and will exalt you to the sides of the north.[1945] But it is another thing when you realize "the summer shall be past, and the harvest ended, and your souls not saved."[1946] Then will they lament: "O that I had repented, and had not killed the prophets, and stoned them, and cast them out. Yea, in that day ye shall say: O that we had remembered the Lord our God."[1947] When all men stand before God and realize He did expect obedience, sacrifice, consecration, chastity and a godly walk of all who are saved, then many who profess to follow Him when it was to their vanity and pride will find they cannot profess to follow Him when it is to their shame and condemnation. They will, with the accuser, join in denouncing the Lord. They will also compass the camp of the saints and make war against them and their Lord.

[1945] Isaiah 14:12–13 "How art thou fallen from heaven, O Lucifer, son of the morning! *how* art thou cut down to the ground, which didst weaken the nations! For thou hast said in thine heart, I will ascend into heaven, I will exalt my throne above the stars of God: I will sit also upon the mount of the congregation, in the sides of the north:"

[1946] D&C 45:2 "And again I say, hearken unto my voice, lest death shall overtake you; in an hour when ye think not the summer shall be past, and the harvest ended, and your souls not saved."

[1947] Helaman 13:33 "O that I had repented, and had not killed the prophets, and stoned them, and cast them out. Yea, in that day ye shall say: O that we had remembered the Lord our God in the day that he gave us our riches, and then they would not have become slippery that we should lose them; for behold, our riches are gone from us."
3 Nephi 8:24 "And in one place they were heard to cry, saying: O that we had repented before this great and terrible day, and then would our brethren have been spared, and they would not have been burned in that great city Zarahemla."

The Lord of the vineyard has done all He could, and respected the agency of men. The arguments at the end of the Millennial Day will prevail. John reports that the number of those who align with the accuser will be so much greater than the camp of the saints, that they will "compass the camp of the saints about" because their numbers so vastly exceed the mere "camp" of the righteous they will be able to entirely surround them.[1948]

These rebellious branches are "burned with fire"[1949] or, as John describes it, "fire came down from God out of heaven, and devoured them."[1950]

This then leads back to the major themes of the allegory. It was included by Jacob for us so that when these things come to pass we are not left surprised or wondering why we were not warned by the Lord.

[1948] Revelation 20:9 "And they went up on the breadth of the earth, and compassed the camp of the saints about, and the beloved city: and fire came down from God out of heaven, and devoured them."

[1949] Jacob 5:77 "And when the time cometh that evil fruit shall again come into my vineyard, then will I cause the good and the bad to be gathered; and the good will I preserve unto myself, and the bad will I cast away into its own place. And then cometh the season and the end; and my vineyard will I cause to be burned with fire."

[1950] Revelation 20:9 "And they went up on the breadth of the earth, and compassed the camp of the saints about, and the beloved city: and fire came down from God out of heaven, and devoured them."

THEMES FROM JACOB 5

Themes from Jacob 5, Part 1

There are important themes in Zenos' allegory. Here are five of them:

1. The Lord of the vineyard controls overall history through His involvement and the involvement of His servants. However, they can only accomplish two things: 1) removing the bad, bitter fruit by cutting away branches and burning them, and 2) encouraging the good, natural fruit by pruning, grafting, nourishing and laboring. Whether or not the natural fruit reappears is left to the tree itself. Mankind cannot be compelled to be good. As agents of their own, they are free to choose. No amount of ministering will force the natural fruit to appear. The Lord and His servants can only present the opportunity.

2. The tree and its branches are prone to repeatedly producing bitter fruit. Producing natural fruit does not come easily. From the beginning, the tree was prone to loftiness and pride. It required cutting away, scattering and destroying the main top in order to have a chance to cause the natural fruit to reappear. This is the tendency. As soon as people learn they are "called" they will presume they are "chosen," even though these are two entirely different things. The

Lord of the vineyard has learned by sad experience that it is the nature of almost all men that they begin to exercise unrighteous dominion over one another as soon as they have a little authority as they suppose. This is why He does not distribute, and cannot confer, the priesthood on mankind through generations of hand-me-down lines of authority. As soon as it is abused, it is lost. And when the Lord says "amen to the priesthood of that man" he is powerless to give it to another.

3. The Lord has occasionally come to the vineyard. On one occasion He labored directly within the vineyard, choosing to mingle with the scattered branches and to personally minister among them. This produced a period of production throughout the vineyard. However, it was short-lived. The vineyard lapsed into bitter fruit everywhere. There came a point where the entire vineyard produced nothing but bitter fruit, in every part of the Lord's possession. When that time came, the Lord determined to labor a "last time" in the vineyard, and to bring a "few servants" to assist. Again this return would involve His personal appearance, but it took the form of periodic appearances with His servants, as in the First Vision and Section 76. When He appears He confers authority. Joseph and Sidney both "received of His fullness" when He ministered to them.[1951] Indeed, no one can behold His glory and not receive of His fullness.[1952] To receive His priesthood, He must redeem from the fall[1953] and thereby receive Him.[1954] This is not an appearance in the heart, but is rather a per-

---

[1951] D&C 76:20 "And we beheld the glory of the Son, on the right hand of the Father, and received of his fulness;"

[1952] D&C 84:22 "For without this no man can see the face of God, even the Father, and live."

[1953] Ether 3:13 "And when he had said these words, behold, the Lord showed himself unto him, and said: Because thou knowest these things ye are redeemed from the fall; therefore ye are brought back into my presence; therefore I show myself unto you."

[1954] D&C 84:35 "And also all they who receive this priesthood receive me, saith the Lord;"

sonal appearance, The idea it is something merely in the heart is an old sectarian notion and is false.[1955]

4. In the Lord's last labor in the vineyard, the commencement of the work does not signal the end of His involvement. Once begun, He will continue to labor with the tree to encourage it to produce fruit. He will send servants who will labor with all their might to bring the fruit about. However, it will be the tree's response and not the Lord's nor His servants' work that will bring again the natural fruit. This will take a long time before the roots are able to take hold again. The grafted branches will require pruning and additional work before they respond and return to respect and take nourishment from the natural roots. What was shocking and hard to bear with will need to be accepted in humility and gratitude before the natural fruit can appear once more.

When the natural fruit begins to appear, the Lord will begin to trim away the bad to make way for the good to prevail. Therefore, those who fight against the natural fruit will be cut down. Even those who entertain high positions will be struck down if they oppose the return of the Lord's natural fruit.[1956] The Lord of the vineyard controls which branches are allowed to survive with His tree, and not the tree itself. The inclination to produce the lofty and high minded remains the tendency of the tree. But those unwanted and unproductive branches will be cut away, burned, and not allowed to interfere with the natural fruit.

[1955] D&C 130:3 "John 14:23—The appearing of the Father and the Son, in that verse, is a personal appearance; and the idea that the Father and the Son dwell in a man's heart is an old sectarian notion, and is false."

[1956] D&C 85:7 "And it shall come to pass that I, the Lord God, will send one mighty and strong, holding the scepter of power in his hand, clothed with light for a covering, whose mouth shall utter words, eternal words; while his bowels shall be a fountain of truth, to set in order the house of God, and to arrange by lot the inheritances of the saints whose names are found, and the names of their fathers, and of their children, enrolled in the book of the law of God;"

Themes from Jacob 5, Part 2

Here are five more themes:

6. The work of the last labor will not be abandoned. The Lord did not establish the restoration of the Gospel only to abandon it. Though it will take some time before it produces natural fruit, the Lord intends to stay with the grafts, labor with them, and trim away as necessary. Joseph Smith suggested the church needed to stay together, and the Lord's hand would continue to watch over the church. As they have left, the splinter groups have all fallen into neglect, and ultimately abandonment. Whether it was Sidney Rigdon, the William Marks/Emma Smith "reorganization", the William McLellin departure, or the various "fundamentalist" movements, the temporary prosperity or success has ultimately ended in collapse and failure.

The Lord intends to work within the church until the natural fruit reappears. Though the church may not be synonymous with the "Gospel," it is the means by which the Lord preserves the Gospel. To see the Lord's hand, all you need to do is be near to the laboring full-time missionaries. The Lord *does* bear testimony to the investigators that the Book of Mormon is true, and Joseph Smith was His prophet, and the revelations are trustworthy, and the sincere soul should receive baptism at the hands of the elders of the church. I received this testimony when I investigated, and have received also the blessings associated with fellowship among others who accept and believe in the Book of Mormon, Joseph Smith, the restoration scriptures, and all the associated practices we have inherited. Though we have departed somewhat from the roots that came from Joseph's ministry, at this moment, for the first time, the church has begun publishing *The Joseph Smith Papers*. We are the chosen generation who can see the records for ourselves. The ability to take nourishment from the roots has become more of an opportunity for us living today than any of the prior saints, from Joseph's day till ours. Thanks be to the church for opening this valuable library that has remained unavailable to the common church member for these last three or four generations. It is as if the Lord has finally moved, despite all we have done to forget our beginnings, to make important change possible and return to His foundation by giving us the original records.

7. The natural fruit involves more than just the regrafting. The establishment of the church was the necessary first step, but the prophecies do not mention The Church of Jesus Christ of Latter-day Saints as the target church. The revelations speak of another name for the Lord's church.[1957] The temporal church is essential to produce another group within it. They are not going to reappear as a group disconnected from the temporal church, but instead from within it. The Gospel net will gather all manner of fish, but the angels will gather the good and cast away the bad.[1958] Being gathered into the net is not the sign of being good and worthy of gathering by the angels. It is only the first step. There is another step beyond that which requires the virgins to have oil in their lamps in order to be with the Bridegroom.

8. The history of the tree is told from the most ancient of our preserved history until the distant end of a millennium of peace.

[1957] D&C 76:54 "They are they who are the church of the Firstborn."
D&C 78:21 "For ye are the church of the Firstborn, and he will take you up in a cloud, and appoint every man his portion."
D&C 88:5 "Which glory is that of the church of the Firstborn, even of God, the holiest of all, through Jesus Christ his Son—"
D&C 107:19 "To have the privilege of receiving the mysteries of the kingdom of heaven, to have the heavens opened unto them, to commune with the general assembly and church of the Firstborn, and to enjoy the communion and presence of God the Father, and Jesus the mediator of the new covenant."
Hebrews 12:23 "To the general assembly and church of the firstborn, which are written in heaven, and to God the Judge of all, and to the spirits of just men made perfect"

[1958] Matthew 13:47–49 "Again, the kingdom of heaven is like unto a net, that was cast into the sea, and gathered of every kind: Which, when it was full, they drew to shore, and sat down, and gathered the good into vessels, but cast the bad away. So shall it be at the end of the world: the angels shall come forth, and sever the wicked from among the just"

There is no other history that will take off in a different direction. The tree is fully accounted for in the allegory. You needn't look for another, separated, surprising or unaccounted for sequence of events or long interruption of the Lord's labors. He is working NOW and it is currently underway. The story is complete. Although the reappearance of the natural fruit is not immediate, it is going to reappear. When it does it will be in the young, tender growth. The high minded and lofty which are barren and tend to grow in their own self-interests, but do not seek the welfare of Zion itself will be trimmed away. The Lord's hand will be most apparent inside the church, not outside of it. But likely in a young, tender place where nourishment from the roots has taken hold. Watch, therefore, and you will not be mistaken when it begins. This is, after all, the Lord's work, and it is marvelous in the eyes of those who can see it.[1959]

9. Although there are many different groups of people, the Lord's work has always focused on the House of Jacob and the potential for it to return to covenant status as the House of Israel. This is the "natural fruit" that the Lord seeks to have return to His vineyard. Although having some religious connection to God is desirable, the "harvest" is looking for this particular kind of "natural fruit" to preserve against the season. This kind of fruit requires the very same thing Joseph was so excited about in his last few talks in Nauvoo. The Elijah Talk followed on the history retold in *Passing the Heavenly Gift*, and goes to the heart of this need to reconnect with "the fathers in heaven," or the original Patriarchal Fathers who were chosen by God as His. It requires us to track back, reconnect to the roots of the restoration, and return to belief in doctrines long neglected if we want to participate in the Lord's work. The Lord invites all to know Him, to come to Him and to form this connection with Him. However, if you are wait-

---

[1959] Mormon 9:16 "Behold, are not the things that God hath wrought marvelous in our eyes? Yea, and who can comprehend the marvelous works of God?"

ing for the process to be unfolded in a weekly Gospel Doctrine class, you will first need a new manual. Nothing of these topics remains in our formal curriculum, though the information is still available if you will search for it.

10. The Lord has actually considered burning the entire vineyard before, and fully intends to burn all but the natural fruit in the future. The risk of the entire earth being cursed at His coming is not just an idle notion designed to make us luke-warm in our church affiliation. It is intended to cause us to work out our salvation with fear and trembling.[1960] When we think our simple affiliation with our church is enough, we are deceived and show disrespect to the requirements of the Lord's plan. The best scriptural passage to put the problem into context is Mormon's description:

". . . Do ye suppose that ye shall dwell with him under a consciousness of your guilt? Do ye suppose that ye could be happy to dwell with that holy Being, when your souls are racked with a consciousness of guilt that ye have ever abused his laws? Behold, I say unto you that ye would be more miserable to dwell with a holy and just God, under a consciousness of your filthiness before him, than ye would to dwell with the damned souls in hell. For behold, when ye shall be brought to see your nakedness before God, and also the glory of God, and the holiness of Jesus Christ, it will kindle a flame of unquenchable fire upon you." (Mormon 9:3–5)

[1960] Philippians 2:12 "Wherefore, my beloved, as ye have always obeyed, not as in my presence only, but now much more in my absence, work out your own salvation with fear and trembling."
Mormon 9:27 "O then despise not, and wonder not, but hearken unto the words of the Lord, and ask the Father in the name of Jesus for what things soever ye shall stand in need. Doubt not, but be believing, and begin as in times of old, and come unto the Lord with all your heart, and work out your own salvation with fear and trembling before him."

That day will come; now, if you prepare for it, but it will come. If that day "burns you up," then you were not natural fruit.[1961] Therefore, it makes sense to do what is needed now, repent, call on His name, and live by every word which He imparts so you may see His face and "know that [He is.]"[1962]

Themes from Jacob, Part 3

The most striking theme of all is the Lord's patience. The work of the vineyard is never immediate. It is generational. Those who enter the vineyard impatiently expect the Lord's work will result in reordering the world for them while they spend their brief moment here.

There has been some confusion in Historic Christianity over the New Testament era expectation of the "end" of things. One of the questions Hugh Nibley asked was "the end of what?" He parsed through the material and arguments and suggested the "end" was of the church itself. The world would continue on, but the church would end. That is one of the themes of Jacob 5. The labor in the vineyard to bring back natural fruit is always against opposition. The success is brief. It requires considerable effort to coax the natural fruit back into production, and when left untended it quickly lapses back to wild, bitter fruit.

The Lord of the vineyard has never been in a hurry. The allegory was originally composed by Zenos in the time of the united Kingdom, some 2,900 years ago. It tells the story of Israel for the next 5,000 years. Jacob put it into his writing approximately 2,400 years ago when the events were only at about verse 14 of the allegory. This

---

[1961] Malachi 4:1 "For, behold, the day cometh, that shall burn as an oven; and all the proud, yea, and all that do wickedly, shall be stubble: and the day that cometh shall burn them up, saith the Lord of hosts, that it shall leave them neither root nor branch."

[1962] D&C 93:1 "VERILY, thus saith the Lord: It shall come to pass that every soul who forsaketh his sins and cometh unto me, and calleth on my name, and obeyeth my voice, and keepeth my commandments, shall see my face and know that I am;"

allegory was important to Jacob. It is also important to when Jacob's record would be restored again. We are now at about verse 55, the era when the Lord and servants are trying to bring again some small appearance of natural fruit in the vineyard. We want the fruit from verse 73 to appear long before the story predicts it will return. We expect it to have begun as soon as He sets His hand to the labor by calling Joseph Smith. The allegory allows for no such interpretation. We want that because we think ourselves "natural fruit" and worthy to be saved against the season.

There is a great preliminary work with only the grafting back at first. It started with Joseph Smith. That graft hasn't taken hold yet, nor produced fruit. It wasn't intended to do so at the start. The graft will require the branches to take nourishment from the original roots; hence the notion of "restoration," but the roots from which nourishment is to be taken are quite ancient. At first it is likely (measured by our conduct and preaching) that the only aspiration of the graft is to become merely another New Testament era faith, and not to find nourishment from the ancient roots which run back to the beginning. It is apparent, however the natural fruit will not reappear until the original, first generation teaching's of man, which were in the beginning, return again at the end.

The Brother of Jared was redeemed from the fall, and was taught about the history of man from the beginning. Enoch's vision included the story of man from the beginning until the end. Moses also. The vision on the Mount of Transfiguration included a similar visionary show of mankind's history from the beginning. The reason Zenos composed, and Jacob transcribed this vision of the history of Israel through the end was because they shared in that instruction of what the Lord is trying to bring back into His vineyard. Joseph Smith was not being inadvertent when the accounts of Moses and Enoch, in the Book of Moses were restored. Nor when the Book of Abraham was revealed. These, as well as the Book of Mormon, pre-date the New Testament era. They tell about an original, ancient faith which was to return again so there would be fruit, or in other words, the hearts of the children would turn to the fathers.

When we take our reckoning from the New Testament era and claim ourselves to be like the other "Christian" faiths, we are not looking to the rock from whence we came. We are not taking nourishment from the roots. We now hardly understand Joseph's preoccupation with the most ancient of themes and religion. Joseph now seems antiquated to us, and he hardly began to introduce the ancient faith which is still to come.

God's patient cultivation of the tree can continue for so many generations as needed, and will linger without the return of natural fruit so long as we choose not to take nourishment from the original root where the strength lies. The Lord of the vineyard creates the conditions which allow growth, but it is the tree itself that must respond and grow.

Our impatience and expectation that God has given us all we need, and everything He intends for us to have, precludes us from taking in what we still lack. God may intend to yet reveal many great and important things pertaining to the kingdom of God, but it will fall on deaf ears if we think we have everything we need for our salvation and exaltation already restored to us.

God's very long-term view contrasts sharply with our 'must-be-in-our-lifetime' outlook. Generations come and go and think themselves saved while God waits patiently for natural fruit, willing to take nourishment from the strength of His Gospel, to finally reappear. Proud and vain men strut about proclaiming how special they and their cultic-following are before God, while God pleads for our repentance, humility and willingness to return to Him. Lofty branches still need trimming and only produce bitter fruit still. We witness how blind, fallen men think it is sufficient for the branches to feel themselves vindicated by reason of their loftiness. If our present form of "Zion" wasn't "prospering" then we might be more acutely aware of our sickness, sores, disease and stench. We use the measuring rod of Babylon and conclude we are among the greatest of people rather than the standard of heaven against which we are loathsome, bitter fruit.

It is good the Lord of the vineyard is patient. It is good He waits for natural fruit to begin to appear before the next round of cutting down and casting into the fire. We should be grateful for His patience, but never fooled by it. His hand does not stay because we deserve it, but instead from His hope there will yet reappear the natural fruit He can lay up against the coming season.

CRITICISM OF THE CHURCH

I do not believe it is at all useful for anyone to criticize the church. When I write, I try to explain what I believe, avoid any direct criticism and leave the rest alone. I also explain history. It is my effort to grapple with the inconsistencies and omissions that plague the understanding of anyone who looks carefully into doctrine and history. Since the traditional stories we hear repeated in the normal discussions cannot be reconciled with primary historical materials, I make the effort to come to grips with the challenges and then to explain my understanding. I know there are others who grapple with the same issues. They receive the benefit of my efforts which I hope proves to be faith promoting.

What I do not do is force my opinions on others. When I teach in church, I use the church's materials and scriptures. I have written eight books. Seven of them are about the Book of Mormon, the Gospel of Christ, and the prophecies given to us. They are written to be faith promoting and bring people to Christ. If someone wants to read what I've written, they have to go to the trouble of finding it. They then have to purchase it and read it. As for the eighth book, *Passing the Heavenly Gift*, it is my attempt to explain the issues I have grappled with as I have read and studied the Gospel and our history. If people have gone to the trouble of finding and buying that book, they have already learned about some upsetting issues and are trying to reconcile the matters for themselves. If they're already trying to find answers, then they can look at what I've written to help them. On the other hand, if they are completely content with what they hear from the inside sources of the insular Mormon community they have no reason to have even encountered what I've written. Unless they have searched into the matter and made the discovery for themselves, my own ward members are unaware I've written books on church doctrine and history. I am not sold at Deseret Book stores, not advertised in any LDS publications, and I do not do advertising or book signings.

The church is an important and valued part of my life and the lives of my family. I attend weekly, and very much enjoy associating with my fellow ward members. I do not understand why people go out of their way to provoke a dispute with the church. If you belong, then follow the rules. If you're unwilling to follow the rules, then why belong?

If in your own studies you find there are issues, then you should search for answers. I've done that. I've found answers and I am willing to state what I believe and to defend why I believe it. It is on display for those who are anxiety-filled and uncertain after learning of problems in doctrine, history, practice and scriptural interpretation. All I have done is help the fellow-explorer who has encountered the many issues which are not adequately understood or taught as yet.

When someone thinks they know all the answers, and can give the chapter-and-verse answer from some Deseret Book publication of a former or current general authority, I have no dispute with them. They are free to believe as they wish. They are free to consider only "orthodox" (although there is no such thing in Mormonism) sources and to confine their inquiries to the traditional stories. However, there are so many saints who no longer do that and who are in a crisis of faith as a result. Someone needs to take seriously the problems and attempt to give answers. If you have no crisis, don't know there are issues, and think all is well with everything then you shouldn't be reading either this blog or much of what I've written. I am writing for those who want to know what the scriptures say. I am writing to those who are interested in the prophecies in the Book of Mormon given to us, the Gentiles. I am writing for those who wish to seek the Lord and Savior. I am writing for those who wish to strengthen their testimony of the Gospel of Christ. I am writing for the troubled, the searching, and the inquiring open soul who honestly wants to believe in the truth but has become alarmed at what they've discovered about our faith.

There are answers to the problems. I offer my conclusions as a consequence of my own search and discovery. It is my belief the Lord is pleased by this effort, and has actively assisted me in doing so. I also know there are a great many who are offended by my work, and that I am unpopular among many of the saints. The Strengthening the Members Committee does not approve of what I am doing. I believe myself more accountable to the Lord than to them.

In the last book I wrote, I divided the church's development into four phases. That is a convenient way to see how and why the church has changed. I am completely converted to my faith, but the version I believe in is the first phase, the original faith which Joseph Smith was developing methodically line-upon-line from the beginning in 1820 through his death in June 1844. It is the foundation of my relationship with God. I rejoice in that faith, and have found God through practicing it. I recognize there are many fellow latter-day saints who hardly understand that version of the church, and dis-prefer it to what is the fourth phase. While I explain my beliefs, and I willingly accept fellowship with anyone who shares faith in the restoration, I do not expect the church or anyone else to adopt a first phase view of Mormonism. It is largely gone. In that respect I am also antiquated. But as an antique Mormon I try to be low maintenance and not require anyone to accommodate me. Instead I'll accommodate them.

I believe God still speaks, and will do so with anyone who follows the steps Joseph Smith followed. I would not want anyone to follow me, and have never even invited anyone to do so. I think everyone should follow Christ, who will lead them to the Father. I think Joseph Smith is the most current prophetic example of the Gospel of Jesus Christ, because he was in Christ's presence and rescued from the fall. That IS the Gospel. I do not worship Joseph Smith, but have tried to replicate the religion he held, and through it to come to know God. It has worked for me.

The church introduced me to Joseph Smith, gave me the Book of Mormon, Doctrine and Covenants, Pearl of Great Price, baptism, ordinances and covenants. I took it all in, accepted and have honored the things I've received from the church and been benefited as a result. The church has my gratitude. I would not want to injure it. When there are others who are disaffected from the church, and who have discovered issues or problems, they are welcomed to look into what I've written as my best effort to state what I believe and why.

In writing I try to be candid. I know there are those who trust in fourth phase Mormonism who resent, even revile against me and what I write. I'm content with that. What God thinks matters a great deal more to me than what some errant blogger hiding behind a pseudonym puts on some discussion board. I am not a coward and intend to stand accountable for everything I write. I make no apologies for my faith. It is honestly and deeply held. As a result of study and prayer I think I know what I am talking about. Those who have spent only a fraction of the effort I have devoted to my religion cannot affect me by their criticism.

Long ago I realized this honest approach would disqualify me from being popular. It makes me "too suspect" for any significant church callings. That is perfectly fine. It was never the intention to become popular or successful in religion anyway. Only being true to what I believe matters. Everything else is, in a word, vain.

So if you want criticism of the church, you will have to look elsewhere. I try to avoid it. I would encourage others to search into what they believe, and stop complaining about what others believe. Search it out for yourself and be content to believe in what you find.

Mormonism is the last place where God touched mankind. It is the place where His hand will begin again in moving mankind upward. Therefore it is where I intend to faithfully remain.

Criticism of the Church, Part 2

Frailty or insecurity in the mind of a person oftentimes interferes with the ability to cope with facts or truth. For example, a secure and healthy woman can be told "the horizontally striped dress you have on makes your hips and shoulders look large." She will thank you for pointing it out, and take it into account. She may or may not change the dress. It is, after all, merely appearance. But an insecure and fragile woman whose self-consciousness interferes with interpreting facts will have a different reaction. She may think the person pointing it out to her hates her, thinks she is fat, even ugly. She will resent the remark and never pause to think there was no criticism or hidden insult in the observation.

Facts are not criticism. Opinions which differ from traditional historical opinions that I have fully explained and gathered the evidence from the sources to support, are also not criticism. If an event occurred and is accurately retold, it is not criticism even if the event is troublesome.

When it comes to evaluating our faith, indeed any faith, there are moments where two things are going to happen: First, you will encounter things you simply do not understand. For those issues, you may struggle with dissonance, or the inability to resolve the question sometimes for years, as I have. That is perfectly norMalachi It means you have more work to do. It does not mean you are wicked, lack faith, or are out of harmony with God because you are unable to understand a proposition. For me, plural marriage was a difficult topic which caused me to leave it unresolved for over two decades. It was not something I had time to resolve. During that time, the issue was an admitted "problem" for my faith. But despite that, I had a testimony, continued active in the church, paid tithing and served in callings. From time to time, when the topic was being discussed, I listened, asked questions, considered what others thought, and kept the matter in the mental file-drawer to be sorted through at some point. During that time many Latter-day writers took the effort to gather and publish histories of the practice. They aided me as I pondered the question. It was literally only a couple of years ago before I finally reached a conclusion. I've never fully explained my conclusions or why. I have, however, mentioned the matter in *Passing the Heavenly Gift*. That is a broad-brush treatment, and not an elaboration of my full understanding on the subject. I am now comfortable with how *I* view the subject.

Second, you are going to encounter information that proves what you believed before is wrong. It may be wrong because it was not true, or because it was poorly understood, or because it was based on a story or incident that never happened. It may be wrong because someone you trusted was mistaken, or they were dishonest. Whatever the discovery that reveals things in a new light, you will undoubtedly find along the path of faith that you were wrong at some point about some things in your religion. I've encountered that a lot since becoming a Mormon. When you encounter such things you have a choice to make—Either you can react with dismay and bitterness, or you can sort through what adjustments now need to be made, and proceed with faith and security in God to sort it out. In other words, you can act like the secure woman who was told the horizontal stripes had an unintended effect on her appearance, and proceed forward with that in mind.

There are those who have never ventured into our history. They don't want to do so. They feel insecure and frail, unable to encounter the material because of fear that it will unhinge them from what they value. I get that. In the case of *Passing the Heavenly Gift* I'm not writing to even address them. For the life of me, I can't understand why such a person would even read that part of what I've written. It was certainly not intended for them. The most frail and insecure of all, however, are those who have never read anything I've written and yet presume to be able to evaluate the intentions and even value of the work I have and am doing. I am not a critic of the church. I have never been one.

I have never said the church does not have the sealing power. Instead, I have discussed the scriptures and teachings of Joseph Smith, the revelations in the D&C, and Joseph's public addresses, the critical moments when the authority has been conferred, and both how and why it is given. There are three chapters in *Beloved Enos*, and several chapters in *Passing the Heavenly Gift*, and some material in *Eighteen Verses*, along with a paper on Elijah in which I discuss things relating to the topic. In none of that have I ever said the church lacks sealing power. In *Beloved Enos* I discuss an example from President Monson where I refer to its use. I also concede regularly the claim by the church that it has it and I do not question that claim. Never have.

The fact that the power to seal is given in only one way is very clear in the scriptures and teachings of Joseph Smith. That is a fact. That fact has been shown in what I've written. Therefore, there are several facts which ought to be considered. First, in scripture, the sealing power comes to man by the voice of God and in no other way. Second, I have never said and don't claim the church lacks that authority. Third, the church claims to have such authority, and I do not question the claim.

Frail and insecure church members, particularly those who presume they have the right to evaluate the faith of others, are well advised to first ground themselves and their own testimony before deciding if an accurate observation about "horizontal stripes" is really an insult or merely a fact.

Here is a sample of the kind of foolishness my wife brings to my attention from various blogs:[1963]

Quote:

> *1. Have you ever been criticized by church leaders? A: No. I've never been criticized nor asked to stop writing by any church leader. Not from my bishop, stake president, nor any higher authority. I have had some contacts, but they have been private, and encouraging me to continue. There have been a number of people who have returned to church activity because of what I've written. Those results are viewed with some support. The criticism I am aware of, some of which has been quite harsh, has come from overanxious church members who have not read the things I've written.*

> *If this Q&A with DS was not in the last few weeks, then it could be true. The investigation by the church is currently in progress. I know that his stake president has spoken with him at least once recently and probably will again. I have a pretty good idea of what will likely happen, but I can't say much about it. —JayE*

[1963] For original formatting and information on internet blog referenced above, see post at denversnuffer.blogspot.com dated April 26, 2012.

Quote:

> *Originally Posted by JayE: I have a pretty good idea of what will likely happen, but I can't say much about it.*

If you're not going to say anything about it, then why even mention something like this? —NRA

Quote:

> *Originally Posted by JayE: If this Q&A with DS was not in the last few weeks, then it could be true. The investigation by the church is currently in progress. I know that his stake president has spoken with him at least once recently and probably will again.*

It could be that his stake president did not criticize him, but merely asked him some questions. The Q & A is the result of an interview he did on Mormon Stories (a podcast) about a week ago, so I'd say it was created within the last few days. —Toni

---

Interesting that there are those who are "in the know" from inside the church who feel at liberty to gossip on the Internet about things such as this. What kind of an organization are they running? Why would the church pretend to have confidential conversations between members and leaders if there are going to be such leaks from within the COB?

Shame on all those involved. Shame on those who refuse to discuss openly the important issues rather than resort to subversion of members through back-channels.

For the Strengthening the Members Committee I have another thought for you: "The wicked flee when no man pursueth: but the righteous are bold as a lion." (Proverbs 28:1). That was Solomon. Today, if it were me, I would say instead: "Grow a pair. For the faithful tire of dealing with eunuchs."

If I err in doctrine, and you have several million words of mine propounding doctrine in very public places then correct the error. Show me the mistakes. Teach me the better view of history. Show the better argument. If I err, I will gladly be instructed. But effeminate men hiding inside a tower who lack the testicular fortitude to confront me and debate the truth are unworthy of any serious consideration. They have chosen to hide from the arena in which ideas are doing battle. Anybody creeping about behind a pseudonym when they dare to comment at all is in sharp contrast to my own public disclosure, public accountability and public defense of the faith I hold as true.

Here's another truth for the self-righteous eunuchs accusing me of wanting the glory of leading my own following: You can't find a picture of me on this blog, or in any book I've written, or in the advertising to the very few speaking engagements I've accepted. You can look into the Chiasmus Conference at which I spoke and you'll find that there is no picture of me in any of the material advertising it, nor in the book when it came out. My picture isn't in any of the material from the Portland Conference I spoke at last year. I'm not looking to be recognized. It is my IDEAS that are advanced, not me. I am nothing. I don't matter. You shouldn't recognize me, pick me from a line-up, or think you know me. I do not do that. Even the interview with John Dehlin was predicated on it being a voice recording, *not* a video. If it were a video, I would have turned it down. I'm not a publicity hog, and offer no competition to the folks who want a following. I do not want one. I do not accept speaking invitations. I turn down dozens of them and rarely speak because I do NOT want to attract attention to myself. I want the IDEAS to have a life, not me.

If you want to search for men seeking to rival the Brethren, take a look at CES. For example, one of my my former Bishops is able to fill a stake center to overflowing mid-day with Mormon housewives who dote on the man. I can assure you I have no intention of trying to accomplish anything similar. I KNOW that what I've written is deeply offensive to many, many church members. It has no advantage apart from being honest, and the honesty of the material is accompanied by my sincere belief in it also being TRUE. If it is wrong, then grow a pair and openly confront the ideas, tell us your name, give us your basis for contradicting the material, and act like you are confident in your beliefs. Or keep your skirts on and snipe from the sidelines, but never expect me to respect the frail and insecure who are unable or unwilling to compete in the arena where the valiant are found suffering for the Lord's cause. I occupy a place where insults come from those who ought to be supporting the struggle; making the Lord's cause all the more difficult for those making the sacrifice He has asked be made. It is not pleasant, but it does conform to a law ordained before the foundation of the world upon which blessings are predicated. Those blessings are personal, between God and myself, and worth enduring your attacks. I will not be deterred by weakness and criticism.

I have a testimony of the church. I have and do serve wherever asked. I pay tithes to her. But the horizontal stripes nevertheless are being worn, and they do affect her appearance.

Criticism of the Church, Part 3

I reject the idea it is criticism or "evil speaking" to discuss candidly the church's history. Here is a sample of one fact which I welcome anyone to correct if I am wrong:

It is my conclusion that the Nauvoo Temple was never completed. Those who worked on it, went inside it, participated in work on it, and knew its condition never claimed it was completed. Never. The words used by those who knew about it were carefully phrased. They said it was "considered sufficiently completed to dedicate." That is much different than being completed.

Joseph Smith died before the walls were completed to the second level. The lower part of the Nauvoo Temple was essentially a copy of the Kirtland Temple. The upper levels were not fully designed. The top attic floor was largely open, a few offices at either end and a large, open area in between. When the attic was adopted as the location for endowments, the area was unsuitable because Joseph never lived to work with design and construction crews to adapt the facility for use in endowment work. It did not have the kind of privacy and separate rooms needed to initiate through the ordinance.

Joseph had ordered a large quantity of canvas to cover the outside bowery next to the Temple. The weather made public meetings unpleasant, and many ended early because of rain or snow. The canvas was intended to let these meetings continue despite the weather.

In the winter of 1845, when the pressure to abandon Nauvoo became so great, the decision was made to use the attic space to do the endowments. The canvas was used to partition off areas in the attic and divide the area up so the ceremonies would be possible. The attic was "tented off" into separate rooms where the endowments were performed from December through early February. As they pulled out of town, the church's leadership prayed for the Lord's assistance in completing the Temple. The next day the attic caught fire and the attic area burned. The fire was extinguished, but not without considerable damage to the roof and attic area.

The roof was repaired, but since the attic was no longer going to be used, the interior was again not completed. The rest of the temple interior was never completed. It was merely "considered complete enough" and was dedicated.

A year after the dedication of the Temple and before there was any damage done by the mobs, a newspaper editor from Palmyra, New York toured the Nauvoo Temple and remarked about its condition. Among other things, he observed in an article titled "The Deserted Mormon Temple," these things about various parts of the Temple:

"The first sight we had of it gave us a pang of disappointment, for it looked more like a white Yankee meeting house, with its steeple on one end, than a magnificent structure that had cost, all uncompleted as it is, seven hundred and fifty thousand dollars. But as we approached nearer, it proved to be something worth seeing . . . [In the attic:] The chamber itself is devoid of ornament, and I was unable to ascertain whether it was intended to have any, if it should have been completed . . . [In the basement baptistery, speaking of the font:] It is very plain and rests on the back of twelve stone oxen or cows, which stand immersed to their knees in the earth. It has two flights of steps, with iron bannisters, by which you enter and go out of the font, one at the east end, and the other at the west end. The oxen have tin horns and tin ears, but are otherwise of stone, and a stone drapery hangs like a curtain down from the font, so as to prevent the exposure of all back of the forelegs of the beasts . . . The basement is unpaved . . . [Overall comment:] The whole is quite unfinished, and one can imagine what it might have been in course of time, if Joe Smith had been allowed to pursue his career in prosperity." (*The Palmyra Courier-Journal*, September 22, 1847)

In a 1962 Deseret Book publication, the Nauvoo Temple's state of completion was described in these words:

"Perhaps there were many rooms in the building whose walls were not covered with lath and plaster. Perhaps factory cloth, canvas, or other curtain material covered the walls and ceilings in the upper story rooms. There were some large assembly rooms and many small rooms that were not to be used in the temple ritual, so they were not put in order and beautifully decorated and furnished with the best of equipment. In all such rooms the pungent odor of fresh pine timber, uncovered by plaster, pictures or carpets, greeted the visitors. There may have been many plank floors and stairways uncovered with carpets, and many walls and ceilings presenting an unfinished condition . . . Bare boards in many rooms, large and small, might have been visible, but the rooms that were necessary for the temple ritual were quickly prepared, and the endowment was administered within the new temple though the building was not as elaborately furnished as was the Temple of Solomon in Jerusalem." (*The Nauvoo Temple*, E. Cecil McGavin, Deseret Book, 1962, p. 56.)

The content of Section 124 *is what it is,* and *requires what it requires.* History shows the Temple was only "considered complete enough" and was not in fact complete. The diaries of church leaders commented on the incomplete condition of the Temple. It appears to be a fact that "considered complete enough" to be used in the endowment, and later for purposes of being dedicated, is not the same thing as completed. Subsequently, after the Saints abandoned Nauvoo, and after the Palmyra editor's visit, the building was burned down. Later it was struck by a tornado. Then the remaining, partial structure was considered a hazard and demolished by the City. By the time it was reconstructed, not one stone of the original building remained on the site. Some excavation located the font area, and some artifacts were recovered, but the structure was gone.

My view is that this has some relevance to our history. I think the early Salt Lake City refugees from Nauvoo suffered through great want, difficulty and hunger. Because of their hunger, they were boiling saddles to soften the leather enough to be able to eat it. This was very real privation and seems to represent something other than God's blessings upon them. In the context of Section 124, it is at least plausible it represented God's displeasure, and not His vindication of the Saints. It states,

> "If ye labor with all your might, I will consecrate that spot that it shall be made holy. And if my people will hearken unto my voice, and unto the voice of my servants whom I have appointed to lead my people, behold, verily I say unto you, they shall not be moved out of their place." (D&C 124:44–45)

This was the revelation given in January 1841, three and a half years before he death of Joseph and Hyrum. The "servants" appointed were Joseph Smith, and the new Co-President, prophet, seer and revelator who was also to be ordained to the Priesthood and given the sealing power by the word of God, Hyrum Smith.[1964] The saints were warned that if they failed to complete the temple, according to the revelation that:

[1964] D&C 124:91–95 "And again, verily I say unto you, let my servant William be appointed, ordained, and anointed, as counselor unto my servant Joseph, in the room of my servant Hyrum, that my servant Hyrum may take the office of Priesthood and Patriarch, which was appointed unto him by his father, by blessing and also by right; That from henceforth he shall hold the keys of the patriarchal blessings upon the heads of all my people, That whoever he blesses shall be blessed, and whoever he curses shall be cursed; that whatsoever he shall bind on earth shall be bound in heaven; and whatsoever he shall loose on earth shall be loosed in heaven. And from this time forth I appoint unto him that he may be a prophet, and a seer, and a revelator unto my church, as well as my servant Joseph; That he may act in concert also with my servant Joseph; and that he shall receive counsel from my servant Joseph, who shall show unto him the keys whereby he may ask and receive, and be crowned with the same blessing, and glory, and honor, and priesthood, and gifts of the priesthood, that once were put upon him that was my servant Oliver Cowdery;"

"I will not perform the oath which I make unto you, neither fulfill the promises which ye expect at my hands, saith the Lord. For instead of blessings, ye, by your own works, bring cursings, wrath, indignation, and judgments upon your own heads, by your follies, and by all your abominations, which you practice before me, saith the Lord." (D&C 124:47–48)

It is clear we have history to help us answer the questions: Were they blessed? Were they not moved out of their place? Were they cursed? Did God's wrath and indignation visit them?

None of this is criticism of the church. It is an attempt to understand history and to read the meaning of events through the lens of scripture, rather than through the lens of conceit. Why should scripture not be used to help us understand history? If God chastens those whom He loves,[1965] then why do we fear acknowledging chastening from God? Can't that be a sign of His love? What is the powerful insecurity that prevents us even considering the possibility of an early failure and God's displeasure? Even if the work was interrupted, we can still have faith in the Restoration. After all, the Book of Mormon predicts we will get off track. It also assures us the Lord will set His hand a second time to recover us. The allegory of Jacob 5 also foretells of the eventual return of natural fruit. What fear should we have? Why would we not want to fully understand the Lord's work instead of some alternative carefully composed fiction, or in other words a cunningly devised fable telling us "all is well," when the evidence strongly suggest things are not at all well?

This is not criticism. This is a labor of love to understand fully the Lord's dealings with us and our true standing before Him. Why would we reject it? Because it requires repentance and return to Him? What right do we have to think we don't have to repent? How

---

[1965] Revelation 3:19 "As many as I love, I rebuke and chasten: be zealous therefore, and repent."

much of our story is motivated by pride, contrary to scripture, and inconsistent with facts?

If you attribute ill-will to those who diligently seek the Lord, then we ought to just disband as a religion claiming to follow God, and admit we are content to be a social group instead. We would still qualify for tax-exempt status. Then we won't be encumbered by any of the rigors of what required the lives of Joseph and Hyrum, and which requires the sacrifice of all things, including our own lives if necessary, to produce faith.

"It is in vain for persons to fancy to themselves that they are heirs with those, or can be heirs with them, who have offered their all in sacrifice, and by this means obtain faith in God and favor with him so as to obtain eternal life, unless they, in like manner, offer unto him the same sacrifice, and through that offering obtain the knowledge that they are accepted of him." (Lecture 6:8; *Lectures on Faith*.)

When we will tolerate only praise for one another, and cannot abide correction from the Lord in the revelations He gave us, we are no different than the Zoramites scaling the Rameumptom and proclaiming our conceit.

There is a great difference between pursuing truth, accepting the unpopular role of saying what needs to be said inside a group who does not welcome it, and merely criticizing the church. I utterly reject the idea. I know I am not qualified to be popular, or advance in the organization because of what I write. The organization resents me, and has made that clear. Even as I seek its best interests, I find myself the object of its ire. On the other hand, I have come to know God by the things I have sacrificed for Him, and I would never alter that bargain; even for the whole world.

JOSEPH SMITH
HISTORY

The Joseph Smith-History found in the Pearl of Great Price was composed shortly after John Whitmer left the church and took what history existed then with him. He was the church's Historian at the time. The bitter Missouri conflict left a lot of former top level church leaders disaffected and no longer followers of Joseph or the church. David Whitmer, Oliver Cowdery and several members of the twelve were among them. Some signed affidavits supporting the Missouri citizens' campaign against the church, and were responsible for persuading the legal authorities that there was reason to justify arresting and holding Joseph. This series of events resulted in Joseph beginning again to write the history of himself and his church.

Given the fact he was starting over in 1838, I think the account in the Pearl of Great Price is remarkable. I think Joseph, like Nephi, could measure the importance of events he had lived from the distance of some years' reflection about them than he ever could have as he lived them. What we get in the JS–History is the benefit of Joseph's considered hindsight. He also could write better the meaning, or intent, of the message he received. He could *interpret* the visits, and make much more sense of them than he could when they happened. Nephi did the same thing. His Small Plates of Nephi were a production of his history begun some 40 years after the departure into the wilderness from Jerusalem. He wrote with all the insight and understanding of how the early events led in turn to the later results. He could see the preliminary disputes in the wilderness against the backdrop of the rebellion and rejection of Nephi following the death of their father, Lehi. He could align his visions with his father's, and show how the elder brothers rejected both.

Joseph Smith used the First Vision and his account of Moroni's first visit to foreshadow in the narrative all of his later prophetic work. It was an inspired explanation, using both scriptural and doctrinal coordinates to establish the Divine and angelic origin of his history and ministry. The JS–H is all the more valuable because of this inspired approach. We are better informed about what was really going on in Joseph's ministry because he told the account by using language of scripture to testify of what he experienced.

I want to comment on the process of Divine or angelic communication and how that makes its way into the written record of a prophet. It is more complex and subtle than most readers can conceive. For the most part, we read the scriptures as a completed work, and think the words give us everything we need to understand doctrine. That is not at all the case. We must arrive at the same place as the ones who wrote the scriptures in order to be able to understand what they mean. Until we share the same view, take in the same Spirit, and have similarly been exposed to the direct influence of heaven, the words are incomplete and can be very misleading.

The angel Moroni appeared to Joseph in his bedroom, and took hours to communicate understanding to young Joseph. The version of that visit we have in the JS–H was written about a decade and a half afterwards. It reflects Moroni's meaning and intent, but accomplishes it by supplying direct quotes from scripture. The account we have looks like a doctrine class, with Moroni as gospel doctrine teacher and Joseph as student. It is doubtful, however, there were any "words" exchanged between Moroni and Joseph. It is also unlikely there were "scriptures" used. Instead, the encounter likely consisted of Moroni conveying directly into the mind of Joseph the thoughts of Moroni's own mind. Joseph would later attempt to explain this using these words:

> "All things whatsoever God in his infinite wisdom has seen fit and proper to reveal to us, while we are dwelling in mortality, in regard to our mortal bodies, are revealed to us in the abstract, and independent of affinity of this mortal tabernacle, but are revealed to our spirits precisely as though we had no bodies at all." (*TPJS*, 355)

This makes it seem as if it were less "real" than if it involved normal faculties, but it is in fact far more real, far more precise, and far more communicative to the mind, heart and spirit. It "imbeds" the information within the person. As a result, the impression becomes more clear with time.

As Joseph worked to reconvey the information to us, writing in 1838, he resorts to using scripture to make the meaning clear to us. Moroni is quoting various passages of scripture to Joseph, as described in these words:

> He first quoted part of the third chapter of Malachi; and he quoted also the fourth or last chapter of the same prophecy, though with a little variation from the way it reads in our Bibles. Instead of quoting the first verse as it reads in our books, he quoted it thus:

> For behold, the day cometh that shall burn as an oven, and all the proud, yea, and all that do wickedly shall burn as stubble; for they that come shall burn them, saith the Lord of Hosts, that it shall leave them neither root nor branch.

And again, he quoted the fifth verse thus: Behold, I will reveal unto you the Priesthood, by the hand of Elijah the prophet, before the coming of the great and dreadful day of the Lord.

He also quoted the next verse differently: And he shall plant in the hearts of the children the promises made to the fathers, and the hearts of the children shall turn to their fathers. If it were not so, the whole earth would be utterly wasted at his coming.

In addition to these, he quoted the eleventh chapter of Isaiah, saying that it was about to be fulfilled. He quoted also the third chapter of Acts, twenty-second and twenty-third verses, precisely as they stand in our New Testament. He said that that prophet was Christ; but the day had not yet come when "they who would not hear his voice should be cut off from among the people," but soon would come.

He also quoted the second chapter of Joel, from the twenty-eighth verse to the last. He also said that this was not yet fulfilled, but was soon to be. And he further stated that the fulness of the Gentiles was soon to come in. He quoted many other passages of scripture, and offered many explanations which cannot be mentioned here." (JS–H 1:36–41)

You have two options to explain this retelling of the visit. 1) Moroni said these exact things and a decade and a half later Joseph could remember and quote it exactly as it was spoken, or 2) Joseph could remember exactly the impressions, and drew from scriptures known to him in order to convey to the reader the information Moroni passed into his mind on that evening.

I believe the second is the accurate way to comprehend the interview. Moroni visited with Joseph, conveyed the information precisely as if Joseph had no body at all, and did not rely upon the eardrums, or the vibration of atmospheric pressure, in order to clearly and accurately enlighten Joseph's understanding. Then, when it came time for Joseph to inform us of the event, he resorted to familiar words of scripture to recount the event.

It begs us to ask: "Why?" That is where we turn next.

Joseph Smith History, Part 2

Joseph was still a young man when Moroni visited with him. He was practically a child when he first saw the Lord and the Father. In both encounters, as Joseph recorded his best retelling of the incident, he used the words of scripture to weave his account together.

In the First Vision, when the Lord addressed Joseph, the account tells it in these words:

> I was answered that I must join none of them, for they were all wrong; and the Personage who addressed me said that all their creeds were an abomination in his sight; that those professors were all corrupt; that: "they draw near to me with their lips, but their hearts are far from me, they teach for doctrines the commandments of men, having a form of godliness, but they deny the power thereof."

Or, in other words, Joseph has the Lord borrow from several scriptures:

> "For there are certain men crept in unawares, who were before of old ordained to this condemnation, ungodly men, turning the grace of our God into lasciviousness, and denying the only Lord God, and our Lord Jesus Christ." (Jude 1:4)

> "Wherefore the Lord said, Forasmuch as this people draw near me with their mouth, and with their lips do honour me, but have removed their heart far from me, and their fear toward me is taught by the precept of men." (Isaiah 29:13)

"Not giving heed to Jewish fables, and commandments of men, that turn from the truth." (Titus 1:14)

"Having a form of godliness, but denying the power thereof: from such turn away." (2 Timothy 3:5)

Or, the Lord conveyed into the mind of Joseph an indelible impression of truth, which would remain with him and expand and distill as he pondered on its meaning. When at last Joseph was able to set it out in an inspired retelling, the words of scripture flooded into his mind and equipped him to compose an account that would ring with truth, convey what happened, and testify of the authenticity of the words of ancient prophets, while letting the world know what the Lord's message was to Joseph. But the language, even the quotes, are not what transpired. They are an accurate retelling, but reduced to our form of communication. The Lord's manner of telling is quite different. It is unencumbered by our vocabulary, and conveys pure meaning and intent. Therefore Joseph was able to capture and compose the information with power and meaning to us. But to do so Joseph had to resort to scripture.

Which again, begs the question: "Why?" Why do prophets resort to the scriptures to explain the truth as revealed to them? Why does a new revelation get put into the words of an earlier revelation? Why does a stunning new truth come forth as an exposition of the already familiar words of scripture?

In perhaps his greatest sermon, Joseph drew from and expounded on the scriptures to proclaim new doctrines, unheard of by those who had studied the Bible for two thousand years. As he did so he remarked:

"It has always been my province to dig up hidden mysteries—new things—for my hearers. Just at the time when some men think I have no right to the keys of the Priesthood—just at that time I have the greatest right." (*TPJS*, 364)

He goes on to expound from the Bible on the true meaning of "eternal judgment" and the resurrection, "salvation for the dead," the plurality of Gods, Abraham's teachings, eternal glories and the pre-mortal exaltation of some who lived on the earth. "Sons of God who exalt themselves to be Gods, even before the foundation of the world." (*TPJS*, 375). He used as his text the Bible.

Prophets see the meaning behind the words of scripture, and not the words themselves. This is because having been taught by angels and the Lord, they know the intent. Hence Joseph's proclamation that it is his "province to dig up hidden mysteries—new things" using the scriptures. They are not a sealed book to them.

In like manner the Lord spent most of the day of His resurrection opening the scriptures in a private conversation between Himself and two disciples while they walked on the Road to Emmaus. "Beginning at Moses and all the prophets, he expounded unto them in all the scriptures the things concerning himself."[1966] The Lord could do this because the Lord was there when they were written, and they reflect His mind and His teachings. Therefore, He could see clearly within them the teachings about Him.

To bear testimony of his encounter with the Lord, and with Moroni, Joseph Smith employed the scriptures to expound unto us in all the scriptures the things concerning himself. How like his Master was this servant! Joseph completely mirrored the pattern of the One who can save! We should be able to recognize the Master in the servant! In Joseph's case, the parallel is unmistakable.

[1966] Luke 24:27 "And beginning at Moses and all the prophets, he expounded unto them in all the scriptures the things concerning himself."

Because he had received a dispensation of the Gospel to him from heaven, Joseph proclaimed the truth using scriptures to confirm the message.

> "It is the order of heavenly things that God should always send a new dispensation into the world when men have apostatized from the truth and lost the priesthood, but when men come out and build upon other men's foundations, they do it on their own responsibility, without authority from God; and when the floods come and the winds blow, their foundations will be found to be sand, and their whole fabric will crumble to dust." (*TPJS*, 375–76)

Joseph, having secured the truth from heaven for himself, did not need to build on other men's foundations. He was privileged to declare the truth to us from his own understanding, from his own knowledge and in conformity with his own dispensation of the Gospel.

The scriptures weave together the truth from dispensation to dispensation because those who wrote them had seen the same vision, conversed with the same heavenly hosts, and found the inspired language that allows the truth to be declared.

When Joseph wrote his account in 1838, he had pondered and gained the insight to be able to weave into his history the corroboration of his Divine mandate employing the words of scripture to justify what he taught. He was a prophet indeed! He knew the things of which he spoke. All he needed to do was expound the scriptures to be able to dig up hidden mysteries, new things, for those who would hear him. Those who heard him were amazed, just as the disciples on the Road to Emmaus.

Joseph Smith History, Part 3

Joseph Smith's entire ministry was connected to scripture. It began with an encounter between him and God which he was only able to describe using the language of scripture. It extended to an encounter with Moroni which he again described using a host of scripture to convey the meaning of what the angel impressed into his mind.

It turned to translating a volume of scripture. This required him to take every thought of the ancient prophets and translate them from one language into another. The language of the Book of Mormon repeatedly adopts phrases from the King James version of the Bible to weave together the ancient narrative. Given the circumstances, and what we have been told of that process, Joseph's mind was embedded with phrases that would have seemed familiar to him as he struggled to capture in his own tongue the ideas of the long dead authors. It would not have been derivative from the King James' Bible, but would have sidled alongside it in phrasing, structure and concept.

Just like Nephi's vision of the fullness of God's works, Joseph Smith likewise saw God's unfolding plan. Nephi was forbidden from disclosing what he beheld. To bear testimony, however, Nephi adopted the language of Isaiah to explain his own (Nephi's) testimony. It is important for us to recognize that when Nephi was writing Isaiah, and then expounding on the material he'd etched into the plates, he was acting the role of a prophet. Isaiah's words WERE Nephi's testimony. They allowed him to tell us what the Lord wanted us to know, and to do it using the words of scripture composed by Isaiah.

Jacob accomplished the very same thing. Jacob adopted the words of Zenos, and the allegory we've been reviewing, to testify of the things he had seen and heard from the Lord. I went over how Jacob had, like his brother Nephi, been visited by the Lord. Jacob was also looking for the language to express his own vision. He invited his people to the temple where he was going to deliver to them his own prophecy. When they arrived, he read them the allegory, Zenos' prophecy, the story of the olive tree. When he completed that retelling, Jacob announced the following:

"as I said unto you that I would prophesy, behold, this is my prophecy—that the things which this prophet Zenos spake, concerning the house of Israel, in the which he likened them unto a tame olive tree, must surely come to pass." (Jacob 6:1)

Jacob, who beheld the Lord and was ministered to by Him, bore his testimony and established his prophecy by retelling Zenos' olive tree story.

Christ's great Sermon on the Mount was based on the Law of Moses. The law of retaliation (*lex talonis*) set out in the prior law was contrasted with what the Lord now established as the underlying meaning for that law. Instead of striking back, bear the blow and forgive. Instead of refraining from adultery, remove lust from your heart. Instead of rebuking, harbor no ill will toward your brother.

Christ's entire ministry was based on expounding the scriptures. Interestingly, He forbid us from calling one another "fools" in His great sermon.[1967] Then He called men "fools" for their blind misapplication of scripture.[1968] The same scriptures which, in the hands of the Lord will save a man, are the tools for deceiving men and leading them into destruction when used by the Pharisees and Scribes.

For Nephi, using Isaiah was the perfect means to preach salvation. For Jacob, using Zenos was the perfect means to preach and prophesy about his people and us. For Joseph Smith, using the words of scripture to translate into English the words of earlier prophets was a master work of a man who received a dispensation of the Gos-

---

[1967] Matthew 5:22 "But I say unto you, That whosoever is angry with his brother without a cause shall be in danger of the judgment: and whosoever shall say to his brother, Raca, shall be in danger of the council: but whosoever shall say, Thou fool, shall be in danger of hell fire."

[1968] Matthew 23:16–19 "Woe unto you, *ye* blind guides, which say, Whosoever shall swear by the temple, it is nothing; but whosoever shall swear by the gold of the temple, he is a debtor! *Ye* fools and blind: for whether is greater, the gold, or the temple that sanctifieth the gold? And, Whosoever shall swear by the altar, it is nothing; but whosoever sweareth by the gift that is upon it, he is guilty. *Ye* fools and blind: for whether *is* greater, the gift, or the altar that sanctifieth the gift?"

pel. For Christ, beginning at Moses and all the prophets, He was able to show how necessary His own sacrifice and offering was to fulfill all righteousness.

However, for the blind guides, the use of scripture to develop as commandments the doctrines of men, the Lord only had the term "fools" to describe their wickedness. They would not enter into heaven, and would instead hinder others who followed them from entering.

Joseph was commanded to "translate" the Bible. His Inspired Version was a work which led in turn to some of the greatest revelations of our day. Reading about "heaven" in John 5:29[1969] led to an inquiry which provided Section 76 to us all. The Vision of the Three Degrees of Glory was given because of an inquiry about scripture. Earlier John the Baptist came because of an inquiry about baptism as a result of translating scripture. The work of the Prophet Joseph Smith was intimately linked and could not be separated from the words of scripture.

At one point a calm Lord told His critics to search the scriptures, because His detractors claimed they would have eternal life from what was contained in them. But, He added, they testify of Him.[1970] So it is not merely claiming the scriptures support a proposition that deserves respect, but instead whether the matter taught has underlying it the truth. Joseph's history shows what an adept prophet can do when employing scripture to inform the reader of God's will. In that respect, Joseph Smith does not take a back seat to Nephi or Jacob. It is a marvelous thing to behold; assuming you recognize it as one of the signs that testifies Joseph was indeed a prophet.

[1969] John 5:29 "And shall come forth; they that have done good, unto the resurrection of life; and they that have done evil, unto the resurrection of damnation."

[1970] John 5:39 "Search the scriptures; for in them ye think ye have eternal life: and they are they which testify of me."

Joseph Smith History, Part 4

Once Joseph had an encounter with God through the veil, he hesitated to discuss the matter fully. Even at the end he remained reluctant, even forbidden, to share all he knew from the encounter.[1971] The first attempt to tell someone about the encounter happened only a few days afterwards. He records that it was to a Methodist minister, the sect he had been most impressed with as he investigated the various religions.[1972] This fulfills one of the laws ordained before the foundation of the world[1973] because it is necessary for the Lord's servants, and even the Lord Himself, to first make an offering of the truth to the existing religious authorities before either Christ, or Joseph, or any of His servants could then move forward independent of them.[1974] Query in your own mind what would have happened if the Methodist minister had accepted Joseph's experience as authentic.

[1971] JS–H 1:20 "He again forbade me to join with any of them; and many other things did he say unto me, which I cannot write at this time. When I came to myself again, I found myself lying on my back, looking up into heaven. When the light had departed, I had no strength; but soon recovering in some degree, I went home. And as I leaned up to the fireplace, mother inquired what the matter was. I replied, "Never mind, all is well—I am well enough off." I then said to my mother, "I have learned for myself that Presbyterianism is not true." It seems as though the adversary was aware, at a very early period of my life, that I was destined to prove a disturber and an annoyer of his kingdom; else why should the powers of darkness combine against me? Why the opposition and persecution that arose against me, almost in my infancy?"

[1972] JS–H 1:8 "During this time of great excitement my mind was called up to serious reflection and great uneasiness; but though my feelings were deep and often poignant, still I kept myself aloof from all these parties, though I attended their several meetings as often as occasion would permit. In process of time my mind became somewhat partial to the Methodist sect, and I felt some desire to be united with them; but so great were the confusion and strife among the different denominations, that it was impossible for a person young as I was, and so unacquainted with men and things, to come to any certain conclusion who was right and who was wrong."

[1973] D&C 130:20–21 "There is a law, irrevocably decreed in heaven before the foundations of this world, upon which all blessings are predicated— And when we obtain any blessing from God, it is by obedience to that law upon which it is predicated."

[1974] John 1:11 "He came unto his own, and his own received him not."
D&C 10:57 "Behold, I am Jesus Christ, the Son of God. I came unto mine own, and mine own received me not."

Joseph explains this encounter as follows:

"Some few days after I had this vision, I happened to be in company with one of the Methodist preachers, who was very active in the before mentioned religious excitement; and, conversing with him on the subject of religion, I took occasion to give him an account of the vision which I had had. I was greatly surprised at his behavior; he treated my communication not only lightly, but with great contempt, saying it was all of the devil, that there were no such things as visions or revelations in these days; that all such things had ceased with the apostles, and that there would never be any more of them." (JS–H 1:21)

This theme of the false minister opposing new revelation found its way into the endowment ceremony Joseph later restored. That portion of the ceremony was eliminated in the 1990 temple changes. Before then the endowment taught how professional ministers were men in Satan's employ, but true messengers were angels, sent from God's presence with a message from God. This endowment teaching came from the actual experiences of Joseph's life, as shown above. It is repeated, of course, in the experiences of all those who follow God, are taught by angels, and opposed by professional's making their living from religion. Ultimately there must be a choice between those who come bearing a message from God and those who oppose it, and claim there can't be any such revelation, and that the organized faith they advocate (i.e., Methodist, Presbyterian, Lutheran, Catholic, etc.) is the guardian and possessor of the right to teach *all* truth. They claim to be the spokesmen for heaven and heaven does not really send any messengers apart from themselves. Of course it follows that those like Joseph Smith were "all of the devil" and not to be trusted.

Joseph lived this. As did Christ. The temple rites, until 1990, fortified the endowed against this particular deception of Satan's.

Joseph's history includes an observation about the reactions the religious critics had toward him. It is always the false, pseudo-religious who are offended by the truth; not the atheists or agnostics. The atheists and agnostics allow others the liberty of believing as they wish. The religious are another story. They were the ones who, throughout Joseph's life, worked against him. Ultimately it was the disaffected within the church, and the ministers outside the church, who were directly responsible for killing him.

There is a passing comment in Joseph's history which is so undeniably authentic it leaps off the page. He writes that he was "persecuted by those who ought to have been my friends and to have treated me kindly, and if they supposed me to be deluded to have endeavored in a proper and affectionate manner to have reclaimed me." (JS–H 1:28.) Joseph is absolutely correct. The right way to proceed, if those who claimed Joseph was wrong and they were followers of God, would have been to have treated Joseph kindly, and endeavored in a proper and affectionate manner to have reclaimed him from error. But they didn't! This is a great key to understanding how the plan of God works. It conforms to a law irrevocably ordained in heaven. The false ministers cannot help themselves.

Why was it that the people claiming to be religious were persecuting Joseph rather than trying to persuade him with affectionate persuasion? It is because when men think that they have God on their side, and they do not, then they become abusive. They seek to have control, dominion and power over others in order to *force* the true disciples of the Lord to change and surrender faith. They abuse their position by claiming to follow God, while actually doing the opposite.

They had to follow the law of their master, Satan, who deceived them. This was because only in this manner could Joseph also obey the law ordained by God upon which blessings were predicated. For Joseph to grow, it was required for the men inspired by Satan to be revealed in their true light. They had to suppress, oppose, persecute and defame Joseph because they *could not* "in a proper and affectionate manner" have ever reclaimed him while serving Satan. He had the truth and they did not. Joseph

> " . . . had actually seen a light, and in the midst of that light I saw two Personages, and they did in reality speak to me; and though I was hated and persecuted for saying that I had seen a vision, yet it was true; and while they were persecuting me, reviling me, and speaking all manner of evil against me falsely for so saying, I was led to say in my heart: Why persecute me for telling the truth? I have actually seen a vision; and who am I that I can withstand God, or why does the world think to make me deny what I have actually seen? For I had seen a vision; I knew it, and I knew that God knew it, and I could not deny it, neither dared I do it; at least I knew that by so doing I would offend God, and come under condemnation." (JS–H 1:25)

Joseph was following the law ordained before the foundation of the world, and so were his critics. This is the same battle fought endlessly when God intervenes in the affairs of men.

We see the same thing when King Noah feared that Abinadi may have actually been sent by God. Noah was about to release him, but the priestly committee he surrounded himself with interfered. They aroused the vanity and pride of the king to make him angry. As a result, King Noah did not repent, and instead followed the law of the persecutor.[1975] Joseph Smith lived according to law, and according to law he was persecuted. According to a higher law he was vindicated by God, though like Abinadi it required his life. We are the beneficiar-

---

[1975] Mosiah 17:11–12 "And now king Noah was about to release him, for he feared his word; for he feared that the judgments of God would come upon him. But the priests lifted up their voices against him, and began to accuse him, saying: He has reviled the king. Therefore the king was stirred up in anger against him, and he delivered him up that he might be slain."

ies of Joseph's death. Through it the latter-day work is sealed, and will ultimately triumph. Temporary set-backs will not prevent the final return of natural fruit, and at last Zion itself.

Joseph's history is the story of how one individual obtained salvation by following the laws ordained for saving any of us. It is authentic. He shares details that conform to the same pattern all disciples of the Lord must follow. He is saved, while his persecutors who followed the law of their master, Satan, opposed the truth and were damned. It is always the case. Joseph explained:

> "The world always mistook false prophets for true ones, and those that were sent of God, they considered to be false prophets, and hence they killed, stoned, punished and imprisoned the true prophets....and though the most honorable men of the earth, they banished them from their society as vagabonds, whilst they cherished, honored and supported knaves, vagabonds, hypocrites, impostors, and the basest of men." (*DHC* 4:574)

Joseph was not just a source of new scripture, but his life conformed to the pattern of it. To study his history is to see the hand of God acting again to offer mankind the opportunity to repent and come to Him. The way never changes. The pattern never varies. Occasionally men who are initially following the law of persecuting the Lord's chosen will repent. Mostly they do not. Instead they reject what is offered, and incur the wrath of God. Joseph's life and death are testimony to this ancient, yet still intact, system of law by which men choose to be saved or damned.

Joseph Smith History, Part 5

Joseph's education did not open his mind. Translating the Book of Mormon did not open his mind. He clarifies in his history the point at which his mind did open up. He writes of it:

"so soon as I had been baptized by him, I also had the spirit of prophecy, when, standing up, I prophesied concerning the rise of this Church, and many other things connected with the Church, and this generation of the children of men. We were filled with the Holy Ghost, and rejoiced in the God of our salvation. Our minds being now enlightened, we began to have the scriptures laid open to our understandings, and the true meaning and intention of their more mysterious passages revealed unto us in a manner which we never could attain to previously, nor ever before had thought of." (JS–H 1:73–74)

This was the moment of greatest change. At that moment Joseph's mind greatly expanded.

Later he would provide a description of the effect the Holy Ghost has on one who receives it:

"This first Comforter or Holy Ghost has no other effect than pure intelligence. It is more powerful in expanding the mind, enlightening the understanding, and storing the intellect with present knowledge, of a man who is of the literal seed of Abraham, than one that is a Gentile, . . . for as the Holy Ghost falls upon one of the literal seed of Abraham, it is calm and serene, and his whole soul and body are only exercised by the pure spirit of intelligence." (*TPJS*, 149)

This is in stark contrast to what some people think the "Holy Ghost" is about. They associate sentiment and emotion, rather than enlightenment and intelligence with the presence of this member of the Godhead.

Joseph could understand the meaning of the scriptures because he acquired access to the same source of intelligence which animated the authors when they composed the scriptures. He did not need to seek an "interpretation" or study the methods of Biblical exegesis. He knew what they meant because the enlightenment from God laid open to his understanding the true meaning and even the intentions of things that before were merely "mysterious."

This is what Peter was referring to when he asserted:

"Knowing this first, that no prophecy of the scripture is of any private interpretation. For the prophecy came not in old time by the will of man: but holy men of God spake as they were moved by the Holy Ghost." (2 Peter 1:20–21)

In other words, no one has the right to assert any prophecy means anything because they think they can "interpret" the words, because such right belongs exclusively to the Holy Ghost. The words came (and still come to those who have received priesthood[1976]) from the Holy Ghost, and therefore, the meaning is only given from that source. [Section 68 was addressed to one of those who, in June 1831, was given the Melchizedek Priesthood at Isaac Morley's farm. According to Joseph Smith, that was the first time the Melchizedek Priesthood was given to the Elders of the church. That is another topic.] Notice also, the appearance of John the Baptist was only to provide the means to be baptized. He specifically speaks about some future visit of Peter, James and John, who held the keys of the Melchizedek Priesthood.[1977] Yet Joseph and Oliver received the Holy

---

[1976] D&C 68:2–4 "And, behold, and lo, this is an ensample unto all those who were ordained unto this priesthood, whose mission is appointed unto them to go forth— And this is the ensample unto them, that they shall speak as they are moved upon by the Holy Ghost. And whatsoever they shall speak when moved upon by the Holy Ghost shall be scripture, shall be the will of the Lord, shall be the mind of the Lord, shall be the word of the Lord, shall be the voice of the Lord, and the power of God unto salvation."

[1977] JS–H 1:72 "The messenger who visited us on this occasion and conferred this Priesthood upon us, said that his name was John, the same that is called John the Baptist in the New Testament, and that he acted under the direction of Peter, James and John, who held the keys of the Priesthood of Melchizedek, which Priesthood, he said, would in due time be conferred on us, and that I should be called the first Elder of the Church, and he (Oliver Cowdery) the second. It was on the fifteenth day of May, 1829, that we were ordained under the hand of this messenger, and baptized."

Ghost without any other ordinance and immediately following baptism.[1978] This mirrored my own experience.

So in Joseph Smith's History, we end at the same point where we began: His ministry as a prophet was directly connected with scripture. He walks through events that happened, including an audience with the Father and Son, repeated visits by Moroni, educational instruction given there, and the appearance of John the Baptist, but for Joseph, it was the Holy Ghost which enlightened his mind. When enlightened, the result was his capacity to understand the scriptures. He tunes into the very same frequency from which they originated. Sharing the mind of those who composed scripture, Joseph could understand what the authors meant. Therefore, when Joseph explained scripture to us, it was his right to tell us things we hadn't known before, interpretations we hadn't considered before, and the true meaning of what seems to us mysterious.

As people debate the meaning of latter-day prophecies, and think they can unravel the correct interpretation of such topics as Zion, gathering, priesthood, sealing power, the "one mighty and strong" and many, many other things we learn of from our unique body of scripture, we should remember Joseph's ministry. We ought to stop researching the threads of comments from oftentimes mystified commentators, and instead "ask of God, who giveth to all men liberally" to find the answer. Joseph did. It took him on a journey which resulted in him gaining a dispensation of the Gospel. He did not need to build on another's work, because heaven worked with and through him.

[1978] JS–H 1:73 "Immediately on our coming up out of the water after we had been baptized, we experienced great and glorious blessings from our Heavenly Father. No sooner had I baptized Oliver Cowdery, than the Holy Ghost fell upon him, and he stood up and prophesied many things which should shortly come to pass. And again, so soon as I had been baptized by him, I also had the spirit of prophecy, when, standing up, I prophesied concerning the rise of this Church, and many other things connected with the Church, and this generation of the children of men. We were filled with the Holy Ghost, and rejoiced in the God of our salvation."

Joseph was above all else, the prototype of a Latter-day Saint. Would that all men were similarly Latter-day Saints, who actually believed and practiced the religion restored through Joseph. A religion in which people are able to ask God and get an answer. A religion which Joseph began, but which God has yet to finish. One where no one needs to say to another: "know ye the Lord" because all know Him.

Little wonder the prophecy of Joel spoken of by Moroni was yet to be fulfilled.

Responses to Various Comments

Here, in no particular order are responses to various comments received since we opened comments up a few days ago:

To the fellow wondering if he'd wasted his time serving a mission: I don't think so at all. The work of bringing people to knowledge of the restoration through Joseph Smith, introducing them to the Book of Mormon, and the modern revelations, as well as baptism, laying on hands, sacrament, and other ordinances offered through the church blessed and changed lives. It was a very good thing. Anyone you converted was given a great gift, and your sacrifice will be one of the things the Lord will account for righteousness.

To the one asking how to reconcile my ancestors contacting me while I did ordinances in the Jordan River Temple for them and the possibility we were rejected, I would respond as follows: Rejection of the church is not rejection of the individual. IF (and I have always left that tentative and for each person to decide for themselves) there has been a rejection, that does not mean anything other than the organized efforts were unacceptable. Each individual is accountable for their own conduct. There was a Temple rebuilt by Herod, presided over by wicked men who would kill the Lord, and yet He called it His "Father's house." In that Temple a publican came in and offered a great offering, and was rejected. A widow, however, entered and gave but a farthing, and she was accepted. The difference was not the building, nor the act of paying, but the intent of the individual. In the same Temple there can be acceptable work and unacceptable work proceeding simultaneously.

To the one asking if I would clarify the sealing power: I can tell you there are at least three different ways sealing power is made available. The church purports to have only one of those. I will not be able to do the topic justice in a blog post. It would require a lengthy paper which I will undertake at some point. If there is anyone who thinks they have command of the topic, perhaps they will come out and write something and then I wouldn't need to.

To the one asking if I thought there was a hidden, wise, or heaven-sent reason to change the temple rites in 1990: I can't think of any. It wasn't introduced as a revelatory change, or as an improvement. It was done because the church had the "right" to change it. The church leadership asserted they held "keys" that made them powerful enough to take the changes on and implement them. That is quite different from being either a revelation, a command from God or necessary for salvation of man. The change came about because of the research done in follow-up to an article suggesting dissatisfaction with the temple experience. That article was confirmed in polling of approximately 3,600 families in Canada and the U.S. The whole process was provoked by the members' concerns and dissatisfaction with the temple rites, rather than Joseph having gotten it wrong in the first place. The leadership had two choices—change the members' minds or change the ordinances. They changed the ordinances. I do think, however, that when we give our common consent to the church leaders, and they stand in their offices and make changes, and we then sustain them after the changes are made, that we (meaning the entire church) are accountable for the change, not just the leaders.

Therefore, we (all of us) are similarly situated and cannot just lament a change made by church leaders. All of us are together moving in the direction we move and are all equally accountable for the changes when we continue to *consent* by *common consent* to the implementation of changes.

To the one asking about how I pass the temple recommend question about sustaining church leaders: I sustain them. They have my common consent. I don't think I have any right to call my new stake president last month, but Elder Nelson did. I don't think I have the right to build a multi-billion dollar shopping mall adjacent to Temple Square, but the church leaders did. I don't think I have any right to separate the "tithing dollars" from the "investment dollars" belonging to the Lord, but the church leaders have done that for generations and have the right to do that. I'm not a leader. I appreciate being able to attend meetings and to receive the sacrament. I'm grateful for it. I neither envy nor want to join the leaders. I think they have a heavy and unenviable burden to carry, and do a commendable job accomplishing it.

To the one asking about how I see Zion unfolding: Not the way most people do. I tend to think the scriptures are quite clear. It will be the Lord's work, not man's. It will be initially in the mountains, only later in the plains. It will be the work of angels to organize. The Lord will provide the means, not men. The residents will not be like the typical nosey, overbearing sort who meddles in other's lives, like the Strengthening the Members Committee. In fact, I doubt very much anyone on that committee will be fit to invite, because they presume to judge others rather than to serve humbly and provide by their meek example a fit pattern for living as "one" with others who hold perhaps very different views. Those who come will be open to growing into a unity of faith, not asserting that they have the right to compel agreement on pain of some penalty being inflicted. They will use meekness, love unfeigned, and pure knowledge to persuade one another of the truth. While outside the gate the demanding, compelling, presiding and coercing sorts will be burned.

To the one asking about organized atheism: I agree. Organized atheism is a religion. They do attempt to impose their views and do persecute others, but I was speaking about the individual atheist, and in particular the persecutors of the Prophet. For the most part, they were not interested and didn't care about what Mormons, or anyone else believed. The atheists I know are more broadminded, and tolerant, than the folks in the Strengthening the Members Committee, and a good deal more discrete, too. The Strengthening the Members Committee leak confidential information on the internet, compromise legal issues and the right to claim certain legal exemptions. I think that is a problem for the church, and ought to result in them abolishing the committee, or firing those responsible for this significant mistake.

To the one asking if I can explain the various events in priesthood restoration: I haven't attempted to give that history for a reason. Therefore, I'm not going to undertake that now. I will get to it, but the blog is not the means to accomplish it.

To the fellow who wants to know why I don't provide my books free for download: First, I don't want everyone reading my books. If someone is interested, they must be inconvenienced to do so. That will remain the case. Second, there are others who need to make a living through publishing the books and with whom I have contracts I intend to honor. One of those involved suffered a stroke a few years ago, and is partially paralyzed. It is an honor for me to be able to provide some revenue through the books (though it is not much) for this man and his family. If you think you should have something free, then read this blog. I've put more words here free, (and in the downloadable papers) than in my books. But the books deal with a single topic, and require the entire scope to accomplish the discussion. It must be a sustained discussion. One of the books (*Removing the Condemnation*) is entirely on this blog. I've been encouraged to put the Jacob 5 series in a short book. I may do that, too, but it is available free here. Your suggestion that I'm profit motivated is foolish (and wrong). I'd suggest you borrow from the local library. We've donated books to many Utah libraries, but my wife tells me there are submission guidelines which may keep them from being made available. So I can't control if they actually put them on the shelves, or throw them away, or if people just take them once donated.

To the one asking about lunch: No.

To the one asking if I'd be willing to come and talk at the family reunion: No.

To the one asking if I'd recommend an order to read my books: In the order they were written.

To the inquiry about *Eighteen Verses*: It is a selection of those problems currently facing the church. They are the eighteen most significant issues we have before us today. The verses were selected to allow that discussion to be put into a single volume, and to show how the Book of Mormon remains highly relevant to our current plight.

To the one asking about which one of the Twelve: You've got to be kidding.

To the one asking about a Harley: The Dyna Super Glide. The basic model. You can do whatever you want to customize it and add anything you want. To bump power about 20% just open up the pipes and air intake using the Harley shop's Screaming Eagle slip-ons and you'll notice an appreciable difference just seat-of-the-pants.

More Responses to Comments

On the best sources of LDS history: *The Joseph Smith Papers* is a gold mine of information. The diaries and journals of the inner circles of church leaders are very informative. There was a conscious effort to prevent diaries and journals from becoming public beginning in the early 1900's. There were "resolutions" and "covenants" among church leaders that they would stop putting stuff in their diaries for others to find out later. That didn't always work so well. Today the church requires an agreement to be signed by every new general authority (I forget how many pages it is), but it covers, among many other things, the obligation to turn over to the church the diaries of the general authority when they die. I've been told Elder Oaks was the one sent to retrieve the journals of Elder Neal Maxwell when he died. So there is an effort to stop that kind of information from being "inadvertently" released to the public.

When you read diaries or journals it is not really "history" in the narrative-telling-a-story sense. They read just like life. From one moment to the next they don't have a clue what is coming. They are constantly surprised or frustrated by how it unfolds. For example, there was no plan to abandon plural marriage. There were incremental concessions, intending always to accomplish statehood, after which it would be made legal. So the goal was to do what was needed to get statehood. When the final events take place, the leaders involved were shocked they'd arrived at the point where plural marriage was actually being abandoned. Many of them recorded that if they had known where it would lead, they would *never* have made the first concessions. So as you read the diaries, you find that the leaders wound up in a place they never intended to go, making concessions they believed would let them avoid forsaking a principle they believed in, and ultimately they were out-maneuvered by the Federal Government and corralled into denouncing and forsaking what they thought was a sacred principle.

When the Cowley and Taylor were forced to resign because they wouldn't renounce plural marriage, there were some tense moments among the leaders. George Albert Smith said some things which Elder Taylor (who had seen the Lord and was considered a spiritual giant) took as an improper insult to himself. He confronted and warned George Albert Smith to not do that again, but that didn't stop the preaching against Elder Taylor. So Elder Taylor "cursed" him. The resulting mental and physical health challenges that George Albert Smith suffered were thought by some to have been due to being "cursed" by the resigned apostle Elder John W. Taylor. These sorts of things are not found in the written histories because, well, among other things, Elder Taylor was forced to resign from the Quorum of the Twelve and George Albert Smith became the president of the church. This year we are studying the teachings of George Albert Smith. It doesn't set well to go into this sort of thing when one has been excluded and the other has triumphed into the presidency. So it just sits as an unexplored thread of events, left for those who search into our history to discover. Then once discovered there is always the further question of whether the researcher is candid or protective. If candid, are they pursuing an agenda to belittle the church and our faith or are they honest and sincere. Even if they are not seeking to belittle the faith, and believe sincerely in it, the problem is further complicated by those who want to gag them, and to prevent any telling of events from something other than what the Strengthening the Members Committee thinks is "faithful" to them. So the history of the church is terribly complicated and likely going to be left to either outsiders of good faith (of which there are a few) or those who must fight to retain their membership because insecure and thin-skinned "thought police" are running amok at this moment.

Returning to the question, the best historians (in my opinion) writing recently are Jan Shipps (non-Mormon), D. Michael Quinn (excommunicated), Richard Van Wagoner, Gregory Prince, and Ronald Walker. Several of those are deceased. That is a horribly incomplete list and I'm not going to look at the bookshelves, but give just this off-the-top-of-my-head list. Bushman's work is not as useful as I'd like. His tools are academic and have the weaknesses of his discipline. He does not inspire me. Some of Quinn's work was marred by an agenda rather than objectivity, but that work was important. The second volume of the *Mormon Hierarchy* series is a very important book. The third one has been delayed, but hopefully will be out soon. It is one of the books I've been waiting to read for months. For anyone writing, the sources they use are important, and their conclusions are less so. For what I've written about history, I've tried to "interpret" (history is always an interpretation) through the lens of scripture. Rather than try to conform the story and sources to the theme I want adopted by the reader, I try to let the scripture's themes lead to interpretation of events. Other writers of LDS history are developing what they hope are objective views based on the events as they understand them.

Fortunately the truth always wins. Even if the church decided to spend its vast resources and repository of good-will among the members, the Internet is providing an inevitable transparency to things. There will be "bootleg" copies of diaries and journals. Right now, for example, Yale University received a donation of a considerable volume of material from the church's archives, which some intrepid (but anonymous) soul published in limited numbers of copies. I've spent thousands of dollars acquiring copies of these limited edition books. I try to use my best sense, my faithfulness to the church and the Lord, and my honest reactions to tell the truth about some things in my last book.

On the question asked about the church leaders being "prophets, seers and revelators" the answer is that this is the 'title' given to them in the D&C. It is scriptural in origin. We have always associated the scriptural authorization with the office and therefore anyone who fills the office is entitled to hold the title. I don't see where that is a problem. Anyone elected to the office has the title.

We have never considered it necessary to search about and find a "seer" to put in the office. Instead we consider that the office imposes the obligation on them, and the scriptures allow them to use the title, and therefore it is perfectly symmetrical. How can you NOT sustain them as "prophets, seers and revelators" when the scriptures say that is the office they have been elected to fill? Doesn't really make sense. Of course they get to wear the title.

On the German version of the Bible Joseph Smith praised: It was the translation rendered by Martin Luther.